A HISTORY OF
MARRIAGE SYSTEMS

G. Robina Quale

CONTRIBUTIONS IN FAMILY STUDIES, NUMBER 13

GREENWOOD PRESS
New York • Westport, Connecticut • London

Library of Congress Cataloging-in-Publication Data

Quale, G. Robina (Gladys Robina), 1931–
   A history of marriage systems / G. Robina Quale.
      p. cm. — (Contributions in family studies, ISSN 0147–1023 ;
no. 13)
   Bibliography: p.
   Includes index.
   ISBN 0–313–26010–9 (lib bdg. : alk. paper)
   1. Marriage—History. 2. Family—History. I. Title.
II. Series.
HQ503.Q35   1988
306.8′1′09—dc19   87–24957

British Library Cataloguing-in-Publication Data is available.

Library of Congress Catalog Card Number: 87–24957
ISBN: 0–313–26010–9
ISSN: 0147–1023

First published in 1988

Greenwood Press, Inc.
88 Post Road West, Westport, Connecticut 06881

Printed in the United States of America

The paper used in this book complies with the
Permanent Paper Standard issued by the National
Information Standards Organization (Z39.48–1984).

10 9 8 7 6 5 4 3 2 1

To my Parents,
True Partners Ever

Contents

Preface

This is a worldwide history of marriage systems. It goes back to the earliest generations of human life to seek the roots of why and how human beings came to marry, to form lasting mutually helpful offspring-raising relationships like those of social wolves and somewhat less social swans, rather than to stay in kin-linked bands for offspring-raising purposes like chimpanzees and rely on somewhat chance-governed meetings outside the natal band for mating purposes. The book traces the gradual modifications in patterns for making, dissolving, and remaking marriages through the rise of agriculture and herding into commercial-urban societies and on to contemporary industrial-commercial life, comparing lines of development in the major regions of the world. It is primarily meant to be a general history of overall trends rather than a detailed compendium of current data. Also, it is written by one who believes that contemporary American trends illustrate broader worldwide tendencies in significant and at times dramatic ways. Consequently it brings in specific current figures about marriage and divorce rates among different segments of the population only for the contemporary United States, as an illustration of those broader tendencies that are also clearly visible in other contemporary societies. The figures given for other countries and regions are less detailed.

The idea for a history of marriage systems came out of the course in history of family structures that I introduced at Albion College in 1980. Teaching that course heightened my realization that the points in family life at which marriages are made, dissolved, and remade are crucial for understanding how not only families but whole societies operate. I therefore used a year-long sabbatical leave in 1981–82 to put together a first draft of the manuscript. I appreciate Albion College's support for the project, not only through the sabbatical leave, but also through payment of typing costs. During 1981–82 I took part in the University of Michigan Committee on Gender Studies Colloquium. Elizabeth Douvan (psychology), Sherry Ortner (anthropology), and Louise Tilly (now on the history faculty at the New School for Social Research) were especially helpful in sharpening my lines of thought and argument, as were Hugh Gilmore and Aram Yengoyan (anthropology). Both then and since I have continued to hone ideas through discussions with colleagues at Albion College, in particular Elizabeth Brumfiel (anthropology), William Hayes, David Hogberg, Barbara Keyes, and Frances Lucas (all in psychology), and my fellow-historians Geoffrey Cocks, Wesley Dick, Clark Halker, Allen Horstman, Julian Rammelkamp, and Neil Thorburn. Mabel Rammelkamp and Sarah Thorburn also turned my attention to significant points. The experience of being interviewed about my findings by Isabel Wilkerson (then of the *Detroit Free Press* and now of the *New York Times*) helped me to focus my presentation of them, as did the experience of being a commenter on an American Historical Association panel on the ideologies of sexuality, organized in 1984 by Shere Hite. None of the people I have mentioned should be held responsible for any of the conclusions I have reached. The conclusions are mine, and I accept whatever praise or blame others may wish to offer. However, each of them has encouraged me to rethink and clarify in some important way. In addition, Cynthia Harris, history editor at Greenwood Press, Penny Sippel, production editor at Greenwood Press, Barbara Hodgson, copyeditor for Greenwood Press, and Vicky Grant, typist for the final prepublication version of the manuscript, have been most helpful and cooperative. I am grateful to them all, and to all the students on whom I have tried out portions of the manuscript for their responses. They, too, have helped me to clarify the presentation.

Above all, I am grateful to the members of my family, chief among them my parents, Leslie Quale and Gladys Dyer Quale. They have contributed in act and word to the recognition embodied in Chapter 3 that ultimately it makes more sense to assume equal mutual benefit as the initial basis for formation of marriage systems than to assume that marriage systems began as a means of exploiting one group within human society for another group's benefit. The Quales and the Dyers, as I have known them, have illustrated well the value of having, the difficulty of achieving, and the possibility of maintaining that kind of equally mutually beneficial partnership. I am glad to have been born into that pair of families.

A History of
Marriage Systems

CHAPTER 1

Relationships Among Marriage Rules, Kinship Rules, and Socioeconomic Conditions: A Hypothesis of the Spiral-like Development of Marriage Systems

Marriage systems involve the sets of rules used in societies to govern the establishment, continuance, and dissolution of marriage. These include rules concerning who may be married and who may not, among both kin and nonkin. They also include rules concerning the holding and transmission of property or status. However, to try to understand the actual operation of a marriage system by looking at it in isolation from its full context is to behave like a taxonomist rather than like a hunter. The hunter who discerns a leopard in the forest would err profoundly in rushing to attack without considering wind direction, sun position, ground conformation, paths of escape open to the leopard, indications of the presence of other leopards such as its mate or its cubs, indications of the presence of other animals the leopard might be watching for, signals from hunting companions, or indications of the presence of other human beings. The leopard must be seen, to be either avoided or attacked. But the leopard must then be fully related to its context, if the hunter is to escape becoming the hunted.

The functioning of a marriage system also needs to be fully related to the overall economic and political situation within which families and individuals must make their way. That overall situation ought in turn to be looked at historically, for it is constantly changing from the situation for which the currently used rules were made. Sometimes that change may seem as violent as a hurricane. Sometimes it may seem almost glacially slow. But it is never entirely absent. It is always forcing people to rethink what they should do, how they should do it, and with whom they should do it.

Marriage is an alliance, before it is anything else. At a minimum, it is an alliance between the two it brings together. However, in some societies it may take less of their time and attention than it does in others.

Marriage is usually an alliance between the two families from which those partners came. Still, it may be less of a preoccupation for those families in some societies than in others.

Marriage is an alliance whose members ordinarily hope it will be expanded and continued through the coming of children. For most people in most societies, children have until recently been the primary economic supporters of their parents in later years. Children remain a primary psychological support to members of older generations in all societies.

Marriage is often an alliance through which property may be transmitted in some way, or through which status of some type is conferred or confirmed. In particular, marriage normally confers the statuses of wife and husband, which have been and still are regarded in many societies as necessary to being seen as an adult rather than as a child. Some anthropologists, like Peter J. Wilson, in *Man, The Promising Primate* (1980), even suggest that the socially recognized linking of a specific human male to a specific human female and her offspring lies at the root of human beings' differences from other primates.

Marriage is also likely to reinforce the realization—which social theorist Talcott Parsons says, in *Family, Socialization, and Interaction Process* (1960), that the members of every society need to have—that their society includes both kinfolk and other people. Parsons states that a child must move from a sense of the circle of self-and-mother to a sense of self-and-both-parents as a second circle, a sense of self-and-kin-beyond-parents as a third, and a sense of self-and-nonkin-beyond-kin as a fourth one, in order to be a fully effective member of the society into which it is born. That sense of who are kin and who are not is likely to be reinforced at the time of a marriage. Whether the marriage is an alliance between those who are already kin before the marriage, or between those who will only become kin through the marriage (and may not even see themselves as kin until the marriage brings forth children), the advantages and disadvantages of having chosen among the kin or among the nonkin are likely to be thoroughly discussed.

Marriage, as the socially recognized linking of a specific man to a specific woman and her offspring, can be found in all societies. Through marriage, children can be assured of being born to both a man and a woman who will care for them as they mature. Marriage thus helps to define descent, or kinship, or who is kin to whom, whether it links one man and one woman in *monogamy*, one man and more than one woman in *polygyny*, or one woman and more than one man in *polyandry*. In some societies a man may take more of the ongoing responsibility for providing for his sister's children than he does for providing for his wife's children, while his wife similarly expects her brother to take more interest in her children than her husband does. Yet these societies, too, recognize and encourage the husband-father to love his children. The proud military Nayar caste of pre-19th-century central Kerala province in southwest India had a property-holding, marriage, and inheritance system that was an extreme example of stressing the wife's brother's responsibility for his sister's children and deemphasizing the husband's relationship with his wife. Still even the Nayar anticipated that the publicly acknowledged father of a child would take an affectionate interest in it. When the specific political and social circumstances which had led to deemphasizing the husband-father's role changed during the 19th century, that affectionate interest proved so strong that the whole property-holding, marriage, and inheritance system was overturned. Both men and women evidently wanted to be able to treat their spouses as primary partners in raising the children born to them. They clearly did not want to have men continue to be torn between their duty to their sisters' children and their concern for their own, to the distress of women whose own husbands could do little to help them if a brother started giving more to a wife's children than to his nieces and nephews.

The Nayar system stressed the role of a woman's eldest living brother, who remained at home to manage the family property, over the role of her soldier husband (usually a younger son of some other family) who might be lost in battle. It may date as far back as the wars that accompanied the decline of the great Chola empire in southern India in the 12th century A.D. It was certainly well entrenched by the time Europeans reached southern India at the end of the 15th century, for they soon began to describe it, in amazed fascination. Its rise in an era of frequent and bloody conflict, its endurance through centuries of continuing strife, and its overturn after the establishment of an effective peacekeeping central government all demonstrate the vital need to look at marriage systems in their larger social and historical context, if their workings are to be understood in full.

No marriage system develops in isolation from other elements in people's lives. Among the Nayar the eldest brother who stayed home took all responsibility for the economic maintenance of the nonfighting women and children. That made it possible for the husband to take none, and for most men to be gone on military service most of the time. It also made it possible to accept the legitimacy of marriages between a woman and several husbands, each of whom might spend his military leave in her company, and each of whom might on his side be wed to several women. In that way he could go to another of them if the wife he chose to go to first was already entertaining another of her husbands. However, it took the special circumstances of being a hereditary military group to lead to such a marriage system, and to sustain it. The cultivators who grew the crops on lands the Nayar aristocracy held from their Brahmin overlords had very different sets of rules for marriage, property-holding, and inheritance. So did those Brahmin overlords, the ones who relied on the Nayar men to fight their wars. They needed different rules, even though they lived in the same region, at the same time, as members of the same society, and in the same larger political and economic system. As C. J. Fuller makes clear in *The Nayars Today* (1976), they were in different political and social circumstances, so that to look at either cultivator or Nayar or Brahmin in central Kerala in

complete isolation is to stalk the leopard without observing either the sun
or the ground.

Despite the differences among Nayar, Brahmins, and cultivators in central
Kerala, they shared a clear expectation that a woman depended on a man's
leadership in property relations, if not always in other areas of life. In the
harsher climate of the Arctic, however, according to J. S. Matthiasson in
K. Ishwaran's collection *Canadian Families* (1980), the Inuit (often called
the Eskimo) regard their marriages as alliances of full partners. Both spouses
contribute to the family food supply through fishing, for example. Each
partner retains his or her own identity, as well as making a needed set of
contributions to the other's well-being. The husband hunts; the wife prepares the flesh and skins of the slain animals for use. Each partner must
agree to any serious partnership-affecting decision, such as the adoption of
a child from another household which has grown too large, or the establishment of a mutual agreement among couples that if husband A (or B, C,
or D) must go out on a hunting trip, but his wife is unable to go with him
to prepare his gear and process the animals he kills, then whichever other
wife is freest to go will take her place. In the past both spouses would also
have had to agree to the abandonment on the ice of an aging parent or a
newborn infant unwanted by any nearby family.

Among contemporary Inuit that partnership continues. Both men and
women treat their new source of income, in working for the recently arrived
petroleum companies, as only partly to be shared with family for current
needs. They see their earnings also as partly to be saved for the future needs
of children or of self. Both men and women run for the elective local
governing councils, organized some time ago by the Canadian government
as the Inuit began to settle in permanent villages, and only the visitor appears
to think it matters how many women are elected, or how many men.

The Inuit understanding of how to balance individual and family concerns
evolved over the past two thousand years or so under the most demanding
of environmental conditions. An Inuit band cared little about what region
its members might claim rights to gather in, because of the relative unim-
portance of gathering. What mattered was the freedom to rove widely to
hunt, on land or sea, following the mobile fish, caribou, seals, and other
animals. For that, one needed the largest possible network of social relationships, both those that one was born into and those (such as marriage
or hunting groups) that one formed for oneself during one's own lifetime.
Even the household from which one adopted a child, or that of a former
spouse who had decided to leave one for another mate, was part of one's
social network. Maximizing that network was one's primary concern, rather
than making clear who had exclusive rights to use a carefully delineated
plot of ground.

For us in modern Western society it is striking to realize that the Inuit
and we both use the same kinds of kinship terms (in a formal sense) to refer

to our relatives. That may not seem as surprising, though, when we recall that we live today in a market society. Most modern Westerners find that their personal network of contacts seems more important to their well-being than their personal inheritance of the right to grow crops on a given piece of land, even though such rights were all-important to our largely agricultural ancestors. Neither the Inuit nor we formally differentiate between the mother's and the father's side, or between blood-kin (like father's sister as aunt) and kin by marriage (like mother's brother's wife as aunt also). *Agnates* (blood-kin in the male line), *cognates* (a term often used to refer to blood-kin in the female line, in describing systems that strongly emphasize the agnatic links among the male blood-kin, but also often used to refer to all blood-kin in both the male and the female lines), *consanguines* (blood-kin in both the female and the male lines), and *affines* (one's spouse's consanguines and one's own consanguines' spouses, and even one's spouse's consanguines' spouses and one's consanguines' spouses' consanguines) all are seen as members of one's *kindred*. All are potentially of help to one, and may call on one for aid in return, whether the link is consanguine or affine, by blood or by marriage. However, it is usually expected that one's parents and grandparents (one's *ascendants*), one's brothers and sisters (one's *siblings*), one's children and grandchildren (one's *descendants*), and their affinal equivalents will feel closer to one than one's aunts and uncles, nephews and nieces, cousins, and their affinal equivalents. One's ascendants, siblings, and descendants are one's *lineal* consanguines, after all, sharing fully one's own ancestry. Other kin are *collateral* consanguines, sharing other ancestries besides one's own. It is necessary to remind ourselves that Inuit kinship terms function differently from ours in their social context, in terms of indicating comparative status and anticipated levels of cooperation. Yet the formal identity of the terminology pattern, with its adaptability to stressing one's personal network rather than one's place in a descent line, remains striking.

We have grown accustomed in the modern West to seeing our network of kinship relations in a fully *bilateral* way, regarding descent from mother's and father's lines as equally important. Bilateralism fits well with our modern Western insistence—not shared even today in all societies—that in order for a marriage to take place, both the man and the woman must be willing to marry each other. Bilateralism also fits our Western belief that the willingness of a man and woman to marry ought to be based on each knowing the other well enough to feel reasonably certain they will be compatible. What we have learned through scientific studies of genetic inheritance has given rise to the modern Western acceptance of the equal importance of both parents' contribution to the basic physical inheritance of the child. It has also begun to encourage some to wonder whether a child's social inheritance (through its upbringing) ought to be equally the task of both parents rather than primarily of one, since the child is equally from both.

Modern Westerners, and the many other states that have revised their legal systems using Western models, already tend to expect children to inherit property in what lawyers call "equal partible inheritance." All children inherit equally from both parents regardless of whether the children themselves are female or male. That is a common pattern (though by no means universal) among nonagricultural peoples. The Visigoth rovers who conquered Spain from the Romans in the 5th and 6th centuries A.D. established their system of equal partible inheritance so firmly that it remains the legal norm for Spain to this day, despite the destruction of Visigothic rule by invading Arab and North African Berber Muslims in the 8th century A.D. The Visigoths also recognized the right of a woman to manage her own property both before and after marriage, like the Inuit in northern Canada today.

Perhaps the Visigoths were recapitulating part of the earlier experiences of the Greeks and Romans, of whose social institutions we know little before the days of Homer and the semilegendary founding of the city of Rome. By those times agnatic ties were so strongly emphasized that women were regarded as the natural dependents rather than as the natural partners of men. Marriage seemed to ally a man with his father-in-law almost more than with his wife. When we first begin to see the outlines of the social systems of the Greeks and Romans in their laws rather than in their legends, they had already turned from roving the land to cultivating it like those whom they had displaced or absorbed. Evidently they had also decided to stress the right of sons to inherit from fathers, as the easiest way to ensure the orderly transmission of cultivation rights, although that meant that the *patrilineal* father-son bond came to be stressed more than the *conjugal* ties of husband and wife. This use of patrilineality has been the most common method of passing on property rights in societies based on *subsistence agriculture*, in which people primarily produce for their own consumption and seek to maximize their self-sufficiency, rather than produce for a market and buy what they do not grow themselves. However, in some groups (like the Nayar caste) it has been a man's sister's son who has inherited from him the right to manage land on behalf of his own sisters and their children. This type of system is somewhat misleadingly termed *matrilineal* inheritance, in contrast to the patrilineal type in which a man's son inherits from him the right to use land on behalf of himself, his wife, and his own children until his daughters marry into other men's homes and his sons have wives and children of their own.

In most hunting-gathering societies the older relatives of young people play the leading role in arranging their first marriages but take a less important part in arranging any later marriages for either men or women. Still, in many cases the course of the marriage, once arranged, tends to be largely (though not entirely) the concern of the two partners. Both partners retain a sense of autonomy, even while they cooperate with each other in what an anthropologist would call their family of *procreation* (in contrast to their family of *orientation*, the one in which they were raised). In societies based on subsistence agriculture both the formation and the course of marriage tend to be largely, or even primarily, the concern of the families in which the partners were raised. In pre-20th-century China or Japan, for example, it might actually be a cause for the parents of the new husband to send his new wife back to her parents as unsatisfactory, if he became so attached to her that his parents saw him as neglecting themselves. In pastoral-herding societies, too, where the inheritance of animals is as vital as the inheritance of cultivation rights to people in societies based on subsistence agriculture, the formation and often the course of marriage tend to be largely the concern of the two partners' families of orientation. Only in industrial-commercial societies in modern times has it come to be expected that the establishment as well as the course of marriage are primarily the partners' concern. This may seem almost like a circling back toward the attitudes of a number of hunting-gathering peoples. Yet it differs from them in accepting the right of prospective partners to arrange their own first marriages, as well as any subsequent ones. Thus, in broad outline, marriage systems and the rules of property-holding and inheritance associated with them appear to have followed a spiraling path through the evolution of economic, social, and political systems, from hunting-gathering through subsistence-agricultural and pastoral-herding to industrial-commercial societies.

At the hunting-gathering level of economic, social, and political life today, people do not have landed property or large amounts of movable property to transmit as wealth from one generation to the next. They generally have some sense of things to be transmitted, whether ritual obligations to be met by a specific descent line, or knowledge to be shared by a medicine-maker with an apprentice (often chosen from among kin). They may even differentiate between individuals on the basis of these intangible goods of inherited status or transmitted knowledge. However, they do not differentiate between individuals on the basis of possession of tangible goods. Nor do they formally recognize permanent or even long-term political leaders as having a responsibility to maintain order. They only deal with disruptive behavior on an ad hoc basis when it actually occurs.

In contemporary hunting-gathering societies, marriages tend to be partnerships, with some activities shared by both partners and other activities clearly divided between husband's and wife's responsibilities, in varying proportions. Marriage is treated as having the same importance in one's adult life as one's family of orientation had for one as a child. One's parents (or elder siblings, if one's parents are gone) are likely to arrange one's first marriage, but not one's later marriages. Divorce is usually accepted as a solution, if a marriage does not prove agreeable to both. Each partner to the marriage recognizes both self's and partner's obligation to return that childhood care to parents, as they age. Each partner recognizes both self's and partner's obligation to care for the children born to them, so that those children will care for them in their old age in turn. Marriage is also seen as widening both partners' networks of alliances. It makes additional hunting, fishing, and gathering grounds available to them and to their children, and also to their other kin. Not inheritance, but marriage, the establishment of a new set of affinal relationships to complement those of consanguinity, is what enables one to enjoy adult life and meet its obligations. It is in the conjugal family, the family of procreation, that one refines the skills and perfects the qualities of personality which one began to develop in the home of one's parents, with their guidance and encouragement, whether that home was an Inuit igloo or a central African Mbuti camp. We can never know with certainty that that is how marriage was seen by early human hunter-gatherers, of course. But it is common (even though risky) to extrapolate backward in time, in hypothesizing about the patterns of their lives.

At almost every point that sketch of hunting-gathering life today contrasts with the experience of those who live now as subsistence agriculturalists, or who lived that way in the recorded past. Subsistence-agricultural peoples care about inheritance of something outside themselves, that is, cultivation rights in land, however those rights may be defined. If they use hoes and digging sticks, they are likely to move their fields from place to place in a defined region from one growing season to another. Cultivation rights are then likely to be seen in terms of permission on the basis of kinship to cultivate alongside the other members of the group. If they use plows, each cultivator's household is likely to plant and harvest the same piece or pieces of land year after year. Cultivation rights are then likely to be seen in terms of actual inheritance from one generation to the next of the right to use that specific land. Subsistence agriculturalists who use plows are more likely to have clear and fairly sharp distinctions among individuals on the basis of wealth or inherited status than do subsistence agriculturalists who use hoes and digging sticks. That is because plow cultivation tends to be more productive per unit of human labor. It yields more surplus, which can be traded for highly valued durable goods, or even for more land to grow more crops and harvest more surplus. Such added surplus may in turn be reinvested in a kind of incipient agricultural capitalism, or it may be used in ways that will increase one's standing in the society, such as lavish feasting of kin and friends, generous contribution to religious institutions, or discerning patronage of the arts. Plow agriculturalists are also more likely than hoe agriculturalists to have more than one local village level of political organization. Their greater producing capacity can yield tax revenues to support peacekeeping administrative personnel, to maintain order (and collect the taxes needed to support themselves) at levels from district to province to a kingdom or a state that unites all those who share a common linguistic and cultural heritage, or even an empire or a state that includes more than one cultural-linguistic group.

Among hoe agriculturalists, with their usually smaller and simpler societies, inheritance of cultivation rights goes matrilineally or else bilaterally in almost as many groups as it goes patrilineally. Little movable wealth is accumulated to pass on through inheritance, though. In matrilineal and bilateral groups marriage thus tends to expand the set of lands available to each of the two partners, letting the husband use what the wife can claim and letting the wife use what the husband can claim. Among bilateral groups each person may choose to stress only one set of claims (mother's, father's, or spouse's mother's or father's), but if so, then the person's children are free to choose to stress another set of claims instead. Marriage in patrilineal groups does not expand each partner's land-use claims, since a daughter or a sister seldom has strong land-use claims anyway. Still, marriage as well as inheritance tends to be seen as necessary to ensure the resources required for adult life, even for men in patrilineal groups for whom a wife's value lies in her labor contributions, not in her land.

Among matrilineal and bilateral hoe agriculturalists, marriage tends to be seen as largely the partners' concern. However, their respective families of orientation take an even more active interest than among hunting-gathering peoples in its establishment and continuance, both through advice (if not actual direction) in the process of partner-choosing and through ceremonies of mutual gift-giving. Such ceremonies serve in part as reminders to each partner that in the final analysis, cultivation rights are defined more by one's own family of orientation than by the family of orientation of one's spouse. They also indicate acceptance of sons' and daughters' marital partners (and eventually their children) as having a claim to take up their spouses' (or parents') cultivation rights. Marriage systems among matrilineal and bilateral hoe agriculturalists tend to be relatively egalitarian, by comparison with marriage systems among patrilineal hoe agriculturalists and especially among plow agriculturalists (the majority of whom are patrilineal). In addition, matrilineal and bilateral hoe agriculturalists tend to be as permissive as hunting-gathering peoples, with regard to accepting the equal rights of women and men to end a marriage with someone who is proving to be nonsupportive, in either the economic or the psychological sense.

Among patrilineal agriculturalists, on the other hand, marriage is less likely to involve the wife's bringing cultivation rights into marriage. That holds true regardless of whether the society consists of hoe agriculturalists or plow agriculturalists, or whether it consists of kinship-based self-governing groupings of villages or of larger political units. If the society practices equal partible inheritance, as in Spain, the woman may have cultivation rights of her own. Yet even if equal partible inheritance is the rule, she is more likely to be given a *dowry* of movable goods or even money, which represents her share of her parents' movable and immovable property, while her brothers will receive their shares in land at their parents' death. Where there has been relatively little surplus to accumulate in forms of movable wealth, she may not bring a dowry at all. In fact, as in much of Africa, her husband may even provide *bride-wealth* or *bride-service* to her parents, to establish his right to have her labor on his family's land and bear him children. However, when there has been more surplus, there has also been a tendency to see that women share in it. Either a father may provide dowry for a daughter, as was done among the ancient Romans, or a husband may provide a *dower* to a wife at the time of marriage, as was done among most of the Germanic peoples when they began to dominate the western regions of the Roman Empire in the 4th century A.D.

When the father has given dowry, among patrilineal agriculturalists, the husband has been likely to manage his wife's property. When the husband has given dower, the wife has been more likely to have the right to manage her own property. But regardless of whether the establishment of marriage has involved bride-wealth, bride-service, dowry, or dower, it has ordinarily been regarded as the responsibility of the bride's parents to arrange on her behalf. It has not been seen as her responsibility to make her own choice. More often than not it has been the groom's parents' responsibility to arrange the marriage for him too, particularly in bride-wealth and dowry systems.

Among patrilineal agriculturalists marriage has tended to mean the more or less formal transfer of the bride into the husband's family of orientation, as if they were adopting a grown daughter. Her ties to her own family of orientation have been more or less completely severed, so as to emphasize to her that she is now expected to care for her husband's parents' and brothers' interests, and to put his ongoing ties to them even above his new tie to herself. Often she only begins to be regarded as a full member of her husband's family as she brings sons into it. She is often also expected to put the interests of her husband's parents, brothers, and sons above all other interests. That expectation is frequently emphasized by some formal ideology of men's superiority to women and their consequent right to make all significant decisions, even though in everyday life a woman may have a great deal of private influence on her husband and her sons.

Pastoral-herding peoples are almost always patrilineal. That may be because herding was in some sense an outgrowth of hunting, in a parallel to the probable turning from gathering to harvesting and storing to actual planting and tending by women in the Middle East of more than ten thousand years ago. Herding as a way of life apparently arose as an extension of following existing herds to prey on them as hunters, and gradually domesticating them. It seems to have developed out of similar conditions not only in the ancient Middle East, but also in ancient central Asia and Siberia, and even to some degree in western North America after the first European conquerors introduced the horse.

As patrilineal peoples, pastoral herders usually display many of the same social features as patrilineal agriculturalists. They accumulate wealth in livestock, which they usually transmit through some combination of inheritance with bride-wealth, dowry, and/or dower. Bride-service may or may not be part of marriage arrangements. The importance of patrilineal inheritance means an emphasis on the importance of agnatic male-kin links, a reliance on parental involvement in making marriage arrangements, and a weak position for a wife until she has become a mother of sons. It also means everything that those three elements in a social system can imply for the relative statuses of husband and wife, or of men and women in general. However, pastoral herders are more likely than patrilineal agriculturalists to recognize the plight of the younger son who lacks bride-wealth, by devices such as accepting younger sons as additional husbands to the wife taken by the eldest son on behalf of both himself and his brothers, as in parts of Tibet. They are also more likely to recognize the plight of the barren wife whose husband returns her to her parents, by devices such as yielding her a right to use some of her parents' livestock as bride-wealth to claim a wife, as in parts of Africa. She can then designate a man to have children with that wife who will care for their mother and their female father (a literal translation of the type of term used) in old age. Such a solution is possible only where polygyny is practiced, so that a man who takes a barren woman's wife as a secondary wife, or becomes a secondary husband to her if one looks at it in that way, can expect to have children borne to him by a full wife of his own.

Gradually agricultural surpluses became large enough in fertile areas to enable those who obtained such surpluses in rent or taxes from the actual cultivators to accumulate goods, and to stimulate trade through seeking those goods. Commercial and manufacturing activity then began to become increasingly important and even dominant in a growing number of societies. Usually these began as patrilineal plow-agricultural societies. They might be ruled by local people who had earlier achieved high status and who usually continued to practice patrilineality, at least within the ruling group; or they might be ruled by members of some conquering pastoral-herding society who also practiced patrilineality. (Occasionally the conquering group might have been close enough to a hunting-gathering past to have continued its egalitarian traditions through a system of equal partible inheritance, like the Visigoths.) Apparent exceptions to that generalization can be found in Southeast Asia. There states blossomed in the early centuries A.D. that were based on a combination of matrilineal, bilateral, or duolineal hoe agriculture and the provision of local products to long-distance traders between India and China. (*Duolineality*, also called *bilineality*, means that some property descends through mothers to daughters, and some descends through fathers to sons.) Yet, in the long run, even those exceptions may be used to strengthen the generalization that industrial-commercial societies tend to develop along patrilineal lines at first. The rulers of those early Southeast Asian states almost always tended to move toward patrilineality, even though their subjects remained matrilineal, bilateral, or duolineal in their inheritance rules and their family structure. The duolineal society of the Inca in the Andes, before the Spanish conquest in the 16th century A.D., might appear to form another major exception to that generalization. However, among the Inca the wealthy obtained goods through tribute rather than through trade.

Most of us who live in a modern industrial-commercial market economy find that we exchange our skills for the money we need to purchase necessities and comforts, far oftener than we sell tangible items we produce with our own resources. In the process of adjusting to that mode of life in the past few centuries, our ancestors began to find that what enabled them to live satisfying lives was not the cultivation rights or the livestock or the other property they might inherit from a parent. It was their corollaries to the transmitted knowledge and inherited position of the hunter-gatherers—their skills and personal qualities, and their network of potential recommenders or customers or supporters. People in western Europe and its overseas extensions have responded to that growing realization in the past three hundred years by moving increasingly in three directions, much as people in other countries like Japan have more recently begun to respond to a similar realization. First, they have moved toward patterns of married life that look in a number of ways like those of many hunting-gathering societies. Their marriages are alliances of partners who see each other as equally important to the partnership, who make some decisions jointly and some autonomously, and who are primarily concerned with their relationships with each other and with their children, rather than with their parents' families. Second, they have developed the use of equal partible inheritance, to carry their recognition of the fundamentally equal worth of each individual into the transmission of the tangible wealth one may inherit or may accumulate (with or without the active aid of the spouse). Third, they have moved toward self-selection of spouses for first marriages, as well as for later marriages. They have come to believe that because young people are likely not to live in the same community with the members of the families into which they are born, they can make better choices for themselves than their elders can make for them. Equal partible inheritance and self-selection of spouses, both of which acknowledge the primary importance of the individual, have been incorporated into the current Western marriage system in a new and unique pattern. That pattern builds on partnership concepts from the distant past. Yet it has taken an upward movement to a new plane, through recognition of the individual, making the line of development from hunting-gathering societies to industrial-commercial societies not merely circular, but spiral.

Before looking in more detail at the rise and development of marriage systems, however, it is necessary to look at some of the demographic realities within whose limits those systems have had to operate. The constraints they place on what is feasible are genuine. They must be taken into account, along with psychological, social, and economic and political factors, if both the marriage systems of human societies and the cultural justifications given for them are to be understood.

CHAPTER 2

Practical Realities: The Functions of Incest
Taboos, Social Replacement Considerations, and
Ages at Marriage and Death, in the Development
of Marriage Systems

Every marriage system reflects the distilling of insights gained over generations of experience. Many of those insights concern social and economic
relations, and are expressed in terms of things like dowry, dower, bride-
wealth, and bride-service. However, some concern biological matters, such
as genetic fitness and mortality rates. They are expressed in terms of things
like incest rules and marriage ages. It is these biological concerns and their
influences that will be discussed in this chapter.

Almost all marriage systems prohibit marriages between kin who are
closer than cousins of some specified degree, whether first, second, or more.
There have been exceptions. Uncle-niece marriages were accepted in ancient
Israel. Sister-brother marriages were found in Ptolemaic and Roman Egypt,
while Zoroastrians in the Iran of that era used parent-child as well as sibling
marriages. Sister-brother marriages were also practiced among the Inca in
Peru before the 16th-century Spanish conquest. However, these exceptions
have invariably been linked with a strong desire to preserve a sense of purity
of lineage, or else to prevent an inherited set of properties from being
fragmented, as in uncle-niece marriages in Southern India.

The line between who and who may not be married is normally drawn
at some point among the cousins. However, two groups in the same overall
social system may follow different rules with regard to cousin-marriage
because of their differing social and economic positions. For example, in
the southern United States before 1865 inheritance-conscious plantation
owners often married first cousins. Their slaves did not. Not only was first-
cousin marriage avoided by many of the African societies from which they
or their ancestors had been taken. Because they might be sold into another
region at any time, it was good survival strategy to maximize the possibility
of finding kinfolk there by marrying outside the circle of close kin. Still,
owners as well as slaves recognized that too much inbreeding could lead to
an increase in defective offspring. Consequently, among plantation owners

as among those in other societies who have favored first-cousin marriages, care was also taken to bring in new bloodlines periodically.

Genetic studies done in the early 1960s on the population of Tristan da Cunha in the South Atlantic, and reported in David Glass and Roger Revelle's collection *Population and Social Change* (1972), bear out the biological wisdom of maintaining at least some minimal incest rules. Tristan da Cunha received almost no new settlers between 1827 and 1961, when a volcanic eruption forced a temporary evacuation of the island. Six generations of intermarrying among the descendants of the 23 residents of the island in 1827 produced a ratio of inbreeding among those children born after 1950 that approached the inbreeding ratio for the children of a man and woman who are first cousins. Of the 267 residents in 1961, four already had a hereditary blindness-producing disease called retinitis pigmentosa, which is carried on a recessive gene and thus only appears if both parents carried that gene. Another 6 were clearly carriers, and there were eight potential carriers among the children. Thus almost 1 in 15, almost 7% of the population, were victims, carriers, or potential carriers. That proportion would increase in every new generation, unless at least 10% of all future marriages could be with new settlers and their eventual descendants. Moreover, there had not yet been marriages among descendants of four out of the eight among the original 23 who had had the most descendants. Consequently the researchers forecast that other hereditary diseases carried by recessive genes were apt to appear in the future, in addition to retinitis pigmentosa and a few less serious diseases already present. They also noted that the intellectual capacity of the most inbred seemed generally less than that of the least inbred.

Even in a large modern population such as that of Great Britain almost 1 in 50 children has some form of birth defect. Only a few of these are hereditary. The rest come from spontaneous genetic mutation in the individual embryo, or from factors like malnutrition or stress affecting the expectant mother, or even from difficulties experienced in the birth process. But as the figures from the Tristan da Cunha population suggest, hereditary defects can spread with comparative rapidity to a significant proportion of the population if there is constant intermarriage among the members of a closed group. Thus a small social unit would find it advantageous to avoid inbreeding.

Mortality rates have influenced marriage ages at least as much as concerns about inbreeding have influenced incest rules. Marriage ages around the world have tended to rise during the past two hundred years, as improvements in nutrition, sanitation, and the prevention and cure of disease have lowered death rates and lengthened life expectancies. When more people live longer, they can wait longer to marry and have children to grow up and take their places in society. They do not need to have as many children to have enough to survive them and carry on. But it takes time and experience for people to realize that that is possible. Consequently birth rates have not declined as fast as death rates, and we have been experiencing a worldwide explosion in population.

It is hard for us to realize that up until the past two centuries, most people have been intensely concerned with ensuring that enough children were born to continue the effective working of their social and economic systems. We are just beginning to sigh in some relief at what appears to be a slowing down of world population growth since 1975. We have scarcely begun to comprehend the reality, let alone the implications, of the decrease in infant mortality and the accompanying increase in life expectancy that have taken place since the 18th century, when the long series of Eurasian plagues ended and effective smallpox prevention became widespread. The probable multiplication of the Maori invaders of New Zealand from about 12,500 in approximately A.D. 1450 to over 30 times that number in A.D. 1800 demonstrates how rapidly a human population can multiply in favorable circumstances, even when not increased by large numbers of later immigrants. However, the general experience of humankind until within the past two centuries has been an annual growth rate of no more than 1% per year, and often much lower. In England, for example, population grew only an estimated less than 0.1% per year over the whole period from A.D. 1250 to 1700, though some periods saw faster growth and other periods saw great losses, like the era of the Black Death in the mid–14th century. Even in the 18th century, population grew a little less than 0.5% per year. When population growth went well over 1% per year in the early 19th century, the resulting social and economic strains led to large-scale emigration, either to regions still under British rule, like Canada and Australia, or else to the newly independent United States.

E. A. Wrigley has suggested in an article in Charles A. Tilly's collection *Historical Studies of Changing Fertility* (1978) that most people do not begin to think seriously of finding means to limit the number of their children to two or three until average life expectancy at birth grows to more than 40, or long enough for most infants to be expected to live to see their first grandchildren. In populations as separated in time and space as Spain in the 1st century A.D., Macedonia (in modern Greece) in the 14th, the Netherlands in the 17th, and India in the early 20th century, at least ⅓ of those born died in infancy and early childhood. Up to another ⅓ died by the time they were young adults, largely from malnutrition, disease, or accident. Thus it was in fact necessary for a couple to have six children in order to have two survive the parents, where life expectancy at birth was no more than 25 or so. We cannot be surprised, then, that it took about 70 years for people in England and Wales to move from an average of six per family for those married during the period 1861–69 to an average of two for those married during the period 1935–39. It takes time to recognize and act on even a dramatic change in how many survive childhood to adulthood, and how long those who reach adulthood continue to live. By the end of the 19th century, $^9/_{10}$ of all those born in western Europe reached at least 20 years of age. However, only ⅔ did so in the 18th century, and scarcely more than ½ in the 17th century. Even of those, some would die before they married and had children, and many would die before more than one or two were born.

People in every society appear to have thought in terms of trying to have an appropriate number of children so that both they and their children can most effectively use the available resources. Unless the economy is rapidly expanding, providing many new opportunities, that is likely to mean people will think in terms of *social replacement*, or having two children reach adulthood to replace their parents as the parents die. Only as life expectancies at birth move toward 35 to 40, rather than the 25 to 30 of much of 18th-century western Europe, does the number of children needed to ensure that social replacement begin to drop from five or six to three or four. Only as infant and early childhood death rates also drop will the appropriate number of children begin to seem to most people to be about two. For a nation like India, which moved from a life expectancy at birth of 29 at independence from British rule in 1947 to a life expectancy at birth of 54 in 1974, almost doubling life expectancy in one generation, the social consequences are staggering. Even China, where life expectancy increased by about half (to a little over 60) in approximately the same period, is in a more manageable situation than is India. Life expectancies at birth may fluctuate around the new levels of 60 or more they have begun to reach in an ever-growing number of countries, as in most regions in the past they fluctuated around the range of 25 to 35. Those born in the Soviet Union in 1980 have a slightly shorter life expectancy than those born in 1960, for example. However, even with the appearance of new diseases, life expectancies do not seem likely to decline again to anything like their former levels.

The link between expected length of life, death rates, and marriage systems lies in the need for every marriage system to ensure that the average marriage lasts long enough to produce the appropriate number of children for social replacement, or for expansion where that seems feasible, as it did for the Maori between A.D. 1450 and 1800. Where life expectancies are shortest and death rates highest, marriages tend to come earliest. Marriages also tend to come earlier where population expansion seems possible because of locally available opportunities, or where there is some visible area of expanding opportunity to which to emigrate.

Average marriage durations have varied greatly, both from place to place and from period to period. In the decades before the French Revolution of 1789, 12 years was all a French peasant couple could expect. That was only a fraction of the 22 years that poorer English couples could expect at that time, let alone the 30 years that English middle-class couples could expect, even though death (rather than annulment or divorce) was what ended almost all marriages. An average contemporary United States couple can still expect almost 30 years of married life together, even with recent high rates of divorce. Quakers in the United States (who seldom use divorce) can anticipate 44 years or so. But not until the 19th century, as life expectancy at birth began to pass 40 in the region of western Europe and North America, did average marriage durations go much past 20 years for any but the best fed portions of the populations in any country. That point was not reached in the overall region of Latin America, Africa, and Asia until after 1930, about a century later. It came even later, after 1950, in some specific regions, such as India, Pakistan, Bangladesh, Sri Lanka, and Nepal in southern Asia.

The lengthening of average marriage duration in a society naturally increases the number of children likely to be born, if the members of the society do not customarily practice some method of limiting the total number of births. Such limitations may range widely in form. Celibate modes of life may be encouraged, as in 18th-century Spain, where 6% of the adult population were in celibate religious orders. The right to marry may be limited, as in many 17th- and 18th-century German, Swiss, and Austrian villages, which required official permission to marry and gave it only to those couples who could show that they could support themselves and the children they might have. Prohibitions on intercourse after childbirth, which are most common in societies that practice polygyny, may be used to try to prolong the period between births. The Cheyenne Indian effort to forbid a woman to have full conjugal relations for ten years after bearing a live child must surely have been the most extreme example of such a rule.

Other aspects of marriage systems may limit births too. Early marriage for a woman, a common pattern, tends to bring her into active childbearing before her period of greatest fertility. In well-fed modern populations that tends to begin at about 25. Early marriage thus exposes her to the risks of death in childbirth (which are greatest for the unusually young and the unusually old among expectant mothers) or of sterility induced through being infected with a venereal disease by her partner, even before she reaches her most fertile years. Late marriage for a man, another common pattern, may increase by as much as 100% the number of acts of intercourse he will need to engage in to ensure that his partner will conceive, by comparison with a man of 25 or so. It also means earlier widowhood and fewer children for his wife, if she is noticeably younger than he and life expectancies are relatively short. Insistence that marriage is to be for life, once consummated, can limit births as well. Cross-culturally about 5% to 10% of marriages prove sterile. One of the major functions of divorce, in most of the societies that have traditionally allowed it, has been to enable those who found they were not having children to separate and seek new partners.

Child-rearing practices can have a direct influence on numbers of births, both for the current generation and for later ones. The continual lactation practiced by contemporary hunter-gatherer mothers, who carry their infants with them in slings as they forage and briefly nurse them on demand two or three times an hour, has been shown to have a strong contraceptive effect. If early hunter-gatherer mothers practiced the same kind of continual lactation, it may well have kept average birth spacings to something like the four-year average among contemporary hunter-gatherers for as long as human beings continued to live primarily by hunting and gathering. That would mean until no more than fifteen thousand years ago, when fishing began to be added to the human repertoire in a few favored regions. A four-year spacing reflects the natural weaning of the child. By age 3 or so it begins to be able to survive on the same foods as adults and can keep up with the adults as they look for food instead of having to be carried much of the time. If contemporary hunter-gatherer maturation patterns prevailed in early times, a woman would have experienced menarche at 16 or 17, but then would have remained sterile for at least another year or so while she continued to accumulate needed body fat. She would not have continued to be fertile beyond 40, which was also the usual limit for a woman's fertility two thousand years ago as observed by classical Greek and Roman physicians. Thus early women may well have been unlikely to have more than six live births, the number previously shown to have been required to ensure simple social replacement in documented European and Japanese populations in the 16th to 18th centuries A.D.

In the longer run the greater attention frequently given to male infants and children than to female infants and children can reduce the number of women who reach childbearing age in a society. That can lessen total births in future generations. Greater attentiveness to male infants and children may simply reflect a gradual realization, going back to earliest prehistoric human experience, that boys tend to be slightly more vulnerable to disease and accident than girls. However, over hundreds of generations it has grown in some areas to such proportions that there were fewer than nine females for every ten males as recently as 1960 in the western Himalayas above the north India plain. That region was a stronghold of formal polyandry, until polyandry began to decline with improving economic conditions in the past few years. Not until the 1970s did death rates among girls of 19 and younger in India cease to be higher than death rates among boys of 19 and younger. Such a change had long since taken place in most urban industrial-commercial societies.

Contrary to frequent belief, most of those societies that formerly accepted the killing or exposing of unwanted children at birth practiced it on the basis of whether the newborn could be properly fed and cared for, rather than on the basis of discrimination against female infants. Most of them also made some informal provision for women who had just given birth to stillborn infants, or had just lost a nursing infant, to take on a newborn infant whose parents did not want it. But since preindustrial China was among the few societies in which a newborn female infant was clearly much likelier than a newborn male infant to be exposed or killed (while the clearly nondiscriminating societies were likely to be smaller ones such as hunter-gatherers), it seems probable that the total number of female infants around the world who have been at risk of infanticide has been larger than the total number of male infants who have risked that fate, at least in the past two thousand years or so. Higher mortality for women in pregnancy and child-birth in China than in the United States helps to explain why the 1953 census in the People's Republic of China showed 107.5 males of all ages per 100 females of all ages, in contrast to the United States ratio at that time of 98.9 males per 100 females. However, the higher male-female ratio in China also seems to have reflected a tendency for parents not to report female infants as conscientiously as they reported male infants. This tend-ency in turn may reflect earlier attitudes about daughters' comparative im-portance to the family. Such attitudes would almost undoubtedly have influenced choices in previous generations with regard to particular infants' being accepted and raised, or not accepted and not raised.

The shortage of adult women that can result from either conscious or unconscious preferential treatment for male offspring not only decreases total future births, but also influences marriage systems. If it does not force adult men into wifelessness, it is likely to force them into wife-sharing, either as formal polyandry or as an informal recognition that a husband's unwed younger brother may lie with his wife, as in much of Africa and many of the Pacific Islands. It also tends to lead to earlier marriage ages for women than for men. That in turn may only make the shortage of women even worse, since women tend to have more male infants when young and more female infants in later years. And again, with fewer women to give birth in the next generation, there will be fewer total births.

Births are naturally limited in other ways as well. Cross-culturally at least one in five conceptions will result in a natural miscarriage or in a stillbirth because of some defect in the fetus or some incompatibility between its physical makeup and that of the mother. General health and nutrition levels can play a major role. In periods of disease and starvation a woman's body may temporarily shut off the procreative functions and channel every calorie into mere survival. For example, 54% of adult women survivors of one World War II concentration camp were found to have amenorrhea (tem-porary cessation of menstrual periods). They did not begin to experience their normal cycles for an average of 18 to 20 months after their release. Malnutrition or stress experienced by the expectant or potential mother can also contribute to an increase in the likelihood of birth defects, and thus to fewer births in later generations. Jewish women who gave birth between 1945 and 1948, after having been overworked, underfed, underclad, and often physically mistreated in other ways while in Nazi concentration camps, had infants with four to five times the normal number of all types of defects taken together, and almost 19 times the normal percentage of infants with Down's syndrome.

To the degree that both births and marriages reflect periods of scarcity and periods of plenty, the ups and downs of the economic situation may also have an effect on numbers of births. Studies done for France, England, and Japan during the 17th and 18th centuries A.D. show that after periods of high grain prices, which would indicate grain shortages and probably malnutrition as a result, those who were already married tended to have fewer children. These studies also tend to show a drop in numbers of marriages in periods of scarcity and a rise in periods of plenty. Thus a couple's childbearing would tend to be delayed until times were better, lessening even further what might be called the ratio of potential births to actual births in famine periods. The generational effects of such experiences tend to linger too. When there have been many births in a 10-year period of plenty, 20 to 30 years later there will be more young people to marry and begin families of their own than there would be after a decade when famine conditions led to fewer births and also to more deaths than usual among those born. (A significant drop in infant mortality has the same effect as an increase in numbers born, as people in both India and China have recently been learning.) Those more numerous young people are likely, then, to be more cautious about marrying and starting families than the less numerous in smaller *birth-cohorts* (those born in the same period of time). It may not seem that way to contemporaries, who simply observe the greater absolute numbers of marriages, and do not observe the lower percentages of people marrying by the time they reach a given age (such as 25). Certainly that was the case in early-19th-century Norway. However, studies of 18th-century western European populations have shown a kind of continuing though diminishing wavelike effect at intervals of about 30 years, for several generations, with relatively small (or large) numbers of births following each other about 30 years or so apart.

The interplay of birth rates, death rates, and sex ratios has a natural impact on marriage patterns. Only a very few societies have expected the bride to be several years older than the groom. Still, in parts of China before the 13th-century Mongol invasion and in much of rural Korea until the 20th century, early-teens marriage was practiced for boys as a guard against venereal disease, and late-teens marriage was practiced for girls as a guard against too-early pregnancy. Somewhat more societies, like northwest Europe in general in the past several hundred years, may have up to $^1/_5$ or even ¼ of brides who are one to five years older than grooms. But usually it is expected that a bride will be anywhere from one or two to 12 or more years younger than her husband. That means in practice that men—or those who arrange their marriages—tend to look for wives among those younger than themselves, a group that expands as they grow older. However, women—or those who arrange their marriages—tend to look for husbands among those older than themselves, a group that decreases as they grow older.

Women in a small birth-cohort preceded by a large birth-cohort are thus at an advantage in most societies in finding partners because there are more men who are older than themselves. However, women in a large birth-cohort preceded by a small birth-cohort find fewer men who are older than themselves. On the other hand, men in a small birth-cohort preceded by a large birth-cohort are at a disadvantage in finding partners because there are more men who are older than themselves to compete with them for partners. Men in a large birth-cohort preceded by a small birth-cohort have fewer men to compete with for wives. In addition, the effects of birth-cohort size may be either increased or decreased by the later impact of death rates on the number of survivors of any given birth-cohort, as its members reach adulthood. That is especially significant if those death rates are noticeably higher in the preadult years for one sex than for the other.

When death rates for girls and young women are noticeably higher than for boys and young men, women will often tend to marry earlier and earlier, as many potential husbands compete for them. Men in such a society will ordinarily tend to marry later and later, as it becomes harder for them to find wives. Where death rates for girls and young women are not higher than for boys and young men, marriage ages for the two sexes will often tend to approach each other. That appears to have happened in northwestern Europe, and also in parts of central and southern Europe, some time after the 14th century. However, other factors may counteract these tendencies. Both India and China were traditionally short of women. Yet the practice of an extended-family system, in which married sons remained with their parents as dependents, made the parents willing and able to finance their sons' early marriages. In late medieval western Europe, on the other hand, the increasing number of potential wives led to such a rise in the size of the dowry which had to be given with a bride that parents took their daughters off the marriage market by placing them in convents, in preference to furnishing dowries for them. They thereby created an artificial shortage of potential wives. In Florence, for example, by 1427 the mean age of marriage for men was 30, whereas for women it was 17. Still, beneath all the societal and cultural practices that may affect the operation of natural tendencies, those natural tendencies continue to operate. It therefore seems reasonable to suggest that as long as the survival rate of women continues to improve by comparison with the survival rate of men, their marriage ages will continue to become closer. It also seems reasonable to suggest that not only will there be more pairings in which the two are the same age or the man is only slightly older than the woman, but there will also be more pairings in which the woman is slightly older than the man, as in recent centuries in northwestern Europe.

The extended-family system, which in traditional India and China sought to keep married sons at home to aid their aging parents, has taken many forms in different societies. Some of these forms will be discussed in later chapters, for they influence specific types of marriage systems found in specific types of societies. However, no matter what traditional society is being considered, the real possibility of being left without a child to support one in one's later years is another factor that must be borne in mind when looking at how its marriage system developed. When one had to depend on offspring, rather than on some combination of pension plans based on contributions from one's own earnings and support from public funds, the patterns of decision-making about whom and when to marry were naturally greatly affected by that stark reality. It has been estimated both for pre–1800 Europe and for pre–1800 India that one in five to six married couples either had no children in the first place, or else had the experience that at least one spouse outlived all the children born to the couple. At least another one in five would find that they had no son, only a daughter or daughters, as they grew older. That could be disastrous in a society in which it was expected that the son would bear the major responsibility for caring for a parent, because the daughter was perceived as moving out of her father's household into her husband's household at marriage. Social reality often differed from that perception. Sonless parents in pre–1945 China, India, and Japan found ways to persuade younger sons to marry their daughters and move in with them, since younger sons (lacking seniority) were almost always at a disadvantage in an extended family. Childless couples adopted surplus children from more prolific kin. Where lifelong monogamy was not the rule, new pairings were tried. Whatever strategies might be available and culturally acceptable were used. Among those strategies one of the most widespread was the establishment of strong affinal networks, close ties with a spouse's blood-kin to whom one could turn if one's own blood-kin could or would not aid one in extremity. A man in India, for example, might remain sonless, even childless. He might be brotherless, and even sisterless, and thus have no nephews or nieces of his own to whom to turn. But if ties of affection could be built up over the years with his wife's brothers (or even sisters) and their children, then he as well as his wife could hope for their assistance if it were ever needed in later life.

In short, people have sought to maintain what they regarded as appropriate levels of social replacement in many ways, other than direct use of contraception to prevent an unwanted pregnancy, abortion to terminate an unwanted pregnancy, or infanticide to eliminate an unwanted and already-born child. Those other ways have often involved a postponement of marriage, or a refusal to permit marriage for a sizable percentage of the adult population, or an effort to limit the frequency with which a married couple might have potentially reproductive conjugal relations. However, many of those ways are not readily applicable in a modern society, in which job opportunities and incomes are great enough to mean that individuals can largely make their own decisions about when and whom to marry, and how to live their married life. The desirability of the conjugal relationship tends to be perceived in modern societies as great enough so that almost everyone eventually marries, with the exception of the few men and women who choose a profession that requires celibate vows, and those women for whom soldiers' deaths in wartime may have meant a noticeably smaller group of men of appropriate age among whom to find partners. Consequently the use of whatever forms of contraception are regarded by a couple as morally acceptable, from carefully timed abstinence to both chemical and mechanical means, has become widely, though not yet universally, recognized as necessary to maintain the age-old pattern of social replacement as the norm. The use of abortion has also been accepted by many as preferable to the hazards ahead after birth for either a defective infant or an unwanted one.

Clearly, then, marriage ages and marriage systems in general have reflected efforts to ensure that neither too few nor too many will be born, taking into account both mortality rates and available opportunities. That concern for maintaining an appropriate level of births still governs the workings of all marriage systems. The concern to avoid inbreeding that is evidenced in incest rules also still governs all marriage systems. The biological advantages of such rules, as suggested by the experience of the population of Tristan da Cunha, would appear to make it likely that this concern will continue to be strong. Other concerns that have governed marriage systems in the past seem to be less significant as societies evolve, however. The growth of nonfamilial pension plans has made it less important to parents to try to govern their children's marriages, or to keep their children close to them after marriage. The growth of other nonfamilial supports for both minor children and temporarily jobless working-age adults has made it less important to the newly married to seek to maintain close ties with older kin. Thus marriage systems tend to be most flexible of all in the affluent modern urban industrial-commercial societies in which those nonfamilial aids are most available. But even there, biological concerns continue to play their age-old role.

CHAPTER 3

From Consortship to Marriage: Some Hypotheses Concerning Early Marriage Patterns, Based on Hunter-Gatherer and Primate Life

"In the beginning..." there were the early hominids we now term *Homo erectus*, who arose, spread, and died out within the past 2 million years in the land mass of Africa, Europe, and Asia. There were earlier forms also, *Homo habilis* and previous upright-walking hominids with still less developed forebrains. Anthropologists generally agree that *Homo erectus* used both fire and language, as well as tools, but they are less willing to credit *Homo habilis* with the use of language. Still, it seems fairly reasonable to assume that at least by the time of *Homo erectus*, human beings were already organized in kinship-recognizing bands, if one considers the behavior of chimpanzees. (They are the primates closest to human beings in such aspects as the ratio of brain mass to body mass, or the difference in size between the sexes. For both modern humans and chimpanzees, adult females weigh, on the average, just over $7/8$ as much as adult males.) It also becomes reasonable to assume that early hominids lived in kinship-related bands in view of the way contemporary hunter-gatherer peoples live. Their experience appears to be most nearly like the earliest human experience—not just the experience of *Homo sapiens*, the species to which all contemporary human beings belong, but that of earlier forms as well.

It may be questioned whether it is legitimate to infer from some aspects of contemporary chimpanzee behavior that *Homo habilis* and earlier hominids already practiced a form of consortship, in which a particular male and a particular female became lasting partners. After all, today's chimpanzees have had as long as human beings have had to modify their social interaction patterns. Other primates, like the macaques of Japan, have been observed in recent decades to develop new behaviors by near-accident (like washing dirt off sweet potatoes) and to find the results welcome enough to teach them to other members of their own bands. However, a consortship of a long-term nature could have had advantages both for the two consorts

and for their offspring, if early hominids (like most primates) had offspring
who took a long time to mature.

In a lasting consortship the male would presumably share with his female
consort and her offspring the meat of the animals that he and the other
males in a band killed by hunting. The female would also presumably share
the foods she gathered with her male consort, as well as with offspring.
Lasting consortship would thus have obvious survival value for a hunting
male. He might make a kill when the group of males with whom he hunted
found a good opportunity, but he would be apt to spend much time hunting
and little time feeding. A female partner who would provide him with plant-
food staples would therefore be useful. A gathering female would find it
equally useful to obtain from a male consort most of the concentrated meat
protein that would help her nurse and feed her young more easily. She could
then focus her own activity on finding food that could not quickly run away,
forcing her to choose between chasing it and tending offspring who were
too small and weak to keep up with a freely moving adult. Virtually every
adult female would always have young offspring to care for. Thus each
adult female would find it helpful to have her own male consort, just as
each adult male would find it helpful to have his own female consort. A
lasting and monogamous consortship, like that of birds who pair for at least
the length of time required to bring the young to the flying stage, would
have made more biological sense than the bull-and-harem situation of the
northern fur seal, whose young can swim immediately at birth.

Homo erectus almost undoubtedly lived in kinship-recognizing bands.
The probable development of language provided a means of conveying
"Good!" and "Bad!" ("Thou shalt!" and "Thou shalt not!") from one to
another, both among adults and between adults and the young. This could
help make it possible to categorize experiences and perceptions into ever
finer and more useful classifications. The inclination to categorize, which
appears to be quintessentially human in its fullest development, had by then
almost surely led at least to a recognition of who had been borne and raised
by the same mother. It might even have led to a sense of having the same
father, whether in the physical-paternity sense or in the sense of his continuing to be that mother's consort over a long period of time, a "social father"
to them in helping the mother feed and care for them. Offspring of sisters
would also almost surely have had a sense of being closer to one another
than to others with a more distant relationship, or no known relationship.
But whether brothers' children felt especially close would have depended
on what being a male consort meant, in *Homo erectus* minds. At best the
degree to which kinship relations might have been recognized, beyond being
children of one mother, or children of sisters, or children of daughters of
daughters of the same great-grandmother—let alone the degree to which
whatever form of consortship existed might last beyond one cycle of pregnancy and lactation (if even that long)—must remain highly speculative.

What can be said with some certainty is that the probable decrease in hairiness, increase in skin sensitivity, and elimination of long periods of lack of interest in intercourse on the part of females, as *Homo habilis* gave way to *Homo erectus* (and *Homo erectus* in turn gave way to *Homo sapiens*), could have greatly facilitated the development of pair-bonding between one male and one female. The male could be assured of a willing partner in intercourse at any season of the year, as well as a steady supplier of plant food, if he could bond her to him through a combination of meat-sharing and affectionate treatment. The female, on her side, could be assured of affectionate treatment and an ongoing interest in providing meat for her and her offspring, if she could bond him to her through a combination of plant-food sharing and receptivity. Without frozen specimens of *Homo erectus* and *Homo habilis* like the mammoths found in the Arctic tundra, it is impossible to know how far any physiological changes might have progressed before the appearance of *Homo sapiens neanderthalis* somewhat over 100,000 years ago, and then of our own species, *Homo sapiens sapiens*. But in view of the appearance of fire in the repertoire of *Homo erectus*, perhaps already by that time a furry pelt had given way to a lesser degree of hairiness. Moreover, the apparent use of skin garments by *Homo sapiens neanderthalis* would suggest a disappearance of most body hair. Though it appears to have been little recognized before the 1960s, women to this day retain a physiological trace of the estrous cycles of receptivity-nonreceptivity-receptivity found in primates and other mammals. Women still need to reach an identifiable stage of physical arousal, which ordinarily tends to depend on preliminary displays of physical affection, in order to find intercourse pleasurable rather than uncomfortable or even painful. For both partners the preliminary arousal provides an opportunity to develop affectionate feelings that can increase the partners' interest in remaining together.

If pair-bonding already existed among earlier hominids, *Homo erectus* or even *Homo habilis*, it could have had the survival-enhancing result for the female's offspring of ensuring that they would have a steady meat supply from her male consort. It has been suggested that hominid female receptivity developed as a means by which a mother might protect her offspring (by exchanging that receptivity for males' not harming them), in view of the practice among Indian langur monkeys of killing all existing infants when a new male leader leaves an all-male troop and deposes the current male leader of a group of breeding females. However, the groups of hominid remains that have been found do not suggest such a division between all-male bands and leader-and-harem bands. They suggest groupings more like contemporary hunter-gatherer bands, in which the predictability of lasting consortships (comparable to those found in wolf packs or in bird colonies) would probably be a more useful mode of behavior than frequent and less predictable exchange of partners.

It is impossible to estimate how early it began to dawn on male and female hominid minds that a connection could be made between having intercourse and giving birth. It is also impossible to estimate when a male began to care that he, too, had made a contribution to the infant a female bore after his intercourse with her. However, once those thoughts began to circulate, as they could have done with the growth of language, then males would have two main choices. They might try to father many offspring with many females, rather than maintain a consortship with only one female. They would then run the risk of other males also consorting with the females they themselves approached, and being the fathers of their offspring. Or they could try to ensure the survival of offspring they felt sure were theirs, because they had established consortship with the mother through mutual food-provision as well as through intercourse. Females would be apt to prefer the latter course, since it offered more security to themselves and to their offspring. They would therefore tend to make it clear that their pro-vision of plant foods would be reserved for consorts who remained faithful to them, in return for their own faithfulness.

There are enough indications of incipient forms of both consortship and food-sharing, among both nonhuman primates and social animals like wolves, to make it reasonable to believe that hominid males and females developed lasting consort pairings of one male and one female rather early, perhaps as early as *Homo habilis*. Seeking to have more than one consort would have been likely to put them into competition in a way that would not occur if each male or female could expect to have his or her own consort. It has been shown that where resources are limited, planning to cooperate in using them yields more for everyone than trying to compete for them. Only where resources are unlimited—and the supply of consorts of either sex would never have been that—do people obtain more for everyone through competition than they obtain by cooperating with one another.

To try to go past that very general level of hypothesizing to something more specific, with regard to how pairings might have been made either among pre-*Homo sapiens* hominids or among early Neanderthal forms of *Homo sapiens*, is to be necessarily speculative. Among contemporary chim-panzees, females tend to move out toward other groups from their natal bands when they are receptive to intercourse, though not at other times. It seems reasonable that expecting hominid females to move out, and hominid males to stay within the bands in which they had been born, would serve both incest avoidance (shown earlier to be biologically advantageous) and the maintenance of bonds among groups of males who were accustomed to hunting together. It also seems reasonable that early hominid females would agree to such a move because they had recognized that collaborative hunting was more efficiently done by males who were familiar with one another as well as with the terrain, while females' gathering, though often done in company with one another, did not require as much practiced cooperation as hunting. However, it is hard to imagine that the permanent departure of sisters for another band would have been taken with complete nonchalance by either the sisters or the brothers. The lengthening of the maturing process brought older and younger siblings into longer association with one another as they shared the care and tutelage of the same mother and quite possibly the care and tutelage of the same male consort of that mother, a social and probably physical father. Any resulting strengthening of sibling links would not necessarily mean that brothers would choose to mate with sisters, rather than see them leave. However, it would be apt to mean that all would be concerned about the consortships that would be formed.

Chimpanzee females do not enter long-term mutually cooperative systematically food-exchanging consortships. Instead they circulate to other bands, mate, and then return to the natal band to raise their young. They thereby maintain sibling relationships at the expense of any lasting consortship. But comparable human societies are few indeed. The Nayar caste of central Kerala in south India, described in Chapter 1, formerly came closer in some ways than most. Yet even they did not send their women out. The circulating husbands came to their wives instead. The Hopi of the southwestern United States also come close, in terms of sisters remaining strongly linked with brothers. But among them, too, it is the men who move in with their wives, and may move out with little ceremony to return to the homes of sisters, rather than the women being the ones to move readily.

The outward movement of chimpanzee females works not only against their mating with brothers, but also against their mating with their own sons as the sons reach maturity, or with their own fathers if their fathers happen to be members of that troop. Nonetheless, these do happen occasionally, since not all females leave every time they are receptive. Mother-son mating has occasionally been observed among macaques, but only after a long series of battles in which the son was clearly seeking to establish his ranking in the troop's dominance hierarchy as higher than that of his mother. Rhesus monkey males have been observed to be the ones to move, and to avoid their mothers if they become sexually active before leaving. Among hamadryad monkeys newly mature males look for almost-mature females and carry them away to raise as future mates (somewhat as Arapesh men in New Guinea in the 1930s were still taking girls as future wives, to finish rearing them). Sibling ties have less time to develop among nonhuman primates than among human beings. Human beings also have more intellectual capacity to elaborate what being son or daughter of X means to them, far beyond the clear capacity of other primates to recognize and mourn the death of their own mother or their own sibling, or of her own infant for a female. Still, the chimpanzee female tends to protest her own brother's advances as unwanted, even if she is ready at the time to accept other males. That observed behavior may be linked with her being the one to move out. She is more inclined to resist her brothers than they are inclined to avoid her. That may be because she (as a female) has spent more time with their mother than they have. Thus she is more used to seeing them primarily as sibling (and only secondarily as male) than they are to seeing her primarily as sibling (and only secondarily as female). It has been hypothesized that brother-sister avoidance comes naturally in human beings because of early familiarity, which tends to preclude the feeling of mild but discernible novelty that seems to be required for strong and lasting attraction. That hypothesis appears to be supported by the tendency of contemporary Israeli kibbutz youth (raised in communal nurseries) to go outside their own kibbutz when seeking a spouse, and by comparatively low numbers of births and high separation rates in 20th-century Taiwan for men and women reared together because the woman was adopted into the man's family as a young girl to become his wife. Arapesh marital relations, in a hamadryadlike situation, did not appear to be warmly intimate either.

One hesitates to conclude firmly that by the time of *Homo erectus*, hominids followed a pattern of female departure at maturity. However, such a hypothesis is compatible not only with the possibility that early hominid females felt more sense of siblinghood with the sons of their mother than those sons felt toward their sisters, but also with the probability that early hominids recognized that keeping related males together as a hunting team was advantageous to both the hunting males and the females with whom they shared the meat they obtained. (Rhesus monkey males observably prefer to migrate to a troop in which one of their older brothers is already established, when they move out of their natal troop at maturity.) As young males matured they would gradually be brought into the hunting team and thereby become accustomed to it as a primary focus for both their productive activity and their social relationships. Young females would become accustomed to the companionable (but not usually actively cooperative) relationship of gathering alongside their own mothers and sisters and the other females of the band. They could thereby perceive as new females entered that being a newcomer did not need to be strongly disadvantageous, if one were friendly and ready to learn what those familiar with one's new locale were ready to teach one about it. But young males would quickly recognize— and males would convey to females when the band was back together in camp—that it was strongly disadvantageous to have a newcomer with them who did not know the terrain and was not familiar with their signaling system. It therefore seems fairly likely that at least by the time of *Homo erectus* (if not already in the time of *Homo habilis*) a pattern had already been established by which females left at maturity to find mates in other bands, while males stayed together as a hunting team. It also seems fairly likely that the form of mating was a lasting consortship. Such a consortship would have assured mutual food-sharing, needed by both the male wanting plant food (in case the day's hunt was unsuccessful) and the female wanting meat (but too fully occupied with infants and young offspring to take much part in hunts). Even if the band hunted as do the Mbuti in central Africa today (using all adult band members except a few aging child-tenders to drive potential prey into an ever smaller circle, in which the experienced adult men then dispatch it), such a hunt was unlikely to be an everyday occurrence. And though all the adult Mbuti may take part, the actual killing is still the task of the experienced men. There is still a differentiation between the roles of men and women in the hunt.

If it is assumed that lasting consortship was already a reality in hominid life more than a million years ago—an assumption with which not all paleoanthropologists are agreed—the next question is: How were those consortships established? A reasonable first hypothesis, on the basis of the suggestions made above, could be that females left their natal band at maturity to seek consorts in other bands (like many, if not most, female chimpanzees), but then remained in the consort's band (unlike many, if not most, female chimpanzees). However, if that hypothesis is accepted, then the next question is again, How? If chimpanzee females hear the calls of members of other troops (as they range through the outer edges of the territories in which they usually gather food), they will ordinarily leave the troop males and go toward the strange calls if they are currently receptive, but otherwise will join the troop males in going away from the strange calls. Presumably the males do not wish to meet with strangers in strange territory, especially if it is familiar territory to those other chimpanzees. Social learning, of which chimpanzees are certainly capable, may have built into chimpanzee habits an expectation that local males will clash with strange males entering their territory, and with strange unreceptive females. That would be a simple extension of the pattern within each troop of establishing and maintaining a dominance hierarchy. Each adult within the troop is forced by actual one-to-one displays of hostility to "put up or shut up" until one gives in and accepts its subordination to the other in the dominance hierarchy of the troop (until or unless willing to challenge later). The outsider is almost always at a distinct disadvantage in such a situation because of being in strange territory. Chimpanzees evidently try to extend their own troop's territories by crossing in bands into the borders of neighboring troops' territories, attacking and wounding any strays they find, if the neighboring troop does not make enough noise to sound formidable. Thus there would be ample reason for a chimpanzee to fear to enter another territory, unless there were a specific reason (such as female receptivity) for that particular chimpanzee to expect to be welcomed.

Human beings today war on one another in a kind of sophisticated mutual group hunt, band versus band, with one band entering the territory of another. This may be an outgrowth of early hominid response to a realization based on narrowly escaped experience that the lone stranger ran a real risk of being forced to the bottom of a hominid band's dominance hierarchy, or even being killed. Males might well have become willing to move into other territories only in company with other males, in large enough groups either to defend themselves successfully or to engage in some form of successful (but not necessarily fatal) conflict with the members of the local group. If the latter were the outcome, the defeated local group might either be absorbed into a larger dominance hierarchy led by the victorious newcomers, or be forced to leave their former home. In that case they might even move to the newcomers' former territory. That is a purely speculative set of suggestions. However, it is one means of trying to explain the appearance of group warfare among human beings by the time of *Homo sapiens sapiens*.

The rise of warfare may seem far removed from marriage systems. But it may also help to explain why human beings have developed marriage *systems*, rather than leaving the establishing of consortships to chance, as among the chimpanzees. (Which female is ready to seek the company of males? What other band's calls does she hear and follow? Which males in that band are not already currently in a consortship, and/or are dominant enough to feel free to approach her without interference from other males?) Sisters perhaps preferred finding consorts not in their own natal bands. Brothers perhaps preferred staying together. Experience perhaps suggested that if a sister were a consort in a neighboring band, her recognition of her brother if he came into her new band's territory (whether alone or in company with other males) would lessen the likelihood of immediate automatic conflict. She could serve as an introducer, an intermediary who had at heart both the interest of the offspring she had given birth to in her new band and the interest of her sibling. With the development of language for communication she could ask what her brother wanted and why he (and his companions, if any) had come into the territory where she and her offspring lived. Moreover, she would have a real interest in mediating any discord, on behalf of her own offspring and her relationship with her own consort.

The image of woman as peacemaker, and with it the insistence on woman as noncombatant so that she can play that role, may go back far indeed in human and hominid life. It contrasts with the life of chimpanzee troops, in which females not currently nursing offspring have been observed to hunt with males. There have been extremely few instances in which women have taken part in openly and formally organized forms of combat, in the recorded history or even the recorded legendry of human societies in the past five thousand years. Armed women have generally been in one of three unusual situations. They have been specially organized as defense and/or police forces at a royal court, like the royal bodyguard of the rulers of Dahomey before 19th-century European conquest. They have been sworn to celibacy for life, like the Amazons of ancient legend, the Nambikwara of the Amazon basin who formerly had a class of nonmarrying women who fought alongside the men, or the unmarried Albanian and Serbian women who as recently as the early 20th century swore vengeance for a kinsman's death, donned men's clothes, took up arms, and carried on feuds alongside brothers and cousins as lifelong celibates. Or they have been disguised in men's clothing, like the redoubtable stock character in Chinese opera, the general's daughter who assumes male garments to carry on her father's campaign because he lacks a son. The encouragement of almost a unisex form of garb in post–1949 Communist China may have combined well with the centuries-old popularity of such legendary heroines, making it easier for both men and women to begin accepting the changes in traditional gender roles urged by the revolutionary leadership.

Female preference for moving elsewhere at maturity may have begun out of a preference for avoiding brother-sister matings. It may have been complemented almost immediately by male preference for remaining with familiar hunting partners and female recognition of the advantages of being with a group of males who were accustomed to hunting together. But it may then have quickly developed into a further recognition that a hunting party's inadvertent—or even deliberate—crossings into other bands' hunting grounds could be successfully mediated by sisters who were consorts to members of those other bands. That in turn may well have led to efforts to use sisters already in other bands as interested mediators to arrange larger-scale hunting forays on an occasional ad hoc basis, since they would be glad to see both their consorts and their brothers benefit. Once it might be recognized that it was useful to brothers to have sisters in other bands with whom they kept up relations (and to sisters to keep up relations with brothers who might cooperate with their consorts in hunting), that recognition could logically have led to efforts to establish regular exchanges of sisters between bands. Such exchanges, as they might continue, would tend increasingly to strengthen what might originally have been rather haphazardly established bonds. Sister-exchanges theoretically could have begun as early as the time of *Homo erectus*, and perhaps even in the time of *Homo habilis*, if language had been developed by then. However, the development of language would seem to have been necessary, both for the desirability of such exchanges to be recognized (by both females and males, it is worth stressing again) and for their organization to be feasible. In any case it is worth emphasizing that both females and males could have had equally good reasons to find sister-exchanges preferable to having brothers be the ones to move.

The first tentative step toward an organization of sister-exchanges may have come when a female who was already in a new band suggested that she could return to her natal band and invite a younger sister to come in as a consort to a newly matured male, rather than his having to await the arrival of a new female. It seems reasonable to assume that at least by the time of *Homo erectus*, lone males did not readily wander into other bands' territories to seek consorts. Not only might they fear being attacked as trespassers, but they might also fear provoking similar forays in response, to the probable disadvantage of their sisters, who would thus have little opportunity for the kind of choice that even at the chimpanzee level the newly arrived visiting female does exercise in some degree. Hominids capable of using language, as at least *Homo erectus* almost certainly was, would also have been capable of feeling enough empathy with distressed siblings to wish to avoid giving any cause for such distress. They would have been readily able to recognize the natural difference in situation between a voluntary newcomer, who could have some choice of consort, and a consort seized by force. The enduring image of the Neanderthal caveman, dragging off the woman he has just clubbed, may in fact be the last surviving remnant of *Homo sapiens neanderthalis* warnings to young men not to do that, for fear someone would do it to their sisters in return. However, a female could readily serve as a mate-finder, for she could safely go between the band of her consort and offspring and the band in which she had been born.

It is not hard to imagine the rapid growth of such invitations in one band as other females observed how it worked, and the spread of the idea to the neighboring natal bands of that band's consorts as their members saw how it worked, and so on outward from initiating bands. Nor is it hard to imagine that the idea could have occurred simultaneously to females in a number of bands, so that its practice could have spread from a number of centers. (Similarity in social conditions has led to similarity in theorizing in widely separated societies as recently as China and Europe in the late 18th century. Both experienced population explosions, and promptly and independently produced theorists who called for study of ways to slow down population growth.) It is also not hard to imagine that in some bands, older males might have asked their consorts whether there might be a younger sister who could be invited as a consort for a younger brother. The advantages of strengthening ties with neighboring bands would have been fully as obvious to males who found their own consorts satisfactory (and therefore would expect their consorts' sisters to be satisfactory too) as the desirability of having a familiar sister as a fellow-member of her new band would be to a female. Both females and males could also see the advantages in strengthening ties to facilitate joint hunting activity and the like. What seems unlikely is that many parents survived long enough to try to make arrangements for their matured offspring, once the idea of sister-exchange began to spread. It seems likelier that at most, a parent might live to see one or two offspring mated. Whatever influence a parent might have on mate-choice was more apt to be exercised before the actual time of mating.

We can only speculate about the actual parts played by men and women, brothers and sisters, parents and offspring, as a general pattern of sister-exchange may have been adopted, perhaps as early as the time of *Homo erectus*. One thing we can say, though: it would not have worked out neatly. Given the reality of one-child families, at least ½ of all families have historically had an odd rather than an even number of children and could not provide a sister for each brother to exchange for a wife (or a brother for each sister to exchange for a husband, to look at it the other way). Moreover only ½ of all two-child families are one of each, only ⅜ of all four-child families are two of each, and so on. Thus any effort to set up a systematic form of exchange would soon have had to deal with the fact that scarcely one family in five would actually be able to work out an even exchange.

One solution is a section system, or classificatory-sibling system, in which a specific set of one sex is marked out as the group from whom each member of a specific set of the other sex may draw a partner. Section systems were worked out in great detail by western Australian aborigines but not passed on to eastern Australian aborigines until the first half of this century. Such systems are often termed *elementary* (meaning that whom one is to marry is specifically prescribed), in contrast to *complex* (meaning that one is only told whom not to marry, in the form of incest rules and the like). Complex systems supposedly leave the field of choice free, beyond the proscriptions, whereas elementary systems supposedly tell one specifically whom to wed. But reality upsets all theorizing, especially when theories try to divide into neat A versus not-A compartments. In today's United States the only formal prohibitions with regard to marriage partners have to do with incest. Many states accept even first-cousin marriages, which the Australian aborigines do not—they avoid the first and often also the second cousin, whether or not they use a formal section system to prescribe the field of choice. Yet, in point of fact, most contemporary United States residents probably have a maximum of about two thousand persons from whom to choose a spouse because of considerations like geographic proximity, relative age, and acceptable socioeconomic level. A choice among two thousand in today's United States is indeed more complex than a man in Pentecost Island in Vanuatu (formerly New Hebrides) in the southwest Pacific may have, among fewer than a dozen mother's mother's brother's daughter's daughters who are old enough to marry and not already married. However, there are still choices to be made, and each choice is uniquely made for its own mixture of reasons.

It is reasonable to differentiate broadly between marriage systems that say formally whom one may marry and marriage systems that say formally only whom one may not marry. It is also necessary to be aware that the prescriptive system is automatically a proscriptive one as well, since one may not marry those who are not in the proper group. The prescriptive rules take care of the incest rules against close kin to which a proscriptive system tends to be largely confined, unless it is part of a social system such as the caste system in India, which maintains itself through formal proscriptions against marrying people in the wrong social groups. In addition, it is advisable to remember that even the least proscriptive system, in the sense of formal rules, is likely to be somewhat prescriptive in practice. One seldom weds a total stranger, and the circle of those known to oneself, one's family, or one's friends, among whom one's partner will almost invariably be found, is naturally limited.

Even at the earliest periods of fully human life—the experience of *Homo sapiens neanderthalis*, who flourished by at least 100,000 years ago, and that of *Homo sapiens sapiens* from the absorption or replacement of the Neanderthals about 35,000 years ago to the introduction of crop-raising in place of simple gathering about ten thousand years ago—whatever systems of spouse selection were in operation can be reasonably supposed to have involved some kind of choice-making. It is risky to extrapolate backward in time from observations of contemporary hunter-gatherers, for they, too, like more complex societies, have had tens of thousands of years to elaborate their systems. Moreover, they have seldom remained unaffected by pressures from more complex societies. However, if one does extrapolate in that way, it seems likely that the choice was not left entirely to the partners, but was not imposed on them either. In effect, that is how a classificatory system operates. It delineates the circle within which choice is to be made, for both the woman and the man. For every man who must wed a mother's mother's brother's daughter's daughter, there is a woman who must wed a mother's father's sister's daughter's son. But even then, a choice is necessary. One person will look at disposition, putting compatibility above all else, and will suggest to parent or older sibling that he or she thinks A or B appears to be a pleasant person. Or perhaps parent or older sibling, discerning that concern in the young man or woman, will suggest A or B as an easy person to be with. A second, concerned with maximizing food supply, will look at how good a hunter or gatherer the potential spouse may be. A third, concerned for maximizing meat-supply potential, will look at how good the hunting is where the potential spouse's natal band usually hunts. That would be just as applicable for the man hoping to cooperate with an incoming wife's brother's band as for the woman hoping to find a spouse in good hunting territory, and it would apply whether the potential spouse is for the self, for a younger relative, or for a younger fellow-member of the band. A fourth, prudent even beyond considerations of current food supply, will try to ascertain which families have had the healthiest children and the most survivals into later adult life. Such a person would do so out of a wish to do everything possible to ensure continuing support throughout his or her own life, or throughout his or her own child's or sibling's or band fellow-member's life. This set of considerations is still important in rural Spain. The siblings of someone who is seen as physically sickly or mentally unstable are almost invariably passed over as potential spouses by everyone in a village, out of fear that they themselves may later prove sickly or unstable. In effect, they must leave for other places (preferably larger towns), if they want to marry.

These four fundamental kinds of considerations—first, potentialities for compatibility and gratification that are part of the partner's own personal makeup; second, potentialities for current and immediately future economic well-being that are linked to personal qualities of the partner; third, potentialities for economic advantages that are linked with whatever economic advantages the family in which the partner grew up may have had; and fourth, long-range prospects in terms of personal health and qualities for whatever children may be born—have probably been paramount in marriage selection processes for at least the past 100,000 years, and possibly much longer even than that. Whether for a first spouse or for an additional spouse (and there are hunter-gatherer societies today in which a man may occasionally have more than one wife), those are the considerations that must be weighed by both the man and woman, both the man's family and the woman's family. When Muhammad proclaimed to the early Muslims that it was the will of God that a man should not take more than four wives (and even then, only if he could treat them all equally), perhaps the specific number set as the limit carried with it some sense of these four basic considerations and the degree of reasonableness there might be in selecting one wife with each of them in mind.

No marriage system is entirely simple. The strong preference of the Arabs for marrying a patrilateral parallel cousin, a father's brother's child, carries on a tradition that goes back in that part of the world at least to the ancient Hebrews of the time of Abraham, Isaac, and Abraham's brother's daughter Rebecca, four thousand years ago. But even first-cousin marriage may well involve some choosing among sisters or brothers. Witness the story of Jacob preferring Rachel over Leah, in the book of Genesis, when Isaac sent him to his mother's brother to seek a matrilateral cross-cousin marriage with his mother's brother's child. Matrilateral parallel cousins, the children of sisters, and patrilateral cross cousins, one's father's sisters' children (a different grouping from one's mother's brothers' children), may also be favored groups. And when first cousins are prohibited by going back another generation or even more for the desired common ancestor, the number of possible partners is multiplied.

By the time *Homo sapiens neanderthalis* may have started making spouse choices, the human brain was capacious enough to think in terms of burial of those who died, and of making what are usually believed to have been ritual fertility figurines. Both of these activities would suggest a fairly highly developed use of language, and with it a fairly high capacity to classify and categorize. Neanderthals seem to have lived in bands of not more than 50, which is estimated to be about the maximum number of people one person can keep track of fairly closely. That estimate may be borne out by the experience of large communal households in 19th- and early-20th-century southeastern Europe. When they grew much larger than 50, it started to appear advisable to divide so that no one's well-being would be overlooked.

It is extremely risky to extrapolate from contemporary hunter-gatherers to Neanderthals. However, if the ages at which Neanderthals took spouses were comparable to marriage ages observed among hunter-gatherers in the 20th century, then they would have tended to mate at about 17 for women and 22 for men. That would have meant that relatively few survived to see a son take a wife, though more might see a daughter take a husband. (Some Neanderthal men but almost no Neanderthal women reached 50, and most people died before 35 or so.) Women might have married earlier than men for two reasons. First, learning to be an effective hunting-team member, ready to take on the full responsibility for wife and children, may have taken more time than learning to be an effective gatherer. Gathering would not have required such closely coordinated and practiced teamwork. Second, infant, child, and adult mortality rates all would have combined to make it seem advisable for a woman to begin to bear as soon as possible. Given the shorter average life span of women (largely the result of difficulties in pregnancy and childbirth), they may always have been somewhat scarce. Under those circumstances they would be sought after at earlier and earlier ages by men who wanted wives. That eager search would also explain the rise of bride-service and bride-wealth, living with the bride's kin and helping them for a time before taking the bride away, or giving gifts to the bride's kin before removing her to her new husband's band. Only a few contemporary hunter-gatherer societies use bride-service or bride-wealth. Bride-service is not practical for hunter-gatherers, except where local peculiarities of terrain matter less than general knowledge of such things as weather indications or types of ice and snow. Bride-wealth is limited by the usual hunter-gatherer practice of either burying all or most of the deceased person's belongings with the body, or else distributing part or all of them among the surviving members of the band, in a foreshadowing of the equal partible inheritance of peoples like the hunting-roving Visigoths. However, a skilled bow-maker might offer to make a bow for one or more of the men in the intended bride's family, as part of the process of inducing her kin and her to agree that she would come to him. Whether that hypothetical bow-maker would then look for a bride with few male kin to have to make bows for, or one with many male kin to establish bonds of appreciation with by providing them with bows, would depend on his own combination of prudence and industriousness with other qualities.

Important though these various considerations are, they still do not answer the question of why the choices were made that were actually made. Again, it is necessary to be speculative. We can only extrapolate backward from our own mental processes as *Homo sapiens sapiens*, and forward (or perhaps better, sideward across a gulf) from the chimpanzees and other primates we can observe. However, if we make those extrapolations, it seems reasonable to believe that *Homo sapiens neanderthalis* and even *Homo erectus*, having language like ourselves in which to represent absent previous experiences to themselves, tended to respond to current situations by looking for analogies with past experience.

Both hunger and pain, as well as satisfaction of hunger and experience of comfort or pleasure (from something smooth and warm to touch, for instance), may have underlain the complex considerations that went into *Homo sapiens neanderthalis* spouse choices. Those who had known hunger often might care more about the three kinds of economic considerations mentioned earlier than those who had known satisfaction of hunger more frequently; or they might not, depending on the circumstances under which that hunger or that satisfaction had been experienced. Which of those three economic considerations might come to the fore would also depend in large measure on previous experience. Those who had known pain often might care more for personal gratification than those who had known pleasure more often; or they might not, depending again on the circumstances under which pain or pleasure had been experienced. And not only they, but others, would have been influenced by those circumstances too, through the unconscious and/or nonverbal cues they gave to those around them at least as much as through conscious and/or verbal cues. In the first few generations of *Homo sapiens neanderthalis* life there would already have been time for adults to influence children before the children ever had an opportunity to learn to recognize their parents' and other elders' messages and check those messages against their own experiences. If one assumes a continuity between *Homo sapiens neanderthalis* and *Homo sapiens sapiens* through which we are the inheritors of accumulated intergenerational messages of fear and enjoyment in a chain stretching back to more than 100,000 years ago, there have surely been at least three thousand such intergenerational transfers that have affected each of us. Even if one only assumes a continuity of such transmission from the origins of *Homo sapiens sapiens*, more recently, then at the very least a thousand such transmissions appears to be the absolute minimum. When the ancient Hebrews spoke and wrote of the visitation of the parents' sins on the children of their children's children, they may not have been consciously thinking of the expectations that parents unconsciously project toward children. But when one learns that among the Ashanti of Ghana, different levels of aggressiveness are both expected and actually experienced from those males born on different days of the week, one wonders where "innate tendencies" end and where "self-fulfilling prophecies" begin.

All that goes into marriage choices too. It ought not to be ignored as relatively insignificant, in comparison to economic considerations, or in comparison to other more immediately obvious sources of potential gratification such as a partner's disposition or attractiveness. It plays more part than is usually acknowledged in determining which of the four basic classes of considerations mentioned earlier will be given more attention in any specific selection of a spouse, and how that concern will be met, whether it is overtly mentioned by anyone involved or not. Whether the potential partners are essentially left to make their own selection, whether their elders determine whom (or even if) they will marry without consulting them, or whether the selection process involves cooperation between potential partners and their elders (as tends to be the case among contemporary hunter-gatherers), both the potential partners and their elders make their decisions under unconscious intergenerationally transmitted influences. They do not act only in conscious and rationally considered ways.

The realization of the significance of both unconscious and conscious factors in selecting among potential partners, either for one's own self or for another, is more important than a detailed account of which specific peoples use which precise type of prescriptive system. In actual practice, as long as a marriage that is wanted does not violate the most basic of incest prohibitions, it will be made whether or not it follows the expected prescriptive rules. "The Sabbath was made for man, not man for the Sabbath," expresses a human belief of long duration. It is sufficient to acknowledge that many, if not most, contemporary hunter-gatherers do make some effort to recommend some specific group of possible partners as the first ones among whom to look.

David Aberle's listing of 101 hunter-gatherer groups in David M. Schneider and Kathleen Gough's collection *Matrilineal Kinship* (1961) shows that 61% of those peoples are like the Inuit in using bilateral forms of reckoning who are significant kin. (See Table 4.) Thus the recommended group of partners tends to come from a kind of circle around the individual, a circle of second, third, or even fourth cousins who may come from either the father's or the mother's side. Some hunter-gatherers reckon their mother's kin as more meaningful and their father's kin as less important to their immediate everyday lives, even though wives do tend eventually to move to their husbands' bands. If so, and 13% of these hunter-gatherers are matrilineal, then they are likely to choose their spouses from the father's mother's or the father's father's mother's group, as "less incestuous" than those from the mother's or the mother's mother's group. One such group would be the Kutchin of northwestern Canada, who also practice a form of bride-service. They expect the new husband to stay with the wife's band until at least one child has been born, which lets the wife remain with her own mother until that time. Another 19% of these hunter-gatherers are patrilineal, seeing their father's kin as more important than their mother's. They are likely to choose their spouses from the mother's father's or the mother's mother's father's group as "less incestuous." The remaining hunter-gatherers use a double-descent system. They reckon the father's and the mother's lines in a separated rather than a bilateral way, so that men descend from their fathers but not their mothers, while women descend from their mothers but not their fathers. However, they are too few in number to try to construct a theory about how they might select marriage partners.

Sometimes hunter-gatherers encourage direct brother-sister exchange between members of the appropriate groups. That appears to have been the situation among Shoshone in the western plains of North America, with their preference for cross-cousin marriages, which had the effect of promoting such exchanges whenever feasible. Sometimes the direct exchange is delayed, as in the system used by the Murngin of Australia, in which women move out of natal into marital groups in a pattern that takes seven generations to complete. In almost all cases, though, the process of selecting among the available candidates in the recommended or even fairly strongly prescribed group is neither entirely in the hands of the potential partners, nor entirely in the hands of their relatives and other members of their band. Elders tend to have a fairly considerable influence in making the arrangements for a first marriage, for both young women and young men. Second and later marriages, whether after a divorce or after a partner's death, are usually arranged primarily or wholly by the partners themselves. Either in first or later marriages, though, both elders and juniors have some opportunity to consider who may seem to be compatible or appropriate. Meetings between members of different bands take place, perhaps in connection with cooperative hunts, perhaps in connection with periodic religious ceremonies. Members of the band pay visits of varying length to relatives in other bands. These all provide occasions for informal exploration before formal arrangements may finally be made.

Harmonious relationships in a small close-living group are too important for group welfare for anyone to regard compatibility as a negligible consideration. Hunter-gatherers do not put economic concerns first and then expect that a close working partnership will eventually develop, once the two have children to give them a common interest, as agriculturalists have often done. If the partners do not get along well, despite all efforts, then concern for overall harmony within the band tends to mean a fairly ready acceptance of both the dissolution of that marriage and the effort by each partner to find a more agreeable mate. The Inuit carry their acceptance of divorce further than most other peoples, however, in their active expectation that a divorced person's next spouse ought to accept that person's former spouse (and any children) as having a right to fish or hunt or gather in the new spouse's area. In doing so they recognize that those earlier children's well-being is of concern to their own parent, and that a refusal would mean his or her possible estrangement from that next spouse. If the partners fail to have children, divorce and remarriage are also accepted. Those who try to have a child with two or three partners but still do not succeed are likely either to bring a young niece or nephew or two into their family circle (not in a formal adoption, but in some informally recognized arrangement), or simply to associate themselves with a brother's or sister's family as an informally included extra adult.

Potential partners themselves may tend to put their estimates concerning the probability of personal compatibility higher than any of the three economic considerations—the personal livelihood-contributing capacities of a possible partner; the advantages of forming an alliance with a possible spouse's band (whether thought of positively in terms of cooperative hunting opportunities or access to a well-known healer of illnesses, or more negatively in terms of lessening possible clashes over use of hunting lands); or the apparent healthiness and longevity of a potential spouse's family line. Elders tend to take economic considerations more into account, having observed that much incompatibility may be linked to insecurity about livelihood. (It is noticeable, in contemporary urbanized industrial-commercial societies, that divorce rates are highest at the lowest levels of the socioeconomic scale.) Finding a spouse within the band may be welcomed when it can be done, but it is much more usual for the formation of a marriage to be also the formation or strengthening of an alliance with another band.

People frequently move from one band to another, both for reasons of personal compatibility and to equalize use of resources. If brothers quarrel, one may move to the band from which his wife came. If he becomes involved in a quarrel there with one of her brothers, they may move to the band of the husband of one of her sisters. They may then move to another band with another sister's husband, if the wife has not left him by then, or if—for example—he has not brought a hypoglycemic condition under control through the successful hunting that would put more protein in his diet. They may go on changing bands in this way until one of the children is old enough to marry, and thereby provide a whole new set of potential kin to whom to turn. Or it may be current local scarcity rather than quarrelsomeness that leads a couple to move to the natal band of the other spouse, and possibly on to other bands, before they return (if they ever do) to the band in which their marriage began. Current local scarcity in the new husband's region may mean he will begin—and end—his married life in his wife's band, not she in his. The bilaterality favored by contemporary hunter-gatherers makes such movement easier than either patrilineality or matrilineality. The fluidity of membership in the households of city-dwelling aboriginal people in Australia today is the despair of government officials. When social service workers try to calculate unemployment and other social welfare benefits, they find it disconcerting to discover that a household that had 12 members two months ago had eight last month and now has 14, and that perhaps no more than five or six are there all the time, yet all the short-term residents are in some way related to those five or six. However, it is simply the way the Aborigines have always been accustomed to move from band to band. On their side, the Aborigines find it even more distressing to be expected to stay in the same place, instead of changing residences whenever it seems appropriate for personal or economic reasons.

Early *Homo sapiens neanderthalis* bands almost surely must have become accustomed to such patterns as shifting between bands, changing partners yet retaining links with children, and cultivating good relations with bands in neighboring areas by establishing and maintaining alliances with them through marriages. In view of the greater intellectual (and presumably linguistic, meaning also categorizing) capacity of Neanderthals when compared with *Homo erectus*, it seems unlikely that Neanderthals continued any near-automatic early hominid pattern of females moving out and staying out. *Homo sapiens neanderthalis* may even have emerged out of *Homo erectus* forms in part because of the growth in brain capacity needed to handle the growing complexity of mating and residential choices. An increasingly careful balancing of considerations about whom to take as spouse and where to reside may also have been a factor in the further development from *Homo sapiens neanderthalis* to *Homo sapiens sapiens*.

Early *Homo sapiens sapiens* may have been less likely than Neanderthals to reach the age of 50. If so, that could have reflected growing pressure of numbers on available resources. Such crowding would not only lessen the life chances of all in terms of food supply, but would also facilitate the spread of contagious diseases. Food needs were eventually met by changing from gathering plant foods to cultivating them, in the Middle East and elsewhere. However, it took fully 25,000 years for *Homo sapiens sapiens* to move in that direction.

The first demonstrable efforts to provide for a gradually growing population of *Homo sapiens* involved improving tools. By lessening the need to use the teeth, the new tools may have facilitated the skull changes that form the chief difference between the skeletons of *Homo sapiens neanderthalis* and those of *Homo sapiens sapiens*, the disappearance of the heavy jaw and the heavy upper-skull support for it. The extension of *Homo sapiens* range was another means of trying to provide for growing numbers. As the glacial ice caps melted, *Homo sapiens* moved northward from Africa and southern Europe, northward from eastern Asia, eastward across the Bering Strait to the New World, and southeastward from India through Southeast Asia into Australia and the Pacific islands of Oceania. But even with better tools and expansion into a wider territory, skeleton finds suggest that life expectancies may have been a little shorter around 12,000 years ago, when the human population reached a level of perhaps 4 million, than around 100,000 years ago, when it totaled probably less than half of that.

A further response to population growth may have been a tightening up of lineages, a greater attention to what kinship rights might be used to enable one to enter another band. That could have been accompanied by increased concern over marriage formations. The mutually considerate forms of partnership hypothesized in this chapter for the earliest men and women might have given way to an increasing assertion of control over women by men, the hunters and fighters. Men were larger and had more upper-body strength. Men used heavier and deadlier weapons than those that women used on the smaller prey they found while gathering. Men may have increasingly used their greater command of coercive force to arrange women's marriages for them, in efforts to extend the band's hunting range by forming marriage alliances with other bands. Rather than accepting women's equal wish to have a voice in mate selection, out of brotherly empathy with sisters who had grown up with themselves, they might have simply used arguments about the needs of the band to override objections to specific matches.

Such developments are potentially compatible with the observation that agricultural and herding societies bring up their children to be obedient, much more than hunter-gatherers do. An introduction to a need to stress obedience would have helped to prepare some of those early hunter-gatherers to move to agriculture. The first insistence on obedience may have come out of a wish to induce both young women and young men to be more willing to accept the partners selected for them by increasingly carefully calculating elders. Young women, who were still probably more apt to move out at maturity than were young men, may have been even more thoroughly trained than young men to accept their elders' wishes about spouse selection. It is also probable that women married right after menarche, at an earlier age than men. Relative youth could have given them less voice in the selection of a spouse than was given to young men, slightly older at the time of selection.

All of these factors made it probable that women were likely to be seen as "live goods" to be "exchanged by" men, rather than men being seen as in any way exchanged by women. Each time a woman's son marries his mother's brother's daughter, the two women can be seen as working out a matrilateral cross-cousin marriage for the elder woman's son as easily as the two men can be seen as working out a patrilateral cross-cousin marriage for the elder man's daughter. There is more than one hint in marriage customs which have survived in some agricultural societies that marriage can be regarded as a rite of women welcoming women, fully as much as it can be regarded as a rite of a man taking a wife. In much of rural Turkey, for example, the groom's sister still has a larger role in the formal ceremonies welcoming the bride than does the groom himself. However, in contemporary societies as described by contemporary anthropologists, attention tends to be focused on the patrilateral rather than the matrilateral side of the arrangement, even in fully matrilineal and matrilocal groups.

Numerous cross-cultural studies of child-rearing make it seem likely that being brought up to be obedient prepares people for the discipline of agricultural or pastoral life. If so, then a preferential socialization of women to be more obedient than men (so that they would be readier to accept elders' marriage choices, as well as to move into a new band and comply with its member's expectations) would fit with the fairly widely accepted hypothesis that the first steps toward agriculture were taken by women, as the primary gatherers of plant foods. As gathering began to move toward harvesting and storing, and then toward planting, which appears to be the probable order of development, more children began to survive to adulthood. The human population nearly doubled in the six thousand years after the first move toward agriculture (in the sense of harvesting and storing), less than 12,000 years ago. It nearly doubled again in each of the next three millennia. By two thousand years ago, as a result, the human population of the world was almost 50 times what it had been a mere ten thousand years before, something on the order of 190 million or so. Because children in larger families are likelier to be taught to be obedient than are children in smaller families, population growth may have led to even more compliance-training on the part of elders toward juniors.

In summary, these five hypotheses seem reasonable: First, lasting nonexploitative consortships based on females moving out of natal bands were already established by the time of *Homo erectus*. Second, by the time of *Homo sapiens neanderthalis* those consortships were leading to more flexible arrangements about band membership, as increased brain size made it easier to be more flexible. Third, by the time of *Homo sapiens sapiens* increasing pressure on resources was leading to lessened egalitarianism between men and women. Fourth, culturally selective pressures were making women more obedient than men. Fifth, increased training in obedience made it easier for women to adapt themselves to settling down in agricultural life, as a means of meeting the resource crisis, which by ten thousand years ago was beginning to become more and more evident. Women may then have used obedience training with sons, to persuade the men to accept agricultural life too. By the time of *Homo sapiens neanderthalis* human consciousness had almost surely started refining and elaborating a pattern in which social learning had originally played a part not much greater than that played by co-rearing in making female chimpanzees unwilling to mate with their brothers, and therefore desirous of moving out to other troops when in a receptive phase. By the time *Homo sapiens sapiens* came on the scene the resulting preferred (if not actually prescribed) mode of spouse selection for almost all human hunter-gatherer bands was probably some form of classificatory-sibling exchange, seeking for a spouse in a specific kin-linked group. Perhaps we can begin to think of "marriage" as having taken the place of "consortship" when such systematic exchange-patterns began to be worked out, whether these were elaborate (as among the early-20th-century Murngin, with their seven-generation cycle) or simple (as among the 20th-century Mbuti, who merely expected each would-be groom to find a bride from among his own kinswomen for some kinsman of the woman he sought to wed).

CHAPTER 4

Marriage in the Transition to Agriculture and Pastoral Herding: General Considerations and Early Developments

Some time after 10,000 B.C., hunter-gatherers in parts of the Middle East apparently began to recognize the possibility of gathering and storing supplies of cereal grains, rather than immediately consuming what they gathered. They also appear to have begun trying to approach milk-giving herd animals, so as to obtain milk for themselves to supplement flesh foods. As they increased the reliability of their food supplies in these ways, they were of course providing for their own gradually increasing numbers. However, they would then have begun to find it increasingly important to teach their children to be obedient to commands not to dip into the carefully stored supplies of grain, and not to play in ways that might startle the milk-giving animals. As suggested at the end of Chapter 3, habits of obedience to rules set by the group on the basis of experience may have been initially instilled more strongly in women than in men as human numbers increased. Eventually, though, obedience would have become increasingly stressed for all, as disobedient behavior began to be seen more and more as a danger to the group.

Once the simple collecting of naturally growing stands of cereal grains began to be first supplemented and then replaced by deliberate sowing and cultivation of the crop to be harvested, permanent settlements began to take the place of the previous pattern of seasonal base camps. That was probably when bands ceased to live as one group with only minimal spatial separation between each cluster of spouses and offspring in the hours of eating, recreation, and sleeping. Band life had enabled each woman and her young children to stay close together, and at the same time to be with the man who was both her husband and the children's father. But in the new situation of settled life other arrangements soon began to be made.

The first Middle Eastern agricultural villages, from around 9000 to 8000 B.C., show a definite separation between sleeping huts and storage huts. Whether the contents of a given storage hut might be for a given sleeping hut's users is highly uncertain. (In African or Pacific Islands or New Guinea villages today that is the case. But it is risky to extrapolate backward from that.) By about 7000 B.C., however, the pattern of separate sleeping huts and storage huts had changed to one of a single, separate sleeping and storage facility for each family. Clearly a sense of mine-and-thine was being inculcated. With that separation of ours-and-yours within the village, the larger community within which basic family clusters of spouses and children lived must have finally ceased to have the unity of the hunting-gathering band. No longer were a dead man's or woman's possessions apt to be shared among all (as among the Mbuti today) rather than being passed on to the nearest of kin, however "nearest" might be defined. Under such circumstances insistence must have sharply increased that a child must be obedient to adults' commands to leave alone what was seen as others', rather than expecting to share in it as a fellow-member of the co-resident community.

Talcott Parsons' four needed layers for a fully operating social system, outlined in Chapter 1, were assuredly functioning by the time village families began living in separate sleeping-storage units. Those four layers start even before birth with the mother-child pair. The second layer, the father-mother (husband-wife) pair to which birth introduces the child, prepares the child for the expectations of the larger society. That is because husband and wife have their own relationship with each other to maintain, as well as their relationships with the child. Through interacting with the parents (and their separate relationship) the child learns how to interact with others less closely linked to itself. The child can then move to the third level of the larger set of kin to which the child is linked through its parents, and to which each parent is linked either through his or her own parent or through his or her spouse (the child's other parent). As the child learns the closenesses and distances in those relationships it finally becomes ready to interact with the fourth layer, those who are part of the total group that sees itself as a community but who are not seen as active kin to whom one's specific links are known.

The child starts to develop its identity within the basic family, both its social identity (what duties and rights it has in relation to others) and its personal identity (how it will carry out those duties and use those rights). Ordinarily this takes place in strongest relation to the father-mother (husband-wife) pair, though some societies also expect a strong relationship with the mother-mother's brother pair. Through these relationships one learns how to distinguish between the mutually sharing and supportive core group, within which one has a specific personal identity, and those beyond. One gradually learns how to work with those whose expectations are based on an impersonally assessed quality of performance in definite tasks, some of which are important to one assessor and others to another, rather than on kinship. In that way one can grow into what Parsons recognized as the full personality. One can turn from leading to following and back again, as a given situation may require. One can both lead and follow not only in getting a job done, but also in maintaining satisfying working relationships among those performing the task. One can accept both person-centeredness (it's who you are and how you relate to others that count) and performance-centeredness (it's what you do and how well you do it that count).

Parsons has often been described as believing that the ideal basic or nuclear family consists of an *instrumental* (task-oriented) husband and an *expressive* (relationship-building) wife, who teach their son and daughter to be instrumental followers and expressive followers, respectively, as preparation for eventually becoming instrumental husband and expressive wife in their turn. What he actually says is that there is a strong tendency for nuclear families to organize in that way for convenience, in a society in which men usually and women seldom do productive work outside the home. Indeed, he insists that for full self-development, every man and woman needs to learn how to be both leader and follower, in both instrumental and expressive ways, and in both performance-centered (usually nonkin) and person-centered (usually kin or close-friendship) situations. The family gives a child its first practice in interacting with other human beings. Whatever mixture of intergenerational transmission of unconscious messages the parents may pass on with their conscious instruction will therefore naturally affect the child. Nonetheless, the child starts anew in some degree, being genetically unique (or at most, except rarely, genetically identical to no more than a twin or a triplet). Thus the interaction patterns of each child will be unique, even though they may resemble those of others in many ways.

The members of social systems help to shape individuals' behavior and thinking through interactions with them. However, the cumulative effect of an individual's interactions with other members of his or her social system also helps to shape that system and its other members. That is true whether the shaping is toward continuance of patterns (because they are complied with fairly readily) or toward modification of patterns (because they are strongly resisted, seeming to the individual to press too greatly on him or her). The "adopted-in wife" pattern in Taiwan, mentioned in Chapter 3, has been practiced in many parts of China at various times. But it seems as if its use may have fluctuated, as resistance by young people of both sexes to the consummation of such marriages led to reconsideration of whether the resultant lessening in strains between mother-in-law and daughter-in-law was really worth the probable increase in strains between husband and wife. When reversion to the (standard and traditionally preferred) practice of bringing in a strange bride led to too much mother-in-law–daughter-in-law tension in the (standard and traditionally preferred) extended-family household of parents, married sons, and grandchildren, then the adopting-in of future wives would again have seemed attractive as an alternative. In another illustration, extended co-resident families have advantages, like work-sharing and the presence of emotional supporters in time of loss. But they have disadvantages too, in terms of strains and pressures felt by those who live in them. That is clearly demonstrated by the almost universal preference for smaller co-resident units, whenever economic and political circumstances make these feasible.

Even a small and fairly closely kin-linked hunter-gatherer band must distinguish between person-centeredness and performance-centeredness. Otherwise, the band might let a now-senile though formerly effective member counsel them toward a disastrous choice. But not until considerably later than the rise of village life did groups of villages begin to cluster around one or another particularly effective village leader. In this way two-tiered sociopolitical systems came into existence. These were apt to be chiefdoms, in which the chief was expected to use celebrations and feasts to redistribute to the villagers whatever wealth he received. The earliest such groupings probably arose when those in drier parts of the Middle East began to concentrate on raising animals to trade for grain from better-watered neighboring areas. This trade would eventually have required coordination between the leaders of the increasing number of agricultural villages and the leaders of the growing groups of nomad pastoral herders, who themselves began to develop two-tiered tribal coordinating arrangements. As groups of villages in better-watered areas then sought to coordinate their trade with both the nomad pastoralists and the animal-raising villages in drier areas, three-tiered sociopolitical systems came into being, in which top-level leaders were full-time coordinators. These three-tiered systems may be called the real beginnings of statehood. They came into being by around 3600 B.C. in southwest Iran, to bring nomad pastoralists and settled villagers into operating harmony. Within another few centuries even more complex four-tiered systems developed in the plains of Mesopotamia/Iraq. In the cities of the four-tiered systems the full-time religious and political leaders' obligation to redistribute wealth was less important to maintaining their authority than were their development of writing and their use of full-time administrative and military servants. Writing made it possible to keep track of information needed for effective coordination; full-time record-keepers and record-users made it possible to coordinate the activities of increasingly large numbers of people who were doing increasingly different things. The first-tier coordinators in two-or-more-tiered systems tended to remain part-time, engaging in agriculture or herding themselves. But above that level coordination tended more and more to become a full-time occupation, as complexity increased.

That complexification of society probably also resulted in an increased feeling of need to instill habits of obedience early, so as to ease the multiple tasks of the coordinators. But it may well have directly affected the development of more than just the parent-child relationship. Early in the agricultural era obedience to all one's seniors in age, and thus presumably in experience, may have replaced previously free discussion like that among

contemporary hunter-gatherers deciding where to seek food next. In a perhaps largely unconscious extension of the small child's common belief that
men must be more important than women because they tend to be taller
and otherwise physically larger than women, obedience to all those larger
than oneself may have become generalized to an expectation of women's
obedience to men. Or it may have been, as !Kung (Qung) former hunter-
gatherers in Botswana have said to anthropologists, that habits of obedience
by women toward men came out of the change from sleeping together
around a fire to sleeping in separate huts. Around the fire the band argued
things through as a group. But in a hut a man could use his greater upper-
body strength to beat his wife into accepting his arguments out of fear,
rather than by reasoning.

However it may have arisen, that expectation of women's obedience to
men would have reinforced the pattern of juniors' obedience to seniors,
which in turn would have reinforced the expectation that children must be
obedient to adults' commands. All of these patterns would have grown
stronger with the passing of the generations, as population increase and the
growth of villages increased concern for protecting stored grain and avoiding
alarm to milk-providing herd animals. Eventually the relative ease with
which most hunter-gatherer women (like most hunter-gatherer men) could
still leave a marriage and seek another partner might well have come to be
seen as too great for the maintenance of expected levels of obedience. Consequently ease of divorce could have been decreased for women as a means
of putting pressure on them to obey, probably far more than ease of divorce
would have decreased for men. The code of Hammurabi in 18th-century
B.C. Mesopotamia may echo that shift. Under the code a husband could
divorce his wife for any reason he might choose by returning her to her
father with whatever dowry her father had given with her, plus a fine whose
amount had been set in the marriage contract. However, a wife could obtain
divorce only under whatever specific conditions had been set forth in the
marriage contract. The contract ordinarily would not only list the reasons
for which she might seek a divorce, but would also fix the amount she must
pay the husband if she obtained one, since he would have given her father
or her guardian bride-wealth for her. Clearly these laws applied to free
persons with property, not to those who were too poor to exchange bride-
wealth and dowry by contract, or to the slaves who had no recognized right
to marry. We cannot document their marriage patterns.

Hammurabi's code was also the first to try to deter a woman from refusing
to enter a marriage her parents had arranged for her, once the contract had
been signed that was supposed to mark her acceptance of their choice. This
again would indicate a tightening of restrictions on women in particular,
perhaps partly to maintain the general principle of obedience in response
to the increasing pressures felt as populations continued to grow. (In contemporary urban societies a positive correlation exists between the number

of persons per room, in housing surveys, and the number of assaults and homicides reported to law enforcement agencies. The greater the crowding, the more frequent the attacks.) A code of a few centuries earlier showed the woman as given by her parents to her husband in the marriage contract, rather than as accepting him from them. But it also gave her full right to refuse her parents' choice after the contract had been signed.

By the time of written codes governing marriage, rules for the selection of partners had in general changed from prescriptive (whom to marry) to proscriptive (whom not to marry). Essentially this meant incest rules and other general rules such as the one in Hammurabi's code requiring free persons to marry only other free persons, since unfree persons were, by definition, unfree to enter legal marriages. Such proscriptive systems gave full play to the four basic considerations of expected personal compatibility, personal economic contribution, family economic and social position, and family record of health and longevity. However, even among preliterates who might continue to use prescriptive systems, the polygynous Iatmül of New Guinea (who raise garden crops and pigs) serve as a warning against taking any formal marriage rules too seriously. The Iatmül say that they use sister-exchange, cross-cousin marriage at first-cousin level between a man and his father's sister's daughter (or a woman and her mother's brother's son), and cross-cousin marriage at second-cousin level between a man and his father's mother's brother's son's daughter (or a woman and her father's father's sister's son's son). Yet these are incompatible with each other. The Iatmül also say that they do not allow a man to marry his wife's brother's daughter or his mother's brother's daughter, even though women do in fact occasionally marry their father's sisters' husbands or their father's sisters' sons. The observable contemporary situation of people like the Iatmül—or the Purum of Assam in northeastern India, raisers of garden crops and pigs, who simply adopt a wanted bride into the correct group for her intended husband to marry into, if she had not been born into it—makes it difficult to believe that early preliterate peoples rigidly adhered to prescriptive marriage rules. The observed willingness of Aborigines in Australia to regard a wanted spouse as being in the correct group, whether actually so or not, reinforces that doubt. The considerations that might have led people toward various general types of prescriptions and proscriptions are more significant than the details of specific sets of rules, as societies moved from simple woman-exchange systems of the kinds hypothesized earlier for the first hunter-gatherers (whether Mbuti-simplified or Murngin-complicated) to more complex systems, which involved exchanges of goods and services as well as the bestowing in marriage of a woman on a man by her guardians.

The probable earliest pattern of a woman's departure for a new band at marriage is apt to have led to her being seen as bestowed on a man as seeker-recipient. Her guardians were likely to think long and hard about the third of the four basic considerations, the position of the group to be married into, both for her own well-being and for the usefulness of establishing or strengthening ties with a potential husband's band. The groom (or his guardians, if he were young and had never married before) would have been less concerned with that. Because the groom's group would be receiving rather than losing the new bride's services, they would care more about the second basic consideration, her characteristics as a worker.

A potential bride's kin could probably choose among several potential husbands, since childbearing hazards made women scarce in almost all early societies. The recurrence of the theme of suitors having to compete with one another or to perform a difficult task set by the father, in order to win a particular bride, may reflect that early human experience. The man saw himself as receiving the highly prized gift of a wife from her people. That in turn could well have led to requiring a period of working for the bride's kin as part of establishing the marriage. Such bride-service was observed, for example, in 19th-century California among hunter-gatherers who lived a semisettled life, moving only twice a year, up to a summer base in the hills and down to a winter base in the valleys. Eventually such beliefs and practices could lead to the instituting of bride-wealth (a giving of goods rather than of services) and that of dower, gifts to the bride's parents and to the bride, respectively, by the intended husband. All of these taken together—bride-service, bride-wealth, and dower—are the forms described in Jack Goody's listing of 857 nonindustrial societies in *Bridewealth and Dowry in Africa and Eurasia* (1973) as being used in 20 times as many societies (almost all small) as those (usually somewhat larger) that use dowry, that is, gifts from the bride's family that are intended to provide for her well-being after marriage.

Those familiar with anthropological discussions of whether marriage systems are primarily a means of establishing and maintaining alliances, or primarily a means of establishing who is descended from whom, and therefore entitled to inherit various kinds of rights in both tangible and intangible property, will immediately recognize that this discussion thus far appears to favor the alliance theory. However, as previously suggested, questions of right to hunt and gather with a particular band may well have begun to increase in importance as population pressures grew. If so, that would have encouraged the development of a sense of lineage. As hunter-gatherers began to become semi-sedentary—like some !Kung today, or the preagricultural gatherers of cereals and milkers of herd animals in the Middle East of 12,000 or so years ago—and then eventually to turn to the actual raising of crops and domestication of animals, means of allocating land-use rights would have been required. The growth in importance to one's livelihood of being recognized as having a right to use a relatively small specific area well suited to cultivation, not merely to rove through a large region with a variety of natural features, could well have increased a tendency to use descent-from-

X as such a means. Descent from someone who had previously used that land would be an easily understandable as well as enforceable means of allocation.

The remainder of this chapter concentrates on types of lineage systems and how they have tended to correlate with various aspects of marriage systems—who is preferred as a spouse, what exchanges of goods and services may take place at marriage, where the spouses live after marriage, why elders have ordinarily been responsible for arranging at least the first marriage if not succeeding ones, what strains may lead to dissolution of a marriage and how readily such dissolutions may take place. It is important to note here, at the beginning, that a growth in the significance of lineage or descent meant a change in the relative significance of considerations of alliance and considerations of descent or lineage as part of marriage systems. As agriculture took the place of hunting-gathering life, stress on inheritance rights began to receive greater emphasis, by comparison with concern for increasing the size of one's network of alliances through one's own and one's kin's marriage ties with groups with whom one might then hope to hunt or gather in future years. Hunter-gatherer marriage rules tend to maximize one's network of alliances by discouraging or even prohibiting marriages between first cousins. (The Inuit are an exception.) Hunter-gatherers tend to require that a spouse be sought from farther afield, even if that field is then specified as a certain set of second or third or even fourth cousins. However, marriage rules in agricultural societies are more likely to allow at least some forms of first-cousin marriage. Not only can such marriages reconsolidate inheritance rights that were divided among siblings in a previous generation, but they can also strengthen a sense of closeness and mutual support within a given kin group. The kin group may even come to regard that aspect of alliance-building as having at least equal priority with forming new alliances with other families. Although a patrilineal system would reconsolidate inheritance rights most quickly through parallel-cousin marriages between offspring of two brothers, the tensions which can result mean that patrilineal systems allow such marriages much less often than they allow cross-cousin marriages between the offspring of siblings of opposite sex. (Middle Eastern experience, to be discussed in Chapter 8, clearly shows that if two brothers marry women born to two different brothers of their father, the two fathers-in-law may go to great lengths to press their brother to favor the son married to this one's or that one's daughter.) Successive generations of cross-cousin marriages can eventually produce some reconsolidation, if consideration is given to doing so.

Those who study societies in which the making of new alliances receives great emphasis tend to stress the alliance-related aspects of marriage systems, whereas those who study societies in which inheritance rights in land or animals receive great emphasis tend to stress considerations of descent and lineage. Yet inheritance-concerned dowry-users as well as hunter-gatherers are interested in making new alliances. Dowry is often used by a woman's father to attract a husband for her from a family with whom they wish to ally. It is usually found in a society in which commercial activity is important enough to make alliances for commercial purposes valuable, not in a more purely agricultural society. Bride-wealth and/or bride-service, on the other hand, tends to correlate with a stress on lineage. But whether the building of networks of alliances or the strengthening of lineages through giving birth to offspring is emphasized, marriage continues to have two major functions. It gives the children born to it a socially recognized father as well as a mother, and it links the two spouse-parents to the wider society. Marriage symbolically reminds the spouses that they remain part of the larger whole. That symbolic reminder may be parental participation in the arrangement and celebration of the marriage, some form of gift-giving or bride-service, or merely the requirement (as in medieval western Christendom) that the two vow to God as their only witness that they mean to wed, not reporting their marriage to another human being until some time later. However, it is always formally recognized that the marriage concerns more than just the spouses, and that the spouses are to be concerned with more than just each other and whatever children they may have. That formal recognition is likeliest to involve a highly visible ceremony if there has been a substantial presentation of gifts from one side or the other, or if the society is an agricultural or a pastoral-herding one in which the children's rights of inheritance will need the recognition of the marriage for their legitimation.

As groups moved from a roaming hunting-gathering life to a semi-sedentary and then a sedentary one, they developed a strong sense of possession about who could cultivate a given piece of land (or at least cultivate a periodically reallocated part of a given area held either by a kin group or a residential community) and who was entitled to make use of a given animal or group of animals. That was true whether they used animals for agricultural labor as well as food (as in the Middle East since the rise of agriculture there), almost entirely for milk and meat (as in much of sub-Saharan Africa, many of whose people relied until recently on hoe rather than plow agriculture), for labor and meat but not for milk (as in much of East and Southeast Asia), or just for meat (as in the pig-raising cultures of New Guinea, the Pacific Islands, and parts of Southeast Asia). Those groups that went to nomadic pastoral herding as a way of life also developed a sense of possessiveness about their animals.

Because both early and recent agriculture-based societies have relied on descent lines to determine the transmission of cultivation rights and other inheritable goods and rights, it is not surprising that they have also tended to move toward either patrilineality or matrilineality, or occasionally duo-lineality. Hunter-gatherers tend to use bilaterality so as to maximize the scope of networks. But where there is some kind of property to be transmitted to heirs, *unilineality* (using one clearly definable line for transmission of a given set of rights) seems simpler than bilaterality, with its expectation of equal inheritance for and from both men and women. (Duolineality is a special type of unilineality.) Exceptions must be made to any unilineal system for lack of a child of the appropriate sex. However, a *cognatic* or bilateral system always has to cope with the probability that children of one sex—usually the daughters—will move out of the community at marriage (not just out of the household) more often than their opposite-sex siblings. Systems giving equal inheritance rights to both men and women do exist in agricultural societies, as in many Pacific Islands societies and much of Southeast Asia. But they tend to be either what is sometimes called *ambilineal*, as among the Maori of New Zealand, or what is sometimes called *utrolateral*, as among the Iban of Borneo, not strictly cognatic. Ambilineality means that one's lineality is ambiguous, in the sense that one seeks to retain lineal ties with as many as 3 or 4 of one's 8 great-grandparents or even one's children's 16 great-great-grandparents. One continues to help with work and take part in festivals in those kin groups. One may also move one's residence from one to another during one's lifetime as one may think that improves one's own and one's children's opportunities. Utrolaterality means that one makes a definite choice of which of one's own or one's spouse's parental or even grandparental lineages one will enter. Usually one signals that by choice of residence at marriage. One is then bound to that choice and loses one's other affiliations, although one's children might choose another line. Residence is likely to influence the sense of nearness or farness of kinship in any society.

In view of the division of labor already visible in preagricultural societies, in which men worked primarily with animals and women with plants, it is not surprising that plow-agricultural and milk-animal-herding societies have tended to move toward patrilineal transmission of those animals and what is done with them. Nor is it surprising that the much less common practice of transmitting cultivation rights from a man to his sister's son, rather than to his wife's son, is likeliest to occur in hoe-agricultural societies, especially those in which the only sizable domestic animal is the meat-providing pig. In David Aberle's study of 101 hunter-gatherer, 79 pastoral, 188 hoe-agricultural, and 117 plow-agricultural societies, in David M. Schneider and Kathleen Gough's collection *Matrilineal Kinship* (1961), 56% of all matrilineal societies practiced hoe-agriculture. Yet matrilineal societies constituted only 25% of dominantly hoe-agricultural societies. (See Table 4.) Of the hoe-agricultural societies surveyed, 37% were bilateral, 35% were patrilineal, and 3% were duolineal.

As agriculture spread, the growing importance of having a parent from whom one could inherit cultivation rights probably encouraged increased obedience to elders, who might disinherit one if too severely provoked. It probably also led to increased concern for having offspring who would support one in return for those inheritance rights, when age lessened one's capacity to do the heavier work. In a hunter-gatherer group the aging could meet their gradually diminishing food needs by their own gathering and by receiving distributions from the meat supplied by active hunters. They could also still contribute by sharing what they had learned in their long years of experience. But in an agricultural society the need for a continuing capacity to do heavy physical labor would have made it increasingly important to ensure one's future by having offspring. Not only that, but small children could be given simple tasks to do much earlier than they could be trusted to gather wisely or hunt successfully.

The multiplication of tasks as people moved from hunting-gathering to agriculture meant more than that small children were put at tasks as soon as possible. It also meant that the wife-mother had to divide her attention more between nursing infants and doing other chores. One answer, shown to increase each adult's productivity by about 15% in a study of villagers in Chad reported by S. P. Reyna in the *Journal of Anthropological Research* (1976), was to bring clusters of related adults together in extended families, keeping married offspring with parents and accepting other kin into the household (such as those who had lost a spouse). To use the economists' term for increasing the proportion of working adults to children and infirm or aged adults, the extended-family household lowers the *dependency ratio*. It brings more than just the two parents of young children together in the ongoing production unit of the household. The extended-family household is both the ideal and (insofar as demographically possible) the reality of many agricultural societies.

Another answer was to shorten the lactation period by turning to cereal gruel, with or without animal milk. Yet another was to cease using continual lactation, nursing the infant only every two to four hours. That increased its chances of becoming colicky but released the mother to work in the field or garden. The infant was left either in a protective crib or cradleboard, or with an older child or aged person as watcher. This, like early weaning, would have meant that the contraceptive effect of continual lactation would have ceased to be felt. Pregnancy may therefore have begun to occur among early agriculturalists at least two to three times as often as has apparently been the case among early hunter-gatherers. The additional children might have been welcomed, as additional pairs of hands to help with chores from early childhood on. But they would also have raised the dependency ratio, putting more pressure on mothers with several small children to care for than their foremothers would have felt when a child was normally at least three to four years old before its next sibling would be born. As that was recognized, still another answer came to be to extend the probably already familiar practice of taking another spouse. Another spouse meant another adult in the household, as well as insurance for having children if one's first spouse did not give them to one. Women probably did not take additional husbands while the first one still lived, in very many societies. But men ordinarily were freer to take another wife while the first one was still alive.

Polygyny means taking more than one wife at a time. *Limited polygyny*, in which only kinswomen of the first wife are taken as additional wives so as to try to facilitate harmony, has been practiced in almost as many societies as *general* polygyny, or unrestricted choice of later wives. About 39% of the 863 societies surveyed by R. L. and R. H. Munroe, in the *Handbook of Cross-Cultural Human Development* (1981), which they wrote with Beatrice B. Whiting, practiced limited polygyny. About 45% practiced general polygyny. *Polyandry*, or taking more than one husband at a time, has been practiced in fewer than 1% of those societies. (See Table 16.) *Sororate*, or taking a wife's sister as wife, either before or after the first wife's death, is found in both matrilineal and patrilineal societies. About 100 of the 250 nonindustrial societies surveyed in George P. Murdock's *Social Structure* (1965) used either sororal polygyny or the taking of a sister as successor to a deceased wife. *Levirate*, in its true form, as in ancient Israel, means treating the sons sired by a deceased husband's brother as the sons of the deceased. The term is also used, however, to describe husband-succession, or having the wife's sons by a second husband inherit the estate of the first (sonless) one, as well as sharing the estate of their actual father with any other sons he might have had by other wives. The term is even used to refer to widow-inheritance, or merging the estate of a sonless deceased husband with that of a second kinsman-husband. True levirate and husband-succession are found only in patrilineal societies. Widow-inheritance is also found in matrilineal societies, in which it maintains a marriage link somewhat as true levirate does in a patrilineal society. Levirate in its various forms parallels polyandry, which almost always involves brothers' or other close kinsmen's being treated as sharers in the rights of the one who is formally designated as the husband, rather than as full husbands in their own right to the wife. About ½ (127) of the societies in Murdock's 1965 survey used some form of levirate. Some of these also used some form of sororate.

Taking more than one husband limits the number of children fathered by those husbands to those borne by only one wife. It also ensures those children the support of more adults. Taking more than one wife has often been combined with a formal or informal prohibition of intercourse for a pregnant or lactating wife. Even when that is not the case, polygyny has generally been observed to limit the number of children that one woman is likely to bear to not more than six or seven, rather than the 11 or 12 averaged in contemporary monogamous Hutterite colony-communities in the western grain regions of the United States. Both polygyny and polyandry may thus give a man access at all times to a wife, yet they also may keep numbers of births from rapidly escalating.

Because a man in a polygynous society generally adds a second wife only after some years, and a third after some years more, polygyny does not ordinarily deprive men of opportunity to marry. Moreover a man's younger wives are likely to remarry after his death. Often they do so through husband-succession by a brother, or through widow-inheritance by a brother or by a son of an earlier wife. Polygyny only delays the opportunity of some men to marry until they either inherit from or succeed to a deceased husband, or in some way acquire the wealth often needed to obtain a wife in polygynous societies.

Among limited forms of polygyny, sororal polygyny in particular appears likeliest to occur in societies that are not only matrilineal, but also matrilocal. In such societies the husband moves into the wife's family residence, and cultivation rights on family-held land are periodically reassigned. General polygyny appears likeliest to occur when wives move in with husbands, particularly if slavery is also practiced in the society.

The circulation of women among husbands and of men among wives may lessen fertility through spreading venereal disease, in a polygynous society or a society in which divorce and remarriage are acceptable and frequent. Societies with such practices may therefore have had more chance for long-term survival in harsh conditions than more fertile monogamous societies. They did not overstrain the carrying capacity of the land on which they lived by rapidly growing in numbers.

A society might be unilineal, duolineal, or bilateral. It might be monogamous, polygynous (limitedly or generally), or polyandrous. It might practice sororate, levirate, both, or neither. It might favor a three-generation extended-family household joining parents with adult offspring and their spouses and children, or a joint family of siblings and their spouses and offspring, or a simple or nuclear family of husband, wife, and children. In any case, in any period of human history, some process of spouse selection has had to take place in order for a marriage to occur. Some set of concepts as to whom to marry and whom not to marry has had to be applied, whether primarily by the potential partners themselves (as in a modern urban industrial-commercial society in the Western world, with its traditions of individualism) or primarily by others (as in almost all other societies, at least for first marriages and especially for women).

"Whom not to marry" includes the incest prohibition. Only in the rarest instances have kin as close as full siblings been allowed to marry. Fewer objections might be raised to half-siblings marrying, as they still could do in ancient Israel as late as David's time in the 10th century B.C. To lessen the possibilities of jealousy, marriage to the former spouse of a sibling (or of a parent or a child) has also often been prohibited, as has marriage to the parent, sibling, or child of a present or former spouse.

"Whom to marry" often means the delineation of a small preferred group from whom to choose a spouse. Some have preferred certain first cousins, as illustrated by the stories of Isaac and Rebecca, or Jacob and Leah and Rachel, a thousand years before David's time. Out of 487 mostly nonindustrial and largely contemporary societies surveyed by George P. Murdock in an article in the *American Anthropologist* in 1957, 57% disapproved marriage to any first cousin and only 9% permitted marriage to any first cousin, but 34% actively preferred marriage to a specified set of first cousins (2% to a father's brother's child, i.e., a patrilateral parallel cousin, 32% to a cross cousin, a father's sister's or mother's brother's child). (See Table 20.) Such cousin-preferential systems tend to be found most often in Europe, Asia, and the Middle East, and to some extent among South American Indian peoples. (See also Table 22.) They are most apt to be used in societies in which it is regarded as important to recombine property rights fragmented by the rules of inheritance, especially where daughters and sons may both inherit rights to use agricultural land. Both parallel- and cross-cousin marriages tend to imply exchange of spouses also. Noticeably fewer cross-cousin-preferring societies in the 1957 Murdock survey stress one form (13%), rather than favoring both forms equally (19%). Thus the ratio of equal-exchange forms to other forms is about three to two. If one form of cross-cousin marriage is stressed, it is that of a son marrying his mother's brother's daughter, which is used three times as often as that of a son marrying his father's sister's daughter. Where it is the mother's brother's daughter who is preferred, the society is probably patrilineal (more than ⅔ of the time), whereas if the father's sister's daughter is preferred, it is more likely to be matrilineal (about ½ of the time).

The small group from which spouses would preferably be chosen may not be first, second, or more distant cousins. The women of descent-group A may be expected to marry men of descent-group B, whose women in turn marry men in descent-group C, and so on through a social system, in a pattern that may take one of three basic forms. One of these three basic forms of prescriptive marriage system continues the idea of exchange. Like the Murngin kinswoman-exchange pattern among hunter-gatherers, this first basic form of A women to B men, B women to C men, and on around ensures an eventual equal or symmetrical exchange of women over some identifiable number of generations if it is carried out in full. A second form of A women to B men, B women to C men, and so on exchanges women for goods, as among the Purum of Assam, in an asymmetrical cycle that carries no implication of superiority or inferiority for wife-receivers or wife-givers. However, this form does not necessarily result in the men of group A ever receiving wives from a group to which they or their ancestors had sent wives. The third form, more common than the second, is probably also more common than the first among agricultural peoples with their sense of hierarchy. It sends women asymmetrically from lower groups as wives into higher groups, in return for confirmation of not having even lower status. The first and second forms do not create problems by their very nature for the men or women of any particular group in finding spouses. The third form almost inevitably makes it hard for high-level women to find husbands of a high enough level, and for low-level men to find women of a level willing to marry them.

A less prescriptive form of spouse selection sets outer and inner limits within which a mate is to be sought and then leaves the selector free to choose among potential spouses, in terms of whichever of the four basic considerations may seem most vital. Usually the outer limit is set in terms of a residential unit, but in India, for example, it may also be set in terms of some other criterion, like birth into a named socioeconomic group. The inner limit is the incest prohibition. Or the field may be opened to all members of the whole society except the few proscribed as too close in kinship, but those from outside the society may remain prohibited unless they are made acceptable in some formal way. Acceptance may be individual, as when an outsider is accepted as a co-religionist, or when a blood-brother tie is established with a member of another society. (This would make marriage to the blood-brother's own kin incestuous but could open the possibility of marrying someone whom the blood-brother could marry.) Or two societies may agree that the women of one may contract marriages with the men of the other through recognized channels. The least prescriptive form, which most nearly fits the term proscriptive, sets formal inner limits, but not formal outer ones.

Certain kinship-terminology patterns show a greater receptivity than others to a particular form of cousin marriage. It can be helpful to look at the relations between kinship terms and marriage patterns in Dravidian-language societies in southern India, for example, where matrilateral cross-cousin marriage is often favored and the kinship terms actually used in an area may give some clue as to how strong the local preference is. Therefore, kinship terminologies will be briefly discussed.

In what are called Eskimo systems, one's collateral kin (siblings of ancestors, like aunts and uncles, and their descendants, one's cousins) are distinguished from one's lineal kin (ancestors and descendants). One uses the same term for all cousins, and must determine whether or not they are potential spouses by tracing their links to one's own ancestors, if there are prohibitions against too-close cousins. However, one cannot tell by the term for cousin itself whether or not they are eligible. In what are called Hawaiian systems, both lineals and collaterals of the same generation and sex are given the same term. No distinction is made between brother and cousin, or between mother and aunt. Again, something other than kinship terms must be used to decide who may be married. Both of these types go with cognatic or bilateral (and also ambilineal and utrolateral) systems of descent and inheritance, but they carry somewhat different implications. Eskimo terminology correlates with a social structure in which basic spouses-and-children nuclear families are much more significant than are lineages. It also correlates with nonprescriptive marriage systems, in which the flexibility to form new alliances is regarded as even more important than the opportunity to keep renewing existing ones. Hawaiian terminology, on the other hand, correlates with a social structure in which lineages are highly significant. Hawaiian terminology also tends to correlate with prescriptive marriage systems, of the type in which the descendants of certain of one's kin are the prescribed group among whom to find a spouse. This type of system tends to perpetuate alliances between groups, rather than to encourage the formation of new alliances. But a better test of a marriage system's degree of prescriptiveness is probably whether or not the kinship-terminology system has a separate set of terms for affines (consanguines to one's spouse, or spouses to one's consanguines). If it does not, then the marriage system is apt to be so strongly prescriptive that no separate set of terms appears to be needed.

Crow and Omaha systems are the matrilineal and patrilineal versions, respectively, of a basic pattern of distinguishing between generations on the more emphasized side but lumping generations together on the less emphasized side. There is thus a sense of a woman's son taking her brother's place (in matrilineal Crow), or a man's daughter taking his sister's place (in patrilineal Omaha). This tends to work against the favoring of matrilineal cross-cousin marriages for Crow, patrilineal for Omaha, for they seem too close to a woman whose male cousin is equated to her uncle, or too close to a man when his female cousin is equated to his aunt. Where wives move from natal home to marital home in an asymmetrical cycle, of a form that does not eventually return wives from the "last" group to the "first" group to give up its sisters and daughters, there is apt to be a system that is like an Omaha system with a special term. That special term equates a man's wife's father with his mother's brother, since his father's wife would have come from the same group as his own wife. Crow and Omaha or modified-Omaha systems tend to be found where the primary concern is with proscription rather than prescription. There may be some prescriptive rules about who may be married, as in a system in which women move asymmetrically, but these are nonconfining enough so that there is apt to be a separate set of terms for affines.

Dravidian and Iroquois terminologies are, respectively, patrilateral and matrilateral versions of systems that take care to distinguish cross cousins from parallel cousins. Where patrilateral Dravidian terminology is used, there is likely to be a cross-cousin preference for the mother's brother's daughter as wife for a woman's son (father's sister's son as husband for a man's daughter). That in turn is likelier to be the case where the inheritance system is at least partly matrilineal than where it is entirely patrilineal. Its effect in a matrilineal descent and inheritance system resembles a patrilateral parallel-cousin marriage in a patrilineal descent and inheritance system, rather than a cross-cousin marriage in a patrilineal descent and inheritance system. However, cross-cousin marriage is apt to be disfavored or even prohibited where matrilateral Iroquois terminology is used. Iroquois systems, like Crow–Omaha systems, show concern with which kin may not be married. They therefore also tend to have distinct sets of terms for affines. Dravidian systems, like Hawaiian systems, show concern with which kin may be married. They therefore tend not to have separate sets of terms for affines.

Sister- or kinswoman-exchange, cousin-marriage (cross or parallel), and symmetrical group-exchange systems all tend to ensure that men (and women) throughout the society have a fairly equal chance at eventual marriage. Delays are primarily the result of whatever difficulty men may have in meeting whatever expectations exist with regard to bride-service and/or bride-wealth. However, asymmetrical cycling systems may actually impede marriage for some, if they work in a hierarchically status-conscious way. That holds true whether bride-wealth or dowry is used, though dowry is more often found than bride-wealth in a strongly status-conscious system.

Clearly many have been affected by bride-wealth or bride-service expectations. Of all 857 societies on which pertinent information was available in the group of 863 (almost all nonindustrial) studied by Jack Goody in *Bridewealth and Dowry in Africa and Eurasia* (1973), 47% have used bride-wealth, another 11% have used bride-service, and 30% expect no significant exchange of gifts. Just over 6% expect an equal exchange, 3% expect exchange of kinswoman for kinswoman, and just under 3% use dowry. (See Table 23.) However, it is well to recall that 75% of the world's population today lives in the Europe–Middle East–Asia region, in which only 22% of the societies studied have existed. It is also well to know that the listing includes some early societies with written records, along with a great majority of recently observed ones. It is important, too, to be aware that only 10% of today's world population lives in sub-Saharan Africa, where 28% of those societies have existed; only 14% (mostly not in the aboriginal societies focused on) in the Americas, where 36% of these societies have existed; and less than 1% in the Pacific region, where 14% of these societies have existed. Consequently if one wishes to estimate the proportion of people affected, one has to look at region-by-region figures. One also has to allow for the near-exclusion of modern Western societies, whether in Europe, the Americas, or Australia and New Zealand. Bride-wealth (or, less than a tenth as frequently, bride-service) is used in 65% of the surveyed societies in the Europe-Middle East-Asia area and 90% of those south of the Sahara. Elsewhere fewer than ½ use either bride-wealth or bride-service. (See Table 21.) In North America, with 25% of all the societies surveyed, Goody found that 57% of the societies expected no significant gift-exchange. (See Table 24.) Only 31% used bride-wealth (13%) or bride-service (18%). The other 12% used equal gift-exchange. In South America, Goody found 50% using bride-wealth (7%) or bride-service (43%), and in the Pacific Islands, 42% (37% bride-wealth, 5% bride-service).

One might guess that bride-wealth may have been used by perhaps ½ or so of the world's population since the development of agriculture. If that is true, then it would be by far the most frequently used form of sealing an agreement to marry. But when one recognizes the great disparity in size among the societies studied, from thousands to millions, one wonders whether it is possible to estimate relative numbers affected over time by any such set of practices. At most one can say with reasonable confidence that the expectation of some kind of provision of goods—either to the bride's kin from the groom or his kin, or to the bride herself (either from the groom or his kin or from her own kin), or to the groom from the bride's kin to help him to ensure the bride's well-being, or in some mixture of two or more of these possibilities—has probably been part of marriage arrangements for a majority of both people and societies, wherever hunting-gathering has ceased to be the chief mode of livelihood.

The use of bride-wealth has tended to correlate with polygyny, both limited and general. Still, it has also been compatible with monogamy. It has been compatible with all forms of descent systems—patrilineal, matrilineal, duolineal, and even bilateral—though it is least frequent among bilateral peoples and most common among patrilineal ones. Bride-service and equal gift-exchange have been somewhat more compatible with bilateral descent than with other descent systems. However, token or no payments have been most common in bilateral systems, and an equally high percentage of the less common systems of equal gift-exchange have also been in bilateral systems. Bride-wealth, dowry (relatively uncommon), and the also-uncommon sister- or kinswoman-exchange systems have been most compatible with patrilineal systems of descent. Patrilineal societies are also most common—47% in Goody's study of 857 societies as compared with 36% bilateral, 14% matrilineal, and 3% duolineal.

The amount of bride-wealth required has usually been rather uniform throughout a society. It has not always worked against the establishment of lasting social differentiations based on wealth, hereditary status, and power, but it has not always worked for the establishment of social differentiations either. It has meant that a woman of any social level might be married by a man of any social level, if he could gather the needed bride-wealth from his kin or from his own resources. A social system with fairly clear differentiations of wealth, status, and power, but with relatively free intermarriage among them, is often referred to as a system of *estates* rather than of classes.

The use of dowry tends to correlate with both monogamy and discouragement of divorce. That is because it tends to be used as a *conjugal fund*, or conjugal estate, which belongs jointly to husband and wife, and is meant to be passed on to their own children. Dowry tends to be negotiated on an individual basis. It rises not only with the bride's father's wealth, but also with the groom's apparent prospects for the future. Consequently it tends to correlate with a system of *classes*, in which those who are at higher levels by virtue of wealth, power, and possibly (but not necessarily) formal claim to a superior hereditary status do not willingly intermarry with those who are at lower levels. Moreover, because it involves matching the bride's dowry to the groom's prospects, it tends to be used more often in bilateral systems than in any other kind. However, a large dowry may also be used to obtain opportunity to marry a daughter into a higher social level, in a patrilineal system, and thereby to claim some gain in status for oneself and one's kinsmen.

A dowry system tends to delay daughters' marriages without hastening those of sons. Yet it may also lead to the early arrangement of marriages, either to keep the dowry low by obtaining a groom early, or to maximize the time available to collect the promised dowry. But a bride-wealth system both hastens daughters' marriages and delays those of sons. That is because the bride-wealth paid for a daughter tends either to be used to pay bride-wealth on behalf of a son, or to be distributed in repayment to kin who had helped to provide bride-wealth on behalf of the father. Those kin then use it to help provide their younger kinsmen's bride-wealth. Where bride-wealth is extremely high, as among the Igbo of eastern Nigeria, it may be accompanied by relatively late marriage for both women and men. Still, marriage is seldom delayed beyond the mid–20s for either sex. The Lele of the Congo/Zaire basin demonstrate that even high bride-wealth may delay only men's marriages, not those of women. Bride-service, kinswoman-exchange, and equal-exchange systems may delay marriages for both men and women somewhat more than systems with token or no exchange. However, they do not appear to be as consistent in hastening or delaying the marriages of either women or men as bride-wealth and dowry systems appear to be.

What the groom receives with the bride always includes the right to have intercourse with her. It does not necessarily include the right to be in the same household with her, although in most societies it does. In matrilineal societies in particular it does not include the right to regard the children she bears as members of his kin group, unless the society is in some stage of transition toward a duolineal or a bilateral or even a patrilineal form. Then he can obtain rights for his children in his kin group, through additional payments of some kind beyond what may be needed to establish his right to have intercourse with his wife. The descent system is likely to be linked with the place of residence, whether with a hunting-gathering band, on a farmstead or in an agricultural village, with a pastoral-herding extended family, or in towns (which have only begun to hold more than 10% to 15% of any country's people in the past two or three centuries). In patrilineal societies newlyweds more often reside with the husband's kinsmen and their wives and children than in a new residence. In matrilineal societies they more often reside with the wife's kinswomen and their husbands and children (or possibly with one of the wife's mother's brothers who serves as a family head) than in a new residence. In bilateral societies they may choose with some degree of flexibility between the extended-family households (or hunting-gathering bands) of the two spouses' parents and a new residence. In duolineal systems they may go either to the household of the parents of the spouse through whom dwellings are transmitted, or to a new residence. In some matrilineal systems, like the Ashanti of Ghana, a husband may persuade his wife to move from her mother's home on the ground that they will be better off with his mother. He may also continue to live with his mother, while his wife remains with hers, until they have accumulated enough to set up a separate dwelling for themselves. He may even set up a new residence immediately for himself and his new wife, though that is rare. In more amorphous systems, like the technically patrilineal Nyamwezi of central Africa, the husband who gives bride-wealth is entitled to take his wife to his father's residence and to regard the children she bears him as part of his kin group. However, the husband who does not give bride-wealth is not entitled to remove his wife from her father's household, unless he pays for the right later. He may not claim her children as part of his kin group, or transmit property to them, unless he pays for that right later also. But seldom will a society be patrilineal in descent and then expect a newly married pair to live with the wife's family. Only six out of 447 societies were both patrilineal and matrilocal, according to R. L. and R. H. Munroe in the article "Perspectives Suggested by Anthropological Data," in Volume I of H. C. Triandis, editor, *Handbook of Cross-Cultural Psychology* (1980). (See Table 27.) A patrilineal, yet matrilocal society is apt to practice *endogamy*, marriage within the group, within a local community whose members reside fairly close together. In Murdock's 1957 listing of 564 societies, on 428 of which there was sufficient information to determine both lineality and residence, 177 of 181 patrilineal societies were patrilocal. Of 58 matrilineal societies, 32 were matrilocal and 15 were avunculocal, meaning that the couple lived with the wife's mother's brother. All except four of 21 duolineal societies were patrilocal. Even among 168 bilateral societies, 78 were largely patrilocal and 30 largely matrilocal. In general, the establishment of a new residence at the time of marriage has not been common except in already fairly highly commercialized societies, and then largely in the towns.

Kathleen Gough has suggested in *Matrilineal Kinship* (Schneider and Gough, eds., 1961), that matrilineal descent systems may have arisen out of modes of livelihood that involved teamwork among women, such as fishing in some Pacific Islands cultures or planting and harvesting in some African societies. Women's teamwork in fishing or farming would make it desirable to keep kin-linked women together through matrilocality, in the way that hunting teams make keeping kin-linked men together desirable to hunter-gatherers. However, she admits that this is only a tentative suggestion. She is probably correct in saying that the question is not, "Why does a matrilineal society use matrilocality?" but rather, "What special conditions make a matrilineal society move away from matrilocality?" She is probably also correct in suggesting that in general, those conditions tend to involve an increase in total productivity, which makes social stratification possible. With social stratification comes a tendency to place increasing significance on keeping each man's wife or wives with him, so as to share in his status. That is because even in a matrilineal society, men tend to dominate in the public life of politics and war, and are therefore more immediately concerned than women with gaining and maintaining status. Certainly matrilocality seems to correlate with small-scale organization (a society of fewer than 50,000 persons), relatively peaceful relations with neighbors, and little movable wealth to be transmitted to offspring. It also seems to correlate with a mode of life that does not involve working with animals larger than pigs, sheep, or goats. Avunculocality, which moves a man from his mother's (and father's) to his mother's brother's home at some point between puberty and marriage, seems to be a means of dealing with an increase in either movable wealth or the total size of the society. However, that does not necessarily mean that matrilocality led to matrilineality. The two might have developed together. Or the recognition of the greater ease of determining siblinghood than of determining paternity (particularly in groups in which divorce came easily) might have brought a use of matrilineal reckoning. Perhaps the Ndembu of Zambia have gone farthest in the matrilineal direction, in regarding all the children of one mother as full siblings regardless of whether or not they had the same father. Matrilineal reckoning might have preceded rather than followed matrilocal residence in some groups, as they moved from hunting and gathering to agricultural life and recognized a need to simplify transmission of cultivation rights by stressing one parent's line. Matrilocal matrilineality seems to require either a fairly large co-resident group or the establishment of provisions for exceptions. One common exception is that the eldest son of the eldest daughter may take his wife to his own mother's residence, so that he may become the successor to her eldest brother as its male leader.

Whenever exceptions are made to a general rule of residence, there will probably be a special reason, as with an eldest son of an eldest daughter in a matrilineal and matrilocal system. A sonless household in a patrilineal and patrilocal society may bring a husband in to obtain grandsons through a daughter. The Mongo of Zaire, who practice sister-exchange, allow a sisterless man to move to his mother's village and seek a wife from his mother's brother's family. Some kind of special concession may be made with regard to marriage payments. In one village in the Oaxaca valley in Mexico, described by Ira Buchler and Henry Selby in *Kinship and Social Organization* (1968), it was calculated that a potential husband would expect about 50% more in goods with his bride if he were being asked to move into her father's household than if she would be moving into his father's household. The villagers in southern Japan who are described by

Joy Hendry in *Marriage in Changing Japan* (1981) have customarily simply reversed the usual expectations with regard to type and value of gifts given, when a son-in-law moves in with his bride's parents instead of the bride entering his household. These last two examples come from agricultural communities in already commercialized and urbanized societies. Still, they describe modes of handling out-of-the-ordinary situations that it is reasonable to expect might be paralleled in more purely agricultural societies.

The frequency with which a newly married pair is expected to begin married life in the household of one spouse's parents points up the evident value placed on maximizing the number of young and middle-aged adults, in proportion to young children and older people. That value appears to be highest in societies that have moved from the single-band and single-village stage to at least a two-level chiefdom or tribal unit, or even a three-level statehood system of coordination, according to J. W. Berry in Beatrice B. Whiting and others, editors, *Handbook of Cross-Cultural Human Development* (1981). Berry also notes that the fullest development of extended-family structures is in societies in which working with large animals is important. These are the societies most apt to practice polygyny, as well as to incorporate as many married offspring as possible in a family of three or more generations. The next fullest development of extended-family life is in those societies that practice either intensive, almost gardenlike permanent cultivation, like the Chinese and Japanese, or *shifting cultivation*. (See Tables 5 through 14.) Shifting cultivators move from field to field in a cycle that may take a number of years, like the peoples of the New Guinea highlands. They use only about $^{1}/_{6}$ of their cultivable land at a time, and then let it go back to bush which can refertilize the soil after it has been cropped. Permanently co-resident extended-family households of three or more generations, like polygyny, are least prominent in hunting-gathering and urban-industrial societies. Hunting-gathering and urban-industrial societies are also the two types in which network-building is more significant than transmitting cultivation rights and rights to animals. Households in hunting-gathering and urban-industrial societies are more apt to expand laterally, to provide more working adults to support dependents, than to try to keep several generations together to facilitate transmission of rights.

Technically, a *fully extended family* involves more than one set of parents together with their own married offspring and all unmarried offspring. A married couple with their own married and unmarried children and grandchildren is a *lineal family*. A *stem family* is one in which only one married child stays with the parents. Only if all decisions are shared in fully by at least the married pairs (usually represented by the husband alone except in a few matrilineal matrilocal societies), if not the unmarried adults, is it really a *joint family*, like the multigenerational fully extended family form known in southeastern Europe as the *zadruga*. In most joint and extended-family systems the elders arrange the younger members' marriages, since the elders are responsible for the household's current maintenance and future contin-uation. Frequently they are concerned with the links between their own extended household and the larger lineages to which it is linked by descent or by marital ties. That is particularly likely if the society is not only pa-trilineal or matrilineal, but also has some kind of cross-cousin preference. It is especially likely also if the society is one of the much smaller number of patrilineal groups that use patrilateral parallel-cousin marriage.

The larger lineages are of vital importance in a two-level society, in which one can count only on the members of one's own lineage in case of need. In such a society the coordinating leader has little to back his authority other than his own lineage members and whatever affines and other fol-lowers he can attract through displays of ability and generosity. But as a society grows in both numbers and complexity, the governing agencies above the second level (the level of coordinating only a few neighboring villages or a few extended pastoral-herding households) tend increasingly to take over the protective functions previously carried out by lineages. As a result extended households cease to pay as much heed to lineage considerations as before. With the rise of town-based and currency-using commerce and industry as alternatives to agriculture and herding, even the extended-family household ceases to be as essential to individual survival as before. The stresses of maintaining it no longer seem outweighed by its benefits. People consequently tend to cease trying to extend their households from the nu-clear form, which high mortality rates would have made the actual expe-rience of most people much of the time, as Peter Laslett and others have shown in *The World We Have Lost* (1965) and subsequent publications. Instead, people in commercial and industrial societies have divided lastingly into nuclear family households, which still retain many activities of mutual support and sociability with one another. At all stages, however, it has been the elders rather than the prospective partners themselves who have tended to play the larger part in arranging first marriages, whether they had much voice in arranging any later marriages or not. That age-old rule has only been modified in modern industrial-commercial societies, within the past two centuries or so. Even in those other societies that have given the young some opportunity to court each other, parental support for their choice was ordinarily still required in order for a marriage to take place.

The kin of both potential spouses have always taken a keen interest in whom their kinsman or kinswoman might marry. In bilateral systems both sides equally see potential children as potential heirs and supporters. In other systems each side also sees all potential children as potential successors, even though there may be formal rules to limit that possibility. In a patri-lineal society a man's daughter's son may inherit only if none of his sons survive him. In a matrilineal society a woman's brother's son may inherit only if none of her own sons survive her. In ambilineal or utrolateral societies either residence or land-use or work-assistance can be used to signify whether one is to be regarded as a member of a certain lineage. However, members of genuinely bilateral systems tend to think in terms of kindreds rather than in terms of lineages. These kindreds are usually *stem kindreds*, like those of early Norway and Scotland (whom one is kin to by virtue of being a child of A and B, a grandchild of C, D, E, and F, and a great-grandchild of G, H, I, J, K, L, M, and N). Far less frequently they may be *nodal kindreds*, like those of the Lapps (the sibling groups one is linked to by affinal ties between one's sibling group and them—all one's parents' siblings, all one's parents' siblings' spouses' sibling groups, all one's parents' siblings' children, all the sibling groups into which one's siblings and oneself marry). People think only in terms of descent groups, coming down from an ancestor rather than going outward from oneself, where there is a sense of belonging to one line more than to others (whether by the social system's setting of preference or by one's own choice). Even then, memory may be conveniently modified. The patrilineal Siane of New Guinea, whose kinship terminology recognizes a clear difference between a daughter's son (female agnate) and a son's son (agnate), will modify that in the next generation to make the daughter's son's son a clan agnate, and will simply class the daughter's son's son's son as an agnate like any other agnate. The patrilineal Tiv of Nigeria have been accustomed to arguing out in public assembly who may and who may not be recognized as members of a patrilineage, on the strength of being raised within its recognized households even though descended from its daughters. The courtyard unit of co-resident agnates and their wives and children, which is the basic social grouping among the Diola of Senegal, also often includes sons of sisters as well as sons of brothers. Among the patrilineal Chimbu of New Guinea, as many as $^1/_5$ of those men residing on a particular patrilineage's land are not themselves members of the patrilineage, though among the also patrilineal Enga, also of New Guinea, only about $^1/_{10}$ are in that situation. Up to $^1/_6$ of Tiv extended-household heads may be husband or son to a daughter of the patrilineage, rather than a member of the patrilineage to which the extended household supposedly belongs. Such instances are not surprising, in view of the realities pointed out in Chapter 2, that probably one in five to six of all couples before recent times had no surviving child unless they adopted one, and that at least another one in five in any unilineal system only had children of the nonpreferred sex.

Whether or not a married pair are producing offspring (or offspring of the preferred sex) has surely been a major type of strain on the marital tie in almost all premodern societies. Only in very recent times, and only in economically advanced countries, have government-sponsored social welfare systems begun to supplement or replace reliance on the family by those unable to support themselves. In practice, almost every society has enabled those who remain childless either to separate and try again with other partners, or to bring children into their own household to raise as theirs.

Usually such children have been from families that are already linked by birth to one or the other of the two spouses. Usually they have also been treated as breaking most, if not all, of their ties with their natal parents. The incest rule against marrying close blood-kin, if known, is virtually the only such tie left in most modern Western societies, in any legal sense. In what is generally termed *fosterage* rather than adoption, in many Pacific Islands societies, children may return to (or be taken back by) their parents until about the age of puberty. At that time they make their own, more lasting choice. However, if significant bride-wealth or dowry had not been given, and if taking a new wife would not require long bride-service from a man, it appears to have been likelier across the span of human history that the two would separate to seek other partners than that they would seek children to adopt or foster. Only if they had found that they were unusually compatible in habits and temperament would they be apt to stay together in spite of childlessness, if the society accepted divorce and re-marriage as legitimate. Among the nominally patrilineal Yoruba of western Nigeria, for example, who expect bride-wealth to be repaid if there is divorce, the British recorded one divorce for every 29 existing marriages (no matter how long ago they had been contracted) in one district in one year before Nigeria's independence in 1960. The result was a higher frequency of divorce than in the United States of the 1940s to 1960s. Among the Barma of Chad, who use some bride-wealth, it was observed in the 1960s (just after independence had been won from France) that 51% of those who were still childless after two years divorced. However, only 15% of those who had a child within two years divorced. Of all women, 59% had been divorced at least once. Among one group of the Gusii in Kenya, in the 1960s, 27% of the wives had divorced without having borne children, and then remarried. The Gusii also use bride-wealth.

Another point of strain has always been the tension between the mutual interests of the spouses themselves (including their mutual interest in their own children) and the interests each spouse may have in common with his or her own siblings, parents, and other close consanguine kin. Depending on the degree to which divorce and remarriage are regarded as acceptable, that tension might result in a divorce, or it might lead to weakening or even breaking ties with other family members (whether still residing in one house-hold or already living in separate households). Even systems like those of traditional China and India, which appear to cut all formal ties between one spouse (almost invariably the wife) and that spouse's natal family, nevertheless tend to acknowledge the brother of the new husband's mother at a wedding or the brother of the deceased's mother at a funeral. Clearly some ties are recognized as inescapably remaining real. Attempts to require a breaking of ties are usually meant to impress on a new wife that she must learn to get along well with her new husband's parents, siblings, and other kin. But if those attempts are harshly enforced—which is possible only where divorce is not easily available to a wife, or she would simply leave—then they are likely in later years to strengthen her resolve to urge her husband to leave an extended-family household in order to set up a separate household. Only then can she, and not his mother, be the senior woman.

That is how it would tend to work out in a monogamous society, or in one in which only the very wealthy and/or the childless might take either a second formal wife or (more often) a less formally established concubine. In societies in which polygyny is more widely practiced, another major and ongoing source of matrimonial strain can be the co-wives' relationships with one another. Occasionally co-wives become so compatible that they will stay together even though their relationships with their husband are unsatisfactory. But that is uncommon. After all, whatever preference may be given among wives tends to be largely by the husband's decision, not by their own. It also tends to be regarded as something for a man to do cautiously, out of recognition that any hint of favoritism will tend to increase strain. If that strain is really hard for one wife to bear, it may make her seek a divorce from a husband with whom she would otherwise prefer to stay. Matrilocal polygyny might seem a solution, even when the wives are not kin to one another. It is still practiced in the Comoro Islands east of Madagascar in the Indian Ocean, probably as a relic of the times when island men traded over long distances and genuinely sought a wife in every port. But its inconvenience for a husband has generally prevented its being seriously considered unless the wives were also sisters.

One of the reasons compatibility-conscious hunter-gatherer men who take a second wife usually turn to one of her sisters is to try to avoid co-wife strain. Few hunter-gatherers practice polygyny, though. Where it does exist, with two or at most three wives for a few older men, it may almost be considered a means of introduction for the newer wives. They will probably eventually marry some other band member, after their aging husband dies.

Another means of trying to avert co-wife strain is to give each wife a different set of functions. Europeans trading on the West Africa coast in the 17th century A.D. noted that the local merchants tended to have at least three wives. One managed the everyday affairs of the household, one worshiped the gods on behalf of the household, and the rest raised millet and yams to feed the household. The husband's responsibility was to clear fields for cultivation, build and repair houses as needed, tend any animals, protect all household members, and carry on trade—but only in items his wives did not produce, for they were free to sell those themselves.

In polyandrous systems, strains similar to those among co-wives in polygynous systems are likely to be felt by co-husbands. However, the set of strains over "whose children" will receive what is essentially absent, unless the several husbands share more than one wife. In that case, as among the Pahari of the Himalayas in India, it is likely that eventually the household will divide into as many households as there are wives. It is to avoid co-husband strains that polyandrous husbands are almost always close kins-men, even brothers, or else they are not co-resident with their wife.

Divorce in polygynous systems is usually easy for a husband to obtain. It may also be fairly easy for him to obtain in a monogamous system. Divorce in a polygynous system may be relatively easy for a wife to obtain, as well. That is less apt to be the case in a monogamous system. Divorce tends to be easiest for a wife to obtain if the descent-and-inheritance system is ma-trilineal. Then a man is more concerned with keeping his sisters' children's loyalty than with keeping a wife's children's loyalty. Divorce also tends to be relatively easy for either party to obtain where bride-service or a moderate amount of bride-wealth is given by the husband, especially if it is not re-coverable. It tends to be harder to obtain (especially for the wife) where dowry is given by the bride's kin, and must be restored either to them or to her if the marriage is dissolved for any reason other than her own death (or possibly her adultery). Divorce tends to be easiest for either party to obtain where the husband gains the fewest rights and privileges through the marriage, such as not having a right to transmit property to a wife's children (only to his sisters' children), or not having a right to take his wife out of her natal household to reside with him. Divorce in a polyandrous system is apt to be a great deal easier for the oldest man in the household to obtain than for anyone else. However, a younger man is usually allowed to with-draw to form a new household with another wife, if he can manage to support a separate household, and if his departure does not leave the initial household unable to maintain itself.

Where bride-wealth has been high, or where dowry has been used, or where payments made on both sides have been high, there has been a tendency for the payment-receivers to discourage divorce, since it has tended to involve some return of payments. There has also generally been a scaling down, perhaps to nothing, of payments made for a second marriage after a spouse has died. However, if a woman enters a second marriage after a divorce, her new husband, rather than her own kin, may be the one expected to repay the first husband. He may also do it indirectly through her parents, rather than directly to the previous spouse. Levirate tends to take place more often in bride-wealth and bride-service societies than elsewhere be-cause it provides another kinsman with a wife without necessitating a new payment. Sororate, in the sense of obtaining as wife a kinswoman of one who has died, may be practiced for similar reasons. The Subanum of Min-danao in the Philippines, who use bride-wealth, expect the household of a deceased spouse of either sex to provide a new spouse. They also expect bride-service for a period after marriage. Bride-service does not correlate as strongly as high payment levels with discouragement of divorce, for no repayment of service by the bride's family is likely to be expected. The bride's family may in fact encourage her to divorce, because then they are likely to be able to receive more bride-service from another hopeful husband.

A patrilineal, duolineal, or bilateral society is likely to seek means of coun-
teracting that through introducing returnable bride-wealth, if it becomes a
frequent occurrence. A matrilineal society is less apt to do so, because the
children of the marriage are of the mother's line anyway. Where there are
no substantial payments on either side, divorce is also likelier to be accepted
than where there is either kinswoman-exchange or an equal but fairly sizable
exchange of gifts.

Payment-givers may accept divorce when payments are returned. But in
dowry systems, where dowry tends to substitute for a later share in the
inheritance, the dowry-givers are apt to discourage dissolution. If an already
married and dowried sister recovers her dowry (which is often smaller than
her brothers' anticipated shares of the family estate), puts it into the estate,
and then expects an equal division, her brothers might have to lower their
inheritance expectations considerably. That could be awkward, if they had
already pledged a certain dowry for a daughter of their own, for instance.
Such concerns may well underlie the Islamic world's continuing acceptance
of the early Muslim rule about giving only half-shares to daughters, which
in its time was an advance on giving neither dowry nor inheritance rights.
Ordinarily a daughter would already have received something in dowry
from the parents at marriage, so that the dowry plus the inheritance of a
half-share at the parent's death would total approximately the full share of
a son.

The recognition of points of strain in relations between a wife and her
husband's kin, between a husband and his wife's kin, and between co-wives
has led to various efforts to ease those points of strain either through *joking
relationships* or (more often) through *avoidance relationships*. In joking
relationships those who might feel tension are expected to trade "friendly
insults" without inhibition, expressing the real tensions in socially prescribed
ways. This is not the same as expecting them to find close relations easy to
maintain because there are no points of real strain. In avoidance relationships those who might feel tension are expected to be formal and reserved
with one another, as a means of minimizing the possibility of open clashes.
The parents of a husband and a wife are expected to avoid each other in
the Andaman Islands in the Indian Ocean, for example. In a patrilineal
system, a man might be expected to avoid his father's father and his father's
elder brothers (who exercise some real authority over him), joke with his
mother's father (who might come to exercise such authority if he became
his mother's father's heir because none of his mother's brothers survived),
and be genuinely free with his mother's sisters' sons (with whom he would
have little reason to be at odds). In a matrilineal system he might be expected
to avoid not only his mother's brother and his wife's brother, but also his
sister's husband; joke with his father's brothers; and be genuinely free with
his father's brothers' sons. Ordinarily a man is not in a joking relationship
with a woman, unless she is his own sister. He may be genuinely free with

a woman, but that is not a joking relationship. Nor are women usually in joking (as contrasted with genuinely free) relationships with one another, since they are usually under more social restrictions than are men. Normally each spouse is expected to be in an avoidance relationship, formal and cautious, with both of the other spouse's parents, no matter what form the descent or kinship system takes—patrilineal, matrilineal, duolineal, ambilineal, utrolateral, or fully bilateral. It is also common for each spouse to be expected to be formal with the other spouse's siblings and with those siblings' spouses, for there can be strains in those relationships as well.

In summary, we have looked at the roles played by concerns with regard to alliance and descent in the arrangement of marriages, as people moved from hunting-gathering life to agricultural life. We have also looked at possible patterns of modification of previous systems for deciding whom to pair in such arrangements, and at the roles of presentations of gifts or services, residential choice, inheritance patterns, and built-in strains. To illustrate that discussion, we shall look at the experience of precivilized two-level and three-level societies in the Middle East and the pre-Spanish conquest civilizations of Peru and Mexico. In seeking to understand the history of marriage systems in early agricultural societies, it will also be helpful to look briefly at the multivaried experience of agricultural societies in Africa south of the Sahara, in New Guinea and the Pacific Islands, and in other parts of the Americas.

CHAPTER 5

Marriage in Agricultural Societies: From Early Mesopotamia to Africa, the Americas, and the Pacific

The societies to be discussed in this chapter are those of the early Middle East, sub-Saharan Africa, New Guinea and the Pacific Islands, and the Americas. Like the early agricultural societies that preceded the rise of the first states and empires in the ancient Middle East, hoe-agricultural and plow-agricultural societies in most of the other regions remained essentially preurban and preliterate until impinged on by more complex societies—in sub-Saharan Africa first by the Islamic Middle East a thousand years ago and then by the West for the past five centuries; in New Guinea and the Pacific Islands primarily by the West in the past century or so; and in the Americas by the West since the 16th century A.D.

Hereditary landholding and cultivating groups are found both in early Mesopotamian records of 3000 to 2000 B.C. and in 16th century A.D. Spanish conquerors' descriptions of sociopolitical arrangements in the already-civilized states of Aztec Mexico and Inca Peru. They may yield clues about how marital systems evolved among early agricultural peoples. Clearly descent mattered, probably more than alliance within the local land-using group (as recognized by those in the higher levels of the state structure). Descent mattered to those in the higher levels too. It was important enough to the highest royal Inca lineage so that only a full sibling was thought fully worthy of marriage, though at lower levels such marriages (evidently used as a symbol of purity and worthiness to lead) were not allowed. Rank was hereditary both in early Mesopotamia and in the Aztec and Inca states, though modifiable by royal decree. Marriage partners tended to be formally limited to those of one's own rank, whether at the top or farther down the social scale. Marriages also tended to be arranged. The woman's parents or guardians received goods (or services, or both) from the man in return for her joining him as partner, in the work of the household, in intercourse, and in the bearing and rearing of children. Among the early Mesopotamians as well as the Aztecs those children were regarded as being of his line rather than of hers. However, they might activate a claim to the property of their mother's father or brother if he were to die without other close heirs. Among the Inca, though, the children were apparently of both lines, in a duolineal rather than a bilateral way. The men inherited some kinds of rights in a father-to-son succession and the women inherited others in a mother-to-daughter line. Such a system virtually required marriage within a relatively small geographic area. Like the Aztecs and early Mesopotamians, the Inca made provision for a brotherless daughter's son to inherit from her father and for a sisterless son's daughter to inherit from his mother.

In ancient Sumer considerations of transmission of property clearly led to patrilineality. The sense of the patrilineage being the landholder, rather than the individual, was still strong enough in the third millennium B.C. so that anyone who wished to sell land (and sometimes other possessions) had to have the permission of lineage members. Women as well as men might have to be asked for such permission, though it is uncertain whether that was because they were widows of lineage members or because they were daughters who were bearing heirs to their own fathers' properties. Marriage was neolocal, so that the new couple entered a new residence. However, newly married couples might have chosen to live near the husband's kin, or even near the wife's, for the sake of keeping up potentially significant lineage ties. Certainly that has been a tendency in many other later, partly urbanized societies. It is hard to tell whether Sumer had undergone a change from a joint-fraternal inheritance system (in which property either was jointly managed or went from brother to brother until all the brothers were gone before passing on to the next generation) to a patrilineal system in which sons inherited separately. Still, given the persistence of joint-fraternal systems in sub-Saharan Africa until longevity increased enough for a father to expect to live beyond the marriage of his eldest son, it is possible. That kind of change can be seen over a thousand years later, in the Elam of the 16th century B.C., whose practice of levirate may have reflected the earlier joint-fraternal system. We do know that around the mid–24th century B.C., the city-state of Lagash in ancient Mesopotamia forbade polyandry, which is compatible with a joint-fraternal system.

By the mid–24th century B.C. it was already fairly common in Mesopotamia for a man to marry his father's brother's daughter, in order to reunite parcels of land that had been subdivided through inheritance. Perhaps it was at least in part to facilitate such reuniting of land parcels that Hammurabi's code for the empire of Babylon in Mesopotamia in the 18th century B.C. made it more difficult for a woman to refuse the husband to whom her parents or guardians had agreed to give her, once the contract had been signed. However, because the contract itself was technically her own acceptance of the husband, she may still have been able to resist an unwanted contract, as she had previously been able to refuse consummation of a marriage that had been contracted for her between a would-be husband and her guardians. Under Hammurabi's code a wife retained control over her own property, except for whatever the husband had given her as dower (which would eventually be used as dowry for her daughters) or whatever her kin had given her as dowry. The husband also had to give a bride-payment to her kin before the signing of the contract. He would have to forfeit that if he did not go through with the contract, whereas they would have to restore it to him twofold if the contract were not carried out (because of the bride's resistance, for example). He would retain the children in case of divorce or his wife's death, unless his wife was a priestess.

A Babylonian priestess was forbidden to bear children herself. She had to provide her husband with a concubine (either a free woman or a slave) to bear them, and she retained them for her own household whether the marriage ended through death or through divorce. They would not be her heirs, though. She inherited like a son from her father; but everything she had passed back to her father's lineage at her own death, including whatever children had been born to the concubines she might have furnished for her husband. We may see foreshadowed here the practice of woman-marriage, by which a woman in a number of sub-Saharan African societies may arrange in some way to have another woman bear children. These children then regard the first woman as their female father, the one who has made their birth and rearing possible by paying bride-wealth for their mother. They may grow up in the same household with their mother and their physical father, while the female father lives in another household with other relatives; or they may grow up in a household led by their female father and their mother. It is not necessary to assume that woman-marriage emerged because cultural diffusion had taken place between ancient Babylon and the ancestors of contemporary Africans. Still, it is thought-provoking that sub-Saharan Africa, with whose interior the heirs of Sumer in ancient Mesopotamia were already trading by way of Egypt four thousand years ago, is the only region in which such systems are found with any degree of frequency today.

Both dower and dowry were regarded as the common property of the spouses. Because there was such a conjugal fund, as well as an emphasis on assuring the paternity of children through protecting the virtue of unmarried women (or restricting their freedom, if one prefers to describe it in those terms), monogamy was the norm. Protection of unmarried women was carried so far that if a married man lay with an unmarried woman, he had to divorce his wife to marry her, and his former wife came under the legal jurisdiction of his new wife's father. Divorce, as noted in Chapter 4, was obtainable in Hammurabi's Babylon by either spouse. If the marriage were dissolved at the wife's instigation, she would pay whatever fine had been stipulated in the marriage contract out of her own property, just as the husband would pay his fine for a divorce out of his property. Divorce fines were not subtracted from their common property, which would then be divided and restored.

Although monogamy was the rule in Hammurabi's Babylon, a man might choose to take a legal concubine as well as a wife. Doubtless this often led to strained relations with his wife, even if she had agreed to it because she had not borne him children. (Hammurabi's Hittite contemporaries in ancient Anatolia—the Turkey of today—may have forestalled some of those strains by allowing a daughter's husband to inherit, if there were no sons.) A free concubine received no dower from her husband and no dowry from her father. Therefore, she and her legal consort had no conjugal estate, no common property, although her children could inherit from him as if she were his legal wife. If a man recognized a female slave's children as his, they could also inherit (even alongside a wife's or a concubine's children, much as in ancient Israel around that time), and both she and they would become free at his death.

Bride-wealth, dower, and dowry were all significant in Hammurabi's time. However, as the generations passed, dowry came to be increasingly sizable in comparison to bride-wealth. This probably reflected an increasing eagerness by parents to get their daughters married. We do not know whether that was because women became more numerous in relation to men in a slowly urbanizing society, because parents grew more anxious about maintaining status through ensuring that their daughters did not marry downward in the social and economic scale, or because of both of these considerations.

Ancient Egyptians apparently relied primarily on bride-wealth at first, five thousand years ago. However, that gradually gave way to a heavier reliance on dower, and then in the 6th century B.C. to an emphasis on dowry. These changes, like those in Mesopotamia, may have reflected changes in sex ratios, status anxiety, or both. Dower remained significant enough for the Ptolemies of the last three centuries B.C. to ensure that it would be used as dowry for the wife's daughters. Still, as in ancient Babylon, so in ancient Egypt, concubines could be taken without bride-wealth, dower, or dowry, and their children could be recognized as heirs. One wonders whether legal concubinage was the marriage of the poor. A female slave's children could also be heirs, if the father recognized them. Monogamy was a practical reality for all but the highest social levels, but it was not as strongly upheld as a legal norm as in ancient Babylon. Sibling-marriage, practiced by the Ptolemaic rulers and noticeably present among city-dwellers by Roman times in the first two or three centuries A.D. (over ⅓ of marriages listed in several communities), seems to have been an introduction from Zoroastrian Persia/Iran of the 6th and 5th centuries B.C.

As noted at the opening of Chapter 2, not only siblings might wed each other among the Zoroastrians, but even parents and children, to maintain unity among the followers of Ahura-Mazda, god of light. They may simply have been following earlier Aryan custom, in view of the practice of allowing not only step-parents, but also fathers (though not mothers) to wed children among some fellow-Aryans, the pre-Christian Prussians, Lithuanians, and Irish. By the time other Aryans reached India (long before Zoroaster's time) such customs may have given way to polyandry. Polyandry is visible in the early Indian Aryan epic of the *Mahabharata*, as well as among the Medes, Aryan contemporaries of the early Zoroastrians in Iran. The earlier Elamites of Iran had used brother-sister marriage as well as the near-polyandry of the levirate, which allocated a dead brother's widow to a surviving brother.

A son's inheritance of marital rights in any wives his father might leave at his death, except for his own mother, may be related to customs like those of the Zoroastrians. Such inheritance practices were already condemned in ancient Israel by the 6th century B.C. Yet they remained common in parts of the Middle East until Muhammad preached against them in the 7th century A.D. By that time the concentration of women in the households of the rich (who could afford to make marriage contracts, concubinage arrangements, and purchases of slaves) was arousing the attention of social and religious reformers in more than one Middle Eastern region. A century before Muhammad's time one of the demands of a rebel movement against the Sassanid rulers of Iran had been to release concubines and female slaves from wealthy households, so that poorer men might seek them as wives.

The ancient Hebrews followed a patrilineal, patrilocal, polygynous, extended-family, and somewhat endogamous pattern. They experienced the same shifts away from bride-service and bride-wealth to dower and dowry as the ancient Mesopotamians and Egyptians, as they moved from pastoral nomadism on the fringes of Mesopotamia to settled agriculture and city life in the land of Canaan.

After the ancient Hebrews made the land of Canaan into the land of Israel, it eventually became customary for those who were of age to make their own marriage arrangements, rather than accept their parents' or guardians' arrangements. But few indeed were the women who reached that age unwed. As the making of one's own arrangements became accepted, though, disparity in age between the spouses seems to have increased. As a result the husband's authority over the wife was strengthened by difference in age. There may be a symbolic reflection of that larger disparity in age (and the resulting expectation that wives would be more submissive to their husbands) in the two accounts in Genesis 1 and 2 of the creation of men and women. Genesis 1 sees both as being directly created in God's image. Genesis 2, however, sees the woman as being created (like a child from within the body of the mother) out of a portion taken from the man, to be a helpmate for him rather than an image in her own right of the Creator-God.

Growth in the use of dowry may have eased the feelings of daughters, who at first received no inheritance, unless there were no sons. In that case they were also expected to marry kinsmen of their father. Daughters were allowed a share in the inheritance only after the destruction of the Temple in Jerusalem in A.D. 70 and the subsequent dispersion or Diaspora of the Jews. At that time firstborn sons were also formally recognized as having the right to inherit a double share. The interest of the patrilineage in the patriline's continuance was thereby recognized. However, the people of ancient Israel foreshadowed the experience of later commercial-urban societies in their movement into an increasingly urban life after the Diaspora. They no longer continued to exemplify the experience of early agricultural and pastoral ones.

The use of dowry in pre-Diaspora Israel may have lessened the possibility that a husband would use too easily his prerogative of initiating a divorce. (To obtain a divorce a woman had to persuade her husband to initiate it.) In addition, the use of dowry helped to ensure that the widow was not left entirely without resources, even if childless. A woman inherited nothing from her deceased husband, but received only what he had given her when still alive. Thus it was to her interest, not only to the interest of her husband's lineage, to bear sons in her deceased husband's name to one of his brothers in the levirate. Those sons would then be expected to care for her in her old age. Similar considerations apply among bilateral Malagasy and matrilineal Ashanti, when they assign to a childless deceased first husband the offspring of his widow and a brother.

In sub-Saharan Africa, the region in which the world's highest levels of polygyny have been found in recent generations, the variety of marriage systems is so great as to be almost bewildering. For the most part its people have been agricultural for probably at least one to two thousand years and more. Most of them have used hoes rather than plows, although that has begun to change in recent years. The amount and timing of rainfall to replace groundwater used by crops is less predictable in much of sub-Saharan Africa than in many of the world's other agricultural regions, except for Africa's eastern and southern mountains and its western equatorial rain forest. Because rainfall is uncertain, and because soils are poor where tropical heat evaporates moisture (which means dead organic matter decays too rapidly to enrich the soil), some form of shifting rather than permanent agriculture has been the normal mode for most. Humidity or locally prevalent animal diseases prevent the keeping of cattle in a number of areas. Yet where cattle can survive, they are likely to be kept and used as bride-wealth, as well as for the furnishing of milk, meat, and hides. As that suggests, bride-wealth as well as polygyny tends to characterize a great many of those marriage systems, even in all of their variety. Because the great majority of sub-Saharan African societies studied in recent years by anthropologists tend to display patrilineality, patrilocality (or at least living with or near some member of the husband's male kin), polygyny, the use of bride-wealth, and a heavy involvement of women in agriculture, it has been tempting to assume that these societies display the basic characteristics of the earliest agricultural societies. After all, they are located in the apparent cradle of the human species, and they have lived, for the most part, in relatively small-scale agriculturally based sociopolitical systems until the European conquests of the late 19th century A.D. However, there are several pitfalls involved in making such an assumption.

One pitfall is that where agriculture first arose, in the Middle East, it arose in areas where rainfall was probably more predictable than in much of the sub-Saharan Africa of today. Agricultural life then spread to areas where the annual floods of great rivers could be and were channeled through canal systems to irrigate fields. Irrigation made permanent, settled agriculture easy to establish, thereby greatly lessening the likelihood that marriage and inheritance systems would have to be constructed to take account of shifting-cultivators' needs for large amounts of fallow land. Where a household needs only to leave one or two fields uncultivated for every field currently in crops, and may even use the uncropped fields to pasture animals, it can be practical to regard a household's land as household property. That would have been the case in the rotational systems used in most of Europe and the Middle East in at least the first 15 or 16 centuries A.D., and probably before. In such a situation crop land can be placed entirely under the household's management. It can even be made alienable—not just to be rented, but to be sold—by those responsible for the well-being of the household's members. Witness ancient Sumer, where crop land could be sold (with the permission of interested kin), and ancient Babylon, where only the sale of land brought into a marriage as joint or conjugal property by a woman had to be agreed to by the husband as well as by the wife. (She apparently had no comparable voice if he sold land from their conjugal holdings.) But in areas of shifting cultivation at least five to ten times as much land must be available for use as is currently being used. This applies not only to most of sub-Saharan Africa, but also to New Guinea, the Pacific Islands, and much of the Americas (and parts of Southeast Asia). That is partly why they are being treated together in this chapter. Under the pressures of a shifting-cultivation system it is more practical for land to be held by a larger kin-linked group of households, large enough to defend its boundaries from encroachment if necessary. That group should probably be at least the size (interestingly enough) of a large hunter-gatherer band, or about 50. However, it should also probably not be more than twice that large, for a group of more than 100 would be too large for one person to keep track of all its members fairly readily. For such a large group to manage its land, it is preferable for land-use rights not to be alienable. At most the group is only apt to share land-use rights occasionally with some nonconsanguine. That person may be an affine, or a blood brother, or even a formally recognized trading partner; but for some special reason that person may be allowed to live and cultivate with the consanguine core. Only after another generation or so, though, are that person's children likely to be accepted as part of the consanguine core themselves.

Another pitfall is the difference between the realities of life in a fairly well-organized society with a permanent capital and nearby neighbors, and the realities of life in a relatively isolated society of only one or two levels. Permanent capitals already existed in the first Middle Eastern societies for which we have any information whatsoever about legal codes from which to try to extrapolate backward to earlier times. Households there could rely on government armies and police to protect them from external invaders and from internal robbers and thieves. But early medieval Europe, lacking police and standing armies, expected households to turn to locally powerful leaders for protection in the manorial system, which seldom allowed individual rural cultivators' households to alienate land. (The European manorial system is discussed in Chapter 8.) If a society operates only at the level of coordinating a relatively small number of villages, or if it seeks only to coordinate use of agreed-on modes of arbitration between disputants (rather than having permanent formal courts with permanent personnel to handle all significant disputes), then it makes sense to use large local groups like co-resident lineages as operating units for almost all major purposes. In this regard the sub-Saharan African societies may be like immediately preurban and preliterate agricultural societies, which may have felt similar pressures toward patrilineal, patrilocal, and polygynous forms. But in relying on shifting agriculture (because of rainfall and soil differences)—a reliance that presses toward lineage-level rather than household-level landholding practices and also tends to involve women actively in crop-raising—they are not. Consequently it is risky to assume that the very earliest Middle Eastern agriculturalists were as strongly lineage-oriented or as inclined to polygyny as many contemporary African agriculturalists. Before populations rose enough to bring competition for land, those early agriculturalists may well have been more like the ambilineal and utrolateral societies of many of the Pacific Islands. These peoples have not been pressed toward patrilineality at least partly because they have not experienced the constant small-scale warfare of New Guinea (or of much of Africa) over who may use which area. Early Middle Eastern agriculturalists eventually used the establishment of cities and central governments to cope with enforcing usage boundaries, rather than staying at the organizational levels of village and lineage like many African societies. They could do so because they could afford to set aside the surplus needed to support a central government. Steady water supply enabled them to use a permanent rather than a shifting mode of agriculture. Moreover, they increased their productivity by using animal power (through the plow) as well as human energy to till the soil.

A third major pitfall, the last to be pointed out here, is that all of the more recent societies have been impinged on by the ripple effects of commercialization (and especially of industrialization) to a degree far greater than seems likely for preurban Middle Eastern agricultural societies. There is some evidence for limited long-distance trade even before the rise of cities. The capitals of ancient Egypt and Mesopotamia knew the presence of slaves from eastern Africa. But the transformation of the world in recent centuries from an economic system mainly based on small-scale local self-sufficiency (in all but a relatively small number of easily transported and highly valued goods) to an economic system mainly based on large-scale interdependence (with a great deal of reliance on long-distance transportation of even the basic necessities of life) has had its impact even on remote societies. That impact can be dramatic. The Bena of Tanganyika in eastern Africa changed from a matrilineal and matrilocal system to a patrilineal and patrilocal one in the hundred years from 1850 to 1950. They did so in response to new opportunities to acquire movable wealth through trade with Europeans, who for the first time entered the region to compete with earlier and smaller-scale Arab merchants. Bena men used their new wealth to purchase rights from their wives' kin, to take as heirs the children born to them, and to remove their wives to residences of their own choice. Moreover, they did so under conditions set increasingly by Europeans, rather than (as before) by local leaders who might be wary of any change whose effects they were uncertain of being able to control.

Most of the smaller societies of New Guinea and the Pacific Islands only began to have similar experiences even more recently. That may mean that their lower percentage of patrilineality and patrilocality reflects their later entry into a larger commercial world, at least as much as it reflects the absence of large herd animals (usually taken as a major point of differentiation between preliterate agriculturalists in the Americas, the Pacific Islands, and New Guinea, and preliterate agriculturalists in sub-Saharan Africa). It must be acknowledged that preliterate agriculturalists in the Americas also felt the presence of European rulers, and much earlier than did most sub-Saharan Africans. But the Europeans arrived as conquerors and settlers in the Americas. They did not begin as traders, as they did at first in Africa south of the Sahara. Moreover, they had not been preceded in the Americas by a gradually increasing number of other merchants, like the Arabs and their Middle Eastern predecessors in all but the southernmost parts of Africa. Consequently the peoples of sub-Saharan Africa had more time, and at first more freedom, to develop their own responses to their changing situation than did the peoples of either the Americas or the Pacific Islands and New Guinea. Patrilineality and patrilocality in 20th-century Africa may indeed reflect in part the pasturing of large herd animals in many areas. But they may also reflect responses to impinging commercialization— especially to the slave-trading of both Arab and European merchants—and to conquest.

It may be almost impossible to separate the results of impinging commercialization from the results of customary (not newly introduced) use of large herd animals. The complete absence of patrilineality among South American mountain peoples (almost all of whom use bilateral systems), even though they have lived for centuries by pasturing relatively large mountain-dwelling animals such as llamas, suggests with some force that comparative freedom to respond to the introduction of commercial activity tends to lead to patrilineal forms. Where early pastoralists were relatively free to develop their own relationships with early urban centers, patrilineality flourished. Men, not as tied down to child-rearing as women, could engage in trade over longer distances. They were also more prepared than women to protect themselves and their goods in case of an attack or an attempted theft. Yet even this suggestion runs into the difficulty that the Spanish conquerors of the Andean regions adhered formally to a bilateral system, though in practice it was less equal than the duolineality of the previous Inca rulers or their nobles and commoners. The cultural influence of the Inca and then the Spaniards may have had as much influence as any other factor on the Andean pastoralists' bilateral preferences. Probably no single factor ever determines what kind of descent system, and with it what kind of marriage system, a given society is likely to have.

What can be said of sub-Saharan Africa's marriage systems, in statistical terms, is that in the survey of 863 contemporary and precontemporary societies around the world used by the Munroes in the 1981 *Handbook of Cross-Cultural Human Development* (see Table 16) and by Jack Goody in *Bridewealth and Dowry in Africa and Eurasia* (1973) and *Production and Reproduction* (1976), 99% of the sub-Saharan African societies surveyed are polygynous, but only 14% use limited polygyny. The other 85% use general polygyny. That compares with 84% in the world (39% limited, 45% general), 86% in North America (49% limited, 37% general), 80% in South America (55% limited, 25% general), 75% in East Eurasia (62% limited, 13% general) and in the Pacific Islands and New Guinea (52% limited, 23% general), and 62% in the Middle East and Europe (26% limited, 36% general). (See Tables 1, 2, 16, 21, and 24.) However, it is well to keep in mind that the Americas hold 36% of the societies studied but only about 14% of today's world population, whereas East Eurasia holds 11% of the societies and about 55% of the people, the Middle East and Europe hold 11% of the societies and about 20% of the people, Africa holds 28% of the societies and about 10% of the people, and the Pacific realm holds 14% of the societies and about 1% of the people. It is also well to keep remembering that the societies surveyed in most of these regions are not the majority groups in the local population today.

Africa has been a stronghold of polygyny. In the 155 African societies south of the Sahara surveyed by Jack Goody in *The Character of Kinship* (1973), 35% of all husbands had more than one wife. In 131 of those 155 societies the average was 154 wives per 100 husbands. That contrasts with Egypt, for example, where the average proportion of polygynous husbands observed in both the early 19th and the mid–20th centuries A.D. was about 5%. It is worth noting, though, that the incidence of polygyny has gone down measurably in the past century in Africa. The introduction of central government taxation tends to mean that each wife's household is taxed separately, which discourages polygyny. It is perhaps even more important that the introduction of plow agriculture (mainly carried on by men) in place of hoe agriculture (mainly carried on by women) has lessened polygyny's previous economic advantage for a man. Among the Tswana of South Africa, for example, only 11% of the married men had more than one wife in 1946, as compared with four times that many a century before. All of the African marriage systems described in this chapter in the present tense should be recognized as similarly being in a continuing state of change.

The high use of general polygyny in sub-Saharan Africa correlates strongly with the heavy involvement of women in agriculture there. As Jack Goody shows in *Production and Reproduction*, 54% of these societies primarily rely on women to raise crops (8% or under in all of Europe, Asia, and the Middle East, and elsewhere only more than 30% in South America, with 37% there). Around the world 64% of all societies that rely on women as chief crop-raisers practice general polygyny, to 28% practicing limited polygyny. Another 26% of African societies rely on women and men equally for crop-raising (40% in the Pacific realm, 44% in eastern Eurasia, with its heavy reliance on intensive agriculture, 25% in the Middle East and Europe, 26% in South America, and only 6% in North America; however, 68% of the North American societies surveyed are nonagricultural, while not more than 13% are nonagricultural in any other region). Worldwide, 42% of societies in which men and women take part equally in agriculture practice general polygyny, and 40% practice limited polygyny.

The strong reliance on women in agriculture in sub-Saharan Africa also correlates with the requirement that bride-wealth or bride-service must be furnished for a marriage to take place. As Goody shows in *Bridewealth and Dowry*, worldwide, 58% of societies that primarily rely on women to raise crops use bride-wealth, 12% use bride-service, 9% use exchange of gifts or of kinswomen, and 21% have little or no gift-exchange. Of all sub-Saharan African societies, 82% use bride-wealth and another 8% use bride-service. That compares with 62% and 3% in all of Europe, Asia, and the Middle East. In those regions, 21% use token or no exchange and 11% use dowry. (Not over 1% use dowry anywhere else.) The African case contrasts far more sharply with 37% using bride-wealth and 5% using bride-service in the Pacific (29% token or none, 16% gift-exchange, 12% kinswoman-exchange), with 16% using bride-wealth and 13% using bride-service in North America (5% token or none, 13% gift-exchange), and with 5% using bride-wealth and 43% using bride-service in South America (where only token-or-none, at 48%, is used by even more than use bride-service).

The use of bride-wealth in turn correlates with patrilineality. Of the 47%

of world societies that use bride-wealth, 71% are patrilineal, for a total of 33% of all the societies surveyed by Goody. (See Table 23.) Out of 195 bride-wealth-using sub-Saharan African societies, 154 are among the 74% of societies in that region that are patrilineal. This means that 79% of the 82% of African societies using bride-wealth are patrilineal, so that 65% of the total group of sub-Saharan African societies surveyed are both patrilineal and bride-wealth users. This 65% contrasts with only 20% in the Pacific (25 patrilineal out of 47 bride-wealth-using societies, with 34% of all societies patrilineal) and a mere 3% in the Americas (ten of 46, with just under 20% patrilineal). Europe, Asia, and the Middle East are more nearly comparable, with 52% (99 of 118, with 66% patrilineal). Of the few sub-Saharan patrilineal societies that do not use bride-wealth, most use either bride-service—ten of 176—or kinswoman-exchange—eight of 176.

With regard to residence, it is reasonable to assume that the 74% of sub-Saharan African societies that are patrilineal, plus most of the 5% duolineal and 5% bilateral ones, are among the 82% with patrilocal residence. (See Table 17.) It is also reasonable to assume that the 10% avunculocal and 2% matrilocal societies account for most of the 16% matrilineal societies. The rest are presumably to be found among the few who use other forms, including neolocality and ambilocality (by the couple's choice at the time of marriage). Parallel assumptions may be made about correlations between residence and lineality in other regions. However, living with the wife's family is noticeably more common than matrilineality in both Americas, and slightly more common in both the world as a whole and the Europe–Asia–Middle East realm. It is also well to bear in mind that in every system there are exceptions. Among the nominally patrilineal and patrilocal Kpelle of Liberia a man who lacks bride-wealth may obtain a wife by bride-service. But then he must live in her father's family, until and unless he can pay bride-wealth to remove her from them. A woman may actually prefer such a situation because it gives her greater opportunity to maneuver for her own and her children's interests in her relationship with her husband.

In Africa south of the Sahara, as a whole, the tendency is thus toward general polygyny. Usually this is found within a patrilineal and patrilocal framework, especially when it is based on an active (if not actually dominant) reliance on women in agriculture which leads to the giving of bride-wealth. Except insofar as patrilineality and patrilocality may reflect responses to recent external pressures, African marriage systems appear likely to have taken that general form for many generations past. Ordinarily bride-wealth takes the form of cattle or some other durable good. Often it is under the control of the adult men of a lineage group. They are the ones who receive control of the bride-wealth given for women born to the lineage group. They are also the ones who determine who, among the men born into it, is to be aided next in obtaining a wife. Not surprisingly, young African men

in polygynous societies may complain about older men's near-monopoli-
zation of young women. They suspect their elders of using their control of
bride-wealth decisions in order to gain additional wives for themselves,
rather than to enable young kinsmen to take their first wives. Among the
Fang of Gabon, for example, a man must compete for a share in the available
bride-wealth, not only with his own brothers and his own father and his
father's brothers, but even with his father's mother's brothers.

The hypothesis that bride-wealth is a circulating (and also status-equal-
izing) societal fund appears to be supported by the frequency with which
men of various social statuses in bride-wealth-using sub-Saharan African
societies marry women of different social statuses. Among the Gonja of
northern Ghana the equalizing effect of bride-wealth is shown in a study
noted in Goody, *Production and Reproduction*. Not only did men in the
ruling clan take ⅔ of their wives from other, lower levels; in addition, fully
¼ of the men in the class of commoners took aristocratic (though seldom
royal) wives. Bride-wealth also enables older men to acquire additional
wives, yet gives women no effective share in managing the kinds of movable
property involved. In all of these regards it contrasts with dowry, which is
almost unknown in sub-Saharan Africa except among Muslim peoples. The
use of dowry usually means the establishment of a conjugal fund, which
has the effect of giving women a share in inheritance. It also tends to uphold
monogamy. Furthermore, it tends to maintain status barriers because parents seek potential husbands with inheritance prospects commensurate with
the dowry they are prepared to provide. Perhaps the beginnings of social
changes can be perceived in Eric Arnould's article in Robert Netting and
others' *Households* (1984). In the villages he compares in interior Niger,
endogamy is lower and polygyny is higher in a remote agricultural village
than in a village in which women make pottery for sale in a nearby town.
The value of having a skilled potter as a wife appears to lessen the attractiveness of both polygyny and extra-village affinal links.

The practices of polygyny and widow-inheritance mean that both women
and men are likely to experience marriage both with someone older than
themselves and with someone younger than themselves. Men tend to marry
first in the early to middle 20s, but women tend to marry first in the middle
to late teens. That difference in age of first marriage facilitates the continuance of polygyny. Even with the shorter life expectancies of women up to
very recent times, more total woman-years than man-years are available to
be spent in the married state, for the women and men who live at any given
period. Recently age of first marriage for men has declined visibly in at least
some African societies, and age of first marriage for women has risen equally
visibly in many parts of Africa. These changes reflect changes in opportunities for wage work and/or cash-cropping. Men can marry earlier on such
income, while women need not marry for economic reasons as early as they

usually did before. The resulting approach to more equal marriage ages for men and women is apt to produce its own pressure toward the substitution of monogamy for polygyny.

There are broad patterns of variation from region to region in sub-Saharan Africa, within the overall tendency to use general polygyny and bride-wealth. Furthermore, within each region there are many local exceptions to those broader patterns. In general, though, the peoples of both the southern and eastern regions tend toward patrilineal, patrilocal, polygynous, hard-to-dissolve marriage established through bride-wealth payments in cattle. In the central region, from the Congo/Zaire basin to that of the Zambezi, matrilineality is typical (though patrilineality, bilaterality, and some duo-lineality are also found). In matrilineal systems bride-wealth may lead to a wife's eventual departure from her natal household. However, it will not yield rights in her children to her husband, unless the system is moving toward a patrilineal form like that of the Nyamwezi. Divorce tends to be somewhat easier to obtain in the central region, at least in matrilineal systems. That is also true of the western regions from Gabon up through Chad to Senegal. There are more patrilineal systems in the west than in the center. These patrilineal systems use a bride-wealth system too. But only in the interior with its grasslands—not in the coastal rain forest—is bride-wealth likely to be reckoned in terms of cattle, as in the east and south, or among cattle-keeping peoples in the central part.

As a very general rule, the amount of bride-wealth given tends to be lower if the society is matrilineal than if it is patrilineal, or even duolineal, since children will not enter the father's lineage. This corresponds to the fact that in a patrilineal society, the amount of bride-wealth which a husband may recover (if his wife leaves him) is generally lower if he keeps the children than if she takes them with her, either to her own lineage or to that of her next husband.

The amount of bride-wealth also tends to be lower if the society is bi-lateral, though that is not necessarily true if the society is duolineal. Islamic societies tend to have lower levels of bride-wealth because Muslim law requires husbands to give dower to wives. Therefore, husbands are not willing to give much bride-wealth to the bride's kin, unless they are assured that it will in effect return with her as dowry. However, dowry in more than token form is much more frequently found in the Muslim Middle East and in Muslim communities in South and Southeast Asia than in Muslim parts of sub-Saharan Africa.

As another very general rule, only in patrilineal groups (and only in some of them) may a woman pass on to her sons any wealth that she and her husband accumulated and managed as theirs. Normally that wealth reverts to his brothers at his death, and does not pass on to the next generation until the last of his brothers is dead. That is particularly true in the western region from the Sahara down to Gabon. Joint-fraternal inheritance is still a reality for many patrilineal groups in sub-Saharan Africa, particularly in its western parts. In nonpatrilineal groups such wealth reverts automatically to the husband's same-generation or senior-generation heirs, in a similar joint-fraternal inheritance pattern that fails to recognize any kind of conjugal fund. In a different vein, the patrilineal Zulu of South Africa, cattle-keeping agriculturalists, do not formally recognize divorce. Any children a woman may bear to a new partner are counted as her first husband's. That is because he has given her a dower of land and cattle for her children by him which he is not allowed to take back if she leaves him. By marrying him she has become a "female brother" to his brothers, and her sons are without question his inheritors.

As still another very general rule, the function of providing everyone with children is esteemed above all else. Children are seen as necessary to every adult, both to care for them in their older years and to inherit what they may have to transmit. That is what underlies such practices as that of the LoWiili of northern Ghana, who expect a brotherless woman to take a partner to bear grandsons for her father. Only after that duty is fulfilled may the partner pay bride-wealth, marry her, and remove her from her father's household to his own.

The Lovedu of Zambia and the Dahomey of West Africa both enable a woman to pay bride-wealth for another woman. The Lovedu then often leave her free to find her own partner to engender her children, while the Dahomey almost always furnish her with one. The wife-obtaining woman may have to divorce her own husband, as among the Igbo of eastern Nigeria, to ensure that the children born to the woman for whom she pays bride-wealth will be regarded as members of her lineage. In order to pay bride-wealth for a child-bearer, a woman must be able to obtain wealth. She may inherit it, receive it as dower (as among the Zulu), or earn it through trade or through such personal services as divining the future. Among the Zulu the receivers of bride-wealth from a woman for a woman must approve of the genitor to be assigned. He is generally of the husband's lineage, but not the husband himself. Among the Lovedu it may be a noblewoman or the queen who gives bride-wealth for a woman. Then she lets a kinsman or follower take the woman, in return for an obligation to provide a daughter. She gives bride-wealth for that daughter, so that a son of the couple can wed. Eventually, then, she expects to receive a daughter from that son, without bride-wealth. Thus she receives both the original woman and that woman's granddaughter for one bride-wealth payment, doubling her capital (so to speak) in a period of 30 to 40 years. At one time almost $^2/_5$ of women in the Lovedu capital were wives to the queen, though scarcely one in 20 were women's wives elsewhere among the Lovedu.

Whatever the marriage system is, it tends to provide some release for the frustrations of the formally unwed. In Dahomey an older man may pay the bride-wealth that he can afford for a new wife, and then assign her to a younger brother, a son, or even a grandson. The younger man may then eventually inherit her at the older man's death. Among the Rukuba of northern Nigeria a young man is initiated into adult status by living for a time in the household of another man's pregnant wife and practicing fatherhood with her newborn infant. Once recognized as an adult, he may court an unmarried girl. Her parents must find a husband for her if she becomes pregnant by him before they have arranged a marriage for her. They may choose not to accept him, if the young man cannot pay bride-wealth for her, since her demonstration of fertility will make her acceptable to an older man who will simply take her child as his. Among the Zande of central Africa a younger brother has access to his older brother's wife, whom he will eventually inherit anyway. Married Zande men could also sleep with their own wives' younger sisters and with their younger brothers' wives, with permission. Among the Lele of the southern Congo/Zaire basin a village may pay bride-wealth for a "village wife." She is lived with by several of the young unmarried men, and may be approached outside the limits of the village (though not inside it) by other men of the village. High levels of bride-wealth are likely to delay a Lele man's marriage until he is in his mid–30s. As many as $1/_{10}$ of Lele women may have been a village wife at some time, even now, after the practice has supposedly been outlawed for more than a generation.

Yet another means was that formerly found among the Afikpo of eastern Nigeria. One of their matrilineal clans was treated as a slave clan, to whose women any man of any other clan had access at any time. When the British came into the region at the beginning of the 20th century, the members of that matrilineal clan used the British courts to accuse and convict men of rape, if they continued the old practice. The ending of the slave-clan system among the Afikpo benefited the members directly, in other ways besides its women no longer being treated as available at all times. Men of other matriclans had always previously been able to take its women as wives without bride-wealth because they could not be assured of those wives' children's actual paternity. Now men of other matriclans began to take former slave-clan wives from distant villages, claiming that they belonged to nonslave matriclans, and obtaining bride-wealth for their daughters. This in turn enabled their sons (members of the former slave matriclan through their mothers) to claim successfully that they should not be required to pay double bride-wealth, as men of the slave matriclan had always had to do before.

Many contemporary observers have mourned the abrupt breaking up of traditional customs by foreign imperial rulers or indigenous rebels as upsetting social continuity, for which human beings do indeed have a real need. However, it is hard to imagine even them finding fault with the slave matriclan priestesses who began burying their past identity by refusing to keep up their clan shrines, as soon as the British came. Even when beaten severely by men of other matriclans to try to force them to maintain the shrines, they refused. They also encouraged the women of their clan to use the British courts against attackers. It was a dramatic illustration of how a lineage-based local-level social system can be altered by establishing a layer of effective central government officeholders above existing local-level co-ordinators.

The Afikpo are also unusual in having houses and some crop land passed on through patrilineal clans, as well as having personal effects and most crop land go through the original matrilineal clans. The patrilineal clans only began to be formed in the 18th century A.D., as residential defense units to protect from slave-raiders. Before British control began the matrilineal clans received compensation when one of their members was killed—even accidentally—by a member of another matriclan. Children belong to the matrilineal clan among the Afikpo. However, a woman may never marry a second husband from any patrilineal clan from which she has already had a husband.

A duolineal system like that of the Afikpo can only function where the population is fairly dense. Otherwise, people will find it too hard to keep up both sets of relationships, whether land descends in both lines (as among the Afikpo) or, more commonly, only in the patriline (as among the Yako of eastern Nigeria). Among the Yako only movables descend through the matriline. Bride-wealth (given in movables) goes to the kinsmen of the bride's mother, for them to use in making marriages for themselves. The Yako allow a man to adopt his sister's son into his own patriline, but do not let a man's son be adopted into another matriline. That may foreshadow an eventual turn to complete patrilineality, unless the whole system moves instead to bilaterality. During the last 30 years or so of British rule, between 1930 and 1960, the British courts facilitated patrilineal thinking by allowing Yako fathers to keep bride-wealth for their own use in arranging marriages for their own sons. The British courts also let sons keep their deceased fathers' personal belongings, instead of sharing these with a father's mother's kin.

Duolineality may be accompanied by sizable divorce rates. Among the Yako in 1939 at least 30% of the women had divorced or been divorced at least once. Yako husbands might recover a bride-wealth payment if they initiated a divorce. However, they might also have to wait to receive it from the woman's mother's kinsmen, until those kinsmen had received another bride-wealth payment for her from another man. That was almost a mirror image of the ex-husband in the patrilineal Tale system in northern Ghana, who might have to wait for his runaway wife's new husband to begin paying bride-wealth to her father's kinsmen, in order to recover the payment he had made for her.

The Afikpo show how a nonunilineally organized society may experience enough cross-cutting of interests to avert faction-building over issues. All the Afikpo patriclans eventually backed up their male members who were seeking to obtain bride-wealth for their daughters by wives of the former slave matriclan. The patriclans realized that this would help those male members' sons pay at the ordinary rather than at the double rate, making it easier for them to marry and have offspring to increase the patriclan. Lozi and other central African bilaterally organized peoples are far less likely to form lastingly hostile factions than, for example, the overwhelmingly patrilineal Tale (or Tallensi) of northern Ghana. The Lozi organize for some purposes around the father's kin, for other purposes around the mother's kin, and for still others (especially life-cycle ceremonies like child-naming, marriages, and funerals) around all the kin on both sides within specified and equal limits. The technically matrilineal Bemba of Zambia organize daily life around a constantly changing co-residential group made up out of the kindred of the headman, rather than around a kinship line. Even the Tale regard the mother's brother as a protector, whether simply visiting his village or really needing help. They also expect a woman to continue to revere her father's ancestors and to be buried with them. The Ashanti of central Ghana are almost as overwhelmingly matrilineal as the Tale are patrilineal. They let only a woman's daughters cultivate her lineage land after she dies, though all her children may do so while she lives. Yet they let a man pass land to his own sons that he himself has acquired, by clearing it or purchasing it. However, at those sons' deaths it then goes to their mother's lineage. An Ashanti man's children bury him, after supporting him and their mother in old age. But his consent to their marriage, though desired, is not required. It is required for the marriages of his sisters' children, to whom his matrilineal land cultivation rights will descend. Both he and his sister will receive small, nonreturnable gifts from the groom at her daughter's marriage. The men of the bride's matriclan receive the money payment, which must be returned if either party obtains a divorce.

The Lozi do not necessarily regard a child as its mother's husband's. If a genitor can make good a claim that it is his, it is counted as his and he may take it into his household even if its mother is married to someone else. The Lozi emphasize relationships between spouses more than sibling relationships. They base their sense of corporate group membership on co-residence, which may be based on links through either parent of either spouse, rather than on any single lineal principle. They use neither a levirate nor a sororate, as do the Zulu. In fact, they do not allow a man to take a wife's sister as a second wife. They thereby avert co-wife jealousy among close kinswomen, as well as maximize the number of alliances made through successive marriages. These concerns have also mattered to the Zande, who refuse all cross-cousin marriages; the Ashanti, who may not marry anyone of their mother's entire clan or anyone who shares the same great-grandfather on their father's side; and the bilateral Amhara of Ethiopia, who have refused any marriage closer than a sixth cousin on either side. The

Amhara have also recognized a woman's full right to retain (and to inherit) property after marriage, to seek divorce, and to have all children inherit from both parents, or from their mother if not born within a formal marriage. However, where a man is expected to live with his wife's family at the beginning of a marriage (as among the Bemba of Zambia), a man's marriage to a sister of an existing wife may be approved rather than avoided.

Always, whatever marriages with kin may be encouraged or discouraged are meant to support the existing kinship system. They are intended to facilitate whichever element is regarded as more important for a marriage system to emphasize, transmission of property rights or formation of new alliances. Cross-cousin marriages are accepted, or even preferred, among the patrilineal Tswana of southern Africa. However, the Tswana are unusual among Africans in accepting both a mother's brother's daughter and a father's sister's daughter as appropriate wives for a man. Most African peoples who use cross-cousin marriage tend to regard one type as proper and the other as unacceptable. They are apt to prefer the mother's brother's daughter, in a patrilineal society, because she carries little or no paternal capacity to threaten her husband. If the society is matrilineal, like the Suku of the Congo/Zaire basin, or possibly duolineal, as with the Afikpo, the father's sister's daughter may be preferred because the mother's brother does have authority over a man. However, the Ashanti will accept a man's marrying his mother's brother's (wife's) daughter because she will not be of her husband's matriclan. They also accept his marriage to his father's sister's daughter because she will not be of her husband's matriclan. Nevertheless, acceptance of marriage between first cousins of any kind is probably even less frequent in sub-Saharan Africa than the 57% found by Murdock in 1957 in the world at large. Such cousin-marriage tends to correlate more strongly with dowry-using systems (almost absent in sub-Saharan Africa) than with the bride-wealth-using systems that overwhelmingly predominate there. Cousin-marriage also tends to correlate more strongly with bilateral systems (36% in the world, but only 5% in sub-Saharan Africa) than with unilineal, ambilineal or utrolateral, or duolineal ones.

Changes in both natural and social environments have led to changes in African marriage systems. The series of seven terrible famines that fell on the Akamba of Kenya, between 1836 and 1898, resulted in a relaxation of rules of patrilocality. By 1900 a new wife could stay in her natal home to help raise crops until she could be spared to go to her husband's family. Moreover, lengths of cloth were substituted for cattle (lost to drought) as acceptable bride-wealth payments. The conversion of the exogamy-minded Diola of Senegal to Islam at the end of the precolonial era was also followed by changes. For the first time the Diola accepted patrilateral cross-cousin marriages. Evidently this was an indirect response to the matrilateral cross-cousin marriage preference of the Mandinka, from whom they learned about the Muslim faith. The two neighboring branches of the LoDagaa of northern

Ghana, the LoWiili and the LoDagaba, show the LoWiili concentrating more power in the hands of men than do the LoDagaba. The LoWiili have poorer land, yet they also have a denser population. Among the LoDagaba each wife has a separate granary for herself and her children, rather than her husband managing all grain, as among the LoWiili. Movable wealth goes to the mother's kinsmen among the LoDagaba, to the father's among the LoWiili. Land goes from father to son in both groups. LoDagaba daughters may provide (grand)sons for their father's patrilineage before marrying formally, even if they have brothers, rather than only if they do not, as among the LoWiili. Among both groups the widowed or divorced woman is free to return to her father's people with the understanding that her children will continue to belong to their father's kin. Yet, interestingly, a man is less likely to leave his father's farmstead for his mother's brother's among the LoDagaba than among the LoWiili. The father-son bond is so all-important to the LoWiili that the mother's brother appears simply not to be a potential substitute.

One wonders whether the LoWiili's greater emphasis on patrilineality (and the wife's weaker position in not having her own granary) responded to their harsher conditions in terms of both soil quality and crowdedness, or whether the LoWiili's crowdedness (with consequent overuse and impoverishment of the soil) has reflected the line of development of their social institutions. The LoWiili may have come to prefer to concentrate all power in the patrilineage in the days of slave-trading, when peacekeeping was a local rather than a central government responsibility. It is not clear whether they were more subject to either slave raids or internal conflicts than were the LoDagaba. Still, it would be an explanation for their greater degree of patrilineality, if they had had more reason to fear slave-raiding in the 17th and 18th centuries A.D., at the height of the transatlantic slave trade. That would be especially true if their numbers were already putting pressure on the land, whether it was already poorer than that of the LoDagaba or only becoming poorer because of overuse. The LoWiili may have preferred to concentrate the authority to sell a seriously troublesome son or daughter into slavery in the men of only one lineage, the father or his brother. That authority was clearly recognized as a less harsh means of eliminating the unbearably disruptive than killing them. Leaving such authority in the hands of men of two different lineages, the father and the mother's brother, as among the LoDagaba, may have come to seem too much of a strain. The LoWiili might have felt less insecure if they did not have to wonder about having to be responsive to potentially conflicting demands for obedience from two different lineages. Both LoWiili and LoDagaba may even have been duolineal societies at one time. If so, that might have evolved from the bilaterality of a distant hunter-gatherer past in order to handle the difficulties involved in letting cultivation rights in land be transmitted equally through both sons and daughters to both grandsons and granddaughters.

Unilineality of transmission may have been a widely adopted device among Africans for meeting the new perils of the Atlantic slave trade era. Unilineality may also have been chosen as a solution by people in New Guinea, facing conflicts over cultivation rights as population grew. But in the Pacific Islands the choice of many groups faced with population growth may have been to use either ambilineality (a continuing freedom throughout adult life to choose which grandparental or great-grandparental line to live with) or utrolaterality (a lasting choice among one's own and one's spouse's grandparental lines at marriage). In the Americas, at least in the two regions of Mexico and Peru (which were already under centralized governments when the Spaniards came in the 16th century A.D.), the establishment of hereditary landholding communities within which people were to marry may have been an early response to population pressure. Such communities thereby ensured that cultivation rights would not have to be shared with outsiders coming in or members going elsewhere. They generally resolved the incest question by setting fairly clear limits on how closely related a potential wife and husband were allowed to be. Similar communities may also have been an early response to population growth in ancient Sumer, before patrilineality became the general rule. Although patrilineality left women out of the inheritance line, it let at least one partner move away from the natal community. That in turn allowed a wider choice of marriage partners, in an incipiently commercializing society. With the rise of commerce, maximizing networks again began to seem at least as significant as transmitting cultivation rights. It is not surprising that the societies of the Pacific Islands (with their inclination toward permitting choices among potential lineage affiliations) accept both easy adoption and the even more informal fosterage of children. Children move readily among consanguine or affine kin of their parents. This forms another means of balancing population and resources, as first one line and then another may come to have more or less land than its current members really need.

In New Guinea, patrilineal societies appear to predominate among the societies studied. Still, some matrilineal ones are also found, and even a few with elements of duolineality. Clearly a frequent response (or at least companion) to competition over who is entitled to use land has been to bring men together through institutions favoring unilineality in some form. The men's house, which brings all the potential warriors of the village together for most of their activities and thereby builds up their team spirit, has been particularly common in a region noted for its frequent and often ritualized conflicts among neighbors. Not only the previously mentioned Siane, but also the Manga, for example, have developed a kind of terminological amnesia for absorbing sisters' sons into full agnateship in three to four generations. This is useful, since the Manga, like the Chimbu, have been observed to have about $^1/_5$ nonagnate men in their ostensibly all-agnate villages.

Some New Guinea peoples resemble the Siane in prescribing a regular pattern of patrilateral cross-cousin marriages. Such marriages link lineages together in something almost like the section systems of Australian Aborigines, so that one always knows out of what rather limited group one's spouse is to come. Others, like the agnate villages of Gimi, perceive their neighboring agnate villages as belonging to one of three groups: fellow-agnates to work with, matrilineals and affinals to marry into, and foes or rivals to compete with for wives from the villages linked affinally and matrilineally with themselves. A woman born in one of a man's fellow-agnate villages may be taken as a wife into one of his affinal-matrilineal villages, if that particular village treats her natal village as one from which its wives come. Her daughter may then become that man's wife. Thus he may be marrying a woman of his own ancestral line, if that line were counted as passing through the woman's mother. However, the marriage will not be seen in that light. As daughter to a daughter, the woman has effectively lost all ties with her own grandfather. Still other peoples, like the Buin, prescribe both kinds of cross-cousin marriages, through the mother's brother or the father's sister. However, also like the Buin, they do not always practice cross-cousin marriage, but may choose more distant kin, or even nonkin, if a particular alliance is desired. Yet others, like the Chimbu, favor a reduplication of existing ties through new marriages between villages already linked by marriage, while also expecting an equal exchange of wives between villages. The Chimbu formalize the arrangement of betrothals by having the newly eligible young women of one village invite the men of another village to a courting party. The party may or may not be followed by a return invitation to the first village's men by the young women of the second village. If that does not occur, then nothing will result, for the required paired betrothals would not become feasible. Because Chimbu villages go to war over land from time to time (though not as often as in some other groups), betrothals must be arranged in the usually fairly lengthy periods between conflicts. Men with wives from a currently hostile village may either be used as mediators or be recognized in time of battle as having the right to avoid fighting their wives' brothers, fathers, fathers' brothers, and fathers' brothers' sons.

About 11% of Chimbu marriages are polygynous. That does not mean that one man in nine has two wives, in the way that two wives is the most common situation for polygynists in much of sub-Saharan Africa. Rather, it tends to mean that one leader or "big man" in each village has several wives. It is also possible that one or two others, who are looking toward the possibility of succeeding him as "big man," have two or three wives each. Because bride-wealth (commonly used in New Guinea) is fairly large among the Chimbu, each man must draw not only on agnates, but also on his mother's kinsmen, to obtain what he will need to win a wife. He can then expect his wife's kinsmen as well as his own agnates to give presents when a child is born, reaches puberty, and marries, and also when he himself eventually dies. He himself would have received gifts from both his father's and his mother's kinsmen when he was born, reached puberty, and married. He must of course reciprocate, by giving gifts at all the corresponding times to them and to their children. Given that obligation, it would probably be hard for any man to accumulate wives (and the wealth that can come through them, through gifts to subsequent children), if it were not for the reality of land shortage. Nonagnate men often want the favor of a current or potential village leader, enough to offer a sister or daughter as a wife without the usual high bride-wealth payment. They then hope to be allotted land to cultivate, in return.

"To him that hath, it shall be given" is still a living truth of village life in New Guinea. Those men who want favors give wives to those who are already powerful enough to be among a village's recognized leaders, through some combination of descent, ability, personal magnetism, and whatever wealth they already hold. The leaders' wealth-potential is thereby increased. An able son, if he receives all his father's wives (though he does not then treat his own mother as his wife), can build the wealth he inherits to even greater heights. True, the "big man" must hold large feasts fairly often, or those who have been following him may begin turning to a younger man whose lavish competitive feasting shows that he is on the rise. The "big man" cannot simply hoard the pigs his wives help raise for meat. He must share them through the feasting ritual. There is some redistribution through those feasts, as well as through the gifts and favors he must continue to give in response to what he receives in goods and wives. Even so, accumulation is possible.

The somewhat similar practices found in many Pacific Islands societies may reflect a similar origin. Feasting, gift-giving, and wife-receiving are common among the hereditary aristocrats of many Pacific Islands groups. Those aristocrats' ancestors may have parlayed big-man status into hereditary rank, in more isolated island societies. Early settlers' preferred solution to crowding may have been to seek a still uninhabited island to settle, rather than try to expand at a neighbor's expense, with all the disruption to a fledgling social system that warfare might cause. The New Guineans seem to have institutionalized conflict between largely unilineal communities, and to have developed their marriage systems in terms of establishing links between villages that could relieve some of the pains of conflict. The Pacific Islanders come closer to having institutionalized systems of hereditary rank (or at least hereditary lineage) within communities that are noticeably less likely to be largely unilineal, and to have developed their marriage systems around the maintenance of each lineage at a level of social replacement. They do not seem to have striven for an increase in numbers of potential fighting men, which is what seemed to weigh on the minds of New Guineans until extremely recent times. The Pacific Islanders have also tended to favor the firstborn, in transmitting any titles or offices that can be held by only one person.

One of the more distinctive features of Pacific Islands societies, as a group, is the tendency to distinguish fairly clearly among successively more restrictive modes of inheritance. The most inclusive mode is the right to cultivate part of the crop land of a lineage, the right of *ooi* as it is called in the Gilbert Islands of Micronesia (today's Kiributu) near the equator. The next most inclusive is the right to sit in the lineage's meetinghouse, or *bwoti*. The least inclusive is the right to live on the residence land of the lineage, or *kainga*. The Pacific Islanders separate these from each other. They choose which bwoti and which kainga appear likeliest to combine to maximize overall opportunities, while also continuing to cultivate some ooi land in at least one or two other lineages. Bwoti and kainga are usually not chosen in the same grandparental or great-grandparental lineages in which ooi is being used. People try to make their choices maximize their children's opportunities, so that the children may choose in future to activate bwoti meetinghouse or kainga residence rights where ooi cultivation rights have been maintained.

The Malayo-Polynesian peoples, of whom the Micronesians form a branch, seem generally to have favored bilateral-kindred systems in their original Southeast Asian homes. That can be glimpsed even from Chinese travelers' observations of Southeast Asia 15 centuries ago. It can also be seen today among people like the Iban of Borneo. But we may perceive an incipient version of the ooi–bwoti–kainga system in the Iban practice of expecting a newly married couple to make a permanent choice of which multiapartment longhouse to reside in—that of the husband's father's parents, his mother's parents, the wife's father's parents, or her mother's parents—and then to choose which of his or her elder-generation kin to live with, either until they die or until another younger relative marries and moves in. By the time a couple has a child who is old enough to do simple chores, the entry of a second married pair into a household almost always makes division possible. The Iban may simply not have formalized an ooi–bwoti–kainga system yet because they are not faced with the constrictions imposed by living on a relatively small Micronesian island. They are also not yet faced with the degree of population pressure that seems to have brought so many New Guineans—perhaps in part like the LoWiili of northern Ghana—to intermittent warfare and to patrilineality. The duolineality of the Ontong of Java in Indonesia may be another kind of way station on the probable path from bilaterality to unilineality. Like the Yako and Afikpo of eastern Nigeria in Africa, the Herero of southern Africa, and the Nyaro and the Tullushi of the hills of the southern part of Sudan near Ethiopia, the Ontong of Java transmit most if not all land through the patrilineage, and most if not all movables through the matrilineage.

The Trobriand Islanders are among the few Pacific Islanders who use matrilineal affiliation and avunculocal residence. Young men normally turn increasingly at puberty to the mother's brother, who will complete the arrangements for their marriages. Although a marriage is formalized by sleeping with the new bride in the groom's father's residence, it is usually followed immediately by a move to the groom's mother's brother's residence. Young women move at marriage to the village of their new husband's mother's brother. Because young women's marriages are usually arranged by their fathers, in whose villages they remain with their mothers until marriage, a woman never lives with her mother's brother or takes an active part in her own matrilineage's everyday affairs. If a young man's father's village is less short of land than is his mother's brother's, and if his father is influential enough, the father may enable the son to stay with him, despite possible objections from the father's sisters' sons who expect to move in with him. But the son, like his father, is still obliged to share the food he grows with his mother and with his sisters and their children, rather than with his wife and children. His wife and children must depend on what she herself raises, and on what her brothers and eventually her sons may bring to her. (Only current or potential village chieftains in the Trobriands have more than one wife, like New Guinea big men.) Nominally a Trobriand man is expected to marry a kinswoman, a cross cousin through a male ancestor's sister. This is intended to reconcile some of the tensions that result from the practice of feeding the sister rather than the wife. However, only chieftains actually bring a sister's daughter in as wife to a son, or marry a sister's son to a daughter of that sister's husband's sister. By these means chieftains can bolster their own or their sisters' grandchildren's claim to rights in that village, the village of their own birth. Only chieftains and their sisters are powerful enough to resist the pressures that result from the normal heirs' resentment at men who favor their own or their sisters' offspring. Pressures and tensions like these, setting wife against husband and brother against sister, have doubtless worked against a lasting use of matrilineality in other Pacific Islands societies, as well as elsewhere in the world. Such pressures and tensions have also worked against the use of cousin-marriage, which is almost always discouraged for first and even second cousins in the region.

In the Polynesian islands of the southern hemisphere from New Zealand eastward, the outlines of an ooi–bwoti–kainga system like that found in much of Micronesia can also be traced. Some peoples allow open lifelong option, like the Maori of New Zealand, the Samoans, and the Tonga Islanders. Others do not, like the primarily patrilineal Tikopians. The Tikopians let a woman's sons claim part of her father's cultivation rights through her, but only if her brothers will agree. The Tikopians are strongly conscious of the need to prevent rapid growth in population, for the sake of social harmony. They are among the few Pacific Islanders who actively encourage younger children in a large family not to marry. Instead, the

younger offspring are encouraged to foster a child or two born to one of
their elder siblings, as eventual caretaker(s) in old age. The Tikopians also
practice relatively late marriage and coitus interruptus, to limit population
growth.

Unilineal systems with little or no residential choice are more common
in the Melanesian islands (east of New Guinea and north of New Zealand)
than in Micronesia or Polynesia. The Melanesian islands tend to be somewhat larger than the rest, other than New Zealand itself. The matrilineal
Dobu have established perhaps the most demanding pattern of residential
(non)choice for married couples. They move one year from the wife's to
the husband's matrilineage, and the next year back to the wife's, in a two-
year alternating cycle. That is their response to the ongoing need to match
available crop land to the number entitled to use it, and yet to try to deal
with potential tensions in both husband-wife and brother-sister relationships. It may well lead to greater harmony than the general Pacific Islands
tendency to paint the sex through whom more land-use rights are locally
transmitted as the wiser and more competent, in local folktales.

Some Melanesian peoples, like those of Manus in the Admiralty Islands
or Bellona in the Solomons, are rather strictly patrilineal and patrilocal. On
both islands, though, a sonless man may adopt a young boy as a son,
choosing the boy from either his own or his mother's or his wife's father's
lines. Others, like the people of Kwaio in the Solomons, combine a preference
for patrilineage and patrilocality, a willingness to allow a man to move to
his mother's or his wife's father's village, and a kinship-terminology system
which by the fourth generation absorbs such a man's descendants into that
mother's or that wife's father's lineage as full agnates. Among the Kwaio
people, as among the Trobrianders, fully $1/5$ of all adults may stay unmarried,
to help limit population increase. The primarily matrilineal Maenge of New
Britain expect the father to pay most of a son's bride-wealth to his new
wife's kinsmen, and expect the mother's brother to pay most of what his
nephew is expected to give the bride herself. The Maenge acknowledge the
father's contribution by accepting the right of a man's children to inherit
his land rights, in preference to any of his mother's kin except his sisters'
children. They also let a man's children cultivate on his matrilineage's land
while he is still alive. About $1/3$ of their land is cultivated on the strength of
claims through the father, and about $2/3$ through the mother. About $1/3$ of
married couples live in the wife's matrilineal village, $1/3$ in the husband's,
and $1/3$ in the matrilineal village of both spouses. This is possible because
more than one matrilineage is represented in most villages.

In Michel Panoff's report on the Maenge in *Ethnology* (1976), it was
noted that just under $1/3$ of the village headmen surveyed were the sons of
previous headmen, while slightly more than $1/3$ were the sons of sisters of
previous headmen. Almost all of the remaining $1/3$ had some other fairly
close tie with an earlier headman, either through birth or through marriage.

Two out of every five village headmen had married someone from their father's matrilineage, compared with less than 30% among the rest of the male population. That clearly demonstrates a recognition that the strengthening of ties with a father's kin could be useful, where a man shares land-use rights, feast-preparing duties, and (in former years) wartime responsibilities not only with his own mother's kinsmen, but also with those of his wife and his father's mother. He can use those other sets of rights, duties, and responsibilities to ease himself (or at least his sons) into another matrilineage if that seems advantageous. On the island of Manus an ordinary man may further his career as a potential big man by offering aid to a noble who is trying to prepare for a ritual occasion, thereby putting him under obligation to give the commoner gifts and even work-service in return. That would not happen among the peoples of Samoa, Fiji, or Tonga, where nobles would expect to receive such gifts but would not feel obliged to respond in kind. They would only give invitations to take part in feasts and ceremonies, or occasionally grant some favorable judgment in a dispute they might help to mediate. However, the people of Manus have emphasized the individual's rather than the kin group's responsibility for providing what is needed for ritual payments and gifts for child-naming feasts, puberty ceremonies, marriages, and funerals. Consequently lineage and rank mean less than on Samoa, Fiji, or Tonga.

In view of the tendencies toward patrilineality in New Guinea and toward bilaterality (including ambilineality and utrolaterality), matrilineality, and even duolineality in portions of the Pacific Islands, it is not surprising that as many societies in that whole area (34%) are bilateral as are patrilineal. (See Table 24.) Nor is it surprising that 22% are matrilineal and an unusually large almost 10% (12 societies out of 126) are duolineal. This is also the region of the world in which sister- or kinswoman-exchange (12%) and gift-exchange (16%) are most common. Bride-service (5%) is less common than anywhere else but the Europe–Middle East–Asia region (3%), and token or no payment or exchange (29%) is more common than in any other region but the Americas. The use of bride-wealth (38%) is more common in the region than any other pattern. Even so, its frequency is far less than in the Europe–Middle East–Asia region (62%), or in Africa (82%). The attractiveness of keeping kinsmen together, in an agricultural society whose male members may need to form war parties as well as find it helpful to cooperate in field-clearing and feast preparation, is shown by the 63% preference for patrilocal or at least agnatic residence. (See Table 17.) That is striking, when only 34% of the societies are patrilineal in form. It probably means that the larger share of the bilaterally organized and duolineally organized societies tend to prefer that type of residence too. Perhaps to ease some of the potential husband-wife and brother-sister strains, 52% practice only limited polygyny and 24% practice monogamy. (See Table 16.) General polygyny is practiced by 23%, compared with 45% worldwide. The remaining 1% use polyandry, which is not found in the societies looked at by the Munroes in Africa, Europe, and the Middle East, or in the Americas, but only in East Eurasia (3%, none of them large).

Among the mainly nonagricultural societies (68%) of North America token or no gifts are given at marriage by the majority (58%) of all societies. Equal amounts in gifts are exchanged by another 13%. Bilaterality is used by 65% (20% are patrilineal, 15% are matrilineal). (See Tables 21 and 24.) Yet here, too, patrilocality or at least agnatic links have been preferred by 57% in residential choice, although 24% have gone with wife's or mother's kin. (See Table 27.) Limited polygyny (50%, to 36% using general polygyny and 14% using monogamy) has been the preferred pattern. (See Table 16.) Cousin-marriages of various forms, mainly patrilateral or matrilateral cross-cousin pairings in matrilineal and patrilineal societies, respectively, have been relatively uncommon. (See Table 22.) In both North and South America, marriage with second cousins has not been discouraged among those peoples who have been studied, even where first-cousin marriages are disapproved.

Matrilineal-matrilocal societies in North America have tended to be found among those who have either practiced settled agriculture, like the Hopi of the southwestern United States, or combined shifting agriculture with hunting (and/or herding), like the Iroquois of the Northeast, the Cherokee of the Southeast, and the Navajo of the Southwest. These and other matrilineal-matrilocal groups have also tended to accept divorce very readily. For example, it has been estimated that among the Navajo, only ⅓ of women and ¼ of men might still be with their first marriage partner in old age, in view of the incidence of both death and divorce. Men have changed partners more often than have women, living with two or more wives in turn, where a woman might not outlive a husband as a man might outlive a wife. In the past a few hunting-gathering peoples, like the Miurok of central California, who moved only twice a year between the hills and the valleys, tended to live in patrilineal-patrilocal bands that practiced *exogamy* (marriage outside the group, in this case the patrilineal band). Yet similar peoples, like the nearby Yurok, accepted the attempts of band heads to attract the kinsmen of their wives or their daughters' husbands through the use of "big man" feasting, gifts, and favors. Still other hunter-gatherers, like the Papago of New Mexico, practiced bilaterality and band exogamy, forbidding marriage within a growing-season co-resident group rather than within a lineage. A Papago band stayed in one place for a short growing season to raise crops but moved often the rest of the year. The result tended to be that most band members were agnatically linked. However, a daughter and her husband were free to choose to remain with her father, after the initial four days' stay in his household that began the marriage. Because the young woman's parents customarily proposed the marriage to the young man's family, the groom was certain of his welcome. A husband, wife, and children might also move from his to her band (or vice versa), as a tactful refusal of a proposal of a marriage between one of their sons and the daughter of a couple from another band.

As European settlement in North America began to impinge on local peoples, more and more of them found that old patterns needed either adaptation or replacement. The introduction of the horse in the western plains made both herding and new forms of hunting possible. Then the Europeans themselves began to come into the plains, as well as rapidly multiplying in the earlier-settled coastal regions. The Navajo remained matrilineal, finding that men's absence to earn income through wage labor fit that pattern, as had their absence for herding and hunting purposes. However, they had to adapt to longer absences. They also began to allow spouses to inherit from each other, as well as continuing former inheritance patterns that favored the matrilineal kin. On the other hand, the Iroquois turned away from using matrilineality altogether, except for reckoning eligibility for the religious-political leadership post of sachem and maintaining a set of exogamy rules. Under the inspiration of the Quaker-influenced prophet Handsome Lake at the opening of the 19th century, they placed their main emphasis on the husband-wife tie. Iroquois men began joining their wives in agriculture, adopting the plow (in place of the hoe) as a substitute for warfare after they were forced to settle on reservations. They also began stressing their own children's right to inherit the conjugal property that husband and wife now built up through joint effort.

In contrast to North America, only 12% of South American societies studied were not engaged in agriculture. (See Table 21.) Bilaterality (73%) and bride-service (43%) or token or no exchange of gifts (48%) prevailed. (See Table 24.) Among newlyweds 41% were likely to live with the husband's close kin, 40% with the wife's. (See Table 17.) Limited polygyny was practiced by 52%, general polygyny by 27%. (See Table 16.) Cousin-marriages were less frequently forbidden than in North America. Both North and South Americans allowed the marriage of patrilateral parallel cousins least frequently of all. (See Table 22.) A few peoples, like the Apinaye of Brazil, used kinship to define a group to marry into, rather than a group not to marry into. More often the group to marry into was defined by some form of co-residence, as among the Shavante of Brazil, the *calpulli* cultivation corporations among Aztec-era commoners in central Mexico, and the similar *ayllu* cultivation corporations of preconquest Andean Peru. If that were so, then those kin not to marry within the co-resident group were also specified. Contemporary Inca villagers (quite possibly in unbroken continuance of the practice of their ancestors) are organized duolineally. Land-use rights, and the knowledge and seeds for growing some varieties of maize, go from father to son (or to daughter's son, if the father has no son). Animals, and the knowledge and seeds for growing other varieties of maize, go from mother to daughter (or to son's daughter, if the mother has no daughters).

A childless couple's land-use rights, seeds, and animals go to their nearest patrilineal or matrilineal kin of the proper sex.

The still-numerous indigenous peoples of South and Central America are considered more fully in Chapter 12. They were under the rule of early modern Europeans for almost three centuries, which inevitably affected them deeply. They have also continued to be strongly influenced by the modernizing West since their homelands' mostly European-descended leaders obtained political independence from Europe in the 19th century.

In summary it appears likely that as former hunting-gathering bands began to become the nuclei of agricultural villages, the network-building and network-maintaining kinswoman-exchange systems that had probably been at the core of early hunter-gatherer marriage arrangements were gradually modified. In their place came systems whose intent was to define who could make use of cultivation rights. It also appears likely that hunter-gatherer systems of kinship reckoning, which focused on bilateral kindreds (maximizing networks in order to maximize hunting and gathering opportunities), often gave way to other forms. If bilaterality was maintained, or modified to duolineality like that of Inca ayllu groups, then ayllulike co-resident group endogamy (with some incest prohibitions) could have seemed a prudent response, as long as the co-resident group was large enough to make that solution reasonable. However, it is the kind of prudence one would expect of central government officials, concerned for ease of tax collection (and control over individuals) more than for the internal well-being of the corporation or its residents' preferences. Something more like the utrolaterality or the ambilineality of many Pacific Islanders seems more likely to have appealed to the earliest villagers themselves. It would certainly have been more like the freedom to move from band to band that was probably familiar to most hunter-gatherers. Or, alternatively, a duolineality that was not as rigid as the ayllu about requiring co-residence might have emerged, in a form perhaps resembling that of the Yako of Nigeria.

Early in agricultural village experience locally differing circumstances may well have led away from bilateral, utrolateral, ambilineal, and duolineal forms, toward either matrilineality or patrilineality. Matrilineality (and usually relative freedom for women as well as men to change marital partners) was apt to emerge more often in the absence of several kinds of situations than in the presence of any one of them. Those situations included a need for defense, which might be felt where populations were dense; a reliance on large herd animals for milk, meat, hides, or labor; and an opportunity for men to take some regular part in more than purely local-barter trade. Patrilineality tended to become more common where one or more of those three conditions prevailed, as in much of sub-Saharan Africa for the past two thousand years and more. Unilineality could have looked simpler than the alternatives, as a means of transmitting those increasingly important cultivation rights and whatever other property there was to be inherited.

Lineage-managed forms of holding and transmitting land and other property rights probably became the pattern for many, if not most, preliterate agricultural societies, particularly if ambilineal and utrolateral systems are counted as quasi-lineal systems rather than as bilateral ones. Villagers were apt to be increasingly likely to move toward patrilineality, as they found themselves pressured more and more by their own neighbors, by outsiders, or by newly established central governments. Like sub-Saharan African peoples, for whom such shifts have been noted since the middle of the 19th century, early agricultural villagers may also have moved toward patrilineality in response to finding opportunity to establish some form of conjugal fund, through the activities of outsiders and/or central governments. The Inca empire was itself a rather new creation when the Spaniards overthrew it. Perhaps its people had not yet had time to complete a shift toward patrilineality, though such a shift is suggested as possible by the fact that land already went entirely through the male line.

With growing lineage-centeredness came a tendency for married couples to live with or near the leader of the lineage group in which their own and their children's interests would be best served. Often, though not always, a shift to lineage-centeredness also brought expectations of more than merely token gifts to mark a marriage. A woman's work was useful. Even if her children remained members of her own lineage rather than becoming members of her husband's lineage, her services as wife and worker could be seen as worth more than just token gifts, by those who enabled her to give those services to a specific man. Moreover, the husband who gave more than token gifts for her might be less inclined to dissolve the marriage hastily, even if he could receive some of them back. On his side, he might also be surer that his wife (or her kinsmen) would not dissolve the marriage hastily, if he was indeed assured of receiving at least some of his gifts back. In short, bride-wealth was an assurance of seriousness of intent. It was not merely something that could be demanded because women were in short supply, as was usual in most preliterate societies. As the Zulu case demonstrates, dower could be an even more serious assurance of intent. But dowry, the provision by the bride's kin of sizable amounts of household and personal gear and other property for the bride's use, was usually not within the experience of lineage-centered preliterate agricultural societies.

Polygyny was probably infrequent in early hunter-gatherer bands. However, it may have become somewhat more frequent, as agriculture took the place of hunter-gatherer life and made extended-family households more attractive. Not only did polygyny increase the ratio of workers to dependents in extended-family groupings. It also tended to counteract the possibility of an explosion in population, as periodic rather than continual lactation and early weaning on cereal gruels shortened intervals between births for monogamous wives. Certainly polygyny tended to become more frequent where bride-wealth payments might both hasten women's marriages and delay those of men, so that women could expect to outlive at least one husband simply because of difference in age.

In any case, in all early and preliterate agricultural societies the selection of one's initial partner in marriage was probably primarily the task of one's elders, not of oneself. True, in any social system which gave young men and young women any chance at all to see each other, it can almost be taken for granted that they probably gave some indication as to preferences, to someone who could bring those preferences to the attention of the ones who would make the final arrangements. Certainly that was the case in many sub-Saharan African and Pacific Islands social systems, with their institutionalized postpubertal courtship periods out of which appropriate marriages were expected to arise. Men in most preliterate agricultural societies were probably fairly likely to arrange their own later marriages, even if not their first one. For women, however, any opportunity for real choices often depended on whether or not they had shown they could bear children for the all-important lineage. After all, the lineage was a self-protection group that needed numbers for protection, as well as being a rights-transmission group. Even in matrilineal systems potential husbands would tend to shy away from taking probably barren wives, except as an extra pair of hands alongside another wife. A man could normally expect some attention from his own children as he aged, even if their primary allegiance was to their mother's kin. He therefore cared that his wife (or wives), as well as his sister(s), would be fruitful.

In short, tendencies toward patrilineal, patrilocal, polygynous marriage systems are visible, though far from universal, in preliterate agricultural populations. (At least they have been far from universal where the region was not yet affected by population growth, trade, or centralized government.) Those same tendencies were and are even stronger among pastoral-herding peoples. They may even have been reinforced by two factors in herding peoples' lives: first, the preference of most pastoralists for finding opportunity to trade the products of their animals for other goods, rather than subsisting on them entirely; and second, the usefulness of men's greater physical size and upper-body strength in herding larger animals. It is to pastoral-herding societies, important in the development of early commercial patterns as providers of animals to carry goods, that we turn next.

CHAPTER 6

Marriage in Pastoral-Herding Societies

Within the lineage-centered systems of preliterate agricultural societies the first purpose of marriage was to perpetuate the all-important lineage. The lineage's continuance was the chief guarantee of lifelong security for each of its members. The second purpose of marriage was to ensure that newborn lineage members would be formally acknowledged as members, with whatever lineage rights were appropriate. Marriage assured that the newborn came into a relationship sanctioned by the lineage. This permission tended to be more broadly interpreted among matrilineal peoples than among patrilineal or bilateral ones. It might even be as broadly interpreted as it was traditionally among the matrilineal Akan of Ghana. The puberty rites for Akan girls authorized them to bear children for their matrilineage, whether or not the mother had gone through the formalities of marriage through bride-wealth that would transfer her work life and residence to a husband's household. Thus any children born to her were full lineage members with full inheritance rights. Only thirdly was marriage used to create or strengthen alliances with other lineages. Marriage as a source of personal satisfaction to the partners themselves was apparently last on the list of concerns for preliterate agriculturalists.

This ranking of priorities probably developed in a context of increasing pressure of population on available land. Stress on lineage could serve as an easily understood means of distinguishing between who was and who was not entitled to cultivation rights. Only those who were recognized as lineage members could enjoy full participation in the group of those who lived and worked together, as hunting-gathering gave way to agriculture throughout the tropical and temperate zones. As noted at the opening of Chapter 4, that changeover from hunting-gathering to agriculture first took place in the Middle East around ten thousand years ago or more. But another kind of change took place there at almost the same time, with similar results in terms of increasing lineage-centeredness, as some groups came to rely primarily on animal-tending. Sheep, goats, and cattle were herded first. The swifter horses and the desert-dwelling camels were added only after the rise of cities made these animals valuable enough for long-distance travel to be worth the greater effort needed to domesticate them. From the outset, though, herders exchanged animal products and surplus animals with agricultural villagers, in return for surplus crops and for postharvest grazing rights (which also resulted in some fertilization of the villagers' fields). In other regions, far to the north, some groups eventually began to obtain the animal products that formed almost their sole diet by herding reindeer, rather than by hunting and fishing like the Inuit. In the past ten thousand years difficulty in digesting the milk of cattle and other herd animals has become far more scarce among people in animal-herding regions than in, for example, West Africa and Southeast Asia. Those who could not thrive on a milk-centered diet evidently died too young to pass along the associated genes to future generations.

In temperate and subtropical regions herders of animals have tended to live in relatively close relationships with raisers of crops, and eventually with merchants coming out from cities as well. Herders in these regions have needed a mode of organization that would respond to needs for both dispersion and gathering—a scattering of animals and caretakers seeking grazing areas across wide expanses in some seasons, and a regrouping in other seasons either to move on to new base-areas or to engage in trade. They have turned overwhelmingly to patrilineality. Of 66 pastoral societies in the Eastern Hemisphere, in the 564-society survey used by David Aberle in David M. Schneider and Kathleen Gough's *Matrilineal Kinship* (1961), 51 (77%) were patrilineal, eight were bilateral, four were duolineal, and only three were matrilineal.

Most of the bilateral pastoral groups surveyed by Aberle lived in harsh and remote Siberian regions, somewhat as most of the 11 bilateral out of 13 total (2 matrilineal) pastoral societies in the New World lived in harsh and remote Andean regions. Remoteness, even more than harshness, may have had something to do with their using bilaterality rather than turning to a linear system. They may have felt less pressure for tight organization, having less frequent contact with others. Their environment's harshness may also have pressed them toward maximizing individuals' opportunities for choosing groups to be with, so that they came to use bilaterality somewhat as Pacific Islands crop-raisers have used ambilineality and utrolaterality. Certainly the nodal-kindred system of the Lapps would seem to be a means of maximizing the numbers one could call on in case of need, for the Lapps included all the siblings in a set as their reference group rather than measuring kinship outward from the individual. Thus all one's brother's wife's siblings were one's affines, not just one's brother's wife. Special circumstances also must have been needed for matrilineality. For example, there could be a separation between large-animal herding as men's work, taking them far from home, while women stayed more closely clustered and tended smaller animals. This would appear to apply to those branches of the Navajo who combine men's horse-herding with women's sheep-herding, do not raise field crops, and practice little or no gardening.

With 65% patrilineal pastoralists to just over 6% matrilineal in the Aberle list, the hypothesis that the need to work with fairly sizable animals favors men's inheritance rights over women's seems borne out well. (See Table 4.) To the degree that bilateral systems do not disfavor men by excluding them from any inheritance rights, their 24% (to 5% duolineal) frequency means that nine in ten pastoral societies give men full access through their fathers to all inheritance rights. The corresponding percentages among agriculturalists are 43% patrilineal and 36% bilateral, so that eight out of ten give men full access to inheritance through their fathers. But even where women have inheritance rights, pastoralists tend to expect that men will actually hold and manage at least the larger animals.

It is not surprising that marriage systems in most pastoral societies tend to include patrilocality, bride-wealth, and polygyny (general polygyny more often than limited polygyny). These characteristics are apt to be associated with the patrilineality that overwhelmingly prevails in pastoral societies. Pastoral societies' marriage systems are much less apt to show characteristics associated with bilaterality, such as monogamy and use of dower or dowry rather than bride-wealth. A survey of 387 societies by Roy D'Andrade in E. E. Maccoby's *The Development of Sex Differences* (1966) showed that 24 out of 32 pastoral societies were both patrilineal and patrilocal, though it did not note how many of those were polygynous as well. (See Table 3.)

A sharp division of tasks between men and women is found in most hunting-gathering societies. Men seldom gather, and women seldom join in hunting large prey except where encircling-drive methods are used. A sharp division is also found in most agricultural societies. Where plows are used, men grow certain items because they manage the animals, while women grow other items in gardens. Where hoes are used, and both men and women cultivate, some other kind of division is made between what men grow and what women grow—sometimes quite arbitrarily, as may have happened when some kinds of maize were allotted to each sex among Inca commoners in Peru. A sharp division of tasks has been made in virtually all pastoral societies too. Women have generally been made responsible for milking and processing milk into cheese and other dairy products. Men have generally been made responsible for the slaughtering and initial cutting up of animals, and for the removal and initial processing of wool, hair, and hides, even though women may do some of the later processing.

This sharp division of tasks in pastoral societies balances men's overwhelming predominance in the tasks of herding that are essential to the pastoralists' life, by making women necessary. The assignment of dairying to women ensures that a woman who is not currently rearing children can still make a significant contribution to the domestic group to which she belongs. Women in most pastoral societies recognize this clearly enough to protest strongly against any male taking part in milking, particularly if the society is patrilineal. In most groups what a woman (or a man) has not been there to do has simply been left undone.

Polygyny, so often found in pastoral societies from ancient Israel to modern times, helps to ensure that someone is always available to do the needed women's work. The tendency of pastoral groups to cluster in extended-family households structured around kinsmen (brothers, fathers and sons, cousins sharing the same grandfather) helps to ensure that someone is always available to do the needed men's work. In pastoral societies, as in agricultural societies, increasing the ratio of working adult members to those too young or too infirm to do a full day's work makes good economic sense.

Most pastoral societies tend to organize in a pyramidal mode. One's own immediate co-resident domestic group or household (perhaps just parents and unmarried offspring, perhaps more) has clearly defined links of mutual responsibility with other closely related households in a *sublineage*. These links can be activated whenever they are needed, which may be quite often. The closely related set of households in turn has fairly well defined links with the other similar sets of households in the *lineage*, which can be called on when necessary. Depending on the size of the total society and the frequency of need for dealing with outsiders, people are also apt to recognize a larger group of sets-of-households or *clan*, which may in turn have *tribe* links with other clans whose members can be called on. Sometimes a set of households, or a group of sets of households, or a larger group of such groups, is lastingly headed by a specific person or set of persons, as among most Central Asian Turkic-speaking pastoralists. Sometimes leadership is assigned only when it is actually needed, as among many Arabic-speaking pastoralists, like the Bedouin of Arabia or of Cyrenaica in present-day Libya. Which pattern is followed seems to be connected with whether the people of the society stay in one large region, like the Bedouin, coming close to waterholes in dry seasons but fanning out in all directions in wet ones, or remain close together while moving between hills and plains as the seasons change, like the Turkoman. The latter situation seems to be more conducive to a more permanent ordering. That in turn seems to be more conducive to a degree of social stratification, in which a dowry element may even be introduced into the arrangement of marriages.

The Khalka Mongols used a dowry system. The jeweled headdress of the bride was expected to equal the value of the bride-wealth given by the groom. Moreover, the parents of the bride were to provide a dowry of animals to the new couple after three years. Up to that time the woman was not supposed to visit her parents unless one of them was ill. However, the marriage was also not regarded as final until the dowry was delivered. It could be broken more easily before delivery of the dowry than afterward.

Unlike most dowry-users, the Khalka Mongols gave more dowry with a woman who married into a poor family, on the ground that she would need it more. Thus they used dowry to equalize, rather than primarily to maintain barriers between economic levels. They also did not allow marriages between those of noble rank, for all nobles were regarded as members of the single clan of Genghis Khan. By the rules of clan exogamy, formed to minimize interclan rivalries and promote group-wide solidarity, they therefore had to marry into other (i.e., commoner) clans. This is unusual, if not unique, along dowry-users, in actually requiring both a circulation of high-ranking women into lower-rank households and a circulation of low-ranking women into high-rank households. The descendant of a noblewoman could only marry the child of a nobleman after four generations had passed. The use of dowry to equalize economic situations may well have stemmed from the concern of high-rank parents for their daughters' well-being, once the circulatory marriage system had been accepted. Apparently this unusual system arose from a recognition that something must be done to forestall clan rivalries, which otherwise could have followed the establishment of a hereditary elite through the predominance of the descendants of Genghis Khan in the 13th century A.D.

Whether among the Khalka Mongols or in any other lineage-conscious society, a household group's members know both the *span* (how far one goes laterally to first and second cousins and beyond) and the *depth* (how far one goes ancestrally to grandfather or great-grandfather or beyond) of each of their operating lineage segments, for each set of purposes for which sublineage, lineage, clan, or tribal cooperation may be required. Usually the largest group is a *sib*. That means that it consists of all who are descended from a named ancestor. (Lineage members can trace their links with other members of their own lineage more readily than they can with others in their clan or tribe.) Clans and lineages keep on growing with each generation. They form new subdivisions when previous divisions become too large to work with easily. Often those new subdivisions are defined in terms of descending from Son A of Wife X rather than from Son B of Wife Y of the common ancestor. They may even be defined in terms of descending from Son H of Wife M of Son A of Wife X, rather than from Son K of Wife Q of Son A of Wife X. In any case, they will exclude anyone who cannot claim that specific named ancestor. Sometimes, however, the largest group is a *sept*, defined by how far back the common ancestor is and therefore changing with every generation. It may also be a kindred (usually bilateral), defined by the closeness of relationship to the individual who seeks support. Unlike a sib or a sept, a kindred is not a lineage segment, whether membership is counted according to the individual (as among modern Greek shepherds) or according to the individual's sibling-group membership (as among contemporary Lapps). However, the limits of duties are equally clearly defined. The only difference is that the level of mutual obligation depends on the other's kin-distance from oneself, rather than on common membership in a sib or sept. Among the Greek shepherds, before the practice of feud was effectively stopped, one was bound only to seek vengeance for one's own parent, sibling, child, or child's child; but other modes of mutual support were to be expected from and given to others, out to second cousins, first cousins' children, and siblings' grandchildren. Mutual obligations might include contributions to bride-wealth required for a lineage segment or kindred member to take a wife; or distributions of bride-wealth received for a daughter or sister of a lineage segment or kindred member; or contributions to the dowry of a woman of the lineage segment or the kindred. Dowry obligations are usually limited to a daughter, sister, niece, or granddaughter, as among Khalka Mongols and modern Greek shepherds.

In any society that requires bride-wealth or dowry to marry, those who do the major providing will expect to have an active voice in the selection of the spouse. Those who are expected only to provide one or two animals in a bride-wealth herd of 30 or more can do no more than register disapproval by refusing to cooperate, however. The gatherer of the bride-wealth can usually proceed without that aid, either by obtaining an extra animal or two from someone else or by persuading the bride's kin to accept a delayed completion of the payment, out of the animals to be born in future into his own herds.

The wandering nature of pastoralists' lives tends to mean that there are only few and brief opportunities to see members of other households informally. Thus there are not apt to be courting rituals like those of many Pacific Islands village societies, with their young men's houses to which a youth may take the young woman he is courting. Instead, most of the selection process is in the hands of a young person's parents and possibly those parents' siblings. Even where young warriors were traditionally free to be with young unmarried women, as among the pastoral Masai and Samburu peoples of eastern Africa, they were expected to remain within limits that stopped short of actual conception. Moreover, young women's parents looked for husbands for them in age-grades older than the young warriors' age-grade. They sought men who were no longer liable to die in battle unless the conflict were so serious that older men were also sent to fight. Among users of dowry, however, freedom for young women and young men to be together is usually unthinkable. A dowried woman ordinarily needs much more dowry if her capacity to be faithful to her husband seems doubtful than if she seems entirely innocent of previous experience. Bride-wealth users have also tended to favor premarital virginity in women, although that sentiment tends to be stronger in patrilineal-patrilocal societies (like those of most pastoralists) than in other types of societies.

Parental control of marriage arrangements may have reached an extreme among the Chukchee of Siberia. The groom's parents could return the bride up to 18 months after the marriage, even if the groom wanted to keep her.

They could also choose a grown young woman as wife to an infant son. They might then expect her to find a consort to bring children to her husband's family, or they might provide her with a consort who would live with her till her husband was mature enough to consummate the marriage in his middle or late teens. Such a parentally provided consort could be a man of the husband's family who had himself been similarly married as a child and then been left without a wife in his adulthood. He might also be infirm or even dead by the time the youthful husband reached sufficient maturity to claim his wife.

In pastoral-herding societies in which bride-wealth is used a man must usually turn to his sublineage or even his lineage for the cattle he needs to take a wife. His own household is seldom wealthy enough to provide what he will need. Young men complain of elders who want to take second wives before a younger man has even one. However, elders must be cautious about doing so. The fathers of eager young men usually press their own sons' claims vigorously, since a married son brings another woman (and eventually more children) into the extended-family household. That is important to a father of adult sons. It is usually more important to him than enabling one of his brothers to obtain a second wife, unless a first wife has proved barren. In that case, the brother's claim would probably prevail. On the whole, elders do not take second wives (and third wives are a rarity), unless there is no immediately pressing'claim for a younger man of the sublineage or lineage to take a first wife. Even then, as young men point out, such a taking of a second wife is apt to remove enough cattle from households' herds to require a year or more to pass before another set of bride-wealth cattle can be given up, unless the marriage of a woman brings in a set of bride-wealth cattle before that time.

When only cattle could be used as bride-wealth and their own herds were the only source of cattle, pastoral groups in Africa and other bride-wealth-using regions tended, in effect, to parcel out marriages, one for each man, until all fully adult men were married. Only rarely would bride-wealth be provided for second or later marriages when any adult man was still without a wife. Still, a newly matured young man might have to yield to a childless uncle's or a widowed cousin's claim. He might even have to yield to an already influential kinsman's wish for a second or even a third or fourth wife, if that would form or strengthen an alliance with another lineage that even the young man's father agreed might benefit the whole group. However, as commercial activity came to regions that previously had seen little of it, opportunities to obtain wealth increased. This new wealth could either be substituted for cattle as bride-wealth, or be used to purchase bride-wealth cattle (either locally or from neighboring regions). Consequently both younger and older men became less dependent on kinsmen for support in providing bride-wealth. Polygyny may well have increased as a result, not because a greater number of women miraculously became available, but because they were circulated faster. Less time might elapse before a widowed or divorced woman remarried, or there might be a shorter wait after puberty for bride-wealth to be collected and paid by or for a woman's first husband. Certainly the power of lineage elders to govern marriage arrangements was greatly decreased by any availability of commercially earned wealth. By the 1970s few, if any, bride-wealth-using pastoral peoples were still untouched enough by commercialization for lineages or sublineages to control their male members' opportunities for marriage, as they had done until the 20th century.

The few dowry-using pastoralists, like the Khalka Mongols, have tended to live in areas through which considerable amounts of commerce flowed. There, extended-family households could obtain wealth by providing animals and hospitable services to merchants. Thus they could become differentiated in status and power. The opportunity for households to obtain wealth from outsiders also meant that households tended to make their own arrangements for their younger members' marriages.

Dowry systems tend to be more discouraging than bride-wealth systems toward both divorce and widow-remarriage. On the one hand, it can be difficult to endow a woman's second marriage if dowry is not returned. On the other hand, it can be hard to require the husband to return the dowry if it is supposed to be returned, or to require the husband's family to return it if she is left widowed. Such problems might be lessened by a delayed payment of the dowry, as with the three-year wait among the Khalka Mongols, which gave time to prove the couple's fruitfulness or compatibility, or both. In a bride-wealth system in which the bride-wealth has to be returned if there is a divorce, the kinsmen of a wife tend to try to discourage divorce perhaps even more than a husband's kinsmen may want to encourage it, whereas in a nonreturnable bride-wealth system the husband and his kinsmen are the ones to want to avoid divorce.

Divorce has been accepted in most pastoral societies, especially when a marriage has not proved to be fruitful within a reasonable length of time. But divorce has probably been somewhat less frequent among pastoralists than among hunting-gathering peoples or even among those agriculturalists who have not experienced strong pressure against divorce, either by a dominant religion such as Christianity or by an economic factor such as the operation of a dowry system. There may have been almost one divorce for every two marriages in some groups, as among Berber pastoralists in 20th-century Morocco. However, those Moroccan Berber pastoralists were also practicing both kinship endogamy and residential endogamy. Consequently divorces did not mean as much disarranging of alliances as if the partners were from different lineages or different localities. The ability of either Khalka Mongol spouse to obtain divorce for adultery by the other, and of the wife to obtain divorce if mistreated by the husband's parents or siblings, was somewhat unusual among either pastoralists or agriculturalists in its protection of the woman's position. The special nature of Khalka Mongol society, which put high-rank women into low-rank families as wives, was probably at work here too. A divorced Khalka woman could not take a son with her, however—only her daughters. A widow who returned to her parents' household also had to send any sons back to the deceased husband's family when they reached maturity. If the woman had had cause for divorce, she recovered her dowry and could use it to remarry. If she were at fault, she could not; and any later children born out of wedlock were regarded as her parents' grandchildren, but no one else's, when it came to providing dowry and bride-wealth. Still, even that gave some protection to the woman's position. Her children would not be left out entirely, and neither would she. Such attitudes may have come not only from the nobles-to-commoners circulating marriage system of the Khalka Mongols, but also from the doubtless long-ingrained recognition that provision must be made for possible sonlessness. That recognition appears in the institutionalization of paying groom-wealth for a husband for a brotherless daughter, or even just a favorite one whom her father wished to keep in the household—or a divorced one whose dowry had not been returned. In such a case, neither dowry nor bride-wealth would be given.

Pastoralists may appear to have more reason than agriculturalists to want to maximize their networks, since (like hunter-gatherers) they are mobile, and would presumably like access to grazing grounds in as many areas as possible. That might seem to press toward easier divorce than where cultivation rights are all-important. But the wish to keep inheritance lines clear for the transmission of animals tends to make marital stability highly valued. In addition, many pastoralists try to protect themselves from disease and drought (perhaps especially in Africa) by putting some of their own animals out with their own and their wives' kinsmen, and then bringing in some of those kinsmen's animals in return. That tends to make divorce unwelcome because one would have to rearrange one's flocks and herds. Such rearranging would not be impossible, but it could be inconvenient.

Some form of cousin-marriage may be accepted among pastoralists, no matter what kinship system they use. In the Middle East, where the use of patrilateral parallel-cousin marriage (children of brothers) has been favored as a means of reuniting possessions divided through inheritance since civilization began, that is perhaps the most common form. However, it is rare in other regions. Recognition of potentially harmful resulting rivalries seems to have worked against its use. Levirate is also common among patrilineally organized pastoralists, perhaps especially in the Middle East and Africa. Nonetheless, some patrilineal pastoralists use their marriages to maximize their networks, rather than to consolidate their kinship ties to the degree that Middle Eastern pastoralists are apt to do. Middle Eastern pastoralists may choose anywhere from $1/10$ to $1/2$ or even more of spouses from among eligible kin. That is quite different from the Khalka Mongols, who forbade marrying not only the father's kin, but also the mother's, if closer than a second cousin.

Pastoralists tend to rely strongly on kinship ties, since they do not have permanent co-residence (as agriculturalists do) to provide an alternative basis for cooperation when needed. That helps to explain their use of cousin-marriages. Local concentration of agnates may be as high as 90%, as among the Bedouin of Cyrenaica in the 1940s, with only a few cognates and affines pasturing alongside the strong core of agnates in a given region. Or the local concentration of agnates may be as low as 20%, with not only cognates and affines pasturing in the region, but also some who are only affines of cognates and of affines, some with no links in that area at all beyond simple friendship (at least as yet), and even some who may share a socially man-ufactured tie like a sworn-brotherhood pact rather than any kinship created by birth or marriage. Whatever the degree of concentration of agnates, though, high or low, there will generally tend to be one lineage that pre-dominates in each area used by the whole society. The members of that lineage are the same ones whom others in the area see themselves as having and needing links with, in order to stay there.

A largely pastoral people may practice some gardening or crop-raising. The Cyrenaica Bedouin cast lots to determine who will plant and harvest on a given strip of land after one of the infrequent rains, for example, while women among the Jie of Uganda garden around the permanent base-resi-dence from which the men go out with their herds. However, as long as a people primarily rely on the food provided by their animals, their thinking with regard to kinship, marriage, and other social relationships will continue to be dominated by the considerations important to the pastoralist, rather than to the agriculturalist. Among the Tuareg of the western Sahara, for example, who are unusual in being matrilineal (transmitting authority from a man to his sister's son), women are as free as men to initiate divorce. A new husband lives in his wife's parents' household. Yet most (though not all) of the animals are held by men, and tend to be used for their sons' bride-wealth, not for their sisters' sons'. Among the more conventionally patrilineally organized Cyrenaica Bedouin, the husband's father was tra-ditionally believed to see the marriage of a son as signaling the onset of age and weakness, and therefore to need time to get used to the idea. Conse-quently newly married couples have often lived with the wife's father for a time. This may have encouraged (or been encouraged by) the tendency to look for spouses among patrilineal kin.

The pastoralists observed between 1900 and the 1950s in Africa south of the Sahara were perhaps nearest the situation of the earliest pastoralists. Like early herders, they lived in some degree of association with agricultural villagers, and even with states that did not feel the direct presence of Eu-ropean or other large-scale imperial rule until only a few decades ago. Most of the reindeer-herders across northernmost Europe and Asia (except for those in the modern states of Scandinavia, who have been affected by those states' experiences) have felt an imperial Russian presence for the past three centuries. Mongols and other Central Asians began to be squeezed between the expanding empires of Russia and China three hundred years ago. The pastoralists of the Americas have also been under the rule of Europeans (mainly Spaniards), and then of local governments run by settlers of European origin and culture, for an equal or even greater length of time. Shepherds in Greece and Tuareg in what is now Algeria, like pastoralists throughout the Middle East and North Africa, have been involved for many centuries in the active commercial life of their areas. That must have deeply influenced their patterns of life. (To mention modern Greek shepherds in a chapter on the rise and development of marriage systems among pastoralists who primarily subsist on the products of their animals may seem nearly as incongruous as to look at Texas cattle-ranchers. Still, the crime of honor, a husband's almost formally recognized right to retaliate for unfaithfulness in a wife, has been known in both groups. And one practice among some Greek shepherds until recent times bears directly on the apparently universal age-old concern that social replacement, rather than actual increase, should be the norm in practice for all except those who can see real opportunities for more than just two surviving children. Newly married couples slept in the same unpartitioned hut as the groom's parents, and were required to have permission before engaging in marital intercourse.) Peoples such as the Fulani of northeastern Nigeria, the Jie of Uganda, the Turkana and the Masai of Kenya, and the Nuer of the Sudan offer better illustrations than pastoralists elsewhere of what precommercial pastoralists' lives and social systems may have been like, and how their marriage systems may have fitted into their social systems and ecological situations.

The Fulani illustrate well the sharp division between men and women frequently found in pastoralists' lives. Their household camps are divided between men's and women's sides. Once a young man reaches adulthood and marries, he is expected to enter the women's side only to lie with his own wife. A girl or woman (married or not) only enters the men's side to milk the herd, carrying out all processing on the women's side. At circumcision (usually at seven to ten years of age) a boy is betrothed to an infant girl. She joins him in his parents' camp when she matures, bringing household gear provided by her mother, while he has cattle provided by his father. She stays until she conceives or until it appears that she will not. She then returns to her parents' camp, either to bear the child and bring it to weaning or to be given to another husband. After that she either moves to a new camp with the child's father or goes through the cycle again, until she either becomes a mother or is simply taken as an additional wife (barren but still useful as a worker) by an already-married man. Even if she has children, but does not have enough of them, her husband may divorce her. She may also divorce him for failure to maintain a large enough herd to provide for herself and her children. She may then take her sons and her betrothed daughters with her. If she does, her husband must go to his father's camp or to a brother's camp, unless or until he has another wife. A divorced woman who has borne children may not be taken as chief or initial wife, but like an apparently barren one must be an additional wife. However, a young widow who is either expecting or nursing, and can bring the infant with her, would be a welcome chief wife to a man who has found that no woman seems to be able to have children with him. All these arrangements are made for a woman, rather than by her, although a woman who has consummated a marriage must be asked for her consent to them. Adult men who have consummated a first marriage make their own arrangements for any later marriages, assuring the fathers or brothers of prospective wives that the herds they have built up from what they received at their first marriage will provide for what the household needs. Each married couple then begins to give up cattle (from father to sons) and household gear (from mother to daughters) as their offspring marry. When the last son marries he takes the last cattle, and when the last daughter marries she takes the last household gear. Either event will lead the parents to join a son's camp, to live out the remainder of their lives. A woman left widowed with children who are past infancy takes as her unmarried children's guardian her oldest married son, if she has one, or else the oldest living brother of her husband. A deceased man's oldest living brother is in fact expected to take at least one of his brother's widows as a wife. Other brothers may take other remaining widows as wives, if they wish. Thus the marriage system is designed to provide security for everyone from birth to death. Not even lineage segments matter much in Fulani life, which makes the Fulani somewhat unusual among pastoralists. But Fulani camps are small—either a nuclear family or a polygynous one, but not two husbands with wives except when aging parents move in with their son. The Fulani live in the hot dry reaches at the edge of the Sahara, where there is little likelihood that larger groups could find enough pasture to stay together at any time of the year. Consequently it is not surprising that beyond the level of the household-camp group, Fulani kinship ties tend to be rather minimal.

Far to the east, in the dry grasslands of Kenya in eastern Africa, both Turkana and Masai also live in constantly moving encampments, following the herds. But pasturage is better than where the Fulani live, and the moving encampments can be larger as a consequence.

Among the Masai, who developed the age-grade system too far back for us to know how long they may have used it, the men who herd and camp together may have become friends in the age-grade of the young warriors, fully as often as they may be kin. Adult Masai men take their wives and children freely from one encampment to another throughout life, now with a brother or a father's brother's son, now with a friend, now with a mother's brother, now with a wife's brother. For a man's first marriage, bride-wealth is primarily provided by his father or by his oldest brother as his guardian, but neither is apt to treat him as a competitor for bride-wealth. The bride-wealth a man gives for his later wives largely comes from his own herds. Because of the age-grade system, which defers a man's first marriage until his 20s, his father is likely by that time to be either dead or old enough not to be taking wives any more. Potential friction with an older brother is eased by the strong social expectation that the dead father's herds are meant to enable all his sons to wed.

On the other hand, the Turkana organize their encampments in terms of father, wives, married sons, their wives, married grandsons, their wives, and all unmarried offspring, in an extended-family household that may even reach the fourth generation before the death of an aged father leads to a division among his sons. Not all household members stay together in one place. The head plus one or more other men, all with their wives and children, stay together in one main camp. The remaining men take their wives and children into one or two secondary camps, roving through the countryside as rainfall opens up new grazing here or there. A son may go with a wife's brother for a time in that brother's camp, or with a bond-friend, or with a sister's husband. (Bond-friends are established by one formally giving a gift to the other and the other accepting it.) While the father lives, though, the father is the one who makes decisions about giving cattle for bride-wealth on behalf of sons and grandsons, or about distributing the cattle received as bride-wealth (for daughters and granddaughters) to sons and grandsons for their use. As a consequence, although he is likely to take more than one wife for himself while his sons are young, he generally does not do so after they mature. He must first provide wives for his sons, once they reach marriageable age, and then he must provide wives for their sons as they mature. Therefore, heads of households are the likeliest to have more than one or at most two wives, but they seldom have more than three or four.

Sons of the same mother usually stay together as cooperating brothers for a time after a father dies and his herds are divided among each wife's group of sons. But sooner or later concerns for their own sons' interests will generally lead the younger brothers to ask for their portion of the herd and leave. However, as long as the father lives, the only cattle that sons and grandsons may treat as theirs are those that the father grants them as personally theirs. The rest are still regarded as part of the family herds. Thus a man who wants to marry must expect to obtain the bulk of his bride-wealth from his father, unless he is a household head himself. Yet he will also turn to kin and bond-friends, for it helps to show his intended wife's family that a marriage alliance with him is worthwhile, if he can demonstrate that he is able to obtain cattle from others. One Turkana head of household, for example, as reported by P. H. Gulliver in *The Family Herds* (1955), obtained ½ his bride-wealth for a second wife from his own herds; ¼ from brothers, paternal uncles, and patrilateral cousins; ⅛ from mother's brothers, first wife's brothers, and sisters' husbands; and ⅛ from bond-friends.

The Turkana and the Masai have not been in their current areas for as long as the Jie have been in their area in Uganda. It is still debatable whether the Masai and the Turkana were sent wandering by population pressure from within their own ranks, or by pressure from expanding agricultural peoples like the Kikuyu, or by both, though the Masai perceive the Kikuyu as having driven them from former grazing lands. The Jie, near the great interior lakes of East Africa, have rainfall enough to allow gardening to be part of their lives. Rather than a moving main camp and moving secondary camps, they organize their basic unit of father, wives, married sons, their wives, married grandsons, their wives, and all unmarried offspring into a permanent garden-surrounded base camp (in which the wives spend most of their time) and secondary roving cattle-keeping camps (in which the men spend much of theirs). They practice polygyny, though to a somewhat lesser degree than do the Turkana. They average just over two wives for older men, rather than just under three as among the Turkana. Like the Turkana, they expect the basic unit to remain together under the father's headship while he lives; but unlike the Turkana, they also expect it to stay together through the sons' lives, only dividing at the grandsons' generation. And because they tend to keep reworking their own memories of kinship to convince themselves that a great-great-grandfather's son (or even a great-grandfather's son) is really a fellow-grandson, as brothers' lines die out, they tend to end up with a continuation of approximately the same number of household units in the total society. It is an interesting parallel to the "agnate amnesia" of the Siane and others, as noted in Chapter 4.

Like the Turkana, the Jie expect bride-wealth to come largely from the agnates. One first-marriage bride-wealth reported by Gulliver in 1955 came as $^2/_5$ from the groom's father's herd; $^2/_5$ from half-brothers, uncles, and cousins; not quite $^1/_{10}$ from other agnates; $^1/_{10}$ from bond-friends; and just one animal from the groom's mother's brother. Like the Turkana, also, the Jie strongly frown on divorce and seldom use it. That is because the bride-wealth is then distributed in corresponding fashion among the bride's male kin (no bond-friends, though some affines), and would be hard to reassemble. Concern for lineage means that adultery is strongly disapproved as well. However, among both the Jie and the Turkana a marriage is not final (and the bride-wealth is not fully paid) until it has proved fruitful. The groom goes to the bride's home until she bears one child among the Turkana, and two among the Jie. Until then renegotiating or even ending the arrangement may take place at any of the 14 stages the Jie recognize between betrothal and removal to the husband's household. The Turkana are less formal. A barren woman can become a second wife-and-worker to an already-married man. Jie men care more about and interact more with a mother's male kin than with a wife's male kin, which reverses the tendency among Turkana men. That is probably because the Jie are more permanently located in a specific area, as well as because they stay together through more generations before a household may divide. Both Jie and Turkana care about expanding networks through marriage more than they care about consolidating kinship, evidently, for both forbid marriages with too-close members of both the father's and the mother's clans. Because a man will be likely to ask a wife's kin (or a sister's or even a brother's wife's kin) for bride-wealth at some future time, he does not bring two wives into a household from the same clan. That is simply practical. No incest rule would prevent him, or him and his brother, from doing so. He does not even tend to marry the sister of a sister's husband. In short, sister-exchange and cousin-marriage are not part of Jie or Turkana thinking.

The Nuer of the Sudan also practice complete patrilineal exogamy, and among a mother's kin only someone more distant than a fourth cousin may be chosen. The Nuer, who are organized by age-grades, seek to avert strains on age-grade relationships by prohibiting a man from ever marrying the daughter of someone in his own age-grade, or from marrying the daughter of a man who is in his father's age-grade as long as both fathers are alive. To relieve other possible strains in marital relationships they forbid a man to marry a sister or other close kinswoman of his wife. They practice levirate, expecting a man to give his deceased brother children through his brother's widow. They also practice ghost-marriage, in which a man takes a wife on behalf of a childless deceased kinsman, for they believe that after death as well as during life a person must have children for security. That is why they allow a barren woman to contract a woman-marriage, paying bride-wealth for another woman and then assigning a genitor to her. In view of Nuer willingness to see a child in terms of its socially recognized "father" rather than its genitor, it is not surprising that the Nuer accept a man's right to lie with a woman (if she is willing) who is the wife of a close paternal kinsman, as long as he is not too close—a father's brother or a father's brother's son, for example, but not the man's own father or brother. Nor is it surprising that they recognize formal concubinage for a widow, or for a woman who has left her husband, or for an unmarried woman. The unmarried woman's children are simply taken into her father's lineage (unless their genitor pays cattle in order to claim them), while the widow's or the deserting wife's children go into their husbands' lineages.

The Nuer scarcely acknowledge the possibility of divorce once a woman has borne a child to her groom in her father's home and the successive installments of bride-wealth have been paid. A husband may recover all but a few of the bride-wealth cattle if a wife leaves him after moving into his household. But he may prefer not to recover them because then he can claim all the children she may bear as concubine to another man. The wife's family would be well satisfied not to have to return the cattle, for by then they would be long since distributed among her father's and her father's mother's male kin (½ to each side, since each had provided ½ of the bride-wealth for her own mother). It is recognized that bride-wealth cattle may not all be paid by the time the wife enters her husband's household because of temporary losses owing to disease or drought. If not all the bride-wealth is received by the time a couple's eldest son is to be betrothed, and needs bride-wealth of his own, the wife's kin are expected to concede her son's needs and give up their claim to any not yet received. Noncompletion of payment may also be a hedge against the wife's dying before a second child is born. If she dies after the first but before the second child, her kin are expected to return part of the bride-wealth, which may take long negotiations to bring about. The Nuer illustrate the tendency to leave all dairying activities to women, although young Nuer boys not yet initiated into manhood may take part in them. The Nuer also illustrate the practice of polygyny, with probably one in five men on the average having more than one wife. The later beginning of a man's marital career, as compared with a woman's, makes that possible.

In summary, marriage systems among precommercial pastoralists tend to display more concern for networks than among precommercial or preliterate agriculturalists. The distaste of Nuer, Jie, and Turkana for cousin-marriage reflects that concern in a form perhaps less influenced by long association with nearby urban centers than Berbers or Bedouin have been. Pastoralists need flexibility in their choice of grazing grounds as rainfall brings to life first one area and then another. However, pastoralists also tend to display strong concern for marital stability (or at least stability in the assignment of children to lineages) because of the inconvenience of having to renegotiate cattle-lending arrangements or to recalculate expectations with regard to providing and receiving bride-wealth. Pastoralists are few, by comparison with agriculturalists. The special conditions of their lives, usually lived out on the fringes of agricultural regions (even though, as with the Lapps, their herding may antedate agriculture in the area), tend to make them gravitate even more heavily than agriculturalists toward patrilineal forms. These forms in turn tend to correlate with patrilocality and polygyny; but the sharp division usually made between men's and women's tasks helps to ensure that women are valued for more than purely childbearing and child-rearing purposes.

CHAPTER 7

Marriage in Commercializing and Urbanizing Societies: Background and General Considerations

In the overwhelming majority of the relatively simple agricultural and pastoral societies that have been looked at thus far, commercial transactions—even when fairly extensive, like Middle Eastern and European slave trading in Africa up to the 19th century—have tended to rely either on direct barter or on some recognized medium of exchange like cowrie shells whose acceptability did not depend on any central government's having issued it. Not even the early Mesopotamian civilizations and their Central and South American parallels in Mexico and Peru used coined money. They used standard weights instead. One measured out a fraction of an ounce of gold or silver in payment for a purchase, like the Ashanti of recent centuries in West Africa, whose beautifully crafted gold-weights are works of art.

Most of the societies discussed thus far have also been small enough in scale so that they have had only one or at most two levels of formal jurisdiction beyond that of the local community itself. They have only been what Aberle calls "minimal states." They have not reached a size, or a degree of governmental or social complexity, sufficient to be regarded as a fully functioning state. It is in such circumstances that kinship takes on the greatest significance in the operation of the society. The society tends to be dominated by lineage groups, whether in a preset unilineal, a lifelong changeable ambilineal, or a once-chosen utrolateral form. The extended-family household tends to be the smallest functioning unit in such societies far more often than the nuclear type. As reported in a 1972 *American Journal of Sociology* article, "Societal and Family Complexity: Evidence for the Curvilinear Hypothesis," R. L. Blumberg and R. Winch found the greatest likelihood of extended-family household patterns in three types of societies: first, those in which the mean size of the local community is 100 to 1,000 and there is no town of over 5,000 (78%, to 69% in those with at least one town of over 5,000 and 51% in those with a mean community size under 100, in a total of 458 societies for which communities' sizes could be ascertained);

second, those in which there are only one or two levels of jurisdiction above
the local community (83%, to 74% for those with three or more levels and
59% for those with none, in a total of 883 societies); and third, those that
had a hereditary aristocracy (79%, to 66% for those with no significant
stratification other than the possible existence of a distinction between free
and slave, and 70% for those with nonhereditary forms of stratification, in
a total of 851 societies). (See Tables 10 through 14.)

These considerations may help to explain the contrast between Aristotle's
view that the state must control the family lest the family defy it, and
Hobbes's view that the family could be used by the state to inculcate obedience. The city-state of 4th century B.C. Greece was apt to fall into the
community-size and jurisdictional-level pattern of a society that was just
emerging from circumstances in which the extended family and the lineage
it belonged to were most likely to be in a dominant position. But in the
England of the 17th century A.D. lineage and family had long since declined
in importance for the individual. The state was larger and more complex.
Government had taken over many of the regulatory and protective functions
previously exercised by lineages and households. Christian teaching also
played a role. Already in 1563 the Council of Trent had proclaimed for
Roman Catholics that parental refusal to countenance a marriage did not
invalidate it, if it had been blessed by a priest. The priest's officiation was
necessary (though not in itself sufficient) to make the marriage valid, but
the parents' blessing was not. It was the two parties' own consent that was
the other necessary condition for the marriage, along with their both being
free to wed (not only because not already wed, but also because not too
closely related to each other). Even being a slave, which had barred marriage
in the ancient Mediterranean world, had been declared in the 12th century
by the canon lawyers of the church not to be a bar to marriage. England
had already left the Roman Catholic fold by 1563, and Roman Catholic
states like France continued to let disapproving parents disinherit offspring
who refused to wed as parents approved. Nevertheless 1563 stands as a
landmark date in the history of marriage systems. It resoundingly signaled
that for a large sector of humanity, the family was no longer the maker of
marriages. The partners and the larger society were.

Yet 1563 alone may not be the best dividing-line between the experiences
of relatively complex and increasingly commercializing societies, whose marriage systems nevertheless continued to operate within a social system still
dominated by lineage and family, and the experiences of much more complex
modern industrial-commercial societies (first in the modern West, and then
in the remainder of the world as other peoples began to make use of Western
experience). The year 1406, when the bishop of Nantes in France established
the first baptismal registry, may actually be a more significant date. This
was the first listing *by name* of who had been born into each household,
by an institution other than the lineage or the extended family itself. The

census-takers of ancient China and elsewhere listed household heads, along with the numbers and sometimes even the names of those in their households. However, they made no effort to find out who had been born or died between the periodic registrations of those then living. At most they tried to keep track of those who reached taxable adulthood. What mattered was taxable units, not specific infants or adults. The baptismal registry was significant because it institutionalized the concept of the individual as an entity in himself or herself, rather than as existing only within the context of the family. Once the use of baptismal registers began to spread across 15th-century western Europe, marriage and burial registers soon followed. These, too, contributed to a rising sense of individuality in all segments of western European society.

Only after the concept of the individual as an entity has been established as an operating principle in at least one major institution of the society can individuals' preferences be regarded as having some genuine legitimacy, if they conflict with the expectations placed on an individual by his or her family. And only after the legitimacy of individual choice has been established can men and women begin to bring their labor (as well as their products) to the marketplace on the basis of their own decisions, as individuals and as members of nuclear families, rather than primarily on the basis of decisions reached at the level of the extended family or even a lineage segment that includes several extended families. That is why the line between commercializing societies and commercial ones, which could be drawn in many different ways for many different reasons, is being drawn here when some kind of suprafamilial registration system for births, marriages, and deaths begins to be effectively introduced. For western Europe that means the 15th century A.D. For Japan it means the 17th century. For formerly colonial regions, like the Americas or India or Africa or the Pacific Islands, it usually means the period in which a European colonial government was effectively established, whether that was in the 16th or the 19th century. For a region such as China or most of the Middle East, under European influence economically more than politically during the 19th and early 20th centuries, it has usually meant only the period since about A.D 1900.

The family might retain a considerable role in marriage arrangements for a long time after the introduction of a suprafamilial system of registering births, marriages, and deaths. However, once such a system became familiar to most people, its suggestion that even the ordinary individual has some identity other than family membership would have its own effect. The family remained psychologically important, as one of the few groups within which an individual interacted with others on a basis of sharing and giving, rather than on a basis of buying and selling or even bartering goods and services. Nevertheless, personal identity no longer had to rest chiefly on one's family membership.

The process of recognizing a marriage (or its dissolution by divorce, if that were to occur) changed correspondingly. It was no longer primarily a matter for the family. It also became a concern of the suprafamilial registering institution, whether that institution was the church (as in medieval and early modern Europe) or the state (as in more recent times in Europe and elsewhere). Both social and personal identity, one's duties and rights with regard to others and the way one exercised them, began to center less on the family and more on larger and usually more impersonal groups.

As family-centeredness diminished, the nuclear-family household increasingly replaced the extended-family household as the expected form. But that only became possible as schools, hospitals, and pension systems began to supplement reliance on household and kin to meet the needs of the young, the ill, and the aged. Moreover, until governments and/or those who oversaw the use of agricultural land began to deal with individuals rather than with household heads, the convenience of minimizing the number of household heads to have to deal with tended to make those in power oppose the breaking up of extended families into nuclear-family households. In actual experience, at any given time, few societies already urbanized enough for record-keeping seem to have had more than five or six persons in an average household. Better-off families might have eight or more, indicating the probable presence of more than one married couple and their offspring, while poorer ones might have only about three because of early deaths. In addition, few record-keeping societies recorded more than perhaps one in 15 families that actually included three or more generations at any given time. Still, many if not most people in earlier societies were probably in a three-generation family for at least a brief period at some time in their lives.

As long as extended-family rather than nuclear-family households remain the expected form in a society, it is obviously desirable to try to ensure that a newly entering spouse will fit well into the ongoing life of the whole household, not merely into the personal relationship with the other spouse. That tends to give the elders a dominant voice in determining who that new spouse will be, particularly since they will also be responsible for any gifts or ceremonial expenditures involved. Insofar as a lineage segment beyond the household may contribute, its leaders, too, may play a role. Whom to seek a spouse for first, a son or a daughter; whom to seek that spouse among; how much of the household resources to put into the making of the match; which specific possible candidate to approach first—all these are major decisions that matter to the entire household. The household's elders naturally tend to use their age and experience to claim that such decisions are more properly their responsibility than that of the younger members. The younger members may well want to say that they will have to live longer and more intimately with the results of their elders' decisions than will the elders. However, they will only be able to put that feeling into operation when social, economic, and political circumstances give them alternative opportunities and assurances for the future, beyond the traditional reliance on family networks and inheritance of family-held rights.

All of these generalizations are well illustrated in the experience of Europe, the Middle East, and Asia, the regions usually termed the "Circum-Mediterranean" and "East Eurasia" realms in surveys by Aberle, Goody, and others, based on George P. Murdock's great collection of ethnographic data. These are the regions in which city-centered societies first rose and spread. They differ in a number of significant ways from the American, sub-Saharan African, and Pacific Islands realms discussed in Chapter 5. The preindustrial and nonindustrial societies of the Circum-Mediterranean realm (Europe and the Middle East) display 38% monogamy, or over half again the frequency with which monogamy is found in any other realm. (See Table 16.) The whole Europe–Middle East–Asia realm shows only one in five societies lacking in some form of either hereditary or wealth-based stratification, whereas from almost one in two to more than three in four lack such a form of stratification in the other realms. (See Table 18.) According to Jack Goody in *Bridewealth and Dowry in Africa and Eurasia* (1973), the Europe–Middle East–Asia realm is second only to Africa's 82% in making use of bride-wealth, with 62% using bride-wealth. Yet the Europe–Middle East–Asia realm is lowest (3%) in using bride-service and highest (11%) in using dowry (not over 1% elsewhere). It is quite low in equal gift-exchange (3%) and sister- or kinswoman-exchange (none) taken together. South America and sub-Saharan Africa are almost equally low, but North America has 13% equal gift-exchange and the Pacific realm has 28% in both equal gift-exchange and kinswoman-exchange together. Yet the Europe–Middle East–Asia realm is neither low nor high (at 21%) in token or absent gift-exchange (5% in Africa, more than ½ in the Americas). (See Table 24.) The Europe–Middle East–Asia realm is the homeland of plow agriculture. Of the 98 plow-using societies in the Aberle survey of 526 societies, 62 were in states, and another 20 were in minimal states. (See Tables 5 through 8.) The 62 plow-using societies found in states were almost equally divided between 30 patrilineal and 29 bilateral forms, with only two matrilineal and one duolineal. The 20 plow-using societies found in minimal states showed 15 patrilineal, one bilateral, and four matrilineal. Only 16 plow-using societies were in nonstate settings. Of these, nine were patrilineal, four were bilateral, and three were matrilineal. More than nine out of ten plow-using societies had either hereditary or wealth-based social stratification. (See Tables 5 and 9.) This is not at all surprising. Plow-use makes land scarcer in comparison to labor, by enabling a household's members to cultivate at least three times the area they could cultivate without a plow. It therefore tends to lead to a strong distinction between chief cultivators, who have animals and plows, and those agricultural workers who do not have them. Like irrigated agriculture, also more widely found in the Europe–Middle East–Asia realm than elsewhere, plow-use tends to lead to an overall level of productivity that can support more than one social level above even the chief cultivators. In about 80% of the societies of this realm, according to Goody in *Production and Reproduction* (1976), men either do most of the agricultural labor (normal in a plow-using society, like most of Europe and the Middle East) or participate equally with women (normal in an intensively cultivating irrigated-agriculture society, like China and its neighbors, or much of India). However, men are only active in agriculture in about 63% of the societies of the Pacific, 51% in South America, 43% in Africa, and 19% in North America (with its 68% of nonagricultural societies).

In view of the greater productivity of the plow agriculture and irrigated agriculture that are common in Europe, the Middle East, and Asia, it is also not surprising that questions of inheritance are handled differently in those realms than elsewhere. What Jack Goody calls "diverging devolution," a system that in some way ensures that both sons and daughters share in their parents' property, is noticeably more common in those regions than it is elsewhere. Diverging devolution does not necessarily ensure that all will share in a fully equal way, but it does ensure some share to all. Most often daughters are given dowries in money and jewelry, while sons either inherit land or are given cash portions so that the land can be passed on intact to only one son. In Goody's 860-societies survey in *Production and Reproduction* he found diverging devolution in 52% of 161 European, Middle Eastern, and Asian societies (out of 190, for 29 of which sufficient information was lacking). (See Table 19.)

The use of diverging devolution in Europe and the Middle East stems in part from the influence of Christianity and Islam. Both of these religions uphold the right of daughters as well as of sons to receive family property. That influence may also be visible in the 41% of 78 (out of 126) Pacific Islands societies (mostly Christianized by the time of observation) that use diverging devolution, in the 20% of 160 (out of 306) New World societies (many Christianized, particularly in Central and South America, by the time of observation) that practice it, and even in the only 6% (but mostly Islamic) of 193 (out of 238) sub-Saharan African societies that use it in some form. However, sufficient information on inheritance patterns was lacking for 271 of the 860 societies, most of them in the Americas. Consequently the percentages must be recognized as subject to considerable possible error.

The effect of Christianity and Islam on the practice of diverging devolution in turn reflects the codified practice of the Jewish predecessors and contemporaries of the founders of both those faiths. By the opening of the Christian era, even before the destruction of the Temple in A.D. 70 and the great Diaspora that followed it, Jewish families habitually provided dowries for daughters as well as dividing property among sons. In doing so they were following a general tendency toward similar patterns in the long-civilized, plow-using and irrigation-using Mediterranean and Middle Eastern regions. By that time those regions had reached full maturity of settlement. All the land that could be cropped with then-current levels of technology was in permanent settled cultivation. Northwestern Europe did not reach that stage till the 16th century A.D., while India and China only reached it at the end of the 19th century. Both India and China knew overcrowding and famine in local areas long before that time. However, they also had potentially usable agricultural land that was not yet permanently settled. It was still in the hands of local shifting-agriculture or even hunter-gatherer peoples, who had not yet bowed to government efforts to convert them to settled agriculture and thereby open part of their previously claimed area to settlement by others from more crowded areas. Still, general levels of agricultural productivity in India and China were comparable to those of most of Europe and the better-watered portions of the Middle East until the 18th or 19th century, at least in years of favorable weather. In other words, productivity levels could support complex social, economic, and political systems there as well as in Europe and the Middle East. Thus enough wealth could be accumulated to make diverging devolution feasible. It did not seem to be as necessary as in other regions to have a more strictly unilineal transmission of inheritances, for fear that the lineage might fail to be able to continue providing for its members.

The significance of this for marriage systems is that once diverging devolution began to be practiced, whether through dowry at marriage or through actual female inheritance alongside male inheritance, lineage funds tended to give way to a conjugal fund. It is a vitally important transition, when the joint holdings of the two spouses replace lineage holdings as the primary support for the spouses and their growing offspring until the offspring marry and establish conjugal funds of their own. It gives the spouses, rather than the lineage elders, the most prominent role in the selection of their children's mates. It also tends to give the wife more voice in family matters, since she brings tangible assets into the marriage with her, over whose disposition she (or her family) will retain at least some continuing control. And perhaps most important of all, it tends to promote monogamy.

In lineage-fund systems additional spouses can be fitted in fairly readily. It is the father-to-son lineage that counts, in a patrilineal society; or the brother-to-sister's-son lineage, in a matrilineal society; or the mother-to-child and father-to-child lineages, in a duolineal, ambilineal, utrolateral, or bilateral society. A man's having more than one wife, or the far rarer situation of a woman's having more than one husband, does not affect the plural spouses. They do not inherit from the single spouse. Nor does it affect the single spouse, who does not inherit from the plural ones. However, the pressure for monogamy is extremely strong where one spouse inherits from the other in his or her own right, not merely as a guardian of children's rights at most. That holds true whether the surviving spouse inherits from a conjugal fund (to which both spouses have brought something from their parents' property, which then is jointly theirs) or merely recovers what was put into the conjugal fund on his or her behalf. Usually, if it is recovery, it is a woman's dowry from her parents that is recovered. Or one spouse may endow the other with property (usually a woman's dower from her husband), which then remains the endowed one's, and is inherited at the endowing spouse's death from the conjugal fund of which it had been part up to then. It should be noted that dowry is given only for a first marriage. Because it is retained by a widow, a second dowry is not provided for her if she remarries, for she then takes it into that marriage with her. Dower, on the other hand, may be given with conditions attached that require its return to the husband's kin in whole or in part, if a widow remarries. However, that has not been frequently done. Both dower and dowry ensure provision for a widow, unlike bride-wealth and gift-exchange. Consequently, where dower and/or dowry are used (and there is therefore a conjugal fund for children to inherit), there is apt to be pressure against remarriages, unless steps are taken to ensure that the children born into the marriage will not lose some of their expectable inheritance.

The presence of diverging devolution—along with the accompanying tendency for that to go with reliance on a conjugal rather than a lineal fund by the nuclear family of spouses and their unmarried offspring—goes far to help explain the strong tendency toward monogamy as the norm in Europe, in particular, even for pre-Christian societies like those of ancient Greece and Rome. Descent might be reckoned patrilineally in classical times in Greece and Rome. But the use of dowry, which came to be inherited by a wife's children (usually only after both she and her husband died), meant that polygyny made little economic sense. Moreover polygyny could be seen as leading to great tensions between half-siblings, whose expectations of inheritance or dowry might differ markedly because of differences between their mothers' dowries and/or how many full siblings might have to divide that dowry.

In the ancient world the presence of slaves meant that even where monogamy was the legal norm, no well-off man (or woman, for that matter, if she were in a position to make such choices) need lack nonspouse partners in intercourse in the household. Either a slave or a free woman might be taken as a concubine to provide a man with heirs if his legal wife had provided none, in ancient Rome and elsewhere. A woman (slave or free) might be taken informally as a mistress, whose children would not have inheritance rights from their father unless he specifically granted them. In royal circles in medieval Europe a formal marriage (called a *morganatic marriage*) might be contracted between one of royal and one of nonroyal ancestry, with the specific provision that no child or later descendant of that marriage might ever claim the throne. However, monogamous marriage, with the expectation that it would produce the rightful inheritors of what their parents held, has been the norm for centuries in societies as far apart as traditional Norway and traditional Japan. That was beginning to be true even before Christianity was widely accepted in Norway or Confucianism in Japan, though both sets of beliefs reinforced the patterns already forming. Both Christianity and Confucianism have upheld monogamy as an ideal, even though Confucianists recognized a need to provide for heirs that could allow for nonmonogamous relationships. In those monogamy-upholding societies that did allow for concubinage, it was generally confined to those men highest in the social and economic scale. Probably the number of men with concubines in monogamous societies would never have been much greater than one in 80 men in a survey in China in the 1930s who had what they termed "secondary wives," whose children were required to honor the legal wife as their mother.

The practical considerations of avoiding fragmentation of the core supporting property needed by a household and of facilitating governmental record-keeping have often led to pressures to recognize only one heir. Those pressures, however, have always been in tension with the practical consideration of maximizing networks, through having more than one heir on whom to rely. Single heirship also runs counter to parents' usual desire to provide as well as possible for all their offspring who reach adulthood, given the amount of time, effort, and support they have invested. Generally speaking, as a result, heirship of some sort for all offspring (either of both sexes or of one sex, usually in that case male) has tended to prevail unless economic circumstances are extremely tight. This has been accepted even in highly centralized and stratified societies because it lessens the likelihood that any nonelite family will accumulate enough to challenge the elite. Inheritance has tended to be partible, not impartible, in other words. Partibility has not always meant equality, as shown by the 2nd century A.D. Jewish codification of the rule that the eldest son received a double portion. Yet it has at least meant inclusiveness. It has also tended to be accompanied by some mode of providing for daughters as they marry, even if only through furnishing articles of clothing and items of household gear. Nevertheless, strong concern for the viability of the ongoing household has led to devices ranging from the patrilateral parallel-cousin marriage of the Middle East, to the polyandry of Tibet, to the *preciput* (preferred-heir) system of medieval southern France, which let one parentally chosen child be given the bulk of the inheritance even though the others also received a share. It is noteworthy that among the few polyandrous societies known, almost all use diverging devolution. Clearly they are using polyandry at least in part to keep brothers together, so as to avoid having to divide property.

Views of heirship have tended to intertwine closely with uses of bride-wealth, dower, dowry, and equal gift-exchange as formalizing elements in marriage arrangements. Views of heirship have also tended to intertwine with rules about who may and who may not be married among kin. Consequently it will be useful here to look briefly at modes of reckoning kinship as they relate to patterns of inheritance and incest rules, as discussed by Bernard Farber in *Conceptions of Kinship* (1981).

Ancient Israel, ancient Athens, and the chiefdoms of early medieval Switzerland, among many others, used the cone-like *parentela* system of reckoning kinship. In the parentela system all one's own descendants take precedence over one's parent's other descendants, all one's parent's descendants take precedence over one's grandparent's other descendants, and so on. Societies (like most Mongol-speaking ones) in which this kinship-and-inheritance system is used tend to organize factionally around kin groups as the chief maintainers of social order. They tend to be patrilineal, to expect patrilocal marriage, to regard marriage as a sacred lifelong commitment rather than as a simple contract, and to see procreation as the major purpose of marriage. Economic contributions and personal companionship are far less important than procreation in their list of marital priorities. Parentela kinship systems tend to use cousin-marriage, to strengthen kinship ties and to recombine properties divided by inheritance rules (if inheritance is partible). They may even regard one's siblings as so much less related to oneself than one's children that it is not seen as incest for one's sibling to marry one's child, as in both ancient Israel and ancient Athens. Parentela systems have been likeliest to emerge where one lineage (usually the patrilineage) is given primary emphasis.

Ancient Rome followed the somewhat different *civil law* system, which mildly discourages the close-knit kinship groups that tend to accompany the parentela form. The civil law reckoned the closeness of kinship for both inheritance and incest purposes by counting how many links or steps there were from one person to a common ancestor with another person, and then from that ancestor to the other person. Thus an uncle (two up from self to grandparent plus one down) would be closer than a brother's grandchild (one up from self to parent plus three down), in contrast to the parentela form. The civil law system moderately encouraged a feeling of closeness within kin groups. It also moderately encouraged the other features that tend to be associated with the parentela form. However, it introduced an element of having to recognize those in a larger circle as closer than one's own descendants. One's brother was seen as closer than one's own great-grandchild, for example. This forced a slightly broader view of the nature of society on those who followed it.

Even more broadening was the *canon law* system, developed by the Christian church in opposition to faction-promoting endogamy. The canon law took four, the same number of links as in the civil law, as the absolute minimum for legitimate marriage. However, canon law interpreted this as meaning the minimum number of links between oneself and the common ancestor and also between the other person and the common ancestor. Thus the nearest common ancestor for a marriageable pair would normally be a great-great-grandparent to two third cousins, rather than a grandparent to two first cousins. By the 6th century A.D. the acceptance of this system in Christian areas was effectively requiring lineages to use exogamy rather than endogamy as an organizing principle in marriage arrangements. It was not yet cutting down effectively on rivalries between lineages, though. To try to enforce network-building that would bring ties between as many lineages as possible, the canon lawyers proceeded to extend the same incest prohibitions to one's godparents and their blood kin as were applied to one's own blood parents and kin. Christian communities have been virtually unique in using an artificially established kinship such as godparenthood as a basis for prohibiting marriages to others beyond at most the parents, children, siblings, and former spouses of those who formally swore brotherhood or otherwise entered a socially recognized equivalent to a kinship bond. The only significant possible exception may be the kinds of age-grade prohibitions noted earlier for some African societies. In inheritance rules, however, in Christian as in other communities, only the blood kin normally were recognized.

The canon law system followed the pattern that had eventually been established in the civil law, counting kinship equally on both sides. Neither canon nor civil law differentiated between the father's and the mother's side, at least for inheritance and often for incest purposes, as parentela systems generally tend to do. Under the canon law inheritance system one's primary relatives came first. These consisted of one's spouse, and those of both sexes who shared ½ of one's genetic inheritance (as we would now put it), one's children, one's parents, and one's siblings. Secondary relatives who shared ¼ of one's genetic inheritance, one's grandparents, aunts and uncles, nephews and nieces, and grandchildren, came next. Tertiary relatives, who shared only ⅛ of one's genetic inheritance, came after them, like first cousins or great-grandchildren. The customary Chinese mode of reckoning degrees of obligation and responsibility, on the father's side at least, bears a strong resemblance to both the canon law system and the fourth mode of reckoning kinship mentioned by Farber, the *genetic* mode. But the Chinese system added another organizing principle, that of always preferring the senior generation to the younger generation when a choice had to be made.

Unilineage-stressing kinship systems in societies such as China and India often appeared to give a man's brothers precedence over his own descendants as long as an extended-family household remained together. However, they generally recognized a parentela-like form when such a household was divided, giving a deceased brother's sons their father's share. This was appropriate, in view of their unilineal rather than bilateral form.

No specific form of kinship-and-inheritance reckoning necessarily favors the use of bride-wealth, dower, dowry, or equal gift-exchange. All four of these modes of property transferral have been practiced with parentela, civil

law, and canon law or geneticlike systems. However, who provides or receives shares of the bride-wealth, dower, dowry, or mutually exchanged
gifts is directly related to the system of kinship-and-inheritance reckoning.
Those who will in future receive, give; those who will in future give, receive.
The parents and others who give on behalf of one child will receive back
what is given, where there are provisions for return if divorce or death ends
the marriage; or else they will receive correspondingly on behalf of another
child of the other sex. The man who gives his own gifts for or to a bride
expects either to receive gifts for daughters or to retain actual use of what
is given to his wife as long as he lives.

As noted, parentela kinship systems tend to favor some form of kin
endogamy. That tendency becomes especially strong if dowry is used. It is
strengthened even more if dowry can include agricultural land, as well as
either movable goods or residences. In such a case, either cross-cousin or
parallel-cousin marriage can be used to reunite landed properties quickly
and directly in the second generation, rather than only after three or more
generations have passed.

The desire to find a spouse of at least equal standing with oneself for
oneself or one's offspring has favored the use of individually bargained-for
dowry, matched to the status and prospects of the groom, in societies from
ancient Babylon, Israel, Greece, and Rome to India and China. All of these
societies were complex both economically and socially by the time dowry
began to be used. Commercial activity seems to be needed, for either dowry
or dower to come to the fore. Commercial activity also seems to be needed
for the practice of diverging devolution, by way of either dowry or inheritance rights for daughters as well as sons. Diverging devolution appears to
be linked with status considerations. Families that are above the poverty
level evidently use it to try to ensure that none of their offspring are left
entirely without some family-provided means of maintenance.

Families in different socioeconomic groupings in complex, non-kinship-
based, commercially active societies may agree to marry their sons and
daughters to each other. But generally these groupings will be on approximately the same level in some sense—the families of independent craftsmen
and independent small shopkeepers, or of street cleaners and launderers, or
of large landlords and wealthy merchants. If they are not, then usually the
families who receive daughters for their sons will be found to be taking
those brides from a lower level, and expecting a large bride-gift or dowry
to come with them as payment for the improved social standing that comes
with marrying the sons of socially superior families.

Sometimes, as seems to have taken place in early medieval Europe, the
daughter of a recognized noble family might be married to a not-yet-en-
nobled, but rising man. If so, the marriage was apt to be regarded by the
noble family as a means of winning his support for his new wife's family
as well as a means of indicating their recognition of his worth and future

prospects. Left untrammeled by church restrictions on kin endogamy, those noble families might have preferred to turn to some form of cousin-marriage to maintain their status. However, the experience of the ancient Middle East with patrilateral parallel-cousin marriages undoubtedly helped to influence early canon lawyers against any willingness to accept cousin-marriages. So did the somewhat similar operation of the parentela system, which was common among the Germanic peoples when they took control over almost all of the Roman Empire during the early centuries of church history. In both the Middle Eastern and the Germanic systems cousin-marriages tightened up patrilineages, making them even more inclined to open rivalry with other patrilineages than they might have been with more marriage links between different patrilineages. But in a society led by network-encouraging clergy such lineage-centeredness was actively discouraged.

Societies that use patrilateral parallel-cousin marriage usually maintain an even stricter separation between postpubertal males and females than those that practice other forms of cousin-marriages. If a cousin-marrying society's members wish to maintain the elders' power to decide who is to marry whom, rather than give the potential spouses a voice, they must keep marriageable cousins apart. This is harder to do when patrilateral parallel-cousin marriage is encouraged, for the offspring of brothers are likelier to see one another often in a patrilineal system than are the offspring of a brother and a sister, or of two sisters.

Only if a society is matrilocal (which almost invariably means matrilineal also) are two sisters' children apt to see one another frequently. Matrilineal societies would probably show a high incidence of matrilateral parallel-cousin marriage, whether or not they allow some freedom of partner-choice to the young. Yet, astonishingly, matrilateral parallel-cousin marriage is so seldom recognized as taking place that it has remained virtually unsurveyed. Recent investigators in Chinese-culture areas have begun to suspect that it may have been frequent there, however, as parents looked for appropriate partners for their offspring. It could have seemed ideal to bring a bride into the household who would see her mother-in-law as sister to her mother, presumably predisposing her to be accepting and obedient.

Of 190 Europe–Middle East–Asia societies surveyed by Jack Goody in *Bridewealth and Dowry* (1973), 125 (or 66%) are patrilineal. The marriage of a man to his mother's brother's daughter seems to fit the emotional dynamic of a patrilineal society. The wife in such a marriage is the daughter of a nonthreatening, affection-providing figure for the man (his mother's brother). She herself finds that her mother-in-law is her father's sister, also a nonthreatening, affection-providing figure. That contrasts sharply with the patrilateral parallel-cousin situation, in which both spouses have as father-in-law the father's brother, second only to the potentially threatening father in authority. It also contrasts with the comparably threatening situation for a man married to his mother's brother's daughter in a matrilineal society. In matrilineal societies the father's sister's daughter is the less threatening bride, although that mode brings the woman more than ever under her mother's brother's control. Marriage of a man to his father's sister's daughter in a patrilineal society is also acceptable to the husband, since he is not thereby acquiring an authority figure as a father-in-law. However, the wife in such a marriage may find her mother's brother to be more potentially threatening to her, no matter whether it is a matrilineal or a patrilineal society. Nevertheless, the marriage of a man to his father's sister's daughter is accepted in slightly more societies than his marriage to his mother's brother's daughter. That may be because it is viewed as tending to assure the wife's obedience to her new father-in-law.

In 534 societies surveyed by Goody in *Production and Reproduction* (1976) the marriage of the son and the daughter of two brothers was preferred in only 18 societies and permitted in only 41 more; 475 (or 89%) absolutely prohibited it. That is a striking indication of its perceived disadvantages, when one considers that George P. Murdock, in his 1957 article in *American Anthropologist,* found only 277 (or 57%) of 487 societies in the world at large prohibiting all forms of marriage with first cousins. Goody, in another survey of 673 societies in *Bridewealth and Dowry in Africa and Eurasia* (1973), found 475 (or 62.5%, ⅝) prohibiting all first-cousin marriages. In Goody's 673-societies survey the Europe–Middle East–Asia realm showed by far the highest permission for patrilateral parallel-cousin marriage (17.5%). (See Table 22.) The region with the lowest permission for either form of cross-cousin marriage was North America. Among North American societies 13.4% accepted a man's son marrying his father's sister's daughter and 13.9% accepted a woman's son marrying his mother's brother's daughter. The same Europe–Middle East–Asia realm showed slightly more than ½ of all societies accepting one or both of these two forms of cross-cousin marriages. Cross-cousin marriages had even a slightly higher acceptance in the few (27) South American societies surveyed, but in Africa and the Pacific only $\frac{1}{5}$ to slightly more than ¼ accepted one or both kinds of cross-cousin marriages. Cousin-marriages of all types can strengthen lineages; but they can also lead to tensions, both within households and across the whole society.

In brief, as societies have become more complex and more commercialized, their first tendency has been to move toward patrilineality. Increasing wealth has then led them toward diverging devolution, conjugal funds, and monogamy. Where circumstances have been favorable, these developments have evolved toward more recognition of the interests of individuals. The actual experiences of such societies are surveyed in Chapter 8.

Marriage in Commercializing and Urbanizing Societies: The Europe–Middle East–Asia Realm

We have looked at the significance of the appearance of conjugal funds as diverging devolution emerged in early commercializing societies. We have also looked at kinship systems and cousin-marriages in such societies. In addition, we have looked at the establishment of suprafamilial systems of registering births, deaths, and marriages, as social and economic complexity continued to increase. In this chapter we will look at the experiences of complex commercializing societies, from China on the east to England and Ireland on the west, up to the period when suprafamilial systems of registration began to be used in them. The later experiences of these societies are discussed in later chapters.

The development of China's marriage system will be considered first. China illustrates what may happen to marriage systems, as a society moves toward both a more commercial economy and a more bureaucratic society (rather than a hereditary-aristocratic one). China also affords a contrast to early Christian Europe, for Chinese practice did not include the use of extrafamilial religious sanctions for marital arrangements like those of Christendom.

The earliest legal codes governing marriage of which we have records for China come from approximately 2,500 years ago. That was shortly after the introduction of iron-tipped plows increased agricultural production and spurred commercial growth. These codes show that a new wife was already expected to move into her husband's household and to become formally a member of her husband's lineage, giving up her ties to her father's lineage. Yet if her husband failed to support her, she could seek permission from the local government official to return to her father's household so that her father might find another husband for her. (Officials were usually still members of hereditary noble families, but some bureaucratization had taken place. Officials were appointed to their posts from a group of available candidates, rather than inheriting them. One could still inherit social rank.

But one no longer inherited political position, below the level of the rulers themselves.) On the other hand, a husband could use any of seven reasons to return a wife to her parents and seek another wife: disobedience to his parents, sonlessness, adultery, jealousy, incurable disease, argumentativeness, or theft. However, he had to consult his senior male kin, as long as he still had a father or grandfather, a paternal uncle, or an elder brother. Kinship was patrilineal, but the use of a component for "woman" in the character for "surname" suggests that kinship might have been matrilineal when the written language was taking form, more than a thousand years before.

After a few more centuries of economic growth and political reorganization a new code recognized a wife's right to divorce her husband if he had committed a crime, as well as his right to divorce her if she had done so. In fact, divorce under such circumstances was regarded as a duty. The local official could declare the pair divorced whether the innocent party brought suit or not. At that time, about two thousand years ago, cross-cousin marriages in both directions seem to have been common among the hereditary nobility and the wealthy, who had reason to wish to recombine property. Though we know little of those below that level at that time, both types of cross-cousin marriage were frequent at all levels in later eras. However, offspring of brothers were forbidden to marry, perhaps because that was seen as tending to endanger social unity by strengthening lineage-centeredness. In order to uphold the already-established principle that an elder generation should always take precedence over all younger generations, as a means of ensuring juniors' orderly acceptance of elders' direction, any marriages that might take place between cousins of any degree were required to be in the same generation. Widows as well as widowers were expected to remarry. So were those of either sex who were divorced, as long as they had not been judged to be criminals. Nevertheless, widows with children to give them roots within the husband's household were beginning to seek to avoid remarrying. Those divorced because of a husband's criminal conduct were also likely to prefer to stay with their children's father's parents, if they had children. Bride-wealth given by the groom's family to the bride's family and dowry given with the bride by her family were regarded as the formalizers of the marriage. They indicated that both spouses' families had agreed to the arrangement. Evidently bride-wealth and dowry tended to be approximately equal in value at that time. This exchange was apparently practiced throughout society, for social commentators of the period complained that bride-wealth and dowry expectations made it hard for those of modest means to marry.

Population growth in the next few generations resulted in increasing pressures on available agricultural land. Collecting agricultural taxes from a poverty-stricken peasantry became increasingly hard. That in turn led to a breakdown of the fiscal and administrative system, which relied almost entirely on the land tax. China's bureaucratic officials were reluctant to encourage and tax commercial activity. They feared that wealthy merchants might compete with the largely hereditary elite landholders, who effectively monopolized the offices of government by declaring that merchants and their sons (the only others likely to be able to afford to obtain the formal education now needed for eligibility for office) were too profit-minded to be capable of honesty in government service. Merchants' sons, as well as merchants themselves, were therefore forbidden to take the examinations that qualified one for government appointment.

The Chinese fiscal and administrative breakdown coincided with a period of evident population expansion all across the grasslands, from north of the Great Wall of China to the borders of the Roman Empire in western Europe. Rome was plagued at that time by its own fiscal-administrative crisis. The Roman crisis, however, stemmed from a declining population rather than an expanding one. Newly arriving diseases from Asia took their toll in nonresistant Mediterranean populations, who were already straining to maintain themselves on overused soils. In view of the fiscal-administrative crises at both ends of the Eurasian land mass, it is not surprising that both China and Europe then experienced some centuries of "barbarian" invasion and intermingling. China reunified at the end of the 6th century A.D., at about the same time that the successors of the Roman emperor Justinian were having to accept the newcomers' rule in the western part of Rome's former domains.

China's reunifiers proceeded to reenact the marriage code of the preinvasion era, though they added to it the wife's right not to be divorced under three sets of circumstances: if she had no father or brother to go to, if she had mourned her husband's parents with him, or if he had risen from poverty to wealth after they were married. Divorces by mutual consent were also recognized, but it was required that the wife's parents must agree to her being returned to them. For the first time, a wife could sue for divorce if her husband had disappeared for a prescribed number of years (a number that changed from time to time between A.D. 600 and 1900). As before, dowry was to be returned with a wife who was divorced and then returned to her kin, no matter who initiated the divorce. As before, too, the husband expected to recover at least part of what had been given the bride's family as bride-wealth, in case of a divorce, even though he also kept all children who might have been born. It is not surprising, then, that formal divorce procedures had to be gone through for a widow to be married off by her husband's family, or to be returned to her own. The intent there was to prevent her from claiming any inheritance rights in her deceased husband's family, and also to release any claim they might otherwise have on children born to her with a later husband. She did not recover dowry, nor did they recover bride-wealth, as would happen with divorce. In any case, a woman was not to marry another man of her husband's patrilineage.

Cross-cousin marriages continued after the 6th-century reunification of China. However, marriages between those bearing the same clan name were entirely forbidden by the new code, no matter how distant the relationship might be. This presents a bureaucratically inspired analogue (on the patrilineal side) to the efforts of canon lawyers in medieval Christian Europe, both west and east, to weaken lineage-centeredness by requiring lineage exogamy through the extension of incest prohibitions to a broadly interpreted fourth degree. Despite the evident effort to weaken clan-centeredness, the number of recognized clans in southern China fell from about 1,900 to about 500 between the 14th and 20th centuries A.D., even while China's total population multiplied more than fourfold. Clearly clan-centeredness was not weakened in the more mountainous south, which was less easily policed by government forces than were the northern and central plains. Continuing population growth, and resulting increases in competition over claims to land and irrigation rights, tended to lead to outright local conflicts between villages or between lineages. (In south China, even more than in north China, a village tended to be dominated by one patrilineage.) Thus those lineage members who could call on the largest number of clansmen to support them had the best chance to survive. The 500 surviving clans in the south in A.D. 1900 apparently absorbed the other 1,400 over the centuries.

The provisions and expectations of the 6th-century code continued to be maintained in broad outline in succeeding centuries. Additions were made from time to time to the list of crimes for which divorce was required. After the 14th century A.D. those who failed to divorce a crime-committer were punished, instead of an official being recognized as having the right to declare a divorce. In general, though, the use of divorce began to be discouraged in the 11th and 12th centuries. There was a spurt in commercial growth at that time, fueled in part by an increase in both population and agricultural productivity. A new faster-growing rice had been developed that could produce two and even three crops a year in the warmer southern parts of China. The growth in commerce was also fueled in part by the facilitation of sea voyages, through the application of the already-invented compass and astrolabe to navigational use. As a result China was becoming affluent enough so that tea was replacing plain boiled water for drinking, and chairs, or at least stools, were replacing floor mats for sitting, even among the poorest. With rising wealth there apparently was also a rise in both bride-wealth and dowry. Evidently that increase made the expected return of both at a divorce unwelcome enough to lead to a more active discouragement of divorce. Moreover, the conjugal-fund element in a couple's calculations for the future became ever more significant, as both what a husband could expect to inherit when his parents died and what a wife brought in as dowry increased in value.

Brothers normally tended to divide their parents' estate, rather than try to stay together. Each younger brother wished to be sure his own children got all they should have, and was reluctant to entrust the management of the family property to the eldest. For his part the eldest brother might wish to try to keep the brothers together, but he also had to recognize the bickering that was likely to ensue. Brothers normally claimed that it was their wives rather than themselves who could not get along, however. When a family's property was divided, shares had to be set aside to pay bride-wealth for any unmarried or widowed sons and to furnish dowry for any unmarried daughters, before the remaining property could be divided equally among the sons. The division was then lasting, unlike the quasi-divisions that might be made while the father was alive. A father might decide to keep the sons within the family courtyard, with its separate quarters for each married pair and their unmarried children, and yet recognize them and the parents as having separate budgets that were based on identifiably separate incomes from specific lands or occupations. Or a father might decide to retain a common budget for all, even though one or more married sons might not be within the family courtyard, either for lack of room or because of recognized personality clashes that made it advisable for at least one son and his wife to reside elsewhere. However, at the father's death all of the family property was to be recombined and redivided. That made each wife's dowry-contribution all the more important to her husband's plans, since it went to their own children rather than being part of the general division. A woman's dowry might even include land, in many wealthier families. If so, then the land remained the wife's rather than becoming her husband's. It then became part of her children's inheritance.

The Chinese also began to use footbinding in the affluent 11th and 12th centuries. Like tight corseting in 19th-century Europe, footbinding demonstrated a family's social and economic standing through making its women incapable of the kinds of work done by women of poorer families. The Mongol occupation of China in the 13th century evidently reinforced the practice. The enforced immobilization of women then seemed like a protective means of keeping them within the household, safe from the eyes of foreign troops and officials. The Mongol occupation also apparently cut short any tendencies toward a bilateral view of kinship and inheritance that might be hinted at in letting women have land as part of dowry among the wealthy. But tendencies toward bilaterality would appear and develop into fruition not long afterward in the commercial centers of the Italian peninsula, half a world away.

The introduction of footbinding signaled greater wealth in the society. But it also meant a lessened recognition of women's economic contribution as natural and important, even beyond the lower status that accompanied their being expected to leave their parents' for their husbands' households at marriage. The expectation that a daughter would always leave to marry someone else led to the view that a daughter was an expense to raise and provide dowry for, whereas a son was an asset because he remained in the home. Even though bride-wealth must be found to bring in a wife for him, few, if any, thought in terms of daughters-in-law replacing daughters, especially since the gifts given for the bride by the groom's family were not usually in a form that could dowry a daughter.

Out of these sets of presuppositions came the baby-wagons (to collect the corpses of girl infants left on the streets) which horrified 18th-century European visitors to the capital of China. The result was a sex ratio of 110 to as high as 156 adult men for every 100 adult women in various Chinese provinces, as reported in census counts (which tended to undercount women to an extent that is hard to estimate). Far more humane was the practice of exchanging girl infants as brides-to-be among families. The marriage would then be formalized merely by ceremonially introducing the new wife to the ancestors of the husband a year or two after she reached puberty. In such cases a family with a young son and an infant daughter would give the daughter to another family in a similar position, and take either their young daughter or that of a third family that came into the circle of exchange. The families involved hoped not only to save bride-wealth and dowry expenditures. They also hoped to make the relations between mother-in-law and daughter-in-law familiar rather than strange—not only strange, but strained, as they often were for a bride uprooted from her parental home in her middle to late teens and placed among comparative strangers. Even when cross cousins or possibly matrilateral parallel cousins married, those strains were apt to appear in some degree.

Arthur Wolf and C. S. Huang have made a study (published in 1980) of such adoptive marriages on Taiwan in the late 19th and early 20th centuries. They show that couples raised as if brother and sister had less attraction and more aversion to each other than did couples who only met when the bride came in at marriage, if attraction and aversion can be measured by numbers of children born and by the reported number of marital desertions (sometimes by the husband, sometimes by the wife). The authors hypothesize that there may have been a cycle in which an artificial scarcity created by female infanticide would lead to exchanges of infant future brides. The exchanges might then lead to marital difficulty, and a return to the traditionally preferred bringing in of the teenage bride. That in turn could lead to another period of artificial scarcity, as raising daughters to marriageable age was seen as an unrewarded expense, and so on around.

Wolf and Huang suggest that the strength of a tendency for Chinese officials in the late 19th and early 20th centuries to observe infant bride adoption reflected the stages of the cycle they hypothesize (high bride-adoption in the south, in the hillier regions of the northwest, and on the central coast; low bride-adoption in the northern plains and the southwest). Wolf and Huang also suggest that bride-adoption might have spread from area to area as families looked for healthy infants to adopt. They note that a scarcity of females could lead to a greater willingness by a younger son to become a marrying-in husband. Not only might he marry a brotherless daughter, becoming the father of members of her father's clan and the head of a household after her father's death, even though still not himself a member of her father's clan. He might even marry an elder daughter with very young brothers, as a needed young male worker in the household whose seniority in age would continue to give him influence after the young brothers matured. In the latter case, though not in the former, the marriage contract was likely to stipulate that their children would belong to his father's clan rather than to hers. Or in any *uxorilocal* marriage, in which the husband moved into the wife's parents' household, it might be agreed that some children would be assigned to his clan and some to hers. And always, what bride-wealth might be given (if any—there was no dowry, in a uxorilocal marriage) depended on how the children would be assigned. Once a household's elders had decided who might be the most suitable candidates, at least on Taiwan, women took the lead in actually arranging whose daughter would be brought in as a wife, whether in infancy or in maturity. Men took the lead, however, in arranging what man would come in as a uxorilocal husband, either for a daughter or for a widowed daughter-in-law.

Uxorilocal marriages tended to be most common in the late 19th and early 20th centuries in those parts of China where the adoption of infant-brides was also most common, though uxorilocality was found in the southwest more often than bride-adoption. Yunnan province in the southwest was also the one region in which there was both a preliminary sharing of property with sons when they married and a tendency for married brothers to remain together after a father's death. That tendency is shown by average household size in early 20th-century surveys, which listed eight to nine or even more in Yunnan, rather than the five to six of China as a whole, as shown in Chinese censuses from A.D. 2 onward. The larger households of Yunnan also tended to be organized so as to have common residence but not a common budget. Sometimes uxorilocal marriage involved marrying a young (usually childless) widow and fathering children for her deceased husband's family, although in the Wolf-Huang study only 54% of young widows (under 29) remarried. By contrast that study showed almost ⅔ of all widowed men remarrying. Almost $1/5$ of them became uxorilocal husbands, about the same as the overall proportion of uxorilocal to patrilocal marriages. The bride's mother's brother, at least in late-19th- and early-20th-century Taiwan, would never attend a wedding feast for a uxorilocal marriage. He would attend only if his niece was moving (properly) into her husband's family. The groom's mother's brother might also prefer not to attend a uxorilocal wedding feast. However, at least in Taiwan, a man was expected to mourn at the funeral of his mother's brother as if the deceased had been his own father. That was because his mother's brother was the one to decide the division of his father's land among him and his brothers, after their father's death. Thus his mother's brother stood in a relation of real authority to him, at one crucial moment in his life.

It is unclear how patterns on Taiwan might have been affected by the fact that the imperial government of China had initially sought to discourage south China's coastal inhabitants from settling in Taiwan. The island was hard for the mainland government both to govern and to defend, being inhabited by shifting cultivators who were not Chinese. Consequently the imperial government forbade men who went there to clear and cultivate fields to take women and children with them until 1760. With only a few generations of regular settlement by 1900, Chinese in Taiwan might have been more conscious of the worth of women than Chinese of other areas. Yet similarly high frequencies of bride-adoption and uxorilocal marriage were reported in the 19th and early 20th centuries by Chinese and foreign observers in the nonplains area of the mainland, while very low frequencies were reported in the northern plains. This seems to suggest either that there was some correlation between the conditions of life in hilly regions of China and a willingness to use bride-adoption and uxorilocality, or that the plains and the hilly regions were in different phases of the hypothesized cycle of scarcity-adoption-nonadoption-expensiveness-scarcity. Not surprisingly, bride-adoption marriages were formalized at earlier ages for both sexes than the preferred patrilocal kind or the uxorilocal ones. In the Wolf-Huang survey of early-20th-century marriages the *median* (half more, half less) age for bride-adoption marriages was 17 for women and 20 for men, but for both other forms it was 19 for women, and for men it was 23 for patrilocal or 25 for the least welcome uxorilocal form.

Those marriage ages tally reasonably well with first-marriage ages reported for 18th- and 19th-century villages in Japan. The Japanese ages were slightly older for both sexes, though. That may have reflected a greater concern to lessen births by marrying later, which was also shown by greater birth-spacings and lower birth rates (possibly indicating some effort at contraception) than among Chinese. However, Japanese life expectancies and Japanese levels of commercialization and centralization were already comparable to those of western European countries at that time. Consequently we will look only at Japan before the 17th century A.D. in this chapter.

In the early centuries of recorded Japanese history, Chinese cultural patterns were imported in the 6th to 8th centuries A.D. on a massive scale. Yet the Japanese did not adopt the Chinese rules against same-surname marriages or marriages of cousins of differing generations, even though they formally adopted the divorce provisions used in China into their legal code. In practice, the possibilities of inheriting through a mother were much greater than in China. This was particularly true if a wife remained in her father's home, while her husband only visited her. Resulting children would be formally recognized as in his or her line by agreement between the families. Divorce and remarriage appear to have been at least as frequent in pre-17th-century Japan as in pre-11th-century China. The remarriage of both widows and widowers was also taken as much for granted in pre-17th-century Japan as in the China of two thousand years ago.

The visiting-husband system may have come in part from the common pre-13th-century practice of expecting the groom to live with the bride's family for a time, possibly even until at least one child was born. A visiting husband might also have more than one recognized wife whom he visited. He might even be a visiting husband because only the son who was chosen as chief heir was permitted to bring his wife into the family home. Japanese were moving away from equal division among sons by the 12th century A.D., at least among the dominant hereditary nobles and warriors, who were anxious to preserve family position by averting fragmentation of family properties. Where there was a chief heir, the rest of the sons, those of their sisters who were visited wives, and those sisters' children (if recognized as in their mothers' family) were expected to accept his leadership after the father's and mother's deaths. Bride-wealth was given only for the in-marrying wife of an heir-son, or for a visited wife whose children would be in her husband's line. Only with such a wife would any dowry be received too. If a man married into a sonless household as a uxorilocal husband, however, groom-wealth would be given to his family. Adoption seems to have been used more than uxorilocal marriage, though. By the 12th century the Japanese had turned back from the Chinese rule, that only agnates could be adopted as heirs, to their own earlier recognition of sisters' and daughters' sons as legitimately adoptable heirs. All these variations from the Chinese norms reflected the continuing Japanese view of the household as the unit to be concerned with, rather than the patrilineage of which all sons were equally members. For the Chinese all sons were successors to the father, each a potential continuer of the patriline. But the Japanese saw the perpetuation of the household through the chosen heir as the basis of a smoothly functioning society, rather than the perpetuation of the ancestral line in as many descent lines as possible. Social replacement, not expansion, was the concern of the island-dwelling Japanese. That was to be reflected later, too, in the evident efforts at family limitation which kept down population growth between the 17th and 19th centuries.

Far to the west, in the high plateau of Tibet, a similar concern to maintain the household rather than the patriline had long since led to polyandry, even to the point of allowing an uncle and his brother's son to share a wife, or a father and a son to share the father's second wife. That concern had also led to the promotion of religiously sanctioned monastic celibacy. In addition, it had led to allowing unwed offspring to remain in the family so that they did not have to marry for later-life security, among those with land-cultivation rights. If members of landholding families married without permission, they had to move out and become mere day-laborers.

Some speculate that pre-6th-century A.D. Japanese and pre-16th-century

B.C. Chinese may have used matrilineal forms. It seems somewhat more certain that Koreans used matrilineality until the Chinese conquest of northern Korea in the 2nd century B.C. The Chinese noted that Korean husbands moved into their wives' homes at marriage, and widespread uxorilocality is almost always a companion to matrilineality. The Chinese disapprovingly proceeded to enforce changes in what they saw as improper procedures, much as they were to refuse to recognize the previous right of daughters or widows to inherit from their fathers or husbands in Vietnam, a few centuries later. By the time Koreans threw off Chinese rule in the 3rd century A.D., new husbands took their wives into their fathers' homes, and the entire family system revolved around Chinese-style patrilineality. When the Japanese began borrowing heavily from Chinese culture in the 7th century, Korean hereditary noble families were already practicing inheritance by the eldest son to protect family position by keeping family properties consolidated, five centuries before hereditary nobles and warriors in Japan turned to naming a chief heir. Koreans adopted rules against marrying another of the same clan name, borrowing that practice from the Chinese after the Chinese had developed it. They also added rules against marriage between members of different hereditary social strata.

In the 15th century a new dynasty (which established itself in Korea shortly after the Mongols had been driven from China in 1368) set minimum marriage ages as 14 for girls and 16 for boys. In practice, though, Koreans often continued to marry girls in their late teens to boys in their very early teens as the Chinese sometimes also did. In 1900, boys of 14 were still being wed to young women of 20 in Shantung in northern China.

The new Korean rulers also adopted the already long familiar Chinese rules with regard to causes for divorce and conditions under which a wife could not be divorced. Like the rulers of China, they recognized the exchange of gifts to the bride's family and gifts with the bride entering the husband's family as the legitimation of a marriage. Any uxorilocal marriage had to be treated as an exception to the rule. Widows might remarry, as in China. They may have done so less often, for there was no echo in Korea of Chinese social commentators' complaints in the 16th to 19th centuries A.D. that parents were forcing dead sons' widows to remarry, either to get them out of the household or to bring in a son-in-law to work and beget grandchildren for them. Segregation between the sexes increased in post-15th-century Korea, as in post-13th-century China. It increased somewhat more in the southern part of Korea, then thinly settled, than in the north. The increase in segregation may have arisen in part to protect women from the half-merchant, half-pirate visits of enterprising Japanese warrior-traders along the southern coasts after the 14th century. Segregation of the sexes might also have grown because of the infiltration of Confucian moral precepts into popular culture, encouraged by the new dynasty's adoption of Confucian-based marriage rules. If that were so, then the southern location of the

capital might explain more of the difference between north and south than
the vulnerability of the southern coastline.

The remarriage of widows, still usually expected but beginning to be
opposed two thousand years ago in China, was also not originally opposed
in India. Only within the past 2,500 years did India become the land of
sati, the self-immolation of an upper-caste widow on her husband's funeral
pyre. The earliest Vedic codes of three thousand years ago did not forbid
a widow to remarry, and recognized both men's and women's right to refuse
a spouse selected for them by their families. A thousand years later the code
of Manu opposed the remarriage of widows, as showing a lack of proper
loyalty to husbands. Prevention of widow-remarriage also ensured that a
widowed mother would stay with her children, rather than leave them to
aunts and uncles who might care less for their interests than she would.
The remarriage of widowers was not correspondingly opposed as it would
be another thousand years thereafter by bilateral-kinship-using Khmer in
Southeast Asia, when they took Indian social forms as a model. The Hindu
widower in India would remain with his kin after remarriage, whereas the
Khmer widower might move into a second wife's family.

The code of Manu two thousand years ago indicated that a daughter
should be wed within three years of puberty so that her virginity could be
more readily preserved, assuring her husband of her purity and her capacity
for faithfulness. Later writers narrowed that three years increasingly, wanting to assure a bride's virginity even more securely. Finally it became expected that a girl should be betrothed and sent to her bridegroom's home
soon enough to prevent any other man from being with her before she
reached puberty. In the matrilineal Nayar system of visiting husbands the
rite by which a girl became a woman who could legitimately accept visiting
husbands was supposed to be undertaken just before puberty. Each of her
children would then be acceptable in her matrilineage, as long as a visiting
husband acknowledged that it could be his, either by paying the midwife's
fee or by sharing that payment with other visiting husbands who also acknowledged that it could be one of theirs.

The increasing restrictions on women's activity that the code of Manu
signaled probably came largely from three major sources. First would have
been the wish to protect women from kidnapping and rape, in the face of
invasion after invasion from Central Asia and Afghanistan into the north
India plain (sending others southward as refugees, who then became invaders in the south). Even tighter restrictions came after the establishment
of Muslim rule in the north in the 12th to 14th centuries A.D. Second would
have been the wish to maintain the barriers of caste, which had begun to
be a visible system of recognized occupational groups. People could still
move into and out of those groups in the Vedic era, but thereafter the groups
became rigidly divided and hereditary. Strict control of marriage was essential to enforce their hereditary nature. Third would have been the eco-

nomic considerations related to bride-wealth and dowry, which made controlling women's rights to property increasingly important as population pressures grew.

As the rules regarding marriage developed, it seemed as if ensuring a woman's chastity (as a guarantee of the maintenance of caste barriers) came to overshadow all other considerations. Because women had to be married before puberty, husbands rather than wives came to seem to be in short supply. A son could be legitimately wed at any time from birth to death, but a daughter must be wed before age 12. Thus her parents had a shorter time in which to look than did the parents of a son. Consequently, even though it was in fact the women who were scarce, it was their parents who gave gifts to find husbands for them (in the upper castes) rather than receiving bride-wealth for them. One sampling in patrilineally organized north India, as recently as 1960, found a total early childhood mortality of one in three, of whom only one in four had been boys, but two in five had been girls. The probability that this could have resulted from chance, rather than from less careful rearing of girls, was calculated as only one in ten. As in China, so in at least that north India region, daughters were evidently seen as an expense rather than as an asset.

Maintaining a daughter's chastity contributed not only to the maintenance of the position of her family within their caste group, but also to the upholding of that caste group's position within the total system of interacting caste groups. To the high-caste interpreters of sacred scripture who developed the rules that maintained the caste and marriage systems, the most worthy form of marriage was giving a bride with gifts and receiving nothing in return. Equal-exchange was next in acceptability, bride-wealth was third, mutual free choice with no exchange of gifts was fourth, abduction (his choice, without consulting her or her family) with no gift-exchange was fifth, and seduction (his choice, using false enticements so that her or her family's supposed choice was misinformed) was sixth.

In practice, giving a bride with gifts and receiving nothing in return tended to be used most often by two sets of people. The first set consisted of those who were striving to elevate their status by inducing families of a slightly higher level to accept their daughters as brides. Among both priestly Brahmins and their Kayastha assistants in contemporary Bengal in the northeast, for example, "purer" lineages still receive brides-with-gifts from "less-pure" lineages. They are following a ranking that dates back to invasions and political upheavals before A.D. 1500. At that time the Brahmin newcomers, arriving with the conquerors, established themselves at the top of the ranking, and those Kayastha who became their assistants became the leading Kayastha. These marriages of daughters to sons of "purer" lineages serve to validate the "less-pure" lineages' claim to be part of that caste group, rather than be seen as of a lower level. The whole process is called *anuloma*, stroking with the hair. It contrasts with *pratiloma*, stroking against the hair, in which a woman would be married to someone below her family's standing. The second set of gift-givers consisted of those who were anxious to avoid pratiloma by ensuring the proper marriage of a daughter through gifts to the family of an appropriately equal-level bridegroom.

The avoidance of pratiloma was a dominant factor in both the practice of polygyny in some groups of Brahmins and the practice of female infanticide (as preferable to dishonorable marriages) among some groups—warrior Rajputs in the northwest and various others in the north, east, south, and west. For those Brahmins who used polygyny it was because their acceptance of brides from slightly lower levels meant that polygyny was needed to assure proper husbands for their own daughters. Generally the polygynous husband visited all but one of his wives in their fathers' homes, rather than bringing them into his own.

Less careful rearing, rather than deliberate infanticide, probably explains the woman shortage that made polyandry feasible among a number of groups in the harsh environment of the Himalaya mountains. These include the Jaunsar, who may be of pre-Vedic (pre-1000 B.C.) origins. They marry the eldest son formally, with bride-wealth. They then give the other sons access to his wife. When the first son dies the wife is treated as formally the wife to the next brother, and so on down the line. In another Himalayan group, the Pahari, a mid-20th-century study showed some still using polyandry and others not. It was noted that only $^1/_5$ of those in polyandrous villages were under 10 years old, but well over ¼ of those in monogamous villages were that young. Evidently polyandry did indeed lessen the dependency ratio. Among some groups, however, as in parts of Nepal, polyandry in groups claiming a higher status might be made possible by pratiloma, downward marriage for those women left husbandless by the continuance of polyandrous forms. If the offspring of such marriages marry members of the higher group, and their offspring in turn marry members of the higher group, the great-grandchildren of the initial pratiloma marriage are accepted as full members of the higher group. But if the offspring of the initial pratiloma marriage marry into the lower group, and their offspring do the same, then the great-grandchildren are regarded as simply members of the lower group.

If one takes into account what the groom would expect to inherit as part of a newly married couple's resources, then something more like equal-exchange became common among many caste groups in the south. There, land might be included in what came with a bride. At the time of marriage itself the exchange would look as if the groom received more than the bride's family did. But if the groom's expectations were considered, the exchange would look more nearly equal. The picture was more complex in the north. There, land was seldom included in what was given with a bride. Large gifts of jewelry came to be given by the groom's family to the bride in many caste groups. These gifts were almost like a dower-gift, not bride-wealth given to her family for having raised her. They were intended as a resource she could draw on as might be needed, but only while her husband lived. At his death she was supposed to take off all her jewelry and give it to their daughters-in-law and their unmarried daughters, and go in unbejeweled mourning for the remainder of her life. Thus the gifts of jewelry could not really be described as either bride-wealth or equal-exchange. The bride's family gave far less with her, and what they gave was often taken by the bride's new mother-in-law to distribute among her unmarried daughters, as gifts that could be given when they were wed.

In both north and south India, bride-wealth was used more frequently as one went down the socioeconomic scale, until one reached the lower levels. At those levels whatever little there was to be inherited (and it seldom included any land rights) was ordinarily not divided until the parents' death. Then it was divided equally among all offspring, married and unmarried, male and female. Whatever gifts might be exchanged at marriage were mainly for actual wedding expenditures and simple household gear.

Divorce was, for all practical purposes, not recognized among the higher-caste groups. However, life was different at lower levels. There, neither marriage nor remarriage involved much outlay or much effort at maintenance of social status. A wife might leave to find another partner, or be sent away, or even be exchanged for another man's wife by her husband, with relatively little objection on anyone's part.

Marriages were generally arranged by parents, rather than by offspring. Early marriage meant that parents were apt to be still alive to do the arranging, even with the short life expectancies of centuries past. The pattern of arranged early marriage is not surprising. Extended-family households were the norm. Parents' arrangement of their children's marriages was only one expression among many of their control over their children's lives. Other examples include requirements in various north India groups that every woman or girl stop working when a male older than herself entered the women's part of the family compound, or that a woman not talk with her husband outside their sleeping quarters until her mother-in-law had died. The maintenance of the extended family had been recognized in northern India as being of the utmost importance by the time of the code of Manu, two thousand years ago. This may have been in part a defensive response to successive waves of invaders, since patrilineality tends to correlate with experiencing a need for self-defense. In the less disturbed south, matrilineality remained prominently, though not exclusively, present. Even among patrilineal groups in the south, the mother's brother was likely to be seen as a potential guardian.

In the code of Manu the patrilineal extended-family household was urged to stay together through four generations, from great-grandfather to great-grandsons. However, if no division of the family property had yet occurred at the fifth generation, when the youngest generation were third cousins, the household was required to divide. This acknowledged the unwieldiness of a too-large group and the weakening of bonds even among second cousins, as compared with first cousins and brothers. But it may have reflected ancient Aryan custom as well as later experience in India, for the Irish of the early centuries of the Christian era followed the same rules.

It is not surprising, then, to find that incest rules tried to prevent any possibility of rivalry, jealousy, or faction-building through intermarriages within such an extended household. No one was permitted to marry some-one born to his or her father's lineage unless they were at fourth-cousin level, so that they could not possibly have been born in the same household. Furthermore, no one was allowed to marry someone born to his or her mother's father's lineage unless they were at third-cousin level. This had a similar effect, for it prevented a pairing-off of cousins who might have been born in the same household if their mother had wed uxorilocally. Uxorilocal marriages did take place despite the patrilocal norm, to cope with that familiar one in five probability that a couple would have daughters but would lack sons.

These stringent incest rules, and restrictions on the previous practice of levirate, may well have been encouraged by the rulers of the states and empires that flourished in northern India during the centuries before the code of Manu was set down. Such rules could have been seen as weakening the potential power of patrilineages. But documentation for such a hypothesis is lacking. Still, the rules discouraged all forms of cousin-marriage (cross or parallel) so effectively that when Muslim conquerors began coming into the north in the 8th century A.D. from the patrilateral parallel-cousin-preferring Middle East, they gradually set aside that pattern in favor of the long-established local north India rules.

Matters were different in the south, where matrilineality was much more common. There was less concern for preventing a concentration of kinsmen into close-knit factions. There was also less concern for preventing an accumulation of kinswomen who might form a faction within a large extended-family household. Bringing sisters or other women who were closely related to one another into a household as wives could be potentially disruptive in a patrilineal system. Bringing kinsmen as non-property-controlling husbands into brother-led matrilineally organized households would not be nearly as disruptive. (The patrilineal household's wives were married to the property managers. The matrilineal household's husbands were not.) As a result the exclusion rules of the north were largely ignored, at least in the matrilineal groups. Cross-cousin marriage was highly favored, which is not surprising. Matrilineality was often accompanied by land-inheritance (or land-dowry) for daughters, rather than sons inheriting alone. Cross-cousin marriages could thus recombine fragmented parcels over the generations, particularly if two lineages repeatedly made matches as time passed. Lineages would also maintain status (always a concern for every caste group) by continuing to recombine at the same level, avoiding pratiloma even if not achieving anuloma. Similar considerations applied in those fairly numerous caste groups in southern India that allow and even favor marrying a man to a daughter of one of his own older sisters, which recombines properties even more rapidly.

The historical interplay of political, economic, and social-status considerations can be seen in microcosm by looking at the situation of the matrilineal Nayar of central Kerala, described in Chapter 1, and by comparing them with their Nambudri Brahmin overlords, their Tiyyar tenants, and both their Nayar and their merchant-Muslim neighbors in northern Kerala. Some time after the 4th century A.D. the Nayar made themselves local rulers throughout most of Kerala; but by the 14th century they had been largely forced to accept the overlordship of Nambudri Brahmins. The Nambudri Brahmins were probably a group from farther north who had been dislodged by the Muslim invasions, and who claimed Brahmin status for prestige (if they did not already have that status) when they established themselves in central Kerala. The Nambudri used the Nayar men as their military arm. They cemented Nayar loyalty by formally marrying Nambudri younger sons to women of royal level among the Nayar, both in the prepubertal legitimizing rite and in postpubertal visiting-husband arrangements. Thus royal Nayar men would see themselves as fighting for their sisters' sons, their own expected heirs. However, the Nambudri carefully preserved their eldest sons for formal marriage to Nambudri wives, although they did not completely follow the formal incest rules of northern India. They practiced polygyny to ensure their daughters marriage partners. Eldest sons among the Nambudri might be visiting husbands to royal Nayar women also. Only an eldest Nayar brother/son would stay at home to manage the extended household's property, at any of the several levels of the Nayar elite group. He himself would be a formal prepubertal husband and a postpubertal visiting husband to one or more Nayar women, either at his own level or at a level or two below. His younger brothers fought as the Nambudri directed, and took wives to visit wherever they might be quartered. When the conquering British forced the Nayar armies to disband in 1792, this system had to change, of course. Those changes are described in Chapter 11.

The Tiyyar tenants who worked the lands held by the Nayar were matrilineal too. However, they did not follow visiting-husband practices, for they were stationary on the soil. Instead, they used both partly returnable bride-wealth and recoverable dowry. A man could expect to recover at least part of what he had given for the privilege of having his wife live and work in his matrilineal extended-family household, if she left him for her brothers' home without a cause such as nonsupport or mistreatment on his part. A woman could take with her whatever personal and household articles she had brought with her, as well as any children, when she left her husband's home (no matter how slight the reason). Her children belonged to her lineage, not his.

The northern Kerala Nayar also brought the (single) wife into the matrilineally organized household of the (single) husband. Because they had not been brought into the military service of the Nambudri, like the Nayar of the center, they did not need to make provision for a group of peripatetic soldier husbands. The northern Nayar used matrilateral as well as patrilateral cross-cousin marriage to recombine properties and maintain status, like many other groups in southern India. They did recognize a father's role by requiring that a woman's husband, as well as her brother, must agree to the first marriage of each of her children by that husband. But if any of the children contracted a second marriage, his consent was not needed, although the mother's brother's was still required. By then they had left the father's household, either for the mother's brother's residence (as a married man of the matrilineage) or for the husband's mother's brother's residence (as a married woman).

The northern Kerala Mappilla merchant group also maintained a matrilineal system, even after they became Muslim through contacts with Middle Eastern merchants some time before the 12th-century Muslim conquests in the central part of northern India. They continued to display a preference for a man's marrying his wife's sister too. Such a marriage would not require a second large-scale exchange of bride-wealth and dowry, whether she were a polygynous second wife, legitimate for Muslims, or a replacement for a deceased one. However, their fellow-Mappilla in central Kerala turned patrilineal and practiced levirate, giving a widow to her husband's brother. That also meant no new bride-wealth or dowry was required. Quite possibly the central Mappilla shifted to patrilineality because they were dealing with patrilineal Nambudri and saw a change as potentially helpful in obtaining trade-monopoly concessions from them, but the northern Kerala Mappilla turned Muslim in part for the sake of better relations with Middle Eastern merchants, while retaining matrilineality as a link with the locally ruling Nayar group.

In their matrilineality and patrilineality these groups in Kerala differ from the more bilaterally organized groups found in much of Sri Lanka (formerly Ceylon). There, too, property-reuniting cross-cousin marriages tend to be strongly favored. Some, like the Gogiyama Radala group of the southern coast (whose presence on the island appears to date back well over 2,500 years), have been accustomed to what amounts to an equal partible inheritance system, even though the practice of primogeniture for land inheritance was established in order to maintain elite status by the 16th century A.D. A daughter is provided with a dowry of goods, jewelry, and money that is approximately the same in value as the land-inheritance expectation of her eldest brother and the goods-and-money expectation of the other sons.

Others, as in the center of the island around Kandy, have also practiced a kind of equal partible inheritance. They have then distinguished between a marriage in which the daughter leaves the household for her husband's parents' household and a marriage in which she stays with her own parents. If she stays, she is ensured a full share in her parents' estate, but her husband must take his chance on making good his claims to his share of his parent's estate when they die. If she leaves, she may take a dowry of goods, jewelry, and money, or she may choose to take her chance on being able to make good her claim to her share in movable properties when her parents die. Some extremely careful calculations take place as such decisions are made, both by the groom and his parents and by the bride and hers. Still others, like the Vellalar Tamils of the northern coast (who arrived from southern India only within the past ten centuries), have yet other versions of this general pattern of providing equally for all the offspring. Until after the first 16th-century European traders arrived, the Vellalar Tamils used a duolineal-like mode of passing on a mother's land to all her daughters and a father's land to all his sons. Then, perhaps in part because of problems of fragmentation of land parcels (despite a strong preference for cross-cousin marriages), they shifted to providing daughters with their share of what both parents held in movable property, as dowry, and reserving inheritance in land to sons. This may also have counteracted problems of cultivation if a wife's and a husband's parcels were far apart, as the original settlements grew in area. The Vellalar Tamils are discussed again in Chapter 11, in connection with the changes introduced by European presence in the region.

In Burma, close to India's northeastern region of Bengal, neither a caste system nor unilineality of any sort took root among the Burmese people. All offspring could expect to share in inheritance. However, shares tended to differ, according to how much assistance a given son or daughter was acknowledged to have given to the parents when they were alive. A son or daughter who had brought a spouse into the parents' home, and was still there when they died, was virtually always recognized as having primary claim. By the 18th century A.D. it was customary for a young couple to live in the wife's parents' household for two or three years. This usually meant until the weaning of their first child. Then they would leave so that another daughter might take that place, or so that one of the younger sons or daughters might marry and remain. A somewhat similar pattern also prevailed by then in neighboring Thailand. There, however, the two potential spouses might request their parents' permission as often as the parents might make marital arrangements on their behalf. Much the same situation as in Thailand existed in the pre-Spanish pre-16th-century A.D. Philippines. Filipinos were also already bilaterally organized by the 16th century. They were therefore quite ready to accept the bilaterally organized marital usages of their Spanish conquerors. However, conversion to Roman Catholicism in the Philippines introduced the whole panoply of prohibitions against marrying close relatives (out to third cousins) and against marrying god-parents and their closest kin. That differed sharply from Burmese incest rules, which primarily focused on not marrying any descendants of a parent's brother.

A widowed Burmese spouse was technically entitled to only half the couple's property. However, their children seldom claimed their half until both parents were gone. If a divorce took place by mutual consent, each recovered what each might have had when the marriage began, including the household gear that the bride's parents usually provided for her. Each also received half of what had been acquired while the marriage endured, except for what had been received through inheritance. Two-thirds of what had been inherited remained the inheritor's, and $\frac{1}{3}$ went to the other spouse. In divorces for cause, in which one party repudiated the other, the repudiator kept all that was jointly acquired during the marriage. The repudiated one was left with only what had been brought into the marriage, but retained all of what he or she might have inherited. The situation was somewhat different on the island of Java in Indonesia, even though its people were bilaterally organized like the Burmese and tended, like the Burmese, to expect a newly married couple to stay with one spouse's parents (not nec-essarily the wife's) until the first child was weaned. The general tendency among Javanese was for all property other than inheritances to be divided $\frac{2}{3}$ to the husband and $\frac{1}{3}$ to the wife if they divorced, while $\frac{1}{3}$ would go to the surviving spouse at death and the rest to children (if any) or to parents or siblings. However, the situation was always talked over by the two family groups involved, and an individual settlement was agreed on. Thus personal situations could be taken into account, and expectations modified.

Before the leveling of social ranks that followed British conquest in Burma in the 19th century, the hereditary Burmese upper classes also differentiated among types of recognized unions. A formal wife's children had inheritance rights from their father. The children of legally acknowledged consorts of other types did not. However, distinctions of rank among the Kachin people of the southeast hills in Burma were maintained by other means, not by differentiating who might be taken as a wife and who only as a consort. Higher-ranking families among the Kachin each gave daughters to one set of lower-level client families in return for cattle as bride-wealth. These clients were thereby recognized as having a somewhat privileged status, being bride-givers. They used the bride-wealth cattle to give feasts, through which they reinforced their own status. They also received daughters from lower-level families without having to give bride-wealth in return.

Such status-centered distinctions, listing groups from which wives were and were not to be taken or setting conditions under which a group's women might be taken as full wives or in other recognized forms of consortship, have been the universal experience of early commercial societies. These distinctions arose only after two developments took place, however. First, the society had to have a central government that was effective enough to have replaced feuds between lineages as the individual's chief means of securing personal safety. Second, there had to be enough mercantile activity to ensure that almost every household (even in a rural area) produced something that it either sold or bartered for goods and services, at least locally.

As governmental and commercial activity joined agriculture as means of livelihood, elite administrative and mercantile groups began to move from bride-wealth to dowry, especially if they were patrilineally rather than matrilineally or bilaterally organized. The change to dowry signaled, among other things, a decline in their womenfolk's participation in their mode of livelihood, in favor of more strictly household-bound activity. This decline then seemed to lead to a wish to ensure that their women still appear to have economic value, through bringing dowry with them. The use of dowry tended to become a means of maintaining elite status by being used to attract another elite member as husband for a daughter, rather than take a chance on her having to be married to a man of lower standing because no elite member sought her. "Elite" might mean priestly Brahmin in India, government official in China, or simply freeborn citizen in ancient Athens, but the operation of the forces tending toward similar results remained the same.

The result of the move to using dowry—at least in patrilineally organized dowry-using groups—was the establishment of conjugal funds in place of lineage funds as chief support for both the spouses and their offspring, once a marriage had begun. That in turn encouraged monogamy. In matrilineal groups like those of southern India a woman's dowry tended to be reabsorbed into her matrilineage holdings through successive use of close-kin marriages. The conjugal fund might not be fully in the couple's possession until the husband's parents died, but its existence meant a strong concern for making marriage hard to dissolve, and also for discouraging widows with children from remarrying. Where dower (the husband's gift to the wife) rather than dowry replaced bride-wealth, it might establish a conjugal fund, or it might become their daughters' portion as what the husband kept became their sons'. In either case it was likely to be treated as an explicit reward for the wife's having remained a virgin, and to be given only after the wedding night, when her virginity had been proved, as in ancient Rome. Where a woman's right to inherit from either or both of her parents came to be recognized, the tendency to use cousin-marriage to reunite fragmented parcels also came to be strong. That was especially apt to be the case in a bilateral system with partible inheritance (equal or unequal), in which she could expect to inherit landed property, not merely movables. Still, societies that did not recognize female inheritance might also favor cousin-marriage, as a means of strengthening already-established alliances between lineages.

On the southern and eastern shores of the Mediterranean and over into Mesopotamia patrilateral parallel-cousin marriage had been used to reunite land parcels since the time of the earliest city-states, more than four thousand years ago. In Roman times, two thousand years ago, Egyptian city-dwellers even married their own full siblings for that purpose (more than ⅓ of the time in some places). The patrilineally organized Arabs of Muhammad's time, around A.D 600, still allowed half-siblings or even fathers and daughters to marry, not because daughters inherited, because they did not, but for lineage-solidarity purposes. They were largely urban and pastoral rather than agricultural, in their dry but commercially strategic homeland, whose caravan tracks served as the major route for goods coming by sea from India and China to the Mediterranean world through South Arabian ports. They expected sons to inherit all their father's wives except their own mothers, who could be inherited by a son of another wife in that polygynous society. They also expected a childless deceased man's brother to give him posthumous sons through his widow so that they could support her as she grew older. Muhammad's preaching ended all those practices, although the last survived in part in the common practice of taking a deceased brother's widow as an added wife.

Muhammad's teachings revolutionized Arab society, establishing the model for most of the peoples conquered and gradually converted by the Arabs in the first Islamic centuries. Men were limited to four wives, with the proviso that they could keep them only if they treated them all equally. Until this century that proviso was accepted as meaning all wives must be provided with equal maintenance for themselves and each child they bore, and with equal time with their husband as well. Some commentators even recommended using the same timing and technique in intercourse with all of them, while others recognized that equal treatment might mean different timing and technique to give comparable satisfaction to each. In the 20th century that same proviso has been used to justify the establishment of monogamy as the legal norm in several Muslim countries, on the ground that equal treatment of more than one is never possible. However, even after Muhammad's time, men still took concubines beyond the fourth permitted wife, if they were wealthy enough. They still recognized concubines' children as having equal inheritance rights with the children born of legal wives. Until Muhammad's second successor as recognized leader of the new Arab Muslim state forbade it, term-marriage was also recognized. Term-marriage was a marriage contract for a specified length of time (even as short as a day, for the convenience of a traveling merchant). It gave any children full inheritance rights if recognized by the father, but gave no widow's portion to the woman if the man died before the term-marriage was ended. A dissident group whose members did not accept this man's right to be regarded as Muhammad's successor continued to practice term-

marriage into the 20th century, in Iran. There, its legitimacy was upheld by
the successors of the dissidents, in the Shiite branch of Islam, who formed
the overwhelming majority of Iranians.

Muhammad's precepts required men to dower their wives. A man could
only recover even part of that dower if he divorced a wife for serious cause,
such as inadequate care for children. Muhammad also encouraged men to
give dowry with their daughters. The laws he established recognized that
whatever property a woman held at marriage, or inherited during marriage,
remained hers. Those laws also provided that daughters were to inherit half-
shares of both their parents' properties, as well as that sons were to inherit
full shares. A childless widow received ¼ of her husband's property. The
rest went to his parents, siblings, or siblings' children, in that order, with
the same half-to-full share ratio for sisters and brothers or for nieces and
nephews. A widowed mother received ⅛, with the rest going to the children.
These lesser portions for women were justified by later commentators on
the ground that since women received both dower and dowry, their total
shares in the wealth of the community were approximately equal to those
of men. Besides, there was the obvious need to provide for the possibility
(in the case of widows) that a man might leave up to four to have to divide
his estate.

A woman's first marriage was arranged by her father or by a male guardian designated by the father. Usually this would be a father's brother, but
sometimes a mother's brother or even the woman's older brother would fill
the role. If it were the groom's first marriage, the bride's representative made
arrangements with the groom's father or male guardian. If it were not his
first marriage, he could designate his own representative. If a woman married
a second time, she could designate her own representative as a man could.
Her dowry and dower were now in her possession, even though she usually
designated a close kinsman to manage her affairs because of the social
customs that confined her to household life so as to guard her chastity.

A remarrying Muslim woman usually received relatively little dower from
her new husband, and no additional dowry from her own kin. She might
have been either widowed or divorced. If she were divorced, it was probably
by her husband's action rather than by her own. There was almost no way
she could initiate a divorce except to ask her husband to pronounce it. A
man, on the other hand, could simply pronounce the marriage ended. He
could take back a pronouncement of divorce, though, unless he had been
angry enough to make it a third time. In that case, if he wanted to take her
back again and if she were willing, they would have to find a man to be a
husband to her briefly. The laws of Islam required that a woman who was
divorced three times in succession by the same man must be married to
another before she could marry the previous one again. This was apparently
intended to discourage a short-tempered husband from being too free about

pronouncing a divorce. In view of these various provisions, divorce did not necessarily place a serious stigma on a woman.

A remarrying woman would bring only her youngest children (if any) with her, and then only temporarily. They belonged to her husband's lineage, and would be taken by their father's family as soon as they were judged old enough to leave their mother's side, around four to seven years of age.

Such movements of women from household to household in Islamic Middle Eastern society would cause the same upsets in calculations with regard to conjugal funds as in India or China, by their removal of both dowry and dower. However, they were evidently regarded in the Muslim Middle East as more bearable than the continued familial friction that often resulted from incompatibilities between an in-marrying wife and her in-laws, tied together in a Chinese or Indian household in which divorce was scarcely known. This may be in part because Muslim Middle Eastern households, whether polygynous or monogamous in practice, tended to be organized into men's and women's quarters that were almost as rigidly divided as a Fulani herders' camp. (Means were found to ease some of the awkwardnesses that this rigid separation might cause. One of the more unusual ways was for a man to marry a friend's prepubertal daughter, leaving the marriage unconsummated, so that as "kinsmen" they could visit each other's homes freely, and then to divorce her when she was old enough to marry.)

Normally there was only a minimal amount of interaction in a Muslim Middle Eastern household between two spouses, or between either spouse and other household members of the opposite sex, by comparison with the Chinese situation. In a Chinese household each husband and his (one) wife had their own cooking and sleeping facilities, unless the household was organized around only one kitchen. In wealthy households the spouses also had their own separate sitting rooms within the larger household. Any widowed or otherwise spouseless adults were also likely to have separate facilities, until and unless infirmity required that they be taken into a younger family member's quarters. Relatively easy divorce and remarriage would have required more complex readjustments on the part of more people in the Chinese system than in the Muslim Middle Eastern system. In China each husband expected individual attention (cooking, mending, and the like) from his own wife. In the Muslim Middle Eastern system men in general expected such attention from women in general, rather than necessarily from their own wives. A traditional north India household was apt to be like a Muslim Middle Eastern one, both in that regard and in being organized into men's and women's quarters; but the absence of patrilateral parallel-cousin marriage and the comparative rarity of polygyny in India, as in China, may have lessened strains among the household's women enough to make them bearable.

The continued acceptance of polygyny among Muslims probably also played a part in the acceptance of divorce and remarriage. Though it is probable that not more than one in 20 men actually had more than one wife at any given time in most polygynous societies, Muslim or other, both men and women might be apt to invest more emotionally in the ongoing bonds of consanguinity than in a marital partnership that might cease at any time to be an exclusive one. It is significant in this regard that even after marriage, a woman's father and brothers remain the chief avengers of her dishonor in Muslim Middle Eastern societies, in which a woman's chastity is regarded as all-important to safeguard. Any breach of that chastity must be avenged, to maintain family honor and status—so that, among other things, dowries for other women of the family need not be increased to compensate for a poor family-reputation. Among monogamous Christian groups in the Mediterranean area, such as the Greeks, who have held similar attitudes for similar reasons, the husband becomes the primary avenger for his wife. Still the father and brothers may take action if they believe the husband does not act soon enough.

It is risky to use data from one relatively isolated village near the Jordan River in the 1920s to make generalizations about centuries of experience in the many communities in the Arab portion of the Muslim world. Yet, as a sample of a rural Muslim community in a society not yet industrialized, it may be instructive to look at Artas in the 1920s through the eyes of H. Granqvist, as reported in Edwin T. Prothro and Lutfy Najib Diab's *Changing Family Patterns in the Arab East* (1974). The most frequent age of first marriage for women was 14, though men seldom wed much before 20. The husband was thereby assured the authority of age in dealing with his wife. The usual practice with dower was to give most of it at marriage, leaving little to be received at widowhood or divorce. Dowry was largely confined to clothing and household gear. One in eight marriages in Artas were between brothers' children, and another one in eight were between other first cousins. Only one in 20 women had been divorced, of those who had ever been married. More than four in five of these had remarried, though. In numbers, more than twice as many widows as divorced women had remarried. Often they had married a brother of the deceased husband. That helped to account for as high a proportion as one in nine men currently having more than one wife. A 1960s survey in urban communities in Lebanon still found one in ten marriages being made between brothers' children, and one in eleven between the children of other agnates, second or third cousins with fathers who were cousins through their fathers' lines. Another survey in rural Morocco in the 1960s found only two in five marriages to be between persons who were not perceived as kin in any way. A survey in regions of rural Tunisia in the 1960s found proportions ranging from nine in sixteen to five in six marriages between persons born either to brothers or to male cousins in the same patrilineage, or to a mother and a father who were born into the same patrilineage. A strong tendency was noted for the daughters of out-marrying daughters to return as wives to someone. Yet another survey in Albania's mountains in 1929 found only one in twenty-five marriages to be between completely unrelated persons. From these surveys, as from literary sources for earlier centuries, it would seem likely that kin endogamy remained an enduring pattern in the Middle East from biblical and classical through Islamic times. The reported frequent use of both types of cross-cousin marriages in more remote Afghanistan in the 1930s may also be indicative of conditions in the past in the Muslim world. However, the marriage of brothers' offspring was as rare in Afghanistan by then as among Muslims in India, which may reflect some cultural influence from northern India's stricter ancient prohibitions on patrilateral than on matrilateral cousin-marriages.

There are at least seven reasons for the maintenance of high levels of kin endogamy. One is that there are fewer strains in adjustment when the new wife already knows and is known by the members of the household, being kin. A second is that there is a greater coincidence in interests between spouses who are also kin. A third is the recombination of divided properties. A fourth is the strengthening of lineage solidarity and loyalty. A fifth is the maintenance of family status through marriage with obvious equals. A sixth is that there are usually lower expectations with regard to dower, dowry, and other outlays when cousins marry. A seventh is that kin will be concerned to resolve husband-wife quarrels so as to keep the marriage alive, rather than being likely to take sides and thereby deepen rifts.

In favor of exogamy, the three primary considerations usually mentioned are the formation of new alliances; the acquisition of new wealth with an in-marrying wife, if she brings a large dowry; and the potentially greater amenability of an in-marrying wife, if she has no natural allies in her new household and must therefore adjust herself more to her husband and in-laws than they must adjust to her. Alliance-formation may be the most significant of these, in reality. Certainly it seemed to the maker of the Tunisian survey to be a consideration in the minority of marriages that were between nonkin. A study done in rural Turkey in the 1960s showed alliance with other lineages to be the first consideration in choosing marriage partners, rather than kin endogamy. (Historically only the eldest son brought his wife into the household in rural Turkey, and all other sons moved out at marriage.) These rural Turks' concern for alliance-making may correlate with the centuries-old practice in parts of Turkey that a man may not marry the daughter of a man who has stood as either his own or his son's sponsor at the time of circumcision. That may be a partial holdover from godparenthood in Christian times before the Turkish conquest of the 11th century A.D. Like Christian practices concerning godkin, the Turkish pattern provides a means not only of establishing a fictive-kin alliance, but also of requiring people to think in terms of moving beyond even the fictive kin in selecting marriage partners. However, given the degree of centralization, commercialization, and even industrialization in Turkey by the 1960s, the finding that alliance-building was given first consideration then by no means precludes the possibility that kin linkages were seen as more important in earlier centuries.

Several studies were made in the 1950s and 1960s of Lebanese, Libyan Bedouin, and Tunisian lineage members' efforts to form what are termed *affinal networks*, or *affinal sets*. These terms refer to the set of alliances formed by marrying a lineage's members into other strong patrilineages, whose strength is occasionally recognized strongly enough so that a young man will take his mother's father's lineage name rather than his own father's. Useful linkages are kept strong through repetition of marriages, while linkages that prove less useful are given up in order to form new linkages with later marriages. These affinal-network studies illuminate historical accounts of royal and other elite-level marriage-makings, not only in the Middle East, but also in every corner of the world. They demonstrate that in a society that is still largely kin-centered, even though partly commercialized and partly centralized, the marriage choices that elders make are carefully thought through. The elders are concerned not only for their juniors' future, but also for their own. Even choosing a spouse from outside the community may be related to the maintenance of an existing affinal network. It may be undertaken to ensure that the man marrying will not be closely drawn into a new set of local affinal links, and can maintain without interference links with siblings' spouses' families in the community. It may also be undertaken to ensure that the woman marrying will have to move out and make her own new network in her new community, leaving her siblings' network unaffected.

Such niceties of calculation have a long history in the Mediterranean world. In ancient Greece the polygynous chieftains of the Homeric era before 1000 B.C. gave their daughters or sisters in marriage, without receiving bride-wealth, to those allies and followers whose loyalty they wished either to court or to reward. They also gave their daughters and sisters in marriage in return for bride-wealth, from other men who wished to cement alliances with them. They received daughters or sisters with dowry-gifts in marriage from still others who sought their alliance. They might then bestow these women on yet others, with or without receipt of bride-wealth. Women were important enough as alliance symbols so that even a mature woman, left widowed near or past the end of her childbearing years, might be married out by her son for political purposes. Alternatively, she might be sent with gifts to her paternal home, so that her father or brother could arrange a marriage for her if he wished.

Lineage support was all-important in an age when feud was one's only protection. Only gradually did reliance on one's lineage for vengeance give way to reliance on governmental courts to settle homicide cases, by the end of the 7th century B.C. In the 8th century B.C., population pressures were already great enough for the poet Hesiod to recommend that all but the wealthiest men should wait to marry until 30. He recommended choosing a wife who was still in her teens, a pattern that continued to be recommended and followed at least as late as Aristotle's time, in the 4th century B.C. Hesiod also recommended that a man should have only one son to provide for. However, lineage groups clearly still had more control over the marriage arrangements of their members in Hesiod's time than did heads of households within those lineage groups.

At the opening of the 6th century B.C. the reform measures of Solon in Athens broke that lineage-group control. Solon let sonless household heads among the free citizenry adopt an heir, even though the heir must come from among a prescribed set of blood kin. Solon let heirless free citizens bequeath their property by will, also, rather than see it revert automatically to their lineage. (Slaves, being without personal rights, could not marry and so could not have heirs.) Dowry was required for a daughter. Usually it would be at about the level of $\frac{1}{10}$ of the father's wealth. It might be either in land or in money, and was to be managed by her husband. It would be returned to her if she went back to her father or brother (either because widowed or because divorced). But if she were willing to remain in her husband's household after his death, which made her sons liable for her support, then it would be passed on to any sons whom she bore (or, as part of dowry, to daughters).

All sons, in Solon's Athens, inherited equally. Eventually, after conversion to Christianity, this practice became the basis for the expectation that all children would receive equal shares, whether by dowry for daughters or by inheritance for sons. That differed sharply from the Roman practice of allowing a father to favor one son. In a sonless Athenian family one daughter could be designated as transmitter of the household property. She was then required to wed the nearest available patrilineal kinsman. Preferably this was to be a brother of her father. Her uncle might even divorce a current wife, in order to enable his kinswoman to meet that expectation that a son born to the two of them might continue that household's existence. If he wished, he could offer to provide some additional dowry for his former wife's remarriage, besides what he returned with her to her father or her brother. Somewhat comparable provisions to those of Athens were made in the other Greek city-states as well, requiring brotherless daughters to wed patrilineal kinsmen.

The importance attached to continuance of bloodlines, which were the passport in every Greek city-state to recognition of full citizenship with its privileges, meant severe punishment for adultery. In Athens death was the fate of the man who thus interfered with lineage-continuance, and the woman was permanently isolated. This pair of rules was applied in all of the classical Greek city-states but two. Sparta proudly proclaimed that it had no need for any rules because there was no marital infidelity. Gortyn,

on Crete, let the woman pay a money fine and be remarried, if anyone
would have her. Until the Romans brought the Greek city-states under their
control during the 2nd century B.C., Athens also differentiated between the
marriage of a citizen to a citizen's daughter and all other marriages. The
descendants of noncitizens were not supposed to be allowed the privilege
of citizenship, although from time to time lapses of memory might allow
the grandson of a citizen and a noncitizen's daughter to be enrolled if his
father had married the daughter of a citizen.

In Greek city-state life the lineage group still validated citizenship. At
least in Athens the lineage group also retained a right to refuse to allow
return from an exile imposed on someone for having killed one of its members. The maintenance of a woman's connection with her father and brothers, through mechanisms such as returning her dowry with her when she
left a husband's house, was another sign of the primary importance of the
lineage group. Marriage with dowry did not really establish a lasting conjugal fund, any more than it was to do later in the Muslim world. This was
in part because divorce was recognized as relatively likely to take place,
given expectations such as the one that close kinsmen would divorce their
wives in order to marry brotherless heiresses. It was in classical Rome,
rather than in classical Greece, that genuine conjugal funds became possible.
This resulted from a series of developments that gradually modified the
significance of dowry and the forms of marriage, over a period of several
centuries.

In the early Roman republic of the 5th century B.C. the hereditary class
distinction between patricians and plebeians meant that status-maintenance
was already of enough concern to have led to the use of dowry to ensure
a daughter's proper marriage. A distinction was already made between a
marriage in which the woman and the dowry given with her became permanently part of the husband's household (so that if she were divorced, her
dowry did not return with her to her father or brothers), and a marriage
in which the woman and her dowry remained technically under her father's
and then her brothers' legal jurisdiction. In the latter type of marriage, the
husband gave some bride-wealth and some dowry was given with the bride.
The wife lived in her husband's household, and her offspring were recognized as in his patrilineage rather than in hers. Her husband might retain
part of the dowry if he divorced her for some serious violation on her part,
but not if he divorced her to marry someone else for political or other
advantage-seeking reasons, as increasingly occurred in later generations.
Unless she had been divorced for cause, her dowry stayed with her, not
with him—or rather, in the eyes of the law, with her male guardian.

Until the time of the Roman emperor Diocletian in the 3rd century A.D.
a woman remained a legal minor all her life. She always had to be represented
in legal transactions by her male guardian, whether father, brother, husband,
or son. Only after Diocletian permitted a woman to act on her own behalf

when she reached maturity—meaning having been married and the marriage having ended—did it become possible for people to begin thinking in terms of marriage as establishing a conjugal fund, which the wife could inherit in full and manage if her husband predeceased her, just as he could do if she predeceased him.

During the 3rd and 2nd centuries B.C., when wars around the Mediterranean took men of fighting age away from Rome much of the time, the kind of marriage that transferred a woman and her dowry entirely to the husband's keeping fell into almost complete disuse because of its inconvenience. Perhaps in part as a result, divorce became more frequent. So did not marrying at all, to the eventual distress of the first Roman emperor, Augustus, in the 1st century A.D. Though Augustus forbade members of the military legions to marry before their 20-year term of service was over, and forbade men of the hereditary senatorial class to marry actresses, he tried to require marriage as a condition for inheriting property. He also recognized co-habitation by simple mutual agreement between the parties as capable of producing legitimate heirs, if the father recognized them. Such co-habitation was not formalized by any kind of gift-exchange. It could be ended at any time by mutual consent, in contrast to the legal procedures required to register—not permit—the end of formal marriage.

Augustus's regulations applied to Roman citizens, who at that time were still an elite minority in the newly formed empire. Other nonslave groups, like the Jews, were largely allowed to retain their customary patterns. Slaves of course could not marry. Gradually, as Roman citizenship was extended to one group after another as a means of strengthening allegiance to the central government, these rules came to apply to them also. They finally became universal for nonslaves within the empire when citizenship became universal for nonslaves, in the 3rd century A.D. Thus when the Christian church became the official religion of the empire in the 4th century A.D., not only the establishment and dissolution of voluntary co-habitations (legal but unregistered), but also the establishment and dissolution of formally registered marriages, were universally regarded as the affair of the interested parties. Marriage was not the business of the state. This is vitally important to realize in understanding the development of the church's attitudes toward marriage. So is the realization that Roman law recognized the freeborn citizen's right to compensation for property taken for state use, for that recognition gave a strong impetus to the development of individualistic thought, with all it could imply for marriage and family relationships.

As the empire's population began to decline in the 1st century A.D.— probably because earlier overpopulation had overstrained agricultural resources and left undernourished people with little resistance to new diseases from regions farther east—successive emperors tried to use tax benefits to encourage marriage (or at least co-habitation) and procreation. Despite their efforts, population continued to diminish. Soon the Germanic peoples along the northern borders of the empire began to penetrate southward, settling in the eastern half and gradually taking over the western half of the Mediterranean world. By the time of Diocletian and his immediate successors the difficulty of collecting taxes led to an effort to require all who were born to cultivators and other workers to remain in their parents' occupational grouping. The parallel difficulty of continuing to provide subsidized grain supplies, to which Roman citizens had been at least nominally entitled since the late 2nd century B.C., led to an effort to allow formal marriage only to those who actually had a position to inherit. However, the desire to maintain population tended somewhat to counteract the second policy. Continued plagues, continued arrivals of new groups of Germanic peoples, and then the invasion of the empire by the Muslims of the Arabian peninsula in the 7th century A.D. led to the effective loss of imperial control over all but present-day Turkey, the southern Balkans, and parts of Italy by A.D. 700. During that period of upheaval Roman society in every part of Europe south of the Rhine and the Danube was having to adjust to the settling down of newcomers who maintained their own laws, like the Lombards in much of Italy and the Franks and others in present-day France. Roman law continued to be applied only to those born to the already-resident families. It was under these confusing and complex circumstances that the marriage systems of medieval Christian western and eastern Europe were hammered out.

The members of the early Christian church showed little interest in regulating marriage, beyond enjoining fidelity for both partners. Because they believed that the end of the world was at hand, by the 2nd century A.D. they were even encouraging celibacy as preferable to putting one's energy into family life, for both men and women. In the late 4th century, when the church was becoming officially accepted as part of the life of the empire, the emperor Gratian went so far as to decree that a woman could not be required to marry against her will. By then it was beginning to be advocated that a priest should bless those marriages already formally entered by the parties involved. But even the priest's blessing did not become universally expected until the 8th century. Only in the 9th century was a formal marriage ceremony worked out in the western half of what had once been the Roman Empire. Not until even later was one developed in the Eastern church (already somewhat distinct from the Western church, though the final break did not come until 1054). And only after there was a formal marriage ceremony to use did that ceremony begin to be regarded as necessary to make a marriage binding.

In the West the acceptance of the church ceremony as the means of formalizing marriage coincided with the change from seeing marriage as a civil contract to seeing it as a religious sacrament. During the 10th century that change was marked by a general recognition that all cases dealing with the legitimacy of a marriage were to be handled in church courts, not in civil ones. This meant a real change, in terms of family control over the choice of marriage partners. Church courts did not regard parents' prior permission as a necessary condition for a legitimate marriage, as civil courts had done. Church courts also did not make slave status a bar to marriage, as had the courts of ancient Rome. They were more concerned with whether there had been a prior legitimate marriage. If we use as an example the records of the diocese of Ely in England from 1374 to 1382, half the cases brought to the diocesan courts for matrimonial causes involved a claim that someone had committed bigamy.

Church leaders had already decided in A.D. 407 that adultery was not sufficient cause to end a Christian marriage, and in A.D. 458, that not even years of absence could be given as reason to end one. Once consummated, marriage was for life, unless it proved later not to have been entered properly. That contrasted sharply with the Roman Empire's legal code. Only in the 6th century did the civil code follow partial suit, by accepting the dissolution of a marriage only for impotence, five years' absence in foreign captivity, or the desire of one spouse to enter a celibate religious order. The Eastern church eventually accepted divorce with right of remarriage, but no more than three times. The Eastern church accepted adultery as well as impotence as a cause for divorce, and also "spiritual adultery" (i.e., heresy). But the Western church only allowed separation (including complete separation of property), without right of remarriage, for anything other than nonconsummation or initial nullity.

By the 12th century, when the canon lawyers of the Western church came to the conclusion that slavery was no bar to marriage, there were few slaves left in western Europe to whom it could apply. Those who had been slaves on the great Roman estates came to work their lands by what amounted to hereditary right as much as hereditary obligation, once Franks and Lombards and Visigoths took over in a continuing era of population decline (made steeper by plagues from the 6th century on). Gradually the slave cultivators succeeded in rising from that status by finding conjugal partners a level above themselves. These often came from the lowest level of nonnoble Franks or Lombards, who were legally free but could not sell the land they worked as followers of their noble overlords. The children or at least grandchildren of such marriages could then claim the less degraded status, in the confusion of the 5th century A.D. onward. As a result almost no slaves were listed in 9th-century registers of households on monastic holdings, though there were many who were required to give some kind of service, as well as rent, in return for being able to cultivate a piece of land.

Childbearing women were clearly in short supply, since the Franks charged three times as much wergild-payment for killing a woman of childbearing age as for killing an adult man, and the Alemannic code counted an abducted women's children by her abductor as her husband's rather than as the abductor's. It was a reality of life in those troubled centuries that abductions were common. Through at least the 9th century A.D. women therefore tended to be placed—or even to place themselves—in the households of the powerful, for protection from abduction. They might become servants or concubines in noble houses, or servants in bishops' palaces and on manorial estates managed by monastic orders. Thus men's opportunity to marry was even more limited than it might otherwise have been, at least at lower socioeconomic levels. However, because the formal rules tended to give a child the status of the mother (at least below the level of the nobility), a woman or her family would have little reason to prefer an unambitious same-level man as husband to a hard-working slightly lower-level one. That, too, helps to explain the virtual disappearance of slave status through upward marriage. Besides, only the man who was heir to a household's cultivation rights was likely to marry, among those with cultivation rights. If more than one of the heir's sisters was to marry, she was apt to have to marry downward. In cottage-holding households, whose members could only labor for others, no similar limits on sons' marriages prevailed.

The exogamy rules developed by the church by the 6th century, in an effort to weaken the strong kinship groups of the invading Germanic peoples as they converted to Christianity, had the effect of requiring ordinary cultivators also to cast their nets widely in seeking spouses. The canon lawyers' goal was to put an end to private feuds, which might become so disruptive that in one 6th-century instance, the Frankish queen simply had all the members of two particularly belligerent feuding clans slain, as the only way to bring some peace to the area in which they lived. Exogamy rules required marriages to be made between lineages, not within them, thereby breaking down their exclusiveness. However, exogamy rules also gave reason (and backing) to lower-status cultivators in resisting overlords' efforts to get them to find marriage partners on the same estate. Because it was easier to marry upward if one were moving at marriage to another estate, the exogamy rules originally developed to control feuding among the conquerors' lineages turned out also to help local cultivators improve their status. Overlords tried to resist the cultivators' moving at marriage for two reasons. One was that the move usually took the mover into a less restricted and service-providing situation. The other was that a worker was being lost, although that could be accepted if an even exchange could be worked out.

The exogamy rules promulgated by the 6th century A.D. called for avoiding marriage with any blood-kin within the seventh degree, any blood-kin of an earlier spouse within the seventh degree (in the case of a later marriage), any godparent, or any godparent's kin within the seventh degree. If one counted in the Roman civil law fashion, one would have to go four ancestral steps up from oneself to a great-great-grandparent and another four descent steps down to that person's great-great-grandchild, one's third cousin, to find a kinship circle into which to marry. The difficulties of finding legitimate marriage partners within such great restrictions multiplied the labors of the canon lawyers and the church courts. Even if a child's grandparent became its godparent, which would add the fewest to the list of those prohibited, finding a partner could be difficult unless one's social network was relatively wide. Having a grandparent as godparent would make the closest marriageable kin on that grandparent's side a fourth, rather than a third, cousin. Parents were prohibited in A.D. 813 from being godparents to their own children, partly in the belief that this concentrated too much authority into their hands, and partly out of taboos that kept new mothers from entering a church until after the period when baptism usually took place.

It was undoubtedly more than coincidence that the level of third cousin was made the level at which marriage was permissible, if the four-up, four-down reckoning were used. That was also the level next beyond the group of one's own eight great-grandparents' descendants, which was the most frequent wergild-providing-and-receiving group among the newly arrived Germanic peoples. It also corresponds, interestingly, to the eight-line maximum often found among ambilineally organized societies, like Samoa in the Pacific Islands. However, there was much confusion as to the significance of "within the seventh degree," once that number had been fixed on. By the 13th century, if not before, it had been modified to "within the fourth degree" by the reckoning up to the common ancestor. This effectively prohibited third cousins too. It made one's great-great-grandparent's great-great-great-grandchild the closest permissible marriage partner, unless one interpreted the pertinent decree, issued in 1215 by the head of the Western church, in the old Roman civil law way. If one used that reckoning, only first cousins could not marry. Yet even that became possible by special dispensation, not long afterward.

The godkin regulations were also maintained in the West until 1215. At that time they were liberalized to prohibit only the circle of godparents, godchildren's parents, godchildren, and godparents' children. (Godkin regulations were maintained in much fuller form in the Eastern church.) Godkin regulations had proved useful in western Europe in weakening the hereditary nobles' power, not only by preventing them from forming narrow intramarrying circles, but also by enabling estate-dwellers to resist estate-holders' wishes that they marry on rather than off the estate. Eventually estate-dwellers began to multiply the number of godparents for each child, as a means of continuing the former necessity of marrying off the estate. By 1310 the Western church began to limit the number of godparents, as a response. However, only in 1563 was the limit for godparents set firmly at two of the child's own sex and one of the opposite sex. The prohibition on marrying one's godkin was then restricted to one's children's godparents, one's own godparents, and one's own godchildren and their parents. In Spain, at least, godparents continued to take part in the major rituals of a godchild's life until betrothal. There, as in the Eastern church, the godparents were the ones to ask the godchild if this marriage had the godchild's free consent, as was required by church law to make it valid. If the godchild said it did not, then they had the backing of the church to take the godchild into their home and arrange a more welcome match.

The introduction and effective enforcement of the church's far-ranging exogamy rules almost paralleled in time the introduction of dower as the major presentation at marriage, as the Germanic "morning-gift" to the proved virgin after her wedding night. Dower came to take precedence over both bride-wealth and dowry. Among Scandinavians and some others bride-wealth was replaced by dower by the 7th century, though bride-wealth was still given among Anglo-Saxons as late as the 9th century. Already in the 3rd century Roman law had recognized a gift from the groom to the bride (*donatio nuptias*) as legitimate. In the 6th century Roman law came to require a *donatio nuptias*. But the *donatio nuptias* was limited to the amount of the dowry, which was also still required. However, by the 9th century, dowry was no longer even mentioned in the western half of what had been the empire.

Dower offered a measure of the worth to a man of finding a wife. Eventually the amount of the dower was limited to a stated fraction of a man's wealth at the time of marriage. The fraction ranged from $^{1}/_{10}$ among the Visigoths in Spain to ¼ among the Lombards in Italy and ⅓ among the Franks in France. The intent was to protect his potential heirs from possible loss, since what the wife was given remained hers regardless of whether she had children. The dower went to her kin, not to his, if she outlived him and they had no children. The right of a widow to ⅓ of her husband's estate (recognized by Franks and Burgundians in France) also limited his kin's losses if she died without children by him, particularly if she had remarried and had children with another man. By the 10th century dower as either gift at marriage or entitlement at widowhood had become virtually universal in western Christian Europe. Dowry was still used in the dwindling imperial realm in the East, though. Among the newly converted Slavs east of the Danube, old institutions of bride-wealth may have been just beginning to disappear. Dower, which removed wealth from a lineage, was also weakening to kinship groups. That may help to account for the church's encouragement of it in place of bride-wealth, whenever a bride-wealth-using people accepted Christianity.

Among all the Germanic peoples of the West a wife's right to manage whatever property she brought into a marriage was recognized. Most of the Germanic peoples expected that if a wife were widowed, she would inherit part of what she and her husband had acquired during marriage, and would serve as guardian and trustee on behalf of any minor children for their share of the rest. (Adult offspring would receive their share immediately.) Those expectations with regard to women's property rights, whether in the property brought into marriage by the new couple (including dower) or in the property acquired by the pair during marriage, began to dwindle after the 10th century.

In the 11th century church reformers in western Europe began actively to oppose the marriage of clergy. The Western church had never reached a working compromise like that of the Eastern church, in which those who wished to hold high office in the church had to remain celibate (and therefore free to travel), while those whose interest was settled parish service could marry—but only once; no remarriage for widowers. The reformers attacked clerical marriage on the ground that married clergy were too concerned for the well-being of their families to serve their parishioners with an open heart and mind. Unfortunately the campaign for clergy celibacy tended to lead to a defamation of women in general, as tending to distract men from their proper duties and to deflect them toward selfish rather than altruistic thinking. Women's social position was inevitably affected. In the 8th and 9th centuries it was fairly common among the Germans for a man to stress his ties to his mother's or even his mother's mother's kin. That may stem in part from the previously mentioned practice of noble families marrying their daughters to rising, but not yet ennobled men. However, that tendency shaded off thereafter. By the 12th century aristocratic families were firmly organized around an agnate core, though ties to maternal kin might still be significant below that level. For example, in 14th-century Macedonia (in the Eastern church), where about 6% of marriages in one surviving list of monastic holdings were uxorilocal, a family property might still be transmitted through a brotherless daughter to her son. Much the same proportion of uxorilocal marriages is found in western European lists of monastic holdings from the 9th century on. The 11th century saw the rise of the cult of Mary in the West as almost a directly compensating response to the defamation of women associated with the opposition to clergy marriage. Nevertheless the gradual shift that appears to have taken place in sex ratios, as western Europe's population grew and began to become more urban than before, was to have more effect on women's daily lives (as well as on marriage patterns) than either the veneration of Mary as Mother of God and Queen of Heaven, or the 12th-century cult of courtly love, which also tried to elevate the moral and social position of women.

The ending of the period of invasions, by Germanic peoples, by Muslims along the Mediterranean coasts, by Vikings from Scandinavia, by Magyars from Central Asia, was followed by a clearing of forests and an opening of agricultural settlements after A.D. 1000. This period of economic expansion coincided not only with a slight but gradually continuing rise in temperatures, but also with the introduction of new agricultural technology, like heavier plows. These developments in turn meant greater productivity, more surplus for trade, growth in commerce, and a rise of towns. Life expectancies seem to have risen somewhat, from under 30 to over 30. For women in particular the less harsh conditions of town life seem to have improved their chances of survival. Within the towns, particularly at the levels of the population that were better off, women actually began to outnumber men. By the 15th century, from which enough population lists survive for moderately meaningful estimates, women outnumbered men in almost every town. Conditions in the rural areas are less certain.

If relative marriage ages are used as a possible indicator, perhaps the 12th century marks the passage from a shortage of potential wives to a shortage of potential husbands. Young boys were often married to mature women in the 8th and 9th centuries, suggesting a concern to find wives for them in that era of abductions. A surviving list from the 12th century of Genoa in Italy indicates approximately equal ages at marriage there. But in the 13th century, in Florence and elsewhere, mature men began taking younger and younger brides. By 1427 the mean marriage ages in Florence were 30 for men and 17 for women, for first marriages, making the mean age when a child was born 39 for men and 26 for women (78 for grandfatherhood, 52 for grandmotherhood?). The result was that a man would probably die before his son or daughter reached 17, although the mother would probably survive at least a decade longer. As older men wed younger women, increasing numbers of young men were left without the satisfactions and stabilizing elements of married life. (Witness the brawling young Capulets and Montagues of *Romeo and Juliet*.) Many women were also left husbandless by the keen competition for acceptable husbands. How much that had to do with the low remarriage rate of widows is hard to say, but a widow's opportunity to manage the family property probably helped to make many widows actually reluctant to remarry.

The shift from a scarcity to a surplus of women was momentous. In every previous medieval century celibate life for considerable numbers of men had been a virtual social necessity, given the rule that marriage, once entered, remained indissoluble for life. The establishment of Christian monastic orders for men had been in part an answer to that problem. Celibate orders for women existed too, but in smaller numbers. Now a growth in celibate religious orders for women would be a social necessity in its turn. The practice known as *oblation*, or the offering of an infant as a lifelong inhabitant of a monastic house, was also affected. Oblation had been the church's answer to the ancient practice of exposure. From ancient Greek and Roman times through the entire medieval era in eastern and western Europe the term *exposure* of an infant was understood to mean its being offered to others by a parent who was uncertain of his or her ability to provide for it, rather than its being exposed to weather and wild beasts. Medieval Christendom modified this practice to provide for oblation, or offering the young to monasteries and convents. Though that removed them permanently from the marriage market, it at least ensured their maintenance for life. It is still uncertain what proportions of male and female infants may have been offered at any given period. However, one might hazard a guess that part of the pre-12th-century shortage of women came from frequent offering of girls as a protection to them from the previously mentioned abductions of the period through the 9th century. One might also hazard a guess that as women ceased to be in short supply after the 12th century, girls were offered more often than boys as a means of providing for their livelihood.

The 12th century marks the first strong reemergence of dowry. For example, Genoa abolished a widow's right to ⅓ of the household's property, and decreed that a woman's dower from her husband was not to exceed ¼ of her dowry from her parents. Clearly a woman could no longer be regarded as a rare prize, for whom her parents could in effect take bids. The bidding was now the other way around. The change was visible enough so that by the 15th century in Spain, a woman was entitled to a share of her parents' estate so that she could be "placed." Her share could be used either as a dowry for a husband or as an entry fee into a convent. There she could live out to the end a safe and respectable single life, protected by the convent walls for lack of either a husband or a son to take the father's place as her protector.

The strength of Spanish emphasis on a woman's need for such protection probably came in part from the experience of Muslim conquest and rule from the 8th to 15th centuries. It would have stemmed not only from the example of Muslim segregation of women, but also from the concern to keep the daughters of the conquered safe from the eyes of conquerors, which helped to place barriers around women's activities in many regions. However, similar tendencies were appearing in every part of Europe by then. By the early 14th century daughters were being put into convents in both France and Italy, in preference to providing large enough dowries for them to marry. By 1500 13% of all Florentine women were in nunneries. In a different direction villagers in both those regions were likely to express indignation at the remarriage of a widower, or especially a widow, through the charivari in France or the mattinata in Italy. The indignation protested the possibility that children of the second marriage might inherit something that the children of the first marriage had been expecting to receive. It also protested the denial of a still-single woman's chance to marry, if a widow were the one to rewed.

Women lost out legally in other ways as well after the 10th century. In the 12th century France limited a widow to the right to use the income of her dower property. She could no longer pass that property on to others after she was dead. In the 13th century, as part of the Norman conquerors' use of marriage to noble heiresses as means of bringing estates under Norman control, England gave a woman's husband full title to all the movable property she might have when she married. The widow's dower-right third was also returned to her husband's heirs at her death. By 1400, once a woman bore her husband a child in England, he could use all her property as he wished for 29 years from its birth. However, he could not alienate property unless she agreed. The western part of the European continent, on the other hand, did not see a conquering group use that proportion of one in five of all families having daughters but no sons to its own advantage. Perhaps as a consequence the lessening of women's property rights did not go as far as it did in England. Between the 12th and 14th centuries a woman in France became described more often as a "co-actor" with her husband in transactions involving either her or his property, and less often as a mere "consenter," even when it was his and not hers. In Wallonia in present-day Belgium either spouse had lifelong use of all the properties held by the couple if they had had a child before the other spouse died, rather than only the husband-widower having that right. In Spain, too, the widow became full successor to her husband in managing the family affairs. Women's position also began to recover in Italy in the 14th century, once they began to bequeath what they received and controlled as dowry to their daughters, for dowry purposes. By the 15th century more than ⅓ of the average dowry came from the mother. That gave her a stronger voice in marriage choices for her daughters than had been the case before.

During the 13th century, as dowry made its way to the fore as an effective requirement for marriage for all but the poorest, other changes took place too. The church exogamy rules began to be relaxed, on petition. Even first-cousin marriages were allowed among nobility and royalty, as a means of healing quarrels within kin groups. This was a reapplication to a new situation of the initial principle that marriage rules should serve the cause of general social harmony. The concept of men as heads of household flourished, rather than that of spouses as partners. It received support from the argument of Thomas Aquinas that woman was made from man, but not man from woman, at the time of the Creation. Aquinas's expressed wish for greater numbers of births—in the face of what seemed threats from the Muslim world, as the Crusaders of the preceding century began to lose ground in the Middle East—also strengthened existing tendencies to see a woman's role as childbearer and wife as the only legitimate one to allow her to take. It was ironic that these tendencies were being reinforced precisely when women's new outnumbering of men meant that in a monogamous and divorceless system, there was no way to place all women in that role anyway. Women had become a social problem. Putting women in convents was not a satisfactory solution to that problem, any more than accusing them of witchcraft and burning them at the stake. Still, not everything changed in the 13th century. The simple declaration of intent to marry remained enough to make a marriage valid if there were no impediments. A priest's blessing was not yet required, recommended though it was. Among ordinary folk, people still exchanged spouses by what amounted to mutual consent (despite the horror of the clergy), much like the 7th-century Anglo-Saxons, who took for granted the right of both men and women to divorce for reasonable cause and then remarry. Among those well enough off to look up a family tree, it was not usually difficult to win release from an unwanted marriage by finding that the exogamy rules had been transgressed, and therefore the supposed existing marriage was null and void.

The fact that the church's exogamy rules were bilaterally reckoned reinforced the tendencies toward bilateral kinship reckoning which already existed among the Germanic invaders, for such purposes as collecting and distributing wergild compensation or determining who inherited from the childless. In some Anglo-Saxon groups this reckoning of kin obligations and rights went all the way to the fifth cousins on both parents' sides. By the 6th century only Ireland was entirely patrilineally organized. The rest of Europe was organized bilaterally for at least some purposes. There might be reappearances (as in 11th-century northern Italy) of a tendency for brothers and their sons and grandsons to remain together in patrilineal-seeming patrilocal households, almost like the zadruga joint-communal households of 14th-century Serbia, with their rotating or elective leaders to act as representatives to the outside world. But except where patrilineality was encouraged by the policies of overlords, as in the Balkans and also parts of France, even such patrilocal households tended to move toward nuclear and bilaterally linked rather than only patrilineally linked forms.

Brother-households of the zadruga type only began to appear in the parts of Greece taken by western European Crusader-conquerors in the 13th century. They came into being there because the new overlords introduced the rule, followed in parts of France and elsewhere in the west, that if a property were divided among sons, then it would revert to the overlord at their deaths. Russian peasants also used the brother-household form. It was helpful for brothers to stay together as long as possible in the Russian communal village, with its periodic reassignment of land in accord with the size of a household. That pattern dated at least to the 13th century A.D. and probably earlier. Russian peasant villagers recognized the in-marrying of husbands for brotherless daughters. Their households tended to divide at about the time the brothers' children were reaching marriageable age. A Russian woman was expected to have as her dowry enough cloth for all her needs as wife and mother. She brought it into her new household in a chest, to which she kept the key and over whose contents she had absolute control. That was her contribution, which would balance the value of the household gear and cattle her husband would get when he and his brothers divided the household property among themselves.

In southern Italy (held by the Eastern or Byzantine Roman Empire longer than the north and center) daughters and sons always received equal shares, rather than sons being favored as in Lombard-controlled areas. In the Greek-speaking lands of the eastern Mediterranean equal partible inheritance was often achieved, as on Cyprus, by giving each child his or her share at the time of the first marriage. Equal partible inheritance may have made the acceptance of divorce in tbe Eastern church more bearable, since each child had his or her own portion to take from one marriage into another. Somewhat like Fulani herders, Greek Christian parents were supported by their children after the last son or daughter had been wed. Among the Norse, too, a parent who had distributed all lands to offspring was entitled to live with each recipient for a fraction of the year that corresponded to the portion of lands received.

The exogamy rules of the early medieval church effectively precluded recombining properties through cousin-marriage. As a result it is understandable that nobles and others began to develop *primogeniture* (inheritance by the eldest) and similar techniques to favor single rather than multiple heirs. By A.D. 800 the church itself was beginning to attempt to impose succession by the eldest son on its own cultivators in France and Italy, in an effort to avert both fragmentation of property and inconvenience of record-keeping. Almost everywhere in Europe, west and east, the tendency of large landholders was to try to do something of the kind, although the church tended to side against them lest they become too strong. Tenants themselves might prefer *ultimogeniture* (succession by the youngest), as in parts of 14th-century England. That meant less frequent transfer, and every transfer required a payment to the overlord. Ultimogeniture was practiced in the free communal villages of pre–1500 Rumania, with their periodic redistribution of land. The Rumanians were not resisting lords' exactions, though. Like agriculturalists in much of Southeast Asia (or for that matter in England or anywhere), they intended to allow older children to marry and move out, while giving the youngest both the responsibility and the inheritance. The youngest would usually have the fewest other dependents during the parents' old age, after all.

Where traditions of equal partible inheritance were too firmly entrenched to be set aside, as in much of northern Europe (and parts of Italy, Spain, Greece, and elsewhere), an overlord might impose a requirement that one heir buy out the rest by paying them their shares in installments. Bavaria in southern Germany affords one example. But where the classical Roman expectation that a father would favor one heir (but must divide at least $\frac{1}{3}$ among the rest) had continued to have some influence, as in much of Europe near the Mediterranean, any unwed offspring were likely to be allowed to remain at home with that one, favored, married heir, if they gave up all claim to a lesser portion. As early as the 11th century some French noble lineages were allowing only one son to marry. By the 12th century that practice was common in many parts of France. Yet at the same time nobles sought to marry all the daughters they could, to form alliances. In Ireland the still-strong agnatic lineages were also letting only one son per household marry by the 12th century, unless a father had more than one farmstead. In that case one son would be allowed to marry for each farmstead the father had. In lower Austria, farms were being transmitted through remarriage rather than by inheritance by at least the 13th century, in another variation on means of preventing fragmentation. The widow rewed. When she died her husband rewed. When he died his widow rewed. Each time the children of these marriages remained as workers on the farm, or else married onto another farm as opportunity became available. In upper Austria, slightly more productive, the usual practice was for the parents to retire to their own quarters when the heir-son married, turning the management of the farm over to him.

By at least the end of the 13th century primogeniture was being practiced in several areas of western Europe, though it never became accepted east of Poland. Primogeniture was swiftly followed by *entail* (nonalienability) of lands. By the late 13th century, in Castile in Spain, the right of entail was being granted as a special privilege to favored nobles. Entail would counteract the possibility that land given as either dowry or dower might be sold by the woman to whom it was given, diminishing her father's (and eventually her brother's) holdings if it were dowry or her husband's if it were dower. By the 14th century entail almost universally accompanied primogeniture among the nobility of western Europe. In England, as in other commercially developed areas, the use of entail led in turn to giving daughters cash as dowry. It also led to giving younger sons cash portions, rather than land, as their shares in inheritance. At levels below the nobility a father often built a house as dowry for his daughter, as in 13th-century England, or in some other way tried to provide some start in life for all the children but the major heir. By 1500, in England, that usually meant portions in cash. In France and elsewhere portions were still usually in goods, which indicates a somewhat lower level of commercialization. The concept of portioning all but the chief heir, among the nobility in particular, resembled another practice common among peasants and townspeople in most of continental Europe north of the Alps by the 15th century. That practice allowed offspring to take a portion in cash and movables at any time and leave the household. However, they were then denied any share in inheritance at the parents' deaths. This was the reverse of the practice in much of France after the 13th century, which required that any child (son or daughter) who took a portion and left must put it back into the estate when the parents died, so that all the estate could be divided equally among the children. In some areas that enforced return became optional rather than required. Probably it came originally from the practice of the Normans, who required all the sons to restore any portions they had taken when the time came to divide the estate, although the daughters did not return their dowries. Nevertheless, even if one did this, one could still benefit, for one could keep to oneself any increase one had succeeded in making.

In the middle of the 14th century, as all these changes were occurring, the great plague of the Black Death swept through Europe and devoured more than ⅓ of the population. The climate had again begun to cool slightly, lessening agricultural productivity and probably weakening resistance by lowering nutrition levels. The decimation meant new places were opened on farms and in town shops or workshops. New marriages could be made by survivors who could now afford to marry because decimation had consolidated inheritances. There may also have been new thoughts on the importance of individuals. It was less than two generations later, in 1406, that that first baptismal register was introduced. Either in the latter 14th century or in the course of the next century or so, what demographic historians have come to call the "western European pattern" of marriage came to be the norm in most of Europe, west of a line from today's border between Italy and Yugoslavia north to today's border between Russia and Finland. In this pattern five elements stand out. First, both sexes marry relatively late, around the mid–20s. Second, a significant number do not marry at all. Third, age difference between spouses is small. Fourth, members of both sexes tend to have lived in households other than their parents' for at least part of the decade preceding marriage, giving them a varied experience to draw on in creating their own household pattern. Fifth, childbearing begins relatively late for women, which makes population growth less rapid than it would otherwise be as life expectancies increase.

The rise of this western European marriage system is an excellent reason for regarding the 1406–1563 era as a transition time, in the development of marriage systems in European life. It may be an irony indeed that only as this period of transition passed drew to a close did rising commercialization and centralization in western Europe make it possible to install educated clergy in every parish. At precisely the same period when new opportunities for individuals outside the limits of the household were going to make the enforcement of household-centered rather than individuality-recognizing norms almost impossible, the ordinary parish clergy were finally well-enough educated to articulate and try to enforce the household-centered norms developed by the church during the period from Augustine to Aquinas. To the church, marriage was to be monogamous and absolutely indissoluble. Within marriage the primary goals were to be procreation and the proper rearing of the children by the father, with the mother as assistant. Yet commercialization and centralization were making equal partnership and mutual support a more reasonable pattern of spouse relationship. The 16th century saw Martin Luther's declaration that marriage is equal in worth to celibacy in the eyes of God, for the first time in the history of the Christian church. The 16th century also saw the recognition by exploring anatomist-physicians that a woman was physically perfect in her own sex, not (as Aristotle taught) an inferior version of a man. Both of these new concepts undercut the assumptions of women's inferiority on which Aquinas's thought had been based. The anatomist-physicians' discovery that men did not have a "missing" rib also undercut the belief that there was such an ongoing anatomical reminder of woman's being created from the body of man. It should therefore not be surprising that the next several centuries were to see dramatic changes in the interpretation and application of church-developed norms. Once European norms began to change, the local norms in portions of the world influenced by Europe began to be affected, as European merchants, missionaries, and settlers made their way into one region after another, unsettling old patterns and facilitating or even introducing new ones everywhere they went.

CHAPTER 9

Marriage in Industrial-Commercial Societies: Background and General Considerations

A number of changes prepared the way for the shift in western European marriage patterns between the decades from the Black Death of 1348 to 1406, when baptismal registers were introduced, and the decades from the preaching of Luther in the 1520s that marriage and celibacy were equally worthy in God's eyes to 1563, when the Roman Catholic Church proclaimed that the two partners' consent was what was essential in marriage rather than the consent of their families.

When Augustine (A.D. 354–430) preached that indissoluble monogamous marriage was the only true Christian mode, there was a shortage of women which forced men to compete for wives. That shortage made it socially necessary to dignify celibacy as an alternative for men, if neither divorce nor polyandry was to be accepted. Elevating celibacy as morally preferable to marriage was a means of doing so. Women continued to be scarce through the next five centuries of invasions and turmoil. The balance between the numbers of men and of women only began to shift as some measure of peace returned, as population and productivity grew, and as towns (with their somewhat less harsh conditions for women in particular) began to draw immigrants from rural areas. By perhaps the 12th century women became more numerous than men. Women therefore began to want dowry from parents so that they would not have to enter institutional celibate life for lack of potential spouses. Women were no longer sources of bride-wealth to parents, or recipients of more dower from a husband than they might bring in dowry.

This fundamental change accompanied a lowering of status for noble women all over western Europe during the 13th to 15th centuries. The rise of primogeniture and entail among the nobility meant that heirship could no longer be transferred through women. Increasing use of wet-nurses lessened noblewomen's importance in the rearing of their own children, even though its initial purpose was to free them for other household duties.

Primogeniture and entail were meant to ensure the maintenance through the generations of the core property required to support the needs of a noble household. But they carried with them a modification of previous bilateral patterns toward patrilineal inheritance. That inevitably diminished the recognition given to women, even though the church retained a fully bilateral reckoning for incest rules. Wet-nursing was meant to enable noblewomen whose husbands had left on long military campaigns to undertake the full supervision of family properties more quickly than could otherwise be done. When wet-nursing was introduced, in the 11th and 12th centuries, those supervisory tasks still fell to wives when their husbands were away; and from the 11th century onward monarchs began to call on their noble vassals for longer and longer periods of warfare against foes. Even the church began to call on nobles for lengthy campaigns, as the era of the Crusades began. Nevertheless, the use of wet-nurses eventually worked against the position of noblewomen in their own households.

During the Crusader era the courtly love ideal of an ennobling love for an unattainable lady—unattainable usually because already a nobleman's wife—came into being as a kind of secular counterpart to the veneration of the Virgin Mary, mother of Jesus, as Queen of Heaven. The courtly love ideal gave a sublimated outlet for sexual drives, both to noblewomen whose husbands were absent and to younger sons of nobles. Younger sons of nobles needed an outlet. They were being increasingly discouraged from marriage, especially in parts of France, to try to lessen the likelihood of inheritance disputes. Yet the idealization of courtly love, like the separation of noblewomen from the tasks of lactation and child care and the longstanding idealization of celibacy, tended subtly to degrade ordinary straightforward marital life.

The downgrading of the marital relationship helped to enable the Norman conquerors to manipulate the laws of England to deprive English women increasingly of control over their own property. Their intent was to improve the Norman position through marrying Norman knights to Anglo-Saxon heiresses. One result was to make 1066, the year of the Norman Conquest, current news in the United States in 1982. That year's failure of the Equal Rights Amendment to the United States Constitution meant the continuance in some states of laws based on English common law, which followed the Norman conquerors' deliberate removal of married women's and even widows' rights to any property they brought into marriage or inherited while married. Lawmakers in France and elsewhere also limited the control of wives over their own property, but they did not usually limit that of widows. Outside of England it did not become possible for a husband to dispose of any of his wife's movable property without her consent. In England it did. Yet even the peasant wife in Russia was recognized by village custom as having absolute control over the cloth she brought to her husband's household at marriage. What she wove after marriage was to be for their daughters' marriages.

The laws that lessened noblewomen's role in the management of property were primarily meant to aid nobles and keep them loyal to rulers. However, these laws affected wealthy merchants and other townspeople too. They had less effect on the vast majority of the population in the peasantry. Tenure and transmission of cultivation rights usually went by whatever rules prevailed locally, as a result of longstanding local custom combined with hard bargaining between peasants and overlords as both sought to turn custom to their own advantage. Yet peasants also tended consistently to lessen sisters', widows', and daughters' rights in favor of surviving males, echoing what was happening at the higher levels of society.

By the end of the 15th century there was an obvious incongruity between the increasing recognition of the individuality of each human being and the continuing lack of recognition of the individuality of both women and younger sons. Recognition of individuality appeared in the instituting of baptismal and burial registers, which even took note of stillbirths in some areas. That contrasted sharply with the increase in husbands' control over wives' property during the preceding period, and the accompanying diminution of dower and other property rights for widows. It also contrasted with the limits placed on younger sons, not only by primogeniture and entail at upper social levels, but also by the spread of overlords' efforts to simplify their dealings with the peasantry between the 13th and 15th centuries. In western Europe most overlords came to require their cultivating tenants to use some kind of single-heirship, so as to make it easier to collect rents, fees, and dues. In eastern Europe most overlords came to require some kind of rarely dividing extended-family household. In western Europe the inevitable result was a favoring of one son over others. In eastern Europe the result was often the eldest son's dominance over his brothers after their father's death, even though the expressed ideal was brotherly cooperation.

In western but not in eastern Europe that incongruity between recognizing and controlling individuals was resolved for women in at least one direction during the 16th century. Both Roman Catholic and Reformed branches of the church came to recognize a woman's right to put her conscience above what had been preached as her marital duty to obey her husband. Both Roman Catholics and Reformed upheld her right to maintain her church affiliation, and to rely on her pastor's rather than her husband's instructions in matters such as child-rearing, if they were in conflict. But in another direction the incongruity became intensified for women by the antiwitchcraft mania of the age, which branded almost any nonconformity as a possible sign of witchcraft—among women far more often than among men. In the Reformed churches more respect for women was implicit in the recognition of marriage as not morally inferior to celibacy, now that there was no longer a shortage of women to make such lofty rationalizations useful for expecting celibacy of a large number of men. However, greater respect for women was counterbalanced by the tendency to emphasize the role of the father-husband of the household as its head, the one responsible for Christian instruction as ministers replaced priests and veneration faded for the Virgin Mary and the saints. This emphasis on the father-husband's responsibility tended to put the mother-wife into a subordinate role, in the household's religious life. The mother-wife who could turn to a sacramentally ordained priest to counterbalance a father-husband's harshness, in the Roman Catholic fold, probably had more room to maneuver than the mother-wife in the Reformed fold. Still, by the end of the 16th century, both the Roman Catholic and the various Reformed churches were beginning to teach that mutual comfort and solace were fully as important in marriage as the bearing and proper rearing of children.

The view that mutual solace is as important a priority in marriage as procreation had remained standard throughout the centuries in Orthodox Christendom to the east. It may well have contributed to the Greek Orthodox recognition of the importance of basic compatibility, in allowing divorce with right of remarriage (up to three times), and for "spiritual adultery" as well as physical adultery. This limited right of divorce and remarriage acknowledged an individual's right to seek that solace, rather than stay tied to one with whom solace seemed impossible to find. It also fitted the ongoing recognition in both the Roman and the Orthodox branches of the church that the spouses' consent, rather than their parents', was the proper basis for a marriage. Witness again the role of godparents (in Orthodox Christian Greece in particular) in assuring that the bride's and groom's consent were freely given. Witness also what Thomas More's 16th-century contemporaries thought of as a radical suggestion in *Utopia*, that when a marriage between two persons was proposed, each should be able to look at the other entirely unclothed in front of chaperone-witnesses and then be free to refuse or agree.

Given this recognition of mutual solace as a chief priority of marriage, it is not surprising that the 16th and 17th centuries saw considerable acceptance for the extramarital amours of royal and noble husbands. The level of acceptance for extramarital amours on the part of royal and noble wives was considerably lower because of their duty to bear heirs. There was a strong demand that wives' fidelity remain unquestionable, at least until after they had borne what seemed likely to be enough potential heirs. Still, even wives' amours were tolerated in some degree. It was recognized that at the levels of royalty and nobility, marriages were often arranged for purely territorial and property considerations, with little or no consideration of personal compatibility. This grated on people's sensibilities, in an age that was half-consciously starting to recognize the marriage bond's growing importance in comparison to other family ties. Yet it was clear that the centralizing national governments of the time were trying to weaken the power of the great nobles through strict control over their marriages. Dictating whom, when, and even whether a nobleman or noblewoman could marry was as much a part of royal policy as consuming the nobles' wealth by honoring them with visits to their estates, using educated clergy and townsmen in government positions, or ennobling some of the new officeholders, as competitors for royal favor whose presence at court would dilute and weaken the older nobility.

Personal attraction rather than familial arrangement did not begin to receive serious consideration as a primary basis for marriage until the 18th century. Only then did compatibility begin to outweigh the three economics-centered considerations of personal capacity, family property and connections, and family health and longevity, among the four basic considerations suggested earlier as governing human marriage choices. This change took place at first primarily in England. Both economic and political change had proceeded much further by the 18th century in England than elsewhere, either in Europe, in most of Europe's American colonies, or even in Japan, the most commercialized and centralized of Asian states and the only one to have a comparable suprafamilial system of registration. Since the early 17th century the government of Japan had required the registration of all births, marriages, and deaths at a Buddhist temple of the family's choice. This system was instituted and maintained to ensure that no Japanese continued to profess Christianity, after it was prohibited out of fear that its followers cared more for foreign Christian teachers' instructions than for the orders of their own Japanese overlords.

High levels of commercialization and centralization are necessary to a recognition of the appropriateness of both partners selecting each other, rather than at most (for the woman at least) acquiescing or not acquiescing in a parental choice. Acceptance of the appropriateness of the self-selection of partners also requires a recognition of the individual as being of enough direct concern to sacred and secular authorities as an individual, not merely as a family member, to be worth recording at birth. Yet Japan demonstrates that these conditions alone are not sufficient. Something else is also needed.

Something else was also present, in the western European marriage system as described by Hajnal. This was the comparative maturity in age of both partners in first marriages, with both partners tending to have reached the middle or late 20s. That was not the case in Japan, where women tended to marry at a noticeably earlier age than men. True, 18th-century Japanese women were apt to be past 20 when they married, which seems seldom to have been the case elsewhere in Asia, or in the Middle East, Africa, the Pacific, or the Americas. But Japanese women in the 18th century seldom reached the middle 20s without marrying. Japanese men tended to marry first in their late 20s, as in western Europe in the 18th century, but also as in a good many bride-wealth-using societies, in which a young man might have to wait for years to obtain needed bride-wealth aid from his household and lineage segment.

A young woman still in her teens or not long out of them could be more easily propelled into a marriage than could a more mature woman. Others could manage her affairs even more easily if she lacked experience outside the parental household. This was the common situation in Japan, but it was uncommon in western Europe. In western Europe, and particularly in England, a woman was as likely as her husband to have lived in a household that was neither her natal home nor his. She had therefore experienced and observed more than young women in most societies. She also had some possibility, however faint, of support or backing from within that other household (and also from godparents), if she found a proposed marriage to be absolutely unacceptable.

Shakespeare's *Romeo and Juliet*, that great and lastingly popular tragedy of love, was still a warning to its first audiences in the 1590s that to choose one's own spouse, rather than await one's family's arrangements, could bring unhappiness and even death to both oneself and the one chosen. It was only half a century after More's *Utopia* had suggested a need for opportunity to veto a parent's choice. It was hardly more than a generation after the Roman Catholic Church accepted the converse of that right of veto, in forbidding the annulling of a marriage on the ground of parental opposition to it. Yet in the play's sympathy for the young lovers it spoke more insistently to every succeeding later generation of the ultimate pre-ferability of letting partners choose each other, rather than putting family considerations above individual choice. In that it was to England what *Antigone* had been to Athens—a setting forth of the claims of individuality against the rule of family, as *Antigone* had set forth the claims of family against the rule of the state—but in reverse. *Antigone* spoke for the family rule of the past. *Romeo and Juliet* spoke for the individualism of the future. The pair were properly married. Their voluntary vows had been blessed by a priest, who could be perceived as seeing (though Shakespeare barely hints it) that such a marriage might benefit the larger society by bringing an end to the longstanding feud between their families. The play showed the use of their untimely deaths to end that family feud. It pointed a finger of accusation at the families as having caused the married lovers' deaths by their feuding. It spoke to the growing sense among western Europeans—Jews and Christians both—that every visibly kin-linked family was itself part of a still larger family, whether that family was seen as the nation-state (excluding all foreigners), western Europe (excluding all beyond a line from Finland to Austria), western Christendom or all of Christendom (excluding Europe's Jews), or all humanity (but still, for all except perhaps the closest followers of Francis of Assisi, largely excluding nonhuman orders of living beings).

In the long run the tragedy of *Romeo and Juliet* preached that in overriding the interests of the visibly kin-linked family, that larger family (however it might be interpreted) was serving its own interest. The larger family was keeping harmony among its members by limiting the authority of the smaller one. The larger family was seeking to provide more opportunity for individuals to develop their own potentialities, make their own choices, and live their own lives in accord with their own mixtures of potentialities.

For some a sense of the larger social family took an absolutist nation-state-centered turn, as in the line of development that ran from Machiavelli and Hobbes in the 16th and 17th centuries to Mussolini and Hitler in the 20th. Nation-state absolutism often carried with it a belief that all economic activity should be closely controlled by the central government. Only an all-commanding central government, ruling a people who could regard themselves as historical and cultural even if not visibly consanguine kin, seemed to absolutists to be capable of success in the existing competition among nation-states. They saw the nation-state as a kind of hunting-gathering band writ large, but far less egalitarian than actual hunting-gathering bands in its lack of opportunity for nonleaders to take any active part in deciding on plans for the future.

For others a sense of the larger social family took a more egalitarian direction. They were open to the idea that each nation-state was also a member of the family of nations, but they still largely focused on the nation-state. This line of development was followed in the increasingly democratic industrial-commercial capitalist states—first England, eventually all of western Europe, and in varying degree their overseas colonies. In these states economic activity was merely regulated, given rules of fair play but otherwise not controlled by government. The family came to be similarly treated—regulated, given what were intended to be rules of fair play, but not directly controlled. For the upholders of democratic capitalism the nation-state was still the hunting-gathering band writ large, but in its alliance-seeking more than its territory-seeking mode.

For still others a sense of the larger social family took some grander form, beyond the limits of nation-state boundaries—like western Europe, or Christendom. However, that sense was seldom operative in a practical way, except to justify some alliance that included many of the nation-states in that grander form.

For those for whom all humanity was seen as the larger family, this vision might be used to justify overthrowing a single nation-state government (such as the Russian monarchy in 1917) that was failing to meet the openly expressed needs of large numbers of its own people. All too often the call to see all humanity as the larger social family resulted in replacing an old nation-state-centered absolutism with a new absolutism that sought to unite the entire human family behind its ideological banner. Nevertheless, it always carried with it a freeing of the individual from the explicit control of kin. Even though it proceeded to put the individual under the equally explicit control of the central government, it generally did not go so far as actually to arrange marriages. The government might provide opportunities for meeting potential spouses, through its policies and programs. But the final choice of spouses was up to the individuals themselves. The government might assign one to a job, as had the family in the past. But it left one's spouse-choice free, as the family had not.

To a person in a democratic capitalist nation-state, with its emphasis on individualism, the amount of control over individual choices of career, of residence, and of leisure activity in a land such as the People's Republic of China seems oppressive. But to Chinese themselves—newly freed from the even greater control of the old-style Chinese family, and able to choose their own spouses from those among whom they live and work—the new regime is genuinely (even if incompletely) liberating. The aging author of a still-popular novel on the old-style Chinese family, which became the sensation of the literate few when it was first published in 1931, was still being thanked half a century later by young readers for giving them the courage to resist parental pressures to accept unwanted partners. The closeness between the marriage-ages currently recommended in China (25 for women and 28 for men) and the actual marriage-ages of early modern western Europe offers some confirmation of the hypothesis that later marriage for both sexes is needed in a marriage system which accepts mutual partner-choice, rather than parent-choice, as its major means of arranging marriages. The strong effort made in China to ensure that both daughters and sons work with others besides the members of their own families, even in the villages, confirms the hypothesis that opportunity for both sexes to interact with a variety of nonkin of both sexes in situations outside the home is also required in such a marriage system. The lessening of the age difference between spouses, which results from the rise in women's marriage-ages, means less widowhood. This in turn helps to make it likelier that aging parents can maintain their own household if they wish, rather than a widowed parent having to move in with a married son or daughter in order to survive. When parents do reside with a son or daughter, there can therefore be an element of choosing to pool resources, rather than its being a matter of utter necessity. The People's Republic of China also recognizes spouses' right to inherit from each other what individual property there is to inherit in a socialist society. That right did not exist in traditional Chinese practice, which effectively treated a woman as at most a trustee for her sons, whether a trustee for her father (as in a uxorilocal marriage) or for her deceased husband. The acceptance of mutual inheritance rights for spouses serves as a partial parallel to the acceptance of the concept of the conjugal fund in medieval Europe. As shown in Chapter 7, the substitution of a conjugal fund (what husband and wife bring to the marriage and add to while the marriage lasts) for a lineage fund (what is held by the lineage segment to which the couple is attached), as the basis for both the support of a widowed spouse and the eventual inheritance of their offspring, always marks a crucial shift in the history of a marriage system.

In brief, commercialization, centralization, and a suprafamilial mode of registering births, marriages, and deaths (implying that the individual matters as an individual, not only as a member of a family) form one set of the necessary conditions required to make possible the full acceptance of partners' direct selection of each other. Relatively late marriage for women as well as for men, combined with a variety of experience great enough to give both sexes sufficient grounds on which to base a reasonable choice, form the other set of necessary conditions. Direct selection differs from the situations found in parts of Africa, Southeast Asia, and the Pacific (but only rarely elsewhere in Asia and virtually never in the Middle East) before modern times, where young men and women were expected and enabled to become acquainted with each other as part of the process of arranging marriages. In those situations it was indeed expected that the young would give their parents or other adult guardians some indication of their preferences. However, it was also expected that they would accept any parental vetoes, and would let their elders make the final arrangements.

For people to be willing to wait to marry, as part of a marriage system that relies on mutual partner-choice, not marrying young has to appear a viable option. Singleness has to be seen as a situation in which it is possible to live satisfyingly for a number of years, or even perhaps for all of one's life. The lower percentage of married people in urban as compared with rural populations, not only in modern societies, but also to some degree in other societies, may reflect a number of factors. It may reflect in part the fact that women in cities now usually outnumber men, who can thus feel confident that they are not lessening their chance to find a satisfactory partner through waiting. It may reflect in part the frequent tendency of newcomers to maintain ties with their place of origin, and to wait to marry until they are well-enough established to be able to persuade someone from that place to come to join them. More important, however, it probably reflects the greater availability in cities of four sets of opportunities for a single person—jobs; facilities for meeting everyday needs like food, shelter, and clothing; facilities for meeting extraordinary needs like illness; and avocational activities ranging from serious to playful. But there were other elements besides these general factors in delaying marriage, as Europe began to urbanize with increasing rapidity after the 16th century. Some of these were distinctively western European; some were not.

Late marriage linked with parental control of property was not unusual for men in bride-wealth systems, but it was highly unusual for women. Late marriage linked with parental control of property could become usual for both men and women in dowry systems, however. Ordinarily the parental wish to ensure a daughter's marriage to an appropriate husband through using dowry would lead to relatively late marriage for men and relatively early marriage for women. However, that could be counteracted (for the woman) by a system such as that found in much of Greece, which only abolished dowry as a legal requirement for marriage in 1983. There, the betrothal was arranged early, but the actual marriage was delayed until the promised dowry was amassed through the labors of the woman's family.

Not only in Europe but elsewhere late marriage and even singleness might accompany a willingness to retain unmarried adult offspring in the household as workers, at least where monogamy rather than polygyny or polyandry prevailed. Not only in Europe but also elsewhere servants might be expected to remain unmarried. Slaves in many past societies might not be able to contract a legal marriage under any circumstances unless first set free. And not only in Europe but also elsewhere—in Buddhist lands in particular—celibate religious orders might exist as an alternative mode of life for those attracted to them.

What was unusual in Europe, even particular to Europe, was twofold: the acceptance of the celibate life as a moral goal for more than just those who formally entered and practiced it (either from religious devotion or because of family or other pressure), and the placement of maturing offspring of both sexes in others' households, either as apprentices and servants from commoners' families, or as attendants of an ostensibly more exalted sort from more aristocratic ones. Acceptance of the celibate ideal was half-present in India, in the Hindu ideal of withdrawal from household life into a hermit or eventually an ascetic mode once one's first grandson had been born. But the perpetuation of the family was to precede, not to be replaced by, the celibate ideal in adult Hindu life. The celibate ideal was more than half-present among Buddhists, who accepted it as in some sense an eventual necessity for all. However, Buddhists regarded entry into celibate religious life as not necessarily a goal in the current life. It could be a goal in some future life instead. Upper-caste Hindus in India sent their sons into a teacher's household, as students of the scriptures, for the years between childhood and marriage. But daughters did not similarly leave.

Both celibacy and service in another household meant acceptance of a nonmarital form of separation from one's natal family as part (or for the religious celibate, all) of life after childhood. Each meant entry into a different household: the religious household of the monastery or convent, or the employer's household, or the fellow-elite member's household. It did not mean the formation of a single-person household, like almost one in four households in the United States by 1987; but it did acknowledge the status of unmarried maturing-or-mature adult as a real phase of adult life, separate from family life.

Historians of domestic architecture have noted that the introduction of central hallways into the residences of European nobility, and then into the homes of wealthy commoners, marked a desire for greater privacy. Once central hallways began to be used, in the 18th century, household members no longer had to pass through each others' rooms to get to their own. Like the acceptance of a period of unmarried life outside one's own natal home as a normal experience, this meant a greater recognition of individuality. Such acknowledgment of the person as a person, not only as a member of a family, is a necessary condition for self-selection of spouses to seem more appropriate than family arrangement of marriages for their members.

In the course of the 18th century in England very young children were freed from many previous restraints on their physical activity, such as swaddling; but earlier demands were made on them for habits of cleanliness and self-control. These changes in child-rearing also suggest a recognition of the individual, both as wanting freedom of action and as needing to learn reliance on self rather than on others for personal care. Whipping, which reminded the child of the parent's power, came to be replaced by exile to a room or closet as a recommended form of discipline. This suggested the separability of the child from the family as an individual, even while it used the child's desire not to be separated from the family to try to make the child obedient.

Other factors also played a part in the process of acknowledging a distinction between the individual and the family. In the commercializing, urbanizing, and centralizing societies of the 15th century A.D. onward in western Europe it came to be recognized that more than just a few favored or fortunate individuals might change status in their own lifetime, whether from agricultural day-laborer to settled peasant or town-dweller, from peasant to town-dweller, or within a town from assistant to person in charge of a shop or workshop. By the 16th century the inclination to use godparenthood for personal and family purposes (which had brought the Roman Catholic Church to begin limiting the number of godparents in the 14th century) was bringing governments in western European states to forbid peasants to ask townspeople to be godparents, or anyone to ask anyone to be a godparent who was not personally known. Governments were trying to slow the already accelerating pace of social change by forestalling the selection of godparents on the basis of their capacity to facilitate such changes in status. Such limitations were hardly a recognition of individual rights. However, they show that families were trying to aid individual family members, through the selection of godparents who would probably be of more immediate help to that individual than to his or her family as a whole. People were beginning to think in terms of planning for a future which could be different from the past, in that commercializing era. They were no longer thinking only of a future that would keep repeating past experience.

Early modern Europeans still had to think in terms of possible disaster periods of as long as two years of famine and disease. Such disaster periods did not end until the late 17th century in England, the late 18th century in France, and the 19th century in Russia, Scandinavia, and Ireland. Famine and disease helped to keep long-term population growth down to less than

1% per year in most of Europe (and indeed much of the rest of the world) through the 18th century. The lowest growth rates were to be found in the more densely populated areas, the Mediterranean lands and France, which suggests rather clearly that peasants in particular were trying to match births to deaths.

Ideally a peasant couple in an already fully settled region would be survived only by a son to inherit and a daughter to exchange—in effect—for a daughter-in-law. Unless there was access to new land to cultivate (either nearby or able to be moved to fairly readily) or access to other means of livelihood besides working the land (either nearby or accessible to migration), having more than two children would threaten partition of the lands that the household cultivated. The introduction of cash crops could also modify peasants' thinking, if the profitability of cash crops made it possible for a smaller holding to support a married pair and their unmarried offspring.

On the other hand, early modern European day-laborers, both rural and urban, saw children as extra earners rather than as dividers of a nonexistent set of land-use rights. Day-laborers therefore tended to be relatively prolific, as long as wages continued to be calculated on the basis of supporting only the individual worker. That calculation was based on the assumption that the worker was part of a household in which all worked except the very youngest, not on the assumption that a worker might have dependents to provide for. It was a self-defeating strategy for those who thought that paying only enough to support one person would discourage marriage and childbearing, and thus keep the numbers of the poor down to a manageable few. Instead, low pay encouraged marriage as a means of pooling resources. Low pay also encouraged childbearing as a means of having additional incomes to pool, as long as children went to work rather than to school when they were old enough to do simple tasks.

The early-19th-century British campaign for paying a man a "living wage," one on which he could support a wife and children, was intended to end child labor. It was also meant to ensure that the nonworking children would have a mother who was free to tend them. But it played its own role in the demographic transition to fewer children per married couple, for it cut the previous link between income level and number of workers for the nuclear family. It thereby made it economically preferable for wage workers to have fewer children among whom to divide income, rather than to have more children to bring in more income.

The conjugal or nuclear family that was encouraged by the "living wage" movement fitted the needs of an industrializing society well. With the husband as primary wage earner, the nuclear family could easily move as jobs moved, and could manage to be psychologically as well as geographically distant from kin. But that only held true as long as the wife's role consisted entirely of being a provider of services (like baby-tending, previously provided by others while she herself worked) and manager of the family income (shopping, and then preparing purchases for use). As the state began providing services like education, and as couples came to have fewer children, wives in industrial societies began once more to work outside the home. Even before state-provided services and smaller families made that possible wives were already supplementing family incomes by doing things at home, like taking in lodgers and boarders. Such home lodging and boarding houses were also one of the ways the not-yet-married could obtain shelter and food while working in a new locality. However, once married women entered the workplace, they almost always found that the years used to raise children put them behind men, in terms of the kinds of positions and incomes they could attain. Only the few mothers who could obtain enough assistance with daily tasks so that they could remain almost continuously in the work force could hope to achieve positions and incomes comparable to those of men. To do so they had to rely either on kin or on employing the services of others with part of their own income. Despite these realities the ideology of the "living wage" movement was so appealing and pervasive that even the widowed mother (or, later, the divorced one), who was in fact the primary wage earner for her household, was often lumped together with the childless woman and the currently married woman, as "not needing" a "living wage" on which to "raise a family." Women were therefore usually not paid as much as men who were doing comparable work.

The urban merchant or artisan with a business to pass on to an heir was apt to behave (reproductively speaking) like the peasant, rather than like the low-paid day-laborer, unless the business was expanding rapidly enough to make either division or partnership seem feasible in the next generation. (In Japan, from the 17th century onward, a merchant might send a younger son to another city to open a branch shop, in a kind of early chain-store system.) In the 18th century the introduction of inoculation for smallpox brought a new element into family fertility calculations in western Europe. So did the introduction of stoves instead of fireplaces for heating, which made it harder for the plague bacillus to survive. The growing use of quarantine also made it harder for the plague bacillus to spread. Once these and other changes, such as drainage of mosquito-harboring swamps, brought a decline in mortality in western Europe, France became the first country in which fertility also began to decline. People in other countries, such as England, turned to emigration before they began to follow the French in limiting births.

Altogether, from A.D. 1500 to 1950 about 45 million Europeans migrated to North America. Another 20 million Europeans went to Latin America, and 10 million went to Australia, New Zealand, and parts of Africa south of the Sahara. Thus almost twice as many Europeans, 75 million of them, emigrated between 1500 and 1950 as the 15 million taken out of Africa by the slave trade between 1500 and 1900 (mainly to the Americas, but also to the Middle East and India) *plus* the 25 million Asians, mostly from China and India, who went as contract laborers or as free migrants to other parts of Asia, to Africa, and also to some of the Pacific Islands and parts of the Americas between 1500 and 1950.

During the 19th century, when the steamship opened opportunity for voluntary overseas migration to more people (in Asia, too, not just in Europe), some of the European migration came from areas in which partible inheritance prevailed. However, more of it came from areas in which either a single-heir system prevailed, or it was legally possible for one heir to receive the bulk of the parental property and the rest to be given only small amounts. In the latter case the less favored heirs could ask for their portion to use as passage money, even while their parents still lived. Earlier this had been done at marriage (for women in particular) or as a means of enabling less favored heirs to migrate from countryside to city (or from one town to another more apparently flourishing town). In regions of equal partible inheritance, though, an heir's prospects were best if he (or she) remained near home to claim a rightful share when the time came. Early Greek and Italian migrants to the Americas were often married men who left their wives behind to make that claim for them. Only then would it be decided on which side of the Atlantic the couple would reunite.

It is true that China and India, from which most Asian migrants came, were lands of partible inheritance. However, most of those migrants initially expected to return home. They generally went as men alone, even if already married. Moreover, if they did not return, their expected shares might be so small as to seem far less attractive than the promise of a new life in a new place. By the middle of the 19th century the per capita level of production and income in both China and India was noticeably lower than in all but the poorest parts of Europe. In fact, it was beginning to decline visibly from past levels, in parts of those two Asian lands. Consequently what a family might have to pass on to heirs grew less and less attractive, in comparison to the lure of a new start.

Late marriage was of course one means of keeping births down everywhere. Probably one fewer child was born for every three years' delay in marriage after the age of 16, for women. With an average marriage age around 25 for women in many western European communities from the 16th to the 20th century, those women who reached their 40s probably had three fewer children than if they had married at the earlier ages then prevalent in other societies. In the North American colonies of the 17th and 18th centuries, on the other hand, with new lands fairly readily available for settlement, marriage-ages were four to six years younger for both sexes than in western Europe.

One wonders what the full significance of the Black Death of 1348 may have been. At least in England it was followed by rising wages for day-laborers, and by openings for peasants' children on vacated lands and for merchants' and artisans' children in vacated shops and workshops. Day-laborers were suddenly in short supply—a situation that did not last long, not so much because of population growth as because of changes in government policies. These changes enabled great landholders to squeeze peasants into yielding customary privileges. Many of those peasants ended by giving up their holdings and becoming day-laborers. The immediate aftermath of 1348 seems to have been a realization that not only was it advantageous to limit fertility to available opportunity; it could also be stimulating to technological improvements (like the introduction of windmills) to have neither too few nor too many people to make those improvements profitable. Demographer J. J. Spengler has pointed out, in an article in David Glass and Roger Revelle's collection *Population and Social Change* (1972), that the 0.33% per year rate of population growth in England between 1700 and 1800 made possible a savings rate (for capital investment) of up to 6% more of total national income than could have been saved with a population growth of 1% per year. That made a crucial difference in England's ability to forge ahead of other societies in per capita income. The English could afford a relatively high level of capital investment, in transportation (roads and canals), in new industrial inventions, and in the factory buildings in which those inventions could be most efficiently linked to the new power source of steam. In 1700 per capita income in England was probably about the same as in most of the rest of the entire world. There was little noticeable difference between Asia and Europe, Europe and Africa, any of these and the Americas. But by 1800 western Europe as a whole (England in particular) was pulling ahead. So was North America. By 1800 in England per capita income was about 75% higher than in any area outside of Europe and North America, except probably Japan. The growth in the proportion of working adults to dependents, as life expectancies lengthened, also played its part. That was true in Japan also, not only in Europe and North America. In Japan as well as in countries like England, France, and Sweden, fully 60% of the population was aged 15 to 64 by 1750. That proportion rose only slightly between 1750 and 1965. But the percentage above 65 grew, while the percentage below 15 declined, and many people over 65 could and did still contribute productively. As late as 1965, in mainland Asia, Africa, and Latin America, only 54% were in the 15 to 64 age group, with almost none over 65. That made it far harder for people in those regions to produce enough to provide for investment, as well as for necessary consumption, than it was in the lands with a higher percentage in the 15 to 64 range.

Late marriage for both sexes has remained prevalent in western Europe. Only in Spain (45%), France (42%), and Italy (40%) were more than ⅓ of the women married by the time they reached 25 in 1900, according to Hajnal. Marriage ages in other parts of western Europe have declined slightly since then, but only slightly. That contrasts with most Asian, African, and

Middle Eastern lands, where in the mid–20th century more (often far more) than ⅔ of women were married by age 25. Populations grew more rapidly in 19th-century Europe than before, except in still largely agricultural France. That was because both internal migration and external migration were possible, internal migration to nearby cities whose industrial growth opened new jobs and external migration to other countries or even overseas. It was also because of increasing life expectancies, which lengthened from perhaps about 35 in 1750 to about 50 in 1900. That meant not only more children born, because of women's longer lives, but more surviving to reach maturity. As this came to be recognized, from Malthus's day on, two sets of responses emerged: a growing interest in contraceptive methods and an increasing call for limitation of conjugal intercourse. The call for less frequent intercourse was usually linked with an ideology of wifely lack of interest, which differentiated the "good" (and uninterested) wives and mothers from "bad" other women. This ideology resembled a similar distinction long made between "pure" and "impure" women among Spaniards and Portuguese, in particular. For them, and for others who thought similarly, manliness meant either maintaining one's own honor against attacks on it or depriving another of honor by a successful attack. However, womanliness meant maintaining one's own honor despite attacks, and also demonstrating moral superiority to men by self-control in all situations, including intercourse. These two concepts of manliness and womanliness can be summed up in the terms *machismo* and *marianismo*, respectively. They are discussed more fully in Chapter 12, in connection with Latin American experience.

Not marrying at all could of course be another means to limit total births. In that, as well as in late marriage for both sexes, western Europe was unique. In every western European country in 1900 at least 10% of all women were still unmarried at age 45. In both Sweden and Portugal one in five women reached that age unwed. However, in virtually no mid–20th-century Asian, African, or Middle Eastern country were even 5% still unmarried at 45. The usual range was 1% to 3%. That situation was more like the situation in eastern Europe in 1900, where the range was 1% to 4%. Even in the mid–20th century this difference between western and eastern Europe was still visible. It finally began to diminish somewhat after 1950, as marriage became slightly less universal in eastern Europe and slightly more universal in western Europe.

The higher percentages of nonmarrying women in western Europe were doubtless linked to the pattern of later marriage for both sexes. Yet even with the evident tendency of widowers to marry previously unmarried women, at least before the 20th century, it was still the case that more women than men remained unmarried. (In woman-short Taiwan in the early 20th century younger widows married previously unmarried men, thereby enabling more men to marry.) The difference in the percentages of men and women marrying would never be great. Seldom was the percentage of men marrying more than 2% to 3% different in either direction from the percentage of women marrying, either in western and eastern Europe in the first half of the 20th century, or in Asia, Africa, or the Middle East in the mid–20th century But those higher western European percentages of both nonmarrying women and nonmarrying men were also linked to inheritance systems that favored one son as heir, while guaranteeing support for the unmarried siblings as long as they stayed with him. Economic prospects inevitably affected decisions about marriage for younger siblings in such a situation. Could one afford to? Would oneself and one's spouse be able to make a go of it? It was precisely the opposite question to that asked in universally marrying societies (could one afford not to?). In those societies one's family was one's sole reliance, no alternative social institutions being available to provide needed services. However, affordability was influenced by other factors besides inheritance systems. It was also influenced by sex ratio (are the costs of obtaining a satisfactory partner, such as bride-wealth or dowry, too high because of shortage?) and by the probabilities and costs of divorce. These differ between a divorce-disapproving society, such as an overwhelmingly Roman Catholic one, and a divorce-accepting one, such as an overwhelmingly Muslim one. By 1986 the only states in the entire world that did not have legal provisions for divorce and remarriage were Ireland, the Philippines, and three Latin American states, all heavily Roman Catholic.

Early Christian church leaders used scriptural texts to teach that a properly made marriage was indissoluble, in reaction to two very real social problems of that era. One was men's use of divorce without considering the divorced wife's chances for mere survival or trying to work out whatever difficulties existed in the marriage. The Roman legal system did not provide, as the Chinese eventually did, that a man could not divorce a wife who had no natal home to return to. The other problem faced by the early church was the use of divorce by both sexes for personal convenience or advancement, unlinked to any serious difficulties in the marital relation itself. This made it hard to develop any genuinely lasting and mutually supportive relationship. The early church leaders believed that husbands and wives would be more willing to commit themselves wholeheartedly to the maintenance of their marriage relationship, if such potentially disrupting factors were not present.

In upholding marriage as indissoluble the church's leaders were also reacting to social changes in the already rather commercialized and urbanized society of the Roman Empire. For most people in the cities (where most of the members of the early church lived) the reality of life was that once they were married, they no longer had the close ties of earlier generations with parents, siblings, and other blood-kin. They were living in nuclear households rather than in extended families. They therefore needed a sense of permanence in marriage as a substitute for the sense of permanence in blood-kinship, which is invariably strong in divorce-accepting societies.

Blood-kin relationships in every society compete with the husband-wife tie for each partner's attention. Divorce-accepting societies are not the only ones in which a sense of blood-kinship is strong. A sense of permanence in blood-kinship is also strong in some divorce-disapproving societies, like Italy and Spain, which did not allow divorce with right of remarriage until after 1970. But in such societies it is likely to be linked with a strong differentiation between husband's role and wife's role. In such a situation the spouses' need to work together is minimized. Each spouse is therefore free to continue working actively (and in fact often primarily) with blood-kin. Such a system is highly supportive for a widowed person, who has continued all along to regard the blood-kin group as important, and to remain an active and accepted member of it. However, a widowed person finds much less support in a system in which the marital relationship has become by far the most important one in every aspect of both partners' lives. A system of differentiated spouse roles, combined with ongoing blood-kin interaction, can also be supportive to a divorced person. Where divorce takes place, a system in which the marital relation has effectively eclipsed all others in significance leaves the divorced person in an anomalous position.

The marital relationship tends to predominate over blood-kin ties in most industrial-commercial, urbanized, centralized states, for reasons suggested in connection with the 19th-century "living wage" movement. The nuclear family with earning husband and household-managing wife appears to be the most mobile family form, and therefore seems at first to be the best adapted to the needs of an industrializing society. However, as experience has been demonstrating, too-great emphasis on the marriage tie can end by bringing too-great strain. The contemporary interest in family ties beyond the nuclear family in the United States clearly arises from a realization that the marital relationship alone is not sufficient for a sense of personal well-being. It is important. But it is not enough.

There are several major factors in the tendency of the marital relationship to predominate over all others in industrial urban societies. The economic one, ease of movement away from blood-kin (both geographically and psychologically), has already been discussed. Another factor is the belief that individuals ought to select their own marital partners because compatibility is highly important if a marital relationship is to be both close and lasting. That in turn comes out of the recognition of the individual as unique, and as not merely a member of a family. These factors, too, have already been discussed. Yet another factor, linked to them, is the general individualistic tendency to value relationships entered by choice (like marriage) above relationships not entered by choice (like birth into a family).

Still another factor in the emphasis on the psychological and erotic aspects of the marital relation in industrial urban societies is the need to maintain a sense of differentiation in function between the two partners. More and more of the functions of production, education, protection, discipline, recreation, and so on have moved out of the home into other social institutions. The elementary conjugal family has been left with little more than the rearing of very young children, the management of income (including provision of needed household services), and the relief of tensions through mutual supportiveness and expression of enduring affection and acceptance. Yet as more wives work outside the home for monetary income, early child-rearing is increasingly done either outside the home, by an employed worker in the home, or on an equally shared basis by the two spouses. Each of these in its own way lessen differences between the spouses' roles. Income-management and service-providing functions, like shopping and household tasks, are also done increasingly in one of those three ways. As a result the function of providing mutual emotional support and expression of acceptance has tended to become the major ongoing function of marriage (or for that matter of blood-kin ties). Because there is a real need for a sense of having one's own role to play in the conjugal relationship, that in turn has encouraged an increasing emphasis on the erotic element in marriage as an inescapably sex-differentiated and therefore partner-differentiating aspect of the relationship.

Recent unisex fashions may have been in part an effort to counterbalance a too-great tendency in the direction of stressing eroticism. Similarly, the both-sex peer groups found among adolescents and young adults in most modern Western societies (even though there may also be one-sex peer groups for certain activities) may prepare young people to balance the husband-wife relationship with relationships with others. They may enable the young not to put so much stress on the husband-wife relationship that satisfactory role performance is almost impossible because constant and heavy demand for emotional support is being placed on only one person.

As a society tends to move increasingly toward a system of marital roles in which the two spouses act jointly rather than separately, the tendency to stress the erotic element becomes increasingly strong. That tendency applies whether the earlier separate roles were seen as complementary, like the ideal put forth by the "living wage" movement, or as independent. (Separate independent roles are the observed reality of much wage worker life in Britain and the United States. In both countries, among wage-earning groups, spouses minimize what they do jointly and what they do in a complementary way. For most purposes they maintain much closer ties with blood-kin than with each other.) That tendency also applies whether the newer joint roles are seen in terms of actually cooperating in making a decision or doing a task, or in terms of each one occasionally making every type of decision or doing every type of task in addition to the times when they act together.

Eroticism in modern industrial urban societies becomes a means of maintaining an otherwise disappearing sense of mutual need based on difference in spouses' roles. As erotic and other emotional elements are stressed the tendency to seek divorce grows also. Divorce comes to be seen as a needed release from a relationship in which the other partner does not appear likely to provide the emotional satisfactions wanted by the divorce-initiating partner. As Talcott Parsons suggested in *Family, Socialization, and Interaction Process* (1960), the divorce rate does not measure the strength or weakness of the institution of the family. What it measures is how willing or unwilling people are to put up with dissatisfaction. Divorce in a modern society is usually a change in relationship rather than a complete break in relationship, at least for those with children. Both partners still ordinarily take an interest in their offspring. They also ordinarily work out some means for both to express that interest—even for the jobless father who disappears so that his wife can get a divorce on grounds of desertion and obtain some form of public aid, and who returns after the children have reached an age at which their mother no longer receives aid for them.

Role-stress, as Parsons calls the dissatisfaction that leads to divorce if it is sharp enough, is indeed at the root of divorce. Where divorce is difficult or impossible, it leads to desertion, or to some provision for legal separation without right of remarriage in a case of flagrantly harmful behavior by one spouse. Many Western societies have found it hard to acknowledge that when dissatisfaction is strong enough, when the factors underlying it are strong enough, and when the ideal of lifelong indissoluble marriage is not accepted as religiously binding by one or both of the parties, then either there must be provisions for divorce with right of remarriage, or there will be desertions—and subsequent liaisons which do not provide the legal protections of marriage for the partners to those liaisons or to any children they may have. It has been especially hard for those Western societies whose early patterns were molded by the Roman Catholic rather than the Greek Orthodox Church to begin regarding marriage as a form of contract (potentially breakable under specifically defined circumstances) rather than as an indestructible sacrament. Yet those changes in attitude have slowly been coming about. All but a few overwhelmingly Roman Catholic countries have legalized divorce. Since about 1920 most European countries (eastern as well as western), Canada, Australia, New Zealand, and the United States have made it easier to obtain a divorce on grounds other than adultery, nonsupport, and physical cruelty, the grounds on which the Roman Catholic Church has long allowed formal separation (including separation of property and arrangements for the innocent spouse to rear any minor children) without right of remarriage. Moreover, the 1982 revision of the Roman Catholic code of canon law (last previously revised in 1917) allows far more discretion to bishops in defining the impediments that make a supposed marriage invalid than the 1917 code, which in turn gave more discretion to them than did its predecessor. (The declaration that a marriage was invalid does not delegitimize any children born to it.) One of those impediments is listed as immaturity. Thus a Roman Catholic couple may be able to obtain a declaration that their supposed marriage was invalid. They may then enter what are seen, not as remarriages, but as valid marriages.

A number of factors may lead to the role-stress that may end in divorce. The difficulty of providing emotional satisfaction if the marital relation is the only one turned to for a feeling of affection and support is an emotional factor, already discussed. The correlation between low income and high divorce rates is an economic factor, also previously mentioned. In particular, a low income based on hourly wages is a source of great role-stress for working-class husbands and wives who accept the "living wage" ideology of the complementary marriage of breadwinner and homemaker, but then find that they cannot achieve it because of layoff decisions in which they have no real voice. Flexibility in retaining or laying off workers is helpful to the managers of economic enterprises. But it is extremely unhelpful for a worker who may be laid off at any time, as a result of decisions by groups such as boards of directors of corporations (or individuals such as a plantation owner-manager) in whose decision-making that worker has no opportunity for input. Those who seek to promote stable marriages in an industrial society might well take note of the relatively low divorce rate in industrialized Japan, where divorce is still almost unknown among those workers who enjoy the security of lifetime employment in the larger firms.

The maturity factor in marital role-stress is also important. The younger the marriage-age, by and large, the greater the likelihood of an eventual divorce, in a society in which partners select each other and may divorce each other also. If the divorce does not come in the first few years, when the risk is greatest, then it may come later, if dissatisfaction becomes high enough to seem unbearable to one or both partners. Even a feeling of having missed something by marrying so young, and wanting a period of unmarried maturity like that which others had before marrying, may cause enough dissatisfaction to lead to a divorce.

On the whole, marriage-ages have been declining in all Western societies in the 20th century. If maturity is one factor in the divorce rate, it should then not be surprising that divorces have increased in frequency. But there may be another factor in the growth of the divorce rate in recent decades. This factor is suggested by the role played by economic uncertainty—uncertainty of livelihood—in contributing to the role-stress and dissatisfaction which make divorce rates higher among hourly-wage workers than among salaried employees. A sense of uncertainty of life itself, in the post–1945 era of nuclear weaponry, may also be a factor in higher role-stress, as reflected in higher divorce rates in most countries in the past generation. That sense of uncertainty exists. A 59-nation survey of teenagers in 1986 showed that 40% of them thought a nuclear war likely. Concern over nuclear weaponry was probably not much of a factor in the sudden peaking of divorces right after World War II in many countries, as young returned service members and the young spouses they had married found that they had not known each other long enough or well enough to make a satisfactory choice. After that wave of divorces, divorce rates again declined. But as big-power rivalry began in the 1950s to be expressed increasingly in testing and stockpiling nuclear military devices, it may have come to be more of a contributor to rising divorce rates than has been generally realized, whether in the United States, in the Soviet Union, or elsewhere.

The 1976 survey by Hugh Carter and Paul Glick, *Marriage and Divorce*, indicates an increase in the divorce rate from 1965 to 1973 in the countries of the developed world. (See Table 27.) That increase was minimal in Japan and Israel, compared with the Soviet Union, the United States, Britain, Canada, Australia, or continental western Europe. Increases from 1932 to 1965 in divorce rates had been even greater, except in France. (See Table 26.) The Carter and Glick survey also indicates an increase in the percentage of marriages that were entered both by men under 25 and by women under 25, during the years 1965 to 1973 in the developed countries. The only exceptions were for Sweden and for a very minute drop in the percentage of marriages entered by women under 25 in the United States and in Canada. There were few sizable changes in the number of marriages per one thousand persons (all ages) per year between 1965 and 1973. However, there was a somewhat noticeable drop in the marriage rate in Austria, Denmark, West Germany, Sweden, and Switzerland, and there was a visible rise in Ireland and Israel. Nevertheless, divorce rates per one thousand persons were still less than $^1/_5$ of marriage rates in 1973 in all but nine of the countries surveyed. (See Table 25.) Denmark showed 2.5 divorces to 6.1 marriages per one thousand persons. Egypt, included for purposes of comparison as a Muslim developing country, showed 2.1 divorces to 9.4 marriages per one thousand persons. Finland showed 1.8 to 7.5, West Germany 1.4 to 6.7 (in 1972), Sweden 1.9 to 4.7, Switzerland 1.3 to 6.2, the United Kingdom (England and Wales) 2.4 to 8.6 (in 1972), the United States 4.4 to 10.9, and the Soviet Union 2.7 to 10.0. The highest marriage rates listed were in the United States. By 1983 only Israel still had a divorce rate less than $^1/_5$ of its marriage rate, in the group of countries listed in Table 27.

Divorces were apt to come before age 35, or even age 30, rather than later, according to Carter and Glick. Divorces were also apt to come in the first three to seven years of marriage, rather than earlier or later. Earlier divorce meant more likelihood of remarriage. Remarriage could enable the children living with a divorced parent to live in a two-parent household again at that parent's remarriage. However, it would also mean having to work out relationships among children and parents that involved including a step-parent in the family circle while the corresponding natal parent was still alive. That was highly unlike earlier experience with second marriages in these countries. Formerly the corresponding natal parent was likely to be dead, since almost all marriages were broken by death rather than by divorce. The Inuit of the Arctic managed to work out step-parent relationships in a divorce-accepting society, on a basis of cooperation among natal and step-parents for the benefit of the children. However, for people in previously divorce-disapproving societies, working out such relationships required rethinking the nature and function of both marriage and parenthood.

The percentage of divorces that involve children did not change much in most of the countries surveyed between about 1950 and about 1960. (See Table 28.) However, in the United States they rose from 45.5% in 1953 to 60.2% in 1962, and in Norway they fell from 68.8% in 1950 to 56.9% in 1957. Nor did the divorce rate per one thousand currently married couples, probably a more meaningful figure than the divorce rate per one thousand persons, change nearly as dramatically between 1935 and 1964 as the divorce rate per one thousand persons. The divorce rate per one thousand couples tripled in the United Kingdom, for example, from a starting point only $1/_{11}$ of the level in the United States. Yet the divorce rate per one thousand persons in the United Kingdom multiplied by eight times, from a starting point only $1/_{13}$ of the level in the United States. In the United States itself the rate per one thousand married couples rose from 7.8 to 10.7, or less than half again, while the rate per one thousand persons rose from 1.3 to 2.5, or almost double.

Divorce was indeed more common in the developed world by the 1970s. But as the Egyptian example shows, divorce rates in the developed world were not dramatically higher than might be found in the developing world, in countries often thought of as family-centered. And the United States, whose crude divorce rate was about twice as high as Egypt's in the 1970s (and far higher than that of other developed countries), is also the country with by far the youngest average age at marriage of all developed countries. This strongly suggests that youthful marriage may lead to a high divorce rate, where both marriage and divorce are matters in which the partners' choice determines what is done.

In the western Europe of the 16th through 19th centuries, then, the means by which people sought to match fertility both to mortality and to economic opportunity included celibacy, late marriage, migration, and fertility control. The incidence of celibacy tended to increase after 1500. That was true not only in Roman Catholic lands, where convents could provide women with a respectable alternative to marriage, but also in the lands of the Reformed churches. The incidence of celibacy tended to be especially high among the elite, who were concerned to preserve family property undivided. About ½ the elite of Milan and Florence had never married at age 50 between A.D. 1600 and 1750, and about ¼ of the elite of Geneva in 1700 and $1/_5$ of the nobility of England between 1730 and 1780. But even in a whole nation as many as ⅛ might never have married at 50, as in Sweden between 1850 and 1900. However, understanding and use of measures to control fertility could alter that, as shown among nobles in 18th-century Genoa and Milan and among the whole population in 19th-century Spain. In both those situations the percentage who never married fell in tandem with the fertility rate of married couples, which was falling even though life expectancies were scarcely rising at all.

Postponement of marriage might be linked with economic situation. In Denmark in 1787 more than ½ of the men in their 20s who were independent craftsmen, shopkeepers, and the like were already married, in contrast to fewer than $^1/_{12}$ of the men in their 20s who were still apprentices or servants. However, it was also a means of lowering the number of children a couple might have. That is why it is significant that the overall western European average age at first marriage, from at least A.D. 1600 to at least A.D. 1850, was about 25 for women and 28 for men. In fact, it was 28 for women and even more for men by 1850 in the Netherlands, Belgium, and Switzerland, where 16% to 20% of all women remained unmarried. Taking a bride older than himself was an obvious way for a man to lessen the number of his children. In one district in Norway in 1801 almost ½ the brides in first marriages for both partners were older than the groom. Almost $^1/_5$ of them (about one in 11 of all brides in the district that year) were ten or more years older than their husbands. That contrasts greatly with Russia before 1900. The opening of new lands for cultivation and settlement in the era of Russian expansion across Asia from the 17th through 19th centuries meant an early-marriage, high-fertility pattern like that found in most of Asia, Africa, the Pacific, and much of Latin America well into the 20th century. That pattern was encouraged by the organization of the villagers under their overlords. Cultivation rights were not really heritable, but depended on how many were in a household at periodic times of redistribution of fields. Villagers lived in extended-family households and used equal partible inheritance. Each of these factors favored early marriage and high fertility, even if life expectancies had not been short and infant mortality had not been high.

Only recently has that early-marriage, high-fertility pattern begun to change in regions such as Asia. An article on changes in Asian marriage patterns in the *Journal of Family History* in 1980 by Peter Smith surveyed a number of non-Communist Asian countries, using data for a year between 1970 and 1975 for most of them. He found that only in the Philippines in 1970 and in Burma in 1953 did fewer than 95% of women marry. More than 95% of men also married, except in Sri Lanka in 1971, in Burma in 1953, and in the rather special situations of Taiwan in 1975, Hong Kong in 1971, Macao in 1970, Singapore in 1970, and Sarawak and Brunei in northern Borneo in 1970, with their numerous and mostly male refugees from the mainland of China (refugees from either poverty or Communist rule). Marriage-ages for women rose in every part of Asia in the 20th century. By 1970 Taiwan, Sri Lanka, and Japan had actually reached western European-like proportions (of 60% to 65%) of all women over 15 having been married. Of the rest, only Singapore, the Republic of Korea, the Philippines, Malaysia, Thailand, Hong Kong, and Sarawak were approaching that level. Indonesia and the countries of South Asia (Pakistan, India, Nepal, and Bangladesh) ranged from 85% to more than 95% of all women over 15 already wed.

As life expectancies have lengthened, those high rates of early marriage (at least for women) and the still high fertility rates associated with them have continued to mean high population growth rates. That also means increased production must be used for consumption rather than for investment, which slows down the implementation of plans to promote the economic growth desired to provide more goods and services to those already born. In the long run lengthening life expectancies can lessen the dependency ratio. In 1982 the United Nations Fund for Population Activities predicted a life expectancy in the developing states of mainland Asia, Africa, and Latin America of 63 to 64 by the year 2000. That level had already been reached by the 1970s in Sri Lanka, Malaysia, and the Republic of Korea (and much earlier in Japan), although in Asia, as a whole, life expectancy was only 56 in 1979. However, in the short run, lengthening life expectancies can mean an increase rather than a decrease in the dependency ratio, until fertility rates start to fall. That has begun to happen. By 1982 world population estimates for the year 2000 were lowered from earlier predictions of 7.5 billion, to 6.1 billion. This was made possible in part by the use of population control programs in 22 of 32 Asian developing states, though only 18 of 50 states in Africa and only 10 in 30 states in Latin America were using them. More important, it was the result of individuals' decisions to control their own fertility, which were beginning to be made not only in those states with population control programs, but in other states as well.

Urbanization in Asia has probably played some part in the decline in early marriages for women noted by Smith, since the percentage currently married in the non-Communist Asian states he studied has dropped more rapidly in urban than in rural areas. In Asia, as a whole, mean average age at marriage had reached 18.2 for women and 23.2 for men by about 1975. The difference in age between spouses was then less than five years everywhere except in India, where it averaged about seven. Smith suggests that worldwide, ages at first marriage are converging on the early 20s. Marriage-ages in Europe and other late-marrying societies have been declining somewhat, in response not only to the availability of effective contraception, but also to the greater availability of economic opportunity. That opportunity includes the opportunity for the wife as well as the husband to continue earning after marriage. At the same time marriage-ages have been rising in Asia and other early-marrying regions. That includes the United States, where median age (half more, half less) at first marriage rose by about two years between 1960 and 1980, to about 22 for women and 24 for men.

The worldwide convergence of marriage-ages toward the early to middle 20s for both men and women, and the worldwide spread of the pattern of mutual partner-choice that first appeared in 18th-century western Europe, form a new stage in the development of marriage systems. This chapter has looked at some general implications of those trends. It has also looked at some general implications for marriage (and divorce) of social and economic patterns associated with modern, individuality-recognizing, urban, industrial-commercial life. The next three chapters will look at how those general implications have been illustrated in the experiences of the peoples of Europe, the Middle East—Asia—Africa realm, and the Western Hemisphere and the Pacific, in recent generations.

CHAPTER 10

Marriage in Industrial-Commercial Societies: Europe

The first western European nation to move toward partners' selection of each other was England. English humanist thinkers like Thomas More introduced the idea of reciprocity in the marriage relationship, as preferable to the Norman use of husband-dominance to win control through wedding Anglo-Saxon heiresses. Yet even after the Church of England severed the last ties with Rome in 1534, divorce was only possible through a specific act of Parliament until 1858. It was granted only to men who brought complaints against their wives for either adultery or refusal of intercourse. A woman could only seek separate maintenance, and could only obtain it on grounds of being in physical danger from her husband.

Marriage-ages in 16th-century England would seem to have already reached the mid–20s, for both women and men. That may have been in part because a daughter was expected to receive a cash portion at marriage, as her share of her parents' property. There was need for time to lay that portion aside. It was also more than likely that a younger son would receive a cash portion at maturity. Men were already dying younger than women were, although they married later than women did. They made real efforts to provide by will for their widows, in the Midlands of England in the 16th and 17th centuries. According to Cicely Howell, in Jack Goody and others' collection *Family and Inheritance: Rural Society in Western Europe, 1200–1800* (1976), about half of the widows whose husbands' wills she studied were left with at least one son or daughter over 21 years of age, but about $^{1}/_{6}$ of them had no children. In the same collection Margaret Spufford describes a pattern of bequest for three Cambridgeshire villages between A.D. 1500 and 1800 that gave the eldest son the land but obliged him to provide for his mother's maintenance, his sisters' dowries, and his brothers' cash portions as they reached maturity. Women, too, left wills. At least in Banbury they were increasingly named by their husbands as executrices between A.D. 1550 and 1800. But most of the bequeathing and control of property remained in the hands of men, given the turn that English common law had taken in Norman hands. For the propertyless the Poor Laws of the end of the 16th century gave a powerful institutional push toward thinking in terms of conjugal rather than extended families. That was because the Poor Laws made only one's parents, spouse, or offspring responsible for one's maintenance. Those lacking support from any of these sources became the parish's responsibility to feed. The Poor Laws may thereby have facilitated industrialization, by making married couples more willing to move away from kin who had no obligation to assist them anyway in time of need.

In the 17th century some diminution of the husband's and father's authority took place among the English nobility. Marriage contracts began to provide for guaranteed income for wives as well as widows, and to establish guaranteed portions, given by both spouses' parents, for the offspring of the marriage. By the end of the century that comparative independence for offspring was giving them some leverage, in responding to marital choices suggested by parents. This facilitated the putting forth of the ideal of the spouse as friend, along with the English humanists' ideal of reciprocity in marriage and the church's recognition of mutual solace as a vital aspect of the marital relationship. Fathers still appointed their children's guardians, and mothers only became guardians if the father appointed no one else. Still, the ideal of marriage as a partnership of complementary yet mature and self-reliant persons had taken root.

With the ideal of the spouse as friend came a turn to spouse instead of servant as closest confidant. This was signalized by the shift in domestic architecture to the central hallway, so that servants did not need to pass through one person's room in order to reach another's. It also led to an expectation that as parents, both spouses should give a greater amount of personal attention to their children from the beginning of life. As one result aristocratic mothers began to lactate their own infants, improving the infants' chances for survival. In short, domesticity had begun to flower. The nuclear or conjugal family was beginning to be seen as central. With that flowering of domesticity came the end of the last remnant of the era of courtly love, the social acceptability of a married woman being escorted at a social gathering by a man other than her husband. (Married women could still be so escorted without scandal at least as late as the 19th century, in France and Italy.)

The ideal of marriage for friendship and companionship increasingly led to an acceptance of young men and women meeting at fashionable places like Bath after 1720, once the professional matchmaker had been outlawed. It was feared that a professional matchmaker might, for a fee, introduce a somewhat doubtful person into high social circles. Still, in 1753, the desire for some check on the possible rashness of the young led to legislation requiring parental consent for the marriage of anyone under 21 years of age. The same law allowed Jews and Quakers to marry by their own regulations rather than require an Anglican marriage. However, not until 1836 were Roman Catholics and Dissenters (i.e., all other Christians of a Reformed persuasion) granted the same courtesy.

By the mid–1700s the English aristocracy's family life was far more egalitarian and respecting of individuality than the family life of aristocracies in most of the rest of Europe. That may help to explain why its members were readier than most European aristocrats to accept the political and social changes which were brought by industrialization. By 1784 it was estimated that three in four of noble marriages were self-arranged rather than parentally arranged. As mutual partner-choice became the norm for the nobility, other segments of society began to take it up as well.

In other parts of English society in the 17th century there was apt to be a shortage of men because of emigration, wars, and diseases like the plague, which killed more men than women. That shortage may have affected the Devonshire village of Colyton, which has quite complete parish registers for A.D. 1538 through 1837, when the registration system was changed. By 1700 the average age of women at first marriage in Colyton was near 30, actually slightly older than the average age of men. However, both before 1650 and after 1700 marriage-ages were nearer the all-western-European averages of 25 and 28. They declined by 1837 to about 23 for women and 25 for men, the levels found in all of England in 1851. That was slightly earlier than in continental western Europe at that time. The marriage rate in Colyton increased during the 18th century, but marital fertility declined. That may indicate the use of some form(s) of contraception. During the 18th century family size rose as income fell in all but the poorest households in three Lancashire parishes described by David J. Loschky and Donald F. Krier in the *Journal of Economic History* for 1969. This may support the hypothesis that those with property were likelier to limit their fertility than were those without property. About the same proportion of Colyton marriages (just under ½) were between Colyton people in the late 18th century as were shown in the census for that village in 1851. This made Colyton different from England as a whole. Over the whole of England there were more marriages between people from different parishes in the 18th century than in the 19th century. In many areas that may have been in part because population growth meant a greater number in the home parish among whom to find a spouse. As early as the 17th century the practical limit for finding a spouse in England, as a whole, had risen from 10 miles to 15 miles from one's home parish. Such a change was not recorded in Germany till 1850. In rural West Africa or in rural mainland China in the 1980s the day's walk, represented by the 10-mile figure, is still the practical limit for finding a spouse for the great majority of villagers.

The longer distance from which spouses came may have resulted from felt necessity, so far as women were concerned. Only 15% of women in

England in A.D. 1700 were married by the time they were 24—just ½ as many as the 30% of 1851. The intervening years had seen a shift from small independent farms to a system of tenant cultivation under great landowners. The tenant system facilitated earlier marriages in rural areas because tenants were provided with cottages, rather than with bed and board like the hired workers of the independent farmer of previous years. A tenant farmer would naturally think of bringing a spouse into the cottage to care for household tasks.

The 17th-century Puritan movement had a visible but temporary impact on bridal pregnancy and illegitimacy. Both declined markedly during the 17th century but then rose again during the 18th century to their 16th-century levels. In the 18th century at least, if not the 16th, couples who were eager to marry may have used conception consciously, as a means to press their parents to agree to their immediate marriage.

The impact of economic ups and downs was also visible. Rises and falls in marriage rates followed two to six years after upswings and downturns (five to ten years for births) before to the middle decades of the 19th century. Thereafter the interval dropped to one year for marriages and two years for births. Marriage-ages in England were lower in the 1860s than at any time before or since (though after rising until the 1920s, they began to decline again). But the impact of local circumstances can be seen in a study of the 1861 census by Michael Anderson in the *Journal of Family History* for 1976. Fewer women married in towns and cities, and they married when 18 months older than in agricultural areas. Fewer men married where live-in agricultural labor was the chief employment for men, and they married later if at all. Both fewer women and fewer men married (and married later if at all) where live-in domestic service was the chief employment for women. Men in garrison areas, where men were more numerous, married when 30 months older than in other areas. Still they married in the same proportions as in most other areas. Not only the availability of potential partners but also the freedom to meet with them were clearly factors of vital importance in making marriage feasible, now that self-selection of partners had become the norm.

Those in authority in both the state and the state church in England continued to believe that the imposition of a legal requirement for lifelong commitment was essential to making marital ties as reliable as blood-kin ties. Consequently it is not surprising that only in 1858 was divorce for adultery permitted by law to both men and women. Nor is it surprising that it took another 80 years to add desertion, cruelty, and insanity to the permissible reasons for divorce. (Within a decade the rate of divorce had multiplied by 7 times, though in 1948 it was still far from high compared with many other European countries or the United States.) It took another 33 years, to 1971, to bring new legislation that would let separation suffice to show that the marriage relationship was too seriously damaged for repair, rather than insisting on specific causes' being cited, as in the 1938 law. With about one in six persons over 21 having experienced divorce or separation in 1969 (and one in eleven unwed), it had perhaps become time to recognize that religious sanctions against divorce were no longer heeded by a large segment of the English population, and to make a corresponding change in legal rules.

In England, as in other industrial countries, the marriages of hourly wage working-class couples are likely to follow a separate-role pattern, while the marriages of salaried employees, managers, professional people, and other self-employed persons are likely to follow a joint-role pattern. It was in Elizabeth Bott's path-breaking study of working-class English couples, *Family and Social Network* (1957), that the concepts of complementary-separate, independent-separate, and joint marital roles were first suggested. She observed that working-class couples tended to combine one of the separate types of marital roles with a continuing close connection with kin (and also friends) who had been known since childhood and who were probably also known to the spouse. They did not shift as much of their expressive and emotional life into the marital relation as the economically better-off tended to do.

Another path-breaking study, by Rhona and Robert Rapoport, *Dual-Career Families* (1971), was updated in 1977 as *Dual-Career Families Revisited*. The Rapoports suggest that the experience of the English couples they studied, in which both spouses had held professional or managerial posts straight through the childbearing period of their marriages, showed that these couples had found more need than most couples to set priorities jointly and with care. These couples had found it hard to make friends with couples who did not also have dual-career marriages. They had found it helpful to see the two careers as complementary, whether because actually in the same field (sometimes even as co-workers) or because the career of each expressed some avocational interest of the other. They had also found that the combined time-demands of career, home, and children had required some type of full-time paid assistance in the home, at least until children grew mature enough to share household duties. Each spouse had gained a real satisfaction from the other's career, as well as from the development of their children's capacities. Yet clearly the high value placed on the wife's having borne children (and in the families studied this was indeed valued highly by both partners to the marriage) needed a counterpart in the husband's being recognized by both partners as having something uniquely valuable to contribute, something that the wife either did not contribute at all or contributed much less fully. The Rapoports suggest that these dual-career families provide helpful insights into what is needed for greater personal satisfaction in the growing number of marriages in all socioeconomic groups in which both spouses work outside the home after they marry. External supports like the availability of professional household services are important. But it is even more important for people to consider seriously what qualities to look for in a marriage partner.

Two-job marriages were already visible in Victorian late-19th-century Scotland, as John Holley shows in the *Journal of Family History* for 1981. Where jobs were available for both married and single women in (for example) a local paper industry, 38% of wives worked. That contrasted with 9% or fewer in a tweed-making town with few jobs for either married or single women. Yet in both situations there was a major difference in family behavior between skilled and unskilled laborers' families, which was unrelated to whether or not the wife worked. Skilled workers, able to count on steady income because seldom laid off, gave up the customary feasting of the wider circle of kin at births, weddings, and funerals. But unskilled workers, often out of work, kept up the traditions of feasting as a means of maintaining a network of kinfolk on whom they could call in time of need. The sense of kin remained strong in Scotland. In clans studied by Ian Carter in *Scottish Studies* for 1973 the highlanders still took 64% of their wives from other highland clans between A.D. 1700 and 1900 (92% between A.D. 1500 and 1699), while the border clans still kept up ties with the highlanders by taking 57% of their wives from them between 1700 and 1900 (80% between 1500 and 1699). Some parts of Scotland declined in population after 1800 because of migration to more promising regions, in or out of Scotland. That helps to account for the total imbalance between males and females (all ages) found by E. M. Soulsby in *Scottish Geographical Magazine* for 1972. In 1811 there were 118.5 females per 100 males. In 1961 there were 108.6 females per 100 males. The greatest surpluses of females were found in towns and in rural regions where agriculture was intensive rather than extensive. Given these imbalances, a continuing lateness of age at marriage for women is not surprising, nor is it surprising that a large number of women did not marry at all.

It was Ireland that came to offer the outstanding example of a situation in which large numbers of men, as well as of women, either married late or married not at all. The English conquerors of Ireland tried from 1695 to 1746 to require that all sons should inherit equally, for the English recognized that partible inheritance would weaken their unwilling subjects. Under the old system one son had been favored. He was expected to use his newly married wife's dowry or portion to buy out his father, who would then retire to a separate cottage or a separate set of rooms to live on that amount with his own wife. The unwed brothers and sisters would then remain on the farm as workers and continue to receive support. When the English gave up the effort to enforce equal inheritance for all sons, the old system returned. It was modified for the next hundred years by a new willingness to divide farmsteads and allow more than one son to marry (enabling more daughters to marry too), as the introduction of the potato lessened the amount of land required to feed a married couple and their offspring. When the potato blight of 1845–49 wiped out not only the potato crops, but also $1/5$ of the human population, the old system was revived in full force. However, now the surplus sons and daughters sought to emigrate rather than to stay on the farm, and ultimogeniture began to replace primogeniture. Ultimogeniture became most common among the better-off farmers. They could spare a small cash portion to send an older son to seek his fortune in a nearby town (or in England, or even overseas) with the hope that if he were successful, he would in turn enable both brothers and sisters to join him there. If the oldest son was still preferred as heir, then part of his wife's portion might be used to give the younger siblings a start.

Among those who went to nearby towns, it was common for a young man to start as a shop assistant and learn enough to start his own shop. He would then marry a woman from the countryside, so that her kin as well as his could be relied on to do their trading with that shop when they came to town. Eventually he might do well enough to take in an unmarried sister, who would open up a branch shop that would revert to her brother or to one of his sons at her death. But few married women worked outside the home or the family shop. As late as 1960 only 3% of married women in the Irish Free State worked outside the home, as compared with 23% in the United Kingdom (England and Wales) at that time. Even in 1981 only 29.7% of all Ireland's women (married and single) worked outside the home, fewer than in any other European state except Greece (25%) and Spain (22.1%). In most of Europe the range was 40% to 60%, compared with an almost universal 70% to 80% for European men.

Marriage-ages for women, which had been similar to England's in the 1830s, climbed steeply until 1911. They then began a slow decline. Nonetheless, in 1951 the average age at first marriage in Ireland was still 31 for men and 27 for women. Even in the 1970s and 1980s marriage-ages remained about two years higher than in England. With divorce still unavailable, even though more than $1/3$ of the voters in a 1986 referendum accepted it, prudence in selecting one's life partner was advisable. Still, marriage rates were higher than in earlier decades. In 1980 scarcely more than 27% of each sex aged 45 to 59 were either widowed or never married. Yet in 1926, as Conrad M. Arensberg and Solon T. Kimball show in *Family and Community in Ireland* (1968, 2nd edition), almost 30% of both sexes in the Irish Free State had never married, in contrast with about 10% of men and less than 20% of women in England and Denmark. More townspeople than rural people married in the Ireland of the 1920s, and then proceeded to have fewer children per couple. Townspeople also married earlier, and tended to pair a somewhat higher-status woman with a slightly lower-status man. That undoubtedly reflected the change in the sex ratio after 1870, when for the first time more women than men began to survive into later life in Ireland. The natural result was an intensification of competition for husbands, which could lead to a woman's willingness to marry someone whose status did not quite match her own. It may also have encouraged the continuance of a marriage pattern in which wives did not go out to work (i.e., did not compete with the husband in the workplace).

Concern for the status of a marriage partner (but on the part of family rather than self) was also at the root of the marriage edict of the king of France in 1556. This was the French state's first effort to regulate marriage rather than to continue to leave its regulation to church courts. The edict allowed a parent to disinherit a son until age 30 and a daughter until age 25 for marrying without parental consent. In 1579 the French state required church registration of all marriages. In 1639 the 1556 edict was broadened to allow the disinheritance of any eldest son who married without parental consent, no matter what his age.

Parents in France were still regarded as the proper planners for their children's future. One local inheritance system might, as in Normandy, require all sons to restore whatever portions they had received so that their father's estate could be divided equally. Norman sons' portions were still given in goods, not in cash as in England by the 16th century. So were the dowries of Norman daughters, but they were not permitted to return a dowry and share in the division of the estate. Thus, in effect, the Norman inheritance system still recognized a patrilineal fund rather than a conjugal fund as basic to the social order. Another inheritance system might, as in the south and among the Walloons on the Belgian border, let the father designate which son would receive the bulk of the family property (i.e., the parents' conjugal fund). It might also let the father designate how much (though not less than ⅓) was to be divided among the other children as dowries for daughters and portions for sons. This system tended to work in practice like that of Ireland in enabling only one son to marry. Other offspring often remained on the farm because their portions were too small for them to leave, unless a son could marry into a sonless family. One in ten of 18th-century marriages in Provence brought the husband into the wife's household. Some marriages in Provence were also neolocal, bringing neither spouse into the other's household, but the overwhelming majority continued to bring the bride into the husband's natal home.

Yet another inheritance system might, as around Paris after the Goths passed through in the 5th century A.D., let the parents exclude from future inheritance any child who was given a dowry or portion while the parents lived, and then divide their conjugal fund equally among those who had not yet received something. By the 16th century, perhaps reflecting Norman practice, those who had received something were allowed to return it and then share in the equal division. That led to careful calculations, as marriages were arranged. Still another inheritance system might, as in the Nivernais, recognize an ongoing lineal type of fund in land. In this system, cultivation rights in land that went as dowry with a wife who married into another farmstead would revert at her death to those of her brothers (or her brothers' sons) who were still in her natal home. Correspondingly, if a man moved into a brotherless wife's natal home as her husband, any land-cultivation rights he brought in with him would revert to those of his own kin who were in his natal home when he died. The system in the Nivernais was the peasants' response to their lords' ruling that if a household divided its property among its individual members rather than maintaining a single joint household, it would lose its land to the lord. In 1534 the lords dropped the requirement that a child must be actually in the parental home when the parents died in order to remain in it thereafter. In Franche-Comté, where a similar system existed, that requirement remained in place until the abolition of all feudal dues and privileges in the Revolution of 1789. When commercialization began to provide new markets for goods and labor, the Nivernais type of system lent itself to a modification by which those who left the land might be given a small portion. They could then establish a household in a village or a town. Once married, they would be likely to use a conjugal-fund system rather like that of the Paris area.

The French Revolution began by sweeping away all of these varied and complex inheritance systems, in favor of mandating simple equal partible inheritance for all offspring. The revolutionists also made the registration of births, marriages, and deaths a governmental rather than a church responsibility, in 1792. The power of local custom soon led to a revision in the inheritance laws. The revision limited the inheritance of any one child (unless an only child) to ½ the estate. The familiar regional patterns soon reappeared in appropriately modified versions: equality for all (not merely sons) in Normandy as well as elsewhere in the north, and a tendency to favor one son elsewhere. The ongoing lineal-fund system of Franche-Comté did not reappear, for it had primarily been a self-protecting response to now-vanished overlords' demands. The similar system in the Nivernais had already largely disappeared by 1789 because most peasants had become sharecroppers as increasing taxes forced them to cease trying to hold on to their own land. The old tendency toward stem or joint family life remained. Parents still kept a married child at home as heir. Brothers (with their spouses) still stayed together after parents died. However, sometimes the different married pairs might live in separate residences, only retaining a common budget for basic needs like fuel and salt.

Pressured as they were by overlords' demands, many married French peasants started limiting births toward the end of the 18th century. Probably they learned techniques of contraception from the nobility, who clearly were limiting their fertility by 1700. In some regions, though, the decline in fertility did not begin until after 1850. As knowledge and use of contraception spread during the 19th century, more women (and men) married, although marriage-ages did not change materially from the 25 for women and 27 for men of the 18th century. This clearly suggests that celibacy had been used to keep down total births. Though there were slightly more marriages than there were women in 18th-century France, about 10% of women never married. The remarriages of widows were numerous enough to make that possible—12% of all marriages, according to D.E.C. Eversley, in *Population in History* (1965). That was true even though both widows and widowers tended to prefer to marry previously unwed partners, as Alain Bideau found in one village between 1670 and 1840 in the *Journal of Family History* for 1980. Probably this was intended at least in part to lessen any complications with regard to inheritance by possible offspring of the second marriage.

The sex ratio, and the respective mortality rates of men and women, meant that one in ten or so of all French women in the 18th century never did find a partner. In parts of 19th- and even 20th-century France, considerable numbers still lived out their lives unmarried. Louise Tilly, in the *Journal of Family History* for 1979, found that 97% of women in one rural village in 1886 eventually married, but that in a nearby city in 1872 only 88% did, and in 1906 only 81% did. There were only 92 males per 100 females of all ages in the city in 1906.

In Nimes in 1906, according to Leslie Page Moch in the *Journal of Family History* for 1981, marriage rates were higher among those who had migrated to the city than among those born in it. The study did not show whether that was because the newcomers married each other after arrival, or because they brought in spouses from their home districts. A study of marriages by A. Michel, in C. C. Harris's collection *Readings in Kinship in Urban Society* (1970), showed that in 1959, 40% of all marriages in Paris (with all its in-migrants) were between people born in the same large region within France. In the northern region along the Belgian border 84% of all marriages were between people born in that area. In a sample of 1,646 couples in the governmental department of the Seine, in the Paris area, 72% were born in the same region and 22% in the same commune (the local governmental unit that would correspond to a New England town, a Midwest township, or a Louisiana parish), with 57% residing in the same commune when they married. The same article noted that about ⅔ married someone from a social-occupational level close to that of their own parents. Like still clearly gravitated toward like. However, fewer than 1% married third, fourth, or fifth cousins, the closest kin permitted. Among foreign migrants, Italians were more likely than Spaniards, Portuguese, or North Africans to marry someone not from their own country.

Among the French bourgeoisie, the propertied middle class, as Jesse Pitts noted in Norman Bell and Ezra Vogel's collection *Modern Introduction to the Family* (1968, revised edition), the concern to maintain status by courting only at or above one's own level remained high in the mid–20th century. Consequently, although the couple themselves were the ones to agree that they would marry, they had both generally sought their parents' approval before going far into courtship. Only after the 1950s, when economic growth finally began to become marked enough to bring people to begin thinking in terms of future prospects based on expectations other than those of inheritance, did the bourgeoisie begin to move away from the longtime practice of asking a childless relative to stand as godparent, in the hope that the relative would make the godchild his or her heir.

That change in attitudes, concerning whether to depend on prospects of inheritance or on prospects opened up by one's development of one's own capabilities, marked a fundamental turning from the patterns of at least the previous 1,500 years. It did not yet show up even in the 1980s in any significant increase in a divorce rate that remains low in comparison to other industrial countries. However, France is still one of the most rural-agricultural of all the industrial nations.

The continuingly low divorce rate in France may be linked to experience in the immediate aftermath of the Revolution of 1789 and the century that followed. The revolutionary generation established divorce by simple mutual consent in 1792, in a reaction against the complexities of canon law that had still governed the possibilities for separation or for annulment and remarriage until the Revolution. During the next decade there was one divorce for every four marriages registered in Paris, a figure not matched in the Western world until the close of the 1970s in the United States. That must have seemed potentially disastrous for familiar concepts of parent-child relationships, including the inheritance provisions so important in French calculations until recently. Divorce-accepting societies tend to make use of lineal rather than conjugal funds. Yet in much of France, inheritance was based on conjugal funds rather than lineal funds. Probably as a response, the code enacted under Napoleon between 1800 and 1804 retained the mutual-consent divorce, but limited it by adding many steps to the process, including the use of a family court. The code also reinstated the parental right of disinheritance for a disapproved marriage, but lowered the ages to 25 for men and 21 for women. In 1816, when the monarchy returned, divorce was once again prohibited. It remained prohibited until 1884, long after the French had turned to a republican form of government again. In view of both the continuing rurality of France and the experience of industrializing England, the French divorce rate may remain comparatively low until the end of the 20th century. After all, it took almost a century for the effects of economic and social change brought by the industrial and agricultural revolutions of the 18th century even to begin to be reflected in the provisions for divorce in England, and another century to move from divorce as a punishment for fault to divorce as a recognition of a mutual dissatisfaction too great to be overcome.

In neighboring Switzerland concern that the children of a marriage should not become a charge as paupers on the public funds led over the years to various local regulations to prohibit any marriage unless the local government gave permission for it. These regulations may have been foreshadowed in the 16th century by the Genevan regulations that the city's governing council must give its permission to women under 18 or men under 20 to wed, unless the fathers of the woman and the man had specifically given theirs. Not until 1876 did the last of those sets of regulations give way. As a result, in the canton or district of Lucerne (where regulations were particularly strict), 39% of all women of 50 or over in 1870 were still unmarried. However, as shown in a study of the Zurich region from 1671 to 1792 by Rudolf Braun in Charles Tilly's collection *Historical Studies of Changing Fertility* (1978), it was the most fertile areas that had the highest checks on marriage. These were the areas in which the peasants were most conscious of not wanting to see lands divided because farm holdings were already at optimal size. Where land was poor (and still relatively plentiful in the 18th century) such checks were low or even nonexistent. As a consequence, when industrialization arrived in the form of the putting-out system (by which a weaver, for example, contracted to provide cloth if provided with wool), it was the people of the poorer districts who were more ready to build up a labor force to make use of this new source of income. They went ahead and married, having children who could help to card and spin the wool. They then used what was paid for the cloth to make improvements on their land.

In the Netherlands, on the other hand, and also in Belgium, earlier commercialization and industrialization had meant more opportunity outside the household than was yet available in Switzerland. Therefore, the persistence of a favoring of one son as inheritor of the family land in an agricultural area (as among the Walloons) did not require precluding others from marrying. Instead, it required that they migrate. In the Netherlands they could go to the newly made land of the great 17th-century era of construction of dikes and fields financed by Dutch trade overseas. In both the Netherlands and Belgium they could go to the growing cities, with their commercial and eventually industrial opportunities. The degree to which experience with migration promoted the giving up of the sense of extended family in the Netherlands, in favor of concentration on the nuclear family, may be judged from the existence in the Dutch language of a specific single word for the nuclear family. However, the existence of that term may also show a continuing need to distinguish the nuclear from the extended family, because of continuing frequent interactions with more distant kin. In English, it has come to be virtually taken for granted that "family" means "nuclear family," unless some qualifying word or phrase or other contextual indicator suggests otherwise.

Restrictions on marriage, similar to those in Switzerland and established for similar reasons in similar circumstances, continued to be maintained in much of Germany well into the 19th century. In Bavaria such restrictions were used to limit marriages to those with prospects of inheritance. In effect, they may have taken the place of the expectation that there must be a favored heir, but that he must pay his siblings equal shares of an amount set by the father so that they could marry. That expectation had been given up in the 16th century. In Hanover the restrictions on marriages may have come out of the late 17th-century rule, in at least some districts, that the local overlord must approve the marriage contracts made by peasants in his district. Everywhere in late-17th- and early-18th-century Germany there was a tendency to move toward the favoring of a single heir, if that was not already the local practice. There was also a tendency to limit marriage, insofar as possible, to those who could demonstrate that they and their offspring could expect to provide for their own livelihood. Sometimes a couple tried to force the authorities' hand by conceiving before marriage, but such efforts often failed to win permission to wed.

In Carinthia in Austria, in the late 18th century, people might persuade a priest to marry them; but then each spouse would still have to stay in his or her natal home, for lack of permission to set up separate housekeeping. When the clergy tried to halt this by refusing to marry a couple unless they could live together, the illegitimacy rate soared. Still, the restrictions were kept until the late 19th century. The result was that in 1880, 45% of women 50 or over had never married, which is quite possibly the highest percentage for any district in Europe. In Poland, on the other hand, the family pattern was for all married sons to stay with the parents. The parents approved their children's marriages, though by the 20th century they no longer arranged them, and the widowed of both sexes were actively encouraged to remarry. Perhaps as a result of a continued parental role in marriage arrangements, fewer than one in five peasant marriages in Poland were between a landholding and a landless family, in the decades immediately before the Communist takeover after World War II. That was about the same proportion as in Norway in the 1850s, according to Michael Drake in *Population and Society in Norway 1735–1865* (1969).

Bavaria saw increasing illegitimacy rates after the mid–18th century. Nevertheless the marriage restrictions continued to be enforced until the 1850s. According to the study of one Bavarian village from 1692 to 1939, published by J. Knodel in *Population Studies* for 1970, the percentage of pregnant brides in first marriages for both spouses rose only from 14% in 1692–1749 to 17% in 1750–99 and 20% in 1800–49. Then, after the lifting of the previous restrictions on marriage, it dropped to 14% in 1850–99. It rose again to 20% in 1900–39. Perhaps the old peasant concern for marital fertility was still in evidence. In earlier centuries peasants in many regions had allowed intercourse to the betrothed, so that they might decide whether or not to marry if they found themselves unable to conceive. Even early-20th-century Bavaria was still highly rural, and its peasants were still concerned to maintain family lines. Marriage-ages were high in the village studied. The mean age for first marriage for women was never under 26.6, and for men, never under 27.1. The highest means were 29.4 for women and 30.2 for men, in the first half of the 19th century. Even with the closeness in age of partners indicated by those figures, husbands and wives might be left widowed. The average age for being widowed was in the late 40s before 1800, in the 50s in the 19th century, and close to 60 in the early 20th century. As the loss of a partner came later and later, the tendency to remarry diminished. Before 1800 almost ⅔ of widows and more than ⅓ of widowers remarried. The men who wed again—as almost all of those under 50 did—often remarried within less than three months. The women, most of whom under 40 remarried, often did so within less than six months. After 1800 the proportions of remarrying widows and widowers steadily decreased. Barely one in eight of either sex remarried in the early 20th century. The time before remarriage lengthened too, to more than six months for men and more than four years for women.

One Bavarian village is not all of Germany, of course. But the preservation of its records so that its demographic history can be traced over such a long period is unusual, given Germany's experience with wars and destruction during that time. Nor is one textile town east of Düsseldorf in the Rhineland all of Germany; but as described by W. Koellman in David Glass and D.E.C. Eversley's *Population in History* (1965), Barmen offers some instructive insights into urban marital patterns in an industrializing society. Barmen's population multiplied 25-fold from 1598 to 1910. Most of that growth came after 1889. In 1815, 41% of those who married in Barmen had been born there (51% in 1855), but only 16% (30% in 1855) of marriages were of one Barmen-born person to another, and 34% (though only 25% in 1855) were of persons neither of whom had been born in Barmen. By 1890, when more than 60% of Barmen's people had been born there (for perhaps the first time since the 1850s), migrants had come to the town from distant as well as nearby parts of Germany. They were drawn by the hope of jobs in its mills, but in different proportions as between men and women. From nearby, 124 women came for every 100 men, and from farther away, 70 women came for every 100 men. This indicates men's greater and women's lesser (or their families' greater and lesser) willingness to put a long distance between self and family. By 1907 that figure was up to 132 women for every 100 men from nearby, but still only a little over 71 women for every 100 men from afar. Given those mutually complementary proportions, however, the overall sex ratio in Barmen was only slightly unfavorable to women. The situation was not like that which prevailed in Germany after both world wars, when front-line casualties left proportions that were near five females of all ages for every four males. Still, Barmen is in the western region that Knodel and M. J. Maynes, in an article in the *Journal of Family History* for 1976, describe as being like southern Germany in 1880 in showing the greatest numbers never marrying as well as the latest marriage-ages. At that time the mean age of first marriage in all of Germany was 28.1 for men and 25.5 for women. The percentages of men and women still unmarried at 49 were 8.7% and 11%, respectively. The authors suggested that men married women when they felt they could afford to, whereas women married when they found a man who was prepared to marry. They also suggested that eastern Germany, where marriage was both earlier and more nearly universal, may have been a transition zone to the pattern of universal early marriage common in eastern Europe.

Before moving from central to eastern Europe, however, it would be well to glance at Scandinavia. Eastern Sweden, too, might seem like a possible transition zone to the eastern European pattern, for in the 19th century it had more and earlier marriages than western Sweden. However, that was probably because it was more urbanized than western Sweden. The greater inclination of the hourly-wage worker to marry than of the propertied to marry is the likely explanation.

As in Ireland, so in much of the more southerly crop-raising part of Scandinavia, the pre–1700 pattern tended to be for one favored heir to seek a wife with a large marriage-portion, so that he could pay his father for the farm. His siblings either married out, remained with him as unwed workers, or sought opportunity elsewhere. Some nonheir sons married brotherless heiresses to other farm families. However, in the large northern areas more suited to grazing than to field crops, the divisibility and self-multiplication of herds meant more nearly universal (though not necessarily earlier) marriage. Allowing only one heir to marry could be risky, as pointed out by J. P. Cooper in Jack Goody and others' *Family and Inheritance* (1976). Danish nobles cut their own numbers almost in half from 1660 to 1720 by limiting their marriages. They were trying to preserve family properties within an inheritance system which gave the land to the eldest son, but anticipated that other sons would receive equal cash portions (and daughters, half-portions). As a result the land-receiving heir would finally receive no more than his brothers, having in all probability paid them out of the income from the land. Under these circumstances having many of one's own children marry and have children seemed inadvisable.

As commercialization and industrialization began to spread in the 18th century (and the potato, as in Ireland), more people began to marry in the crop-raising areas of Scandinavia than had done so before. Then, as death rates declined with the introduction of vaccination, returning population pressure led to a slight but real decline in marriage rates by the 1840s. By 1865 more than ½ (instead of less than ½) the population age 15 to 29 was still unmarried. This was true even though mean ages at first marriage went up only slightly from 1841 to 1865 for both women and men, and mean ages at all marriages (including remarriage) remained approximately the same. According to Michael Drake, in *Population and Society in Norway, 1735–1865* (1969), mean ages during 1841 to 1859 rose from 28 to 29 for first marriages for men and from 26 to almost 27 for women, remaining almost 31 for men and about 28 for women for all marriages. In 1865, 11% of men and 15% of women were still unmarried at 50, compared with 9% of men and 15% of women in 1801. About 83% of marriages between 1841 and 1865 were between previously unmarried people. About 10% were between widowers and spinsters, about 5% were between widows and bachelors, and only about 2% were between two widowed persons.

Scandinavia remains a region of relatively late marriage. Except for more industrialized Sweden, it also remains a region with the relatively low divorce rates that tend to be associated with the less urbanized agricultural producers among commercialized European states. That may in turn reflect a sense that there are nearby kin to turn to for emotional support, in a less geographically mobile society. Being close to other family can lessen the strains often placed on the marital tie, when one's spouse is the only other adult family member within call. The reality of such kinship links, for those who live in rural Scandinavia in particular, is evident in phenomena like the lineage books that have been published in most Norwegian districts. These books show who married whom, who begat whom, and where they moved to (if known), for the lineage group associated with every farmstead in the district. They trace each lineage group back to the beginning of church registration of births, marriages, and deaths in the 17th century.

Long-standing courtship patterns, as well as kinship ties, may play a part in low divorce rates. By at least as early as the 17th century, in many parts of rural Scandinavia (and also parts of rural Germany), all village youths called on all village maidens in an organized way. They then gradually paired off, with the acquiescence of their parents. (This system was paralleled, to some degree, by regular community gatherings in rural areas in France, Spain, and other European countries, at which young people could meet and their elders could recognize potential matches.) This may mean that habits of looking for personal qualities which would wear well in marriage, and of not marrying the first one looked at, both of which would be conducive to mature choice and to lasting relationships, have been deeply enough ingrained to survive the commercialization of Scandinavian economic life.

As far as marriage patterns and associated family relations were concerned, eastern Europe presented a very different picture from the West in the period of western Europe's commercialization and industrialization. The 13- to 16-member households of the Baltic regions of Estonia and Latvia, the extended-family households of the Russian mir or collective village, and the large joint families of up to 40 members and beyond of the Balkans were quite unlike the nuclear families that predominated to the west. Large households may have been the norm on the east shore of the Baltic since before the 13th century, when the order of Teutonic Knights established a German aristocracy there. The Teutonic Knights found that the large extended-family household, common among Slavic peoples, was useful to them as a unit on which to levy fees and duties. They therefore encouraged its continuance, by rules comparable to those complained of in 1789 by the peasants of Franche-Comté. As Andrejs Plakans reported in the *Journal of Family History* for 1977, the average household size on one large Latvian estate in 1797 was 17, and 86% of households had at least 12 members. Households generally included at least two married couples and their children, as well as resident workers on the household lands (many of them unmarried young people from other households). Marriage within the confines of the estate was expected, unless the overlord permitted otherwise. As a result almost everyone in the estate's serf population was at least distantly related to someone in every other household. There were also a number of marriages between those with cultivation rights and those without. Marriages, which were arranged by fathers, uncles, and brothers, tended to come later than elsewhere in eastern Europe—almost as late as in western Europe. That relatively late marriage-age has persisted into the Soviet era. The Estonian Soviet Socialist Republic, which is the most urbanized of the Soviet republics and has the highest per capita income, also has the highest age at marriage (and the lowest fertility), the largest percentage never marrying, and the highest divorce rate. Perhaps the strains of urban life counteract the high marriage-age, in bringing about a relatively high divorce rate. Mean marriage-ages for men might be in the late 20s or even 30 or 31 in some other parts of pre-20th-century eastern Europe. According to Thomas H. Hollingsworth, in *Historical Demography* (1969), that was true for the lower Danube valley in 1866, when it was still under Ottoman Turkish rule. But for women, marriage-ages were seldom far past 20 in pre-20th-century eastern Europe outside the Baltic region. In the lower Danube valley in 1866 they were often under 20. This made it highly probable that husbands would be fully a decade older than wives, with all that that could mean for their ability to exercise the authority of age or seniority.

In Rumania, endogamous free villages seem to have been the pattern from the 6th century A.D. (after the last vestiges of Roman authority had disappeared) to the 16th century (after the Ottomans arrived). In these villages the youngest son inherited the parents' home and land rights, while older sons moved out, perhaps even to help form new villages. Most villages sold themselves to local armed lords for protection from Ottoman tax collectors in the course of the 16th century. Their residents thereby lost the freedom to move to another village. Endogamy became required, rather than simply being the most convenient way to find a spouse. However, during the 17th century, most of the villages recovered their residents' freedom of movement by trading payment of taxes for that right. They still owed 6 person-days of labor per year per household to the lord on his own land. By the early 19th century that had been raised to 56 days, once the lords found that they could sell grain to western European markets. That was still hardly more than one day a week, in contrast to the usual two to three days per week required of each serf household in a Russian mir by then. In coastal Dalmatia on the Adriatic Sea, in present-day Yugoslavia, labor services increased from 10 days per extended-family household per year in the 16th century to 90, almost 2 days a week, by the time Austrian conquest ended serfdom there in 1815. When the last labor-dues vestiges of serfdom were abolished in Rumania in 1864, it gave the peasants more control of their own time. However, it was not as much of a release as in imperial Russia when serfdom was abolished there in 1855. In terms of marriage, the Rumanian emancipation also made far less difference than the Russian one. Voluntary village endogamy had remained usual in Rumania after freedom of movement had been recovered, and parents generally took some account of their children's probable preference. But in Russia rules against mir-dwellers leaving without permission had been supplemented by rules enabling overlords to arrange all marriages among the serfs on their lands. Some overlords exercised that authority with attention to ascertainable preferences, and some did not.

The eastern European states that came under Soviet occupation or pressure by 1945 and established Communist governments not long afterward—Poland, Czechoslovakia, Hungary, Rumania, and Bulgaria—continued into the mid–20th century to be regions of almost universal marriage. They also continued to have fairly early marriage-ages, at least for women, and rather low divorce rates. There were some exceptions among pockets of German settlers from earlier centuries who had brought with them the later-marrying patterns of 16th- to 18th-century Germany. Most of the people of these eastern European states were Orthodox, who could divorce, but only after careful weighing of the circumstances by the church. The chief exceptions were Poland (largely Roman Catholic), a religiously mixed population in Czechoslovakia, and some Muslims in Bulgaria. Parental involvement in the arranging of marriages also continued to be visible in most of eastern Europe into the 20th century, especially in rural areas. However, since the 1950s these states have been experiencing a rise in women's (and men's) marriage-ages, a sharp decline in parental involvement in marriage-arrangement, and increases both in the percentage not marrying at all and in the divorce rate. By 1981, in fact, Czechoslovakia was experiencing a two-in-five divorce rate for new marriages. Marriage-ages there had fallen to 20 for women and 23 for men (young, compared with other eastern European states by then), in response to state-provided benefits to encourage marriage and child bearing that had been introduced a decade earlier.

The communal household, or *dvor*, in the Russian mir, the communal household, or *zadruga*, among Serbs (now in Yugoslavia), and the communal households of Slovenes, Croats, Montenegrins, Albanians, and others elsewhere in the Balkans have significant differences. Yet they also show many similarities. All of them have tended to divide at some point after reaching a size of 30 to 50, as more spouses entered and more children were born. The comradeship of brothers became the relative coolness of cousins as the generations passed. Moreover, the household accumulated enough cattle, implements, and other goods so that when division took place, each resulting new unit would be able to take with it a full complement of what its members would need. For the dvor, still very much a reality in rural Soviet life in the 1960s, according to Sula Benet in the 1970 *Transactions of the New York Academy of Sciences*, this usually meant division between brothers after the father's death, about when their sons were reaching marriage-age. In the era of serfdom the overlord had controlled the occupational and marital choices of the serfs. In the short two generations between emancipation in 1855 and revolution in 1917 the dvor head was recognized as having the right to make both marital and occupational decisions for the other members of the household, although he was expected to consult the other adult members of the household as well as the godparents. However, that authority began to be eroded with the reform of 1906, which allowed sons to claim their share of household land at marriage. (The dvor head did not have the authority to beat his wife with a whip, as the serf husband had had until that was made illegal in 1853.) In the Soviet era the dvor head lost the remainder of his authority over household members. However, on the kolkhoz, the collective farm, dvor members still pooled their incomes and managed them jointly rather than separately.

A sonless dvor would ordinarily bring in a *primak*, an in-marrying husband, for at least one daughter. Before the Soviet era the primak brought in an animal or two, as a parallel to a bride's expected dowry of cloth. He gave up all claims to gear or land rights when his natal household divided. He might even take his wife's father's name, once the imperial government required the newly freed serfs to take family names for registration purposes. In the Soviet era the dowries of the past dwindled into a few household articles. These no longer remain under the wife's control, to be shared only with her daughters to increase their dowries. However, village endogamy remains the rule in rural areas, given Soviet restrictions on changing residence without permission. The partners to a marriage now select each other. Unless they are loyal enough to the Russian Orthodox Church to continue to use its incest rules—which proscribe any blood-kin closer than second cousin, or any parent, sibling, or offspring of a former spouse—they may marry even first cousins, aunts, uncles, nieces, or nephews. Only siblings, ancestors, and descendants are forbidden by Soviet law, which was framed to allow for a variety of customary marriage patterns among the many peoples of the Soviet Union.

Once the dvor head lost most of his authority over the life-choices of dvor members, he also lost his previous informal right of access to the wife of any of his sons who might be away for a long time, on labor service or as a military conscript. When such labor or military service might mean an absence of as much as 20 to 25 years, it was felt that the wife's childbearing years should be used to raise sons for her husband. It was regarded as likely to be less divisive within the dvor if the husband's father rather than a brother did so.

Marriage-ages were young in 19th-century Russia. In one central Russia district, 95% of women and 85% of men married by the time they were 21, according to Peter Czap, in David Ransel's collection *The Family in Imperial Russia* (1978). According to Ansley Coale and others, in *Human Fertility in Russia Since the Nineteenth Century* (1979), women's marriage-ages declined (and marital fertility increased) as one moved east and south from the Baltic coast in European Russia in the 19th century. In the 20th century, however, since the Soviet Union came into being after the 1917 Revolution, women's marriage-ages have declined somewhat where they were highest and have risen where they were lowest. As a result, for all of the Russian Federated Socialist Soviet Republic (including most of the European Russia of the 19th century), marriage-ages for both sexes by the 1970s were near the 1914 median ages in the urban and already somewhat industrialized center of Moscow—23 for women and 26 for men.

The Serbian zadruga has now been effectively replaced in Yugoslavia by the nuclear family form. The other variants of the collective household that had been the norm in rural areas before World War II in Yugoslavia, Albania, and much of Bulgaria have also disappeared. In all of them the leader was regarded as a representative for the household to the authorities, rather than as a maker of decisions for its members. He was selected either by lot or by the agreement of the married men as to which one of them should take on the leader's duties. He was expected always to consult with the other married men. He was also expected to consult with the married women, through the leader he appointed from among them, before undertaking any action from purchasing implements to arranging marriages. He virtually never appointed his own wife, for to do so would concentrate too much authority in one couple's hands. Both the zadruga head and the woman he chose as women's leader were responsible for assigning tasks to the household members of their own sex. Tasks might be carried out singly or in teams, but they were generally rotated among members. However, both the head and the women's leader were also expected to pay close attention to individual capabilities and preferences. A new bride was not put on the work list for a year. During her first year she had opportunity to make friends with all the household members, and to demonstrate what she could do through volunteering. (This was almost totally opposite to the situation of a traditional Chinese peasant bride, on whom demands were deliberately made immediately so that she would quickly learn to obey her husband's parents.) Other Yugoslav, Bulgarian, and Albanian collective-household forms were not as democratic as the zadruga. In all of them, though, whether Orthodox Christian, Roman Catholic, or Muslim, what the bride brought with her was hers to pass on to her daughters as part of their dowry. She received no inheritance at her parents' deaths, regardless of what distant governmental authorities or even local religious leaders might say about a daughter's inheritance rights.

All of these collective-household societies practiced endogamy in some form, within the limitations of whatever incest rules their religious affiliation imposed. In Islamic Albania people leaned toward marrying patrilineal kin, like Middle Eastern Muslims. In Dalmatia they sought to marry within the village as much as possible, even after the ending of serfdom lifted restrictions on changing residence. Because a large collective household of 30 or more was seldom without sons, in-marrying husbands were few, but not entirely unknown. Zadrugas and similar forms in Yugoslavia seldom divided before reaching 50, until the 20th century. Then they began increasingly to move toward simply dividing at a father's death. The true ongoing collective form, resembling that of the pastoralist Jie of Uganda, only survived until the 1930s, and then only in the inland Yugoslav regions of Bosnia and Macedonia.

In view of the importance of personal compatibility within a large group like a zadruga or other collective household, it is not surprising that Muslims or Orthodox Christians might use the divorce provisions available to them, if a young wife proved less compatible in the household than expected. Nor is it surprising that any of the groups using large-household forms in the Balkans might use betrothal to allow a trial period of residence before the formal marriage ceremony. That was done at least in the 19th century, if not in the 20th. If the marriage was not formalized, the two were treated as if widower and widow. Each was then expected to marry someone who was either in a similar position or genuinely widowed, rather than someone who had never been married. Virtually everyone married, except that at least in Serbia and Albania, a woman might assume a man's clothing, forswear marriage, and work and fight with the men of the household. Since 1900 these centuries-old patterns have been increasingly replaced by self-selection of partners, nuclear-family households, and older ages at first marriage. These changes have taken place first in the towns (already changing when the 20th century opened) and then in the rural areas. However, divorce rates remain fairly low, even though the various Communist governments have enacted divorce legislation that enables couples to divorce by mutual consent after court hearings.

The marriage and divorce laws of all the eastern European Communist states except Yugoslavia and Albania have largely been modeled on the laws developed in the Soviet Union, after a series of experiments. By 1775, as Jessica Tovrov suggests in the Ransel collection, the nobles of imperial Russia had accepted western European ideals of marriage as companionship and self-selection of partners as preferable, though with parental approval expected. The previous social separation between men and women was gradually eliminated, to facilitate that self-selection. During the 19th century the urban intelligentsia and middle class also accepted these ideals. By the early 20th century they had penetrated the urban working class as well, though not the peasantry. However, no divorce was allowed in the Russian Orthodox Church (unlike the Greek), only annulment. In practice, annulments were available only to the well-to-do, who could afford to take the time to use the church courts. Consequently, when the new revolutionary government decided in 1918 to institute marriage by simple mutual consent (not even requiring registration), the change was so sudden that people had difficulty handling it. Equally unsettling were the abrupt reversals of familiar expectations that resulted when the new government also ceased to recognize spouses' jointly held property as a conjugal fund. (People could hold only personal property, not land or even residences, under the new regime.) Divorce was allowed not only by mutual consent and registration, but by one partner notifying the other and the court that the marriage was ended, which left little room for seeking reconciliation. Furthermore, no provision was made for alimony or child support, on the ground that in the socialist state, where all were equal, women would be working and earning as did men.

In the kibbutz communities that Jewish immigrants from Russia and elsewhere began to set up in the Israel of their dreams in the 1920s, such a system could and did and still does function. (Israeli law took cognizance of the special nature of the kibbutz when the state was established in 1948.) It could function because the kibbutz was a relatively small and supportive group. The kibbutz provided community child care for infants and children, though members learned by experience that children would thrive better if there was a continuing close tie to their own parents, for emotional security. The kibbutz provided sympathetic companionship for each of the partners to a marriage if it ended in divorce, as well as to the survivor if a partner died. Perhaps above all, the kibbutz provided assurance of continuing livelihood for both the former spouses and any children they might have had, if a divorce occurred. So familylike is a kibbutz that those born and raised in the same kibbutz almost invariably marry someone from outside. However, in the Soviet Russia of 1918 and after—devastated by World War I, lacking supportive child-care services, without well-paying work for untrained housewives dumped into the work force by a "postcard divorce," as the unilateral notification type came to be called—the new set of rules proved unworkable.

Like kibbutz members, the Soviet government came to recognize potential advantages in encouraging ongoing parent-child relationships, particularly since child-care services were and still are in short enough supply so that the "babushka," the grandmother, is still very much in evidence as babytender. The Soviets also recognized the need to provide for children's maintenance. Therefore, they reintroduced alimony in 1936, as maintenance for minor children as well as for a former spouse who was too incapacitated to work. Alimony did not go automatically from former husband to former wife, though. It was to be paid by whichever former spouse had the better income. Usually, but not invariably, that meant the man. In addition, the Soviets set an escalating schedule of divorce fees, making each successive divorce costlier for the individual who divorced more than once. In 1944 the formal registration of a marriage was required. The fees required for divorce were sharply raised, and a requirement was added that the couple must be counseled with regard to possible reconciliation before divorcing. By the Soviet Union's Supreme Court's directive of 1949, divorce was to be allowed only for "serious and established cause." The right of an unmarried mother to file a paternity claim was also removed in the 1940s, and a monthly governmental support payment was substituted. Soviet lawmakers probably recognized that the unbalanced sex ratio resulting from losses in World War II—1959 figures showed almost 200 females for every 100 males over 32 years old—was likely to lead to too many such paternity claims to handle. In 1947 the Soviet Union central government took over responsibility for legislation on marriage and family from the various republics. Between 1953 and 1968 the government moved to restore three former policies, in modified form. Some paternity claims were again allowed. Divorce could take place by mutual consent without required reconciliation counseling when no minor children were involved. Unilateral divorce was made possible for those married to persons who were legally missing or legally incompetent or who had been sentenced to at least three years in prison for the commission of a crime.

The official ideal for the Soviet family is the companionship model. Ideally, spouses are expected to share in household decisions and tasks, in a joint rather than a complementary or an independent way. In practice, however, only those husbands born after 1945 give their wives much help in household tasks. Of those who genuinely live by the joint model, a large share are at a socioeconomic level comparable to the English dual-career families studied by the Rapoports. They can therefore employ household workers to carry out many needed daily tasks. In most urban households, as well as in most rural ones, something more like the complementary or the independent mode tends to hold sway despite official urgings. Resultant role-stress (as well as strains caused by overcrowded housing, a chronic complaint) may help to explain the high Soviet divorce rate. By 1982 it was predicted that one in three existing Soviet marriages would eventually end in divorce.

When the Soviet central government took over marriage and family law from the federated republics in 1947, it recognized that greater uniformity was possible across the Soviet Union than before. Increased geographic mobility, and increased settlement of Russian speakers outside the Russian Federated Soviet Socialist Republic, had accelerated social change. In the early 1920s the new Soviet Union had tried to break down parental (mainly paternal) control of marriage and every other aspect of children's lives in its Asian territories. It had introduced and tried to enforce laws much like those established in 1918 in European Russia. However, it had found so much opposition that it had retreated somewhat from the attempt to enforce them. Instead, it turned to measures like requiring school attendance for both sexes and providing opportunity for women to earn independent incomes outside the home. These were seen as needed to prepare the way for moving away from patrilineal patrilocal extended-family forms, used not only by the Muslims of Soviet Central Asia, but also by a good many of the herding peoples of Siberia. Once the nuclear conjugal-family form became the goal of Soviet legislation after 1936, the provision of outside schooling and outside employment continued to be recognized as helpful to establishing the new family form in the Soviet Union's Asian territories. As far as urban centers were concerned, that change had largely taken place by 1968, when the new all-Soviet legislation was finally in place. However, the three-generation family was still found in villages.

One of the types of customs the founders of the Soviet Union were most eager to eliminate was the use of either bride-wealth or dowry, in whatever form. Both bride-wealth and dowry seemed to place a woman on the market, rather than to treat her as the equal of a man. However, that is not how dowry had been viewed in Mediterranean Europe, Greece, Italy, Spain, and Portugal, in all of which dowry continues to be used.

Greece has been the last nation to maintain laws based on the Justinian code of the 6th-century Eastern Roman Empire. Dowry continued to be a legal requirement there for marriage until 1983. At that time the father ceased to be defined by law as the head of the household. A wife was permitted to start a private business without having to have her husband's permission. Civil marriage was finally allowed (the last European state to institute it). Consideration also began to be given to the establishment of divorce legislation like that of 1971 in England, by which the fact of a specified number of years of separation can serve as sufficient evidence of marital breakdown to make divorce possible. With the elimination of dowry and of an Orthodox wedding as legal requirements for marriage, the still-strong roles of godparents and of wedding sponsors may begin to diminish somewhat. However, their usefulness as mediators in a variety of social situations means that they will probably continue to be important as they are in the rest of Mediterranean Europe. Moreover, the experience of Italy, Spain, and Portugal suggests that dowry needs no legal requirement to flourish, where local circumstances and beliefs encourage it.

A woman's dowry is in fact her share in her parents' property in Greece, Italy, Spain, and Portugal. It is delivered at marriage, rather than at her parents' death, so that the marriage may be regarded by both partners to it as establishing an economically sound relationship. The dowry helps to ensure their children's well-being through this guaranteed contribution to their inheritance. The husband will not receive it if the wife dies first, except as a trust for any children. If she predeceases him, it will go to her blood-kin if she dies childless, as in ancient Greece, not to him or to his kin. In pre-19th-century Spain he even had to return any increment earned on it. Because dowry has an economic importance for the family, it is likely that it will continue in practice among many families in Greece, as it has in the others.

What may be affected most by the ending of the requirement for dowry at marriage in Greece may be the marriage-ages of the daughters of the poor, who have had to rely on virtue rather than more than just a token dowry. They will be under less parental pressure to wed early, before they might fall victim to temptation. Brothers had already largely stopped killing their sister's seducer and their seduced sister by 1960, although husbands continued even after that to kill unfaithful wives and their lovers.

The daughters of the propertied in Greece will probably still wed early, if they are from families rich enough to afford a dowry as soon as a suitable match may be found. They will probably also still marry late, if they are from less wealthy families that need time to accumulate enough dowry to attract an acceptable suitor and his family. The ideal of partner self-selection has been accepted at all social levels in the 20th century. Yet it is still coupled with concern for parental approval, which is still likely to hinge in part on the economic prospects of the couple. This in turn is likely to continue (as in Italy, Spain, and Portugal) to mean an expectation that the bride's share of her family property should come to her at marriage. Especially in view of increases in life expectancies, there is real value to a married couple in having the new wife bring her inheritance with her, rather than wait until her parents die. Otherwise, the couple's children may be grown and married before the time to inherit comes.

In northern Italy, where Franks and Lombards had once ruled, sons continued to be favored in inheritance over daughters into the 19th century. However, inheriting sons also inherited the father's obligation either to provide marriage portions for their unmarried sisters or to place them in a convent. In the south the Justinian code's provision for equal inheritance by sons and daughters was honored, to some degree. In practice, this was primarily done by providing dowry, though not always as an equal share. All over Italy dowries increased in size after the 16th century, perhaps reflecting an increasing surplus of marriageable women. One answer was to portion the daughter with a house, as also came to be done in parts of Greece. Another was to ration marriages more closely. Italian families kept control over marriage arrangements well into the 20th century, even though they began in the 19th century to accept some degree of self-selection, by paying more attention to objections raised (and preferences expressed) by the potential partners. Family control of marriage may help to explain why the percentage of women between 18 and 49 who had not yet married was 34% in 1871 and had increased to 36.5% in 1931, even though the mean age of first marriage held steady at about 24. However, World War II casualties (and consequent difficulty in finding partners) probably had more to do than family control with that percentage being 37.3% in 1951, when the mean age at first marriage was still 24. Not until 1971 did legal divorce (rather than only church annulment) become possible in Italy. Once available, though, it began to be used in Italy at a rate resembling that in France. Legal divorce came even later in Spain. Rates were lower there, probably in part because more people continued to accept Roman Catholic teachings, but probably also because Spain was less urbanized.

In 16th-century Spain, as in 16th-century France, concern for the acceptable marriage of children ran especially high among the nobility. In Spain the nobility were effectively definable as those who had property entailed on them by a royal grant. In 1559 in Castile (which included much of Spain) a father was allowed to disinherit any daughter who wed without his permission at any age, and any son who married without his approval before the age of 25. By 1600 a daughter could require in a court of law that her father provide her with a portion either to marry or to enter a convent, if neither the mother nor any of the four grandparents could furnish it. (Spanish and Portuguese convents tended to require an entry fee.) In 1730, 6% of the entire adult population of Spain were in celibate religious orders, with 12% of adult men and 11% of adult women in 1787 having never married by the time they reached 60. Widowers often remarried. They usually married previously unwed women, thereby gaining the use of a second dowry. Widows seldom remarried, however. As widows, they came into the control of their own property, fully so if childless, or in trust for children if they had them.

Even the 1787 percentages of never-marrying men and women were low by comparison with some marriage-controlling areas of Austria, Germany, and Switzerland at that time. By 1900, when 6% of men and 9.5% of women had never married by age 60, the situation in Spain was more like what prevailed then in most other western European countries. Marriage-ages for men rose noticeably between 1787 and 1900, but only slightly for women. Only 10% of men (though 25% of women) were married by age 25 in 1900, compared with 20% for men and 27.5% for women in 1787.

The 20th-century revolutionary experiences of Spain left in place a code of equal partible inheritance. This tends to be interpreted in terms of marriage portions for all but the favored heir among the Basques and others in the north, who were used to either impartibility or a larger share for the preferred heir. However, land has continued to be part of that share for almost all others in the agricultural areas. As a result, holdings have become fragmented over time. Cousin-marriage, in remote enough degree to be acceptable under church incest rules, is often favored as a means of reuniting them. In towns and cities other forms of real estate (among the wealthy at least) may be included in a daughter's dowry, as well as in a son's inheritance. But when that dowry comes to be partitioned among children, a choice may need to be made between fragmentation and some form of buying-out of shares. A dowry of movable property therefore seems better to many. Until economic growth brings a new sense of being able to rely on one's own capabilities, rather than needing to rely largely on inheritance—a sense that did not find its way into the life of France until the 1950s—dowry (as an inheritance in advance) is unlikely to disappear from Mediterranean Europe, whether in Portugal, Spain, Italy, or Greece.

We have looked in this chapter at the experiences of western and eastern European societies with some of the effects of commercialization, centralization, industrialization, and urbanization on marriage systems, in the context of the cultural tradition within which individualism first began to flourish. In the next chapter we will look at the experiences of societies in the Eastern Hemisphere that were influenced or even ruled by Europeans, but in which Europeans themselves did not settle in large numbers. In the chapter after that we will look at the experiences of societies in the Western Hemisphere and the Pacific basin in which Europeans settled and formed new societies.

CHAPTER 11

Marriage in Societies Moving Toward Industrialization and Commercialization: The Middle East, Asia, and Africa

The people of the Middle East, next to Mediterranean Europe, share a number of patterns with their neighbors. One of these is the use of dowry. Like Italians, Spaniards, Portuguese, and Greeks, both Muslims and Christians in the Middle East have preferred not to give agricultural land in dowry. It is understandable that Middle Easterners, both Christian and Muslim, have leaned toward patrilateral parallel-cousin marriage (though not first cousins among Christians). Even though patrilateral parallel-cousin marriage can promote factionalism, it is the quickest means of reuniting properties.

As reported in Edwin T. Prothro and Lutfy Najib Diab, *Changing Family Patterns in the Arab East* (1974), 13% of existing marriages in the overwhelmingly Sunni Muslim Jordanian village of Artas in the 1920s were between patrilateral parallel first cousins. Artas was still relatively untouched by European influence then. Another 13% of marriages were to other first cousins. As recently as 1970, in the commercial center of Beirut in Lebanon, 11% of existing marriages among Shiite Muslims were between patrilateral parallel first cousins. In a Shiite Muslim village in Lebanon, as E. L. Peters noted in Julian Pitt-Rivers's collection *Mediterranean Countrymen* (1963), there was a definite class difference in the degree of kin endogamy. Differing groups clearly had differing levels of concern for maintaining social status by marrying at one's own level, as cousin-marriage would do. They also had differing levels of interest in reuniting fragmented properties, so that their social status would retain an economic basis. Among members of landlord families 15% married a patrilateral parallel first cousin, and almost 22% more married a patrilateral parallel cousin at some further remove. (This total was close to the 41% of parents of students at the University of Karachi and the University of Punjab in Pakistan in 1965 who were cousins of some sort, although only 24% of the students' own already-married siblings were married to kin.) Among offspring of shopkeepers in this Lebanese village 18% married a patrilateral parallel first cousin, and 14% married some other type of parallel or cross cousin. However, fewer than 20% among ordinary peasants married any type of cousin, near or far.

High kin endogamy might be put down in part to lack of other candidates in comparatively isolated villages like Artas, or an Arab village in Israel studied by Henry Rosenfeld in J. G. Peristiany's collection *Mediterranean Family Structure* (1976). There, the mass departure of the people of neighboring villages when Israel was formed in 1948–49 meant a doubling of kin endogamy for both the Muslim and the Christian residents of the village in 1954–69, as compared with pre–1954 marriages. However, isolation could scarcely explain the high kin endogamy still found in Beirut.

In Berber Morocco, in a village studied by Vanessa Maher in Peristiany's collection *Kinship and Modernization in Mediterranean Society* (1976), the proportion of spouses from more than ten kilometers away almost doubled from 22% to 40% in a 40-year span. The villagers had a steady rate of 49 divorces for every 100 marriages during the 20th century, which was approximately the ratio reached in the United States in 1980. In the Kharga oasis in Egypt, kin endogamy was declining, according to A. M. Abou-Zeid in *Mediterranean Countrymen*. By the 1950s people began to use money earned by working elsewhere in order to purchase shares in several wells, as insurance against one well's drying up. They were doing so in preference to following the previous system of each lineage holding on to its own well. The establishment of links with new lineages, with whose members one shared ownership of wells, was beginning to outweigh the maintenance of links within one's own lineage. Circumstances altered calculations, as people's lives were affected by commercialization and by the establishment of a central government strong enough to end fears of blood feuds between lineages. The Kharga oasis provides an almost classic illustration of how both commercialization and governmental centralization influence whether people see marriage more as a means of strengthening the lineage, or more as a means of widening the network. Commercialization clearly replaces reliance on kin for economic well-being with a wider set of choices, while governmental centralization ends a need to rely on kin for physical safety. On the other hand, a less fully centralized government may actually encourage lineage-centeredness. In Morocco, for example, the dissolution of the national legislature in 1965 was followed by a turn to local councils based on representation from neighborhoods, which are almost always dominated by one kinship group. As long as lineages remain strong, high levels of divorce (like that found by Vanessa Maher in the village she studied) are not as disruptive as they are in a society in which the nuclear family is at the center of the social system.

In the 1920s the Arab village of Artas in Jordan showed that 4.5% of ever-married women had been divorced. Almost all of them had since remarried. In addition, 9% of ever-married women had been widowed. Most of them had remarried a brother of the deceased, and most of the rest had also remarried. Eleven percent of Artas men in the 1920s had more than one wife, going down to 8.7% in 1967. Those figures may be compared, on the one hand, with 21% of propertied urban men having more than one wife in Morocco in 1963 (but 2% of propertyless urban men) and, on the other hand, with only 2% of all Sunni Muslim men in Beirut having more than one wife in 1967. Only in 1981 did Egypt, for example, enact legislation to require an existing wife's permission for a man to take another wife. However, in Egypt and elsewhere such clauses could be and were written into individual marriage contracts before polygyny was either outlawed (as in Turkey in the 1920s and Tunisia in the 1950s) or limited by provisions like the Egyptian one. The Egyptian requirement that a current wife must agree to a man's marrying again paralleled a similar provision in a new marriage law in Iran in 1968. That law also allowed a wife to initiate divorce, which was still not possible in Egypt even after the 1981 reform. The new marriage law was a grievous shock to tradition-minded Iranians, who still saw a 10- to 20-year age difference at marriage as preferable, and still accepted the use of specified-term marriage for purposes such as providing heirs if a wife were childless. A divorce rate of one for every five marriages per year seemed perfectly acceptable to them, on the other hand.

Marriage-ages may help to explain the numbers of both widows and divorced women in Artas. The mean first-marriage age among Artas wives in the 1920s was 14. Women's mean first-marriage age in Artas was still only 17 in 1967. However, 22 was the mean first-marriage age for women in Beirut in 1967, whereas men's mean first-marriage ages in 1967 were 24 in Artas and 30 in Beirut. Marriage contracts in the Lebanese town of Sidon in the 1920s actually showed the mean first-marriage age for men to be more than twice that of their brides, 31.6 for men and 14.3 for women, a difference of 17.3 years. By 1960–65 the difference had been more than halved. Mean first-marriage ages in Sidon were 29.3 for men and 21 for women, slightly older than the 27 for men and 20 for women found in Karachi, Pakistan, in 1965. This lessening of difference in age may have helped to decrease divorce rates, as illustrated in the Lebanese town of Tripoli. There were 4 divorces for every 10 marriages per year in 1921–34 in Tripoli, but only 135 for every 1,000 in 1960–64. Compatibility may have been easier to find when both partners were in their 20s than when they were a generation apart. At the far eastern end of the Islamic world in Indonesia, high divorce rates—one for every two marriages in some areas, with perhaps 40% coming in the first year—led to the establishment in the 1960s of government marriage counseling offices to try to bring those rates down. However, the continuing pattern of relatively early marriage there would probably have to change before divorce rates would decline.

Barrenness clearly also continued to affect divorce decisions in the Middle East. In Jordan, in 1964, only 5% of all those married more than ten years

were childless, but 40% of those married more than ten years who sought
a divorce were childless. Nonetheless, after 1940 (perhaps as early as 1920
in some areas) the divorce rate began to decline in most of the Middle East.
The decline parallels the rise in women's ages at marriage, which brought
first-marriage ages closer together for men and women.

Opposition to early marriages for women mainly came from those Middle
Easterners who came in contact with western Europeans. They accepted
western European medical ideas about the preferability of delaying first
childbirth until at least the later teens, though they did not accept western
European willingness to see unmarried women work outside the home. As
Nadia Youssef noted in *Social Forces* for 1972, only $1/7$ as many women in
Pakistan, $1/5$ as many women in Egypt, and $1/3$ as many women in Morocco
worked outside the home at that time as worked outside the home in Chile
in South America. Chileans, too, held strong assumptions about women's
duty to the family being primary in their lives. However, a Middle Eastern
woman could rely on father or brother for economic support if she were
left husbandless, more than a Latin American woman could. The male kin
of a Latin American woman would feel obliged to see her "placed" either
in marriage, formerly (and sometimes even now) in a convent, or more often
now in a profession or at least a steady job. Nevertheless, they have then
come to expect her to make her own way. Spanish and Portuguese legal
tradition has accustomed them to the idea of widows managing their own
affairs. But in the Middle East a woman left alone was and still is regarded
as the responsibility of her male kin. By custom she was not free to move
about outside the home. Instead, she was expected to keep herself incon-
spicuously wrapped from head to toe whenever she had to go out on the
street. Village women were less strict about that than women in towns, for
they were moving among relatively few people, most of whom they knew;
but in towns, or with strangers, they usually also followed that rule. That
expectation lies at the root of the "Islamic modernist" mode of dress increasingly used by educated women in Egypt, Iran, and elsewhere. The
wearer of a head covering that flows over the top part of an ankle-length
long-sleeved gown and leaves the face visible, but not the hair, cannot be
accused of improper exposure of the hair and figure, as were those who
began wearing European dress in the 1920s.

Muslim law's requirement of dower from the husband to the wife also
expresses the view that a woman must always be protected and provided
for. So does the expectation of both Muslims and Christians in the Middle
East that a daughter will bring as dowry most or all of her share in her
parents' personal property. In practice, though, parents might connive (as
in parts of Lebanon) at a daughter's elopement with a suitor whom they
approved. Then she would take no dowry with her, leaving more to divide
among the other heirs. However, parents would insist that a son must marry
properly so that his bride would have to bring her dowry with her.

Formerly it was customary in many Muslim areas for the husband to pay the larger part of the *mahr*, or dower, at the marriage. He would reserve only a small part to pay if he divorced her, or for his estate to pay if he predeceased her. He might not actually pay that last portion, though, if it were really she who wanted a divorce. She might use an offer to forego the payment to persuade him to initiate it, since she could not. In other Muslim areas at least ½ the mahr was reserved for later payment, either within a specified term of years or at divorce or widowhood. The large-later-payment system offers more long-term security to the wife. It has become more widespread in recent times, although it had not yet replaced the large-early-payment system in Artas in 1967. Another variant, often found in Pakistan in particular, has also grown in popularity. In this form a large part of the mahr is left to be paid later, but it is to be paid when requested by the wife, rather than at a specified time. This allows her to pressure her husband by using a threat to request it, if she wishes to influence him for or against some action, and he is not responsive to her arguments.

The large-early-payment system may help to explain the lateness of men's marriage-ages. Its decline may also help to explain the lowering of those ages, and even the decline in the divorce rates, since the large-later-payment system makes divorce costlier if it comes. The dowry system helps to explain the early marriage-ages for women in the past. So does the emphasis on virginity for a woman at her first marriage. It raises her dowry and lowers her mahr if she is not virgin at that time. Emphasis on virginity also accounts for the widespread use of clitoridectomy in Islamic lands and some non-Islamic parts of Africa, as a prepubertal initiation rite to correspond to circumcision for males. Because clitoridectomy has the result of actually depriving a woman of the most excitable portion of her anatomy, it corresponds more closely to castration than to circumcision in a physical sense. It was only declared illegal in Egypt in 1958. It was still legal in many African countries in the 1980s. Clitoridectomy also serves a concern for marital fidelity and the paternity of children, by making a woman less easily aroused.

A study by N. S. Alamuddin and P. D. Starr, *Crucial Bonds: Marriage Among the Lebanese Druze* (1980), shows that virginity remained a factor in the sizes of mahr and dowry in Druze marriage contracts from 1931 to 1974. It also shows that marriages with high mahr (as a pledge of earnestness) were still being used to try to heal factional differences. Mahr was lower for marriages between kin or between neighbors, or if the man held higher status than the woman. Using marriage to end a feud was not just a Middle Eastern technique. In 1979 two politically antagonistic provincial governors in the Philippines sought to cement an alliance with a marriage between two of their children. Nor was using marriage for other political ends a Middle Eastern monopoly, since one of the two was at the same time marrying a son to the daughter of another political leader.

Other factors are more important than mahr and dowry for the recent increase in women's ages at first marriage. One is opportunity for women to study and work outside the home. Another is the decision of government after government from Morocco across to Pakistan between the 1920s and the 1960s to raise minimum ages for marriage to at least 15 or 16. Still, the continuance of dowry among Muslims and Christians, as well as the continuance of mahr among Muslims, means continuing parental involvement in the arrangement of marriages. Parents keep a watchful eye on the resulting affinal set, the shape of the network formed by the family's marriages.

Among Christians, divorce is rare, even where permitted. Among Roman Catholic Maronites in Lebanon, for example, only annulments are allowed. Therefore, the relationship of marriage is permanent enough so that spouses will often use a term for cousin (i.e., lifelong consanguine kin) to refer to each other when talking with third parties. However, among Muslims the preferred term is parent of X, once a child is born. This suggests that in a real sense, the kinship of a married pair is only seen as beginning with joint parenthood. As long as they might still divorce for barrenness, they are not yet fully linked.

The belief that parenthood is what makes marriage is gradually changing. The ideal of marriage-as-companionship is taking tentative root, and marriage is coming to be seen as more important, by comparison with relationships to blood-kin, as economic life commercializes and political life becomes centralized. Deniz Kandiyoti has observed that shift in a central Turkish village, in Peristiany's *Kinship and Modernization in Mediterranean Society* (1976). The village was founded in 1905 as part of a plan to turn nomads into settled farmers. By 1970 the farmers were using tractors, and more than 60% of the households sent daughters as well as sons to nearby towns, to work or go to secondary school. Fewer than one in ten still thought it acceptable in 1970 for the bride and groom not to have met and talked before the wedding, although parental arrangement was still the accepted norm. Moreover the groom, rather than his mother and sisters, met the bride when she came to his father's house for the marriage ceremony. This change clearly denoted that she was really joining her life to him, rather than to them as before.

Centralization and commercialization have played their part in the development of the companionship ideal in marriage and the gradual acceptance of partners' self-selection. But centralization and commercialization alone would not have been enough, as Japan clearly illustrates. Commercialization, centralization, even the institution of registrations of births, marriages, and deaths in the early 17th century—none of these resulted in the establishment of self-selection of partners as the Japanese norm. Women's registered first-marriage ages varied from 19 to as high as 25 in some 18th-century villages studied; but the higher ages may reflect a delay in registering the marriage until it seemed certain that the wife would not be divorced for barrenness or some other cause. The estimated mean first-marriage age for women in 1868 in Japan was 19. Women also did not usually have experience outside the natal home before they married. But most important, the ongoing *ie*, or household lineage, remained the focus of attention rather than the individual. The registration was an accounting of what was happening within the ie, item by item. It was kept according to ie, not in chronological order (all baptisms on a given day, for example) as in the churches of Europe. That pattern was maintained when the government took over the registration task after 1868. Each household's book was separately kept in the local record office. Each legally recognized household head—either the father-husband, or his eldest son after his death—was responsible for keeping it up to date.

Marriage was not necessarily universal. At least one city in Japan showed noticeably fewer locally born married than in-migrants between 1773 and 1871, somewhat like the situation noted in L. P. Moch's article on Nimes in France. A study of one small village between 1778 and 1871, by Akira Hayami in *Keio Economic Studies* for 1968, showed only about ⅔ of women married at 50. Some, but not all, would already have been widowed, like some of the ⅛ of men who had no wife at 50. There was a total of 237 married couples over the whole period. About ½ of the 49 divorced or widowed men remarried, most of them under 40. Eight could not be traced. However, only two of the fifty divorced or widowed women remarried, though nine could not be traced.

Divorce was not uncommon before a child was born, as the one divorce for every three marriages registered in 1885 makes clear, but was rather uncommon after a child came. Among those who could afford to bring or send more than one bride into or out of a household, more than one son might have a wife living with him. But given customs of gift-exchange, these instances were few. Still, a younger son might eventually be enabled to start a new branch household. If he did, then he and his descendants were expected always to acknowledge the main household's leadership. That meant obligations like providing sons to be adopted to keep the main household in existence, and giving its members any other assistance requested.

In rural areas the eldest son was often the only one to have a wife brought in for him. All the other sons had to visit their wives. The husbands of most of their sisters, who also stayed within their natal household, were apt to be visiting husbands too. All the children born became members of their mother's household, under the jurisdiction of its eldest-brother head. The eldest brother's eldest son, rather than any of his brothers, would follow him as head. Before 1600 a man might be a visiting husband to more than one wife, though a woman seldom had more than one visiting husband. After 1600 this was discouraged. The 1898 civil code required monogamy. The visiting-husband pattern may have evolved in part from the pre-13th-century pattern of the husband's staying with the wife's family at the beginning of the marriage, as in early Korea.

The 1898 civil code, not altered until 1946, underlined the concept of dominant household head by authorizing him to control his offspring's marriages until a son was 30 and a daughter 25. Though the 1898 code required monogamy, it liberalized divorce. It added mutual-consent divorce to the centuries-old Confucian-based listing of causes for which husbands (or their families) could repudiate a wife: sterility, adultery, disobedience to parents-in-law, loquacity, larceny, jealousy, and serious disease. Mutual-consent divorce was also available to women. Women had already been allowed in 1873 to seek divorce for desertion, crime, profligacy, and serious illness, if a father, uncle, or elder brother approved. Despite these apparent liberalizations, the divorce rate actually declined from the one divorce for every three marriages of 1885 to one for every six in 1900–04, one for every ten in 1920–24, and one for every 13.5 in 1935–39. The divorce rate rose only to about one for every twelve marriages in a given year, during the first 20 years after the new civil code of 1946. The new code gave women fully equal rights with men to seek divorce. It lowered the age for marriage without parental consent to 20 for both parties. It also ceased to recognize any specific household head. However, the divorce rate did begin to rise again in the 1970s. In 1983 it stood at 1.50 per 1,000 population, not far below continental western Europe, but less than ⅓ of the United States rate of 5.03 per 1,000 population in 1983. Still, the rising divorce rate was high enough to make a divorce, rather than death, the primary cause for single-parent families in Japan by 1984.

Before the 20th century, village youths regulated their own courting, somewhat as in much of Scandinavia and parts of Germany. However, the Japanese village youths may have given less attention to parental approval than the European. Parental approval would matter less to the success of a match, except for those few who would bring a bride to their own homes. Husband-wife relations also remained most nearly equal for the longest time in rural areas. Not only did the wife still often live with her parents, but Confucian ideals (which had begun to limit women's freedom in the upper levels of society by at least the 8th century A.D.) did not begin to enter the villages effectively until the 1870s. Then a new requirement for universal primary schooling brought Confucian precepts to everyone's attention, as part of the moral education which was at the core of that schooling. It is worth noting that in a survey reported by Hiroshi Wagatsuma, in Alice Rossi's collection *The Family* (1978), only 4% of families in Kobe reported that the husband was dominant in family decision-making. The figure in Detroit was 25%.

In the post–World War II era the Japanese husband has tended to expect his wife to run the household and raise the children without what both would see as interference from him. He has also tended to expect her to pamper him, as one would a tired child, when he comes home from work. This is not surprising when one considers that only with the new civil code of 1946 did any man (other than an ie head) become legally equal in household authority even to his own mother. Thus the mother-wife's precedence in household affairs is somewhat ingrained. Yet the terms for "wife" in Japanese are so laden with connotations of a wife's inferiority to her husband that the modern-minded have borrowed the word ("waifu") from English to try to get away from them. "Waifu" is increasingly used as more married women go to work. By 1970 just under 40% of all working women in Japan were married, as compared with just over 60% in the United States at that time.

Japan's industrialization in the late 19th and early 20th centuries opened opportunities to unmarried women to work in the new factories. Factory owners carefully assured parents of their daughters' safety and well-being by providing dormitories and after-work instruction and recreation for them. By 1912 women's mean first-marriage age rose to 23, from 19 in 1868, primarily because young women could now earn part of their own dowry. For centuries a Japanese bride had been expected to bring an outfit of household gear with her as her effective share of the family property, a smaller share than that of her brothers. She is still normally expected to bring such a dowry. However, the groom's education is increasingly replacing the groom's corresponding gifts to the bride's family. Before the late 19th century these were mostly gifts of cloth to make the bride's clothing; but they also included some money and a few items for the prewedding celebrations at her home, before the celebration of the wedding itself at his home.

The hereditary line of imperially appointed commanders who ruled Japan from 1603 to 1868, when they were forced by internal political circumstance to yield control to others around the emperor, carefully regulated what could be given as groom's gift and bride's outfit for every social group. Their intention was to prevent both overspending by the poor and presumptuous display by the nonaristocratic but wealthy. Once those regulations were lifted in 1868, brides' outfits tended to rise in value for reasons much like those for rising dowry costs in 14th-century Italy. The number of women was growing, and their parents wished to maintain or improve social status through obtaining an equal- or higher-status husband. Grooms' gifts also increased, though not as greatly, and began mainly to be given in money. The groom's gift was especially likely to be large if the groom's family saw a possible improvement in status.

Gift-giving would be essentially reversed if the groom moved into the bride's household. That still happens, as when a son-in-law is wanted to carry on a family farm or business. The bride's family then sends a money-gift to the groom's family. The groom brings his contribution (possibly even including a car) to the bride's household, to mark his severance from future inheritance from his own parents. But before the lifting of the restrictions on the spouses' families' marriage gifts in 1868, that kind of reversal of roles remained officially disapproved. Gifts in such marriages were even more severely limited than for the approved type of marriage, in which a wife entered her husband's household. Adoption of a son was regarded as more appropriate.

Among the propertied and the town-dwellers of Japan, marriage arrangements have for centuries relied on go-betweens. Sometimes the go-between was a professional, sometimes a helpful friend or relative. After 1600 the go-between was also expected to make whatever arrangements might be required if there were a divorce. In rural areas, though, the go-between is a recent addition. As better transportation became available in the late 19th and early 20th centuries spouses could be sought from farther away than the next village, beyond the practical limits for the use of the familiar youth-regulated courting pattern. Moreover, that pattern fell into disuse because of disapproval, thanks to the primary schools' instilling of Confucian ideas about the impropriety of conversation between any man and woman not of the same household (let alone between an unmarried man and an unmarried woman).

The go-between, or marriage-arranger, continues to thrive in today's Japan. However, his or her customers are now likely to be the young people themselves, at least in the cities. The modern ideals of marriage-as-companionship and partner self-selection have penetrated, thanks to the encouragement of examples like the marriage of the imperial crown prince to a fellow tennis enthusiast, a few years after the new civil code of 1946 removed the household head's control. Modern urban marriage-arrangers may employ detectives to be sure that their clients are giving accurate self-descriptions, as part of their reassurance to all who come to them. In smaller towns and rural districts that is less likely, since people are apt to know more about each other's backgrounds there. It was estimated by Japan's Economic Planning Agency that in 27% of all marriages in Japan in 1983, the initial meeting of the two was arranged by a professional matchmaker. But in the remainder a friend or a family member might have arranged the initial meeting. In remote rural areas, where this initial meeting is still a new idea, it may be quite brief and formal, rather than the prelude to a series of conversations as elsewhere. Or the two might have met at work (or in school or in some other relatively structured situation) and then sought a friend or family member to act as an informal sponsor-arranger with their respective parents. The initiative is passing from the parents to the potential spouses, as in the England of the 18th century. But it has not yet passed entirely. Given the customary prudence of Japanese who are making important decisions, and especially their tendency to wish to consult with others, the matchmaker-investigator is not likely to fade from the scene in the foreseeable future.

Go-betweens still flourish on Taiwan too, where fewer changes have taken place than on the mainland of China. The marriage laws enacted on the mainland in 1931 still apply on Taiwan. There they replaced the 1898 code of the former Japanese colonial rulers of Taiwan in 1945, when the Nationalist Chinese government recovered the island taken from the imperial government of China in 1895. The 1931 laws forbade polygyny, and defined the spouses (not their parents) as the ones contracting the marriage. They also accepted divorce by mutual consent. On the mainland they were superseded in 1950 by the new Communist government's even more vigorous reforms.

Young people on Taiwan have only started finding their own spouses since the commercialization of Taiwan's economy began opening opportunities to young men and women outside the household. They have often relied on a friend's introduction. But they are ceasing to acquiesce in their parents' arrangements. They are also ceasing to accept the thought that it is best for their parents to take the initial steps, or that it is enough for their parents to let them meet the proposed spouse and then indicate acceptance or rejection.

The half-century of Japanese rule on Taiwan and the application of the Japanese civil code of 1898 during most of that time may be reflected in a tendency to expect that the wife will stick to household matters, on Taiwan as in Japan. But in Taiwan the continuing enshrinement of Confucian thinking tends to give the wife less control within the household than in Japan. Competition for good positions in a relatively small economy, among a growing number of well-prepared people, has tended since the mid–1960s to lead to efforts to send women back to the home, much as after World War II in the United States. This has been frustrating to watch, for those women who had succeeded in combining career and marriage on the mainland before moving to Taiwan in 1948–49. They were relatively numerous in China by comparison with many other Asian countries, for the founders of the Republic of China had done much to eliminate barriers for women. However, unless the economy booms enough to make many new openings available, or unless far more than already are doing so succeed in leaving Taiwan for other areas, the campaign to keep women in the home is apt to continue. So is the concern of parents for their children's marriage choices, even though parental influence over marriage is decreasing.

The marriage laws of 1931 were effectively applied only in the cities of mainland China during the next 19 years. The changes they introduced were taken much farther, and applied much more widely, by the Chinese Communists' 1950 marriage law and its 1980 successor. The new laws recognize the partners, not their parents, as the only ones entitled to agree on or dissolve their marriage. The Communists have eliminated the 1931 laws' recognition of a formal head of household (always male) and a formal family council headed by the eldest living man of the eldest available generation of the patrilineage. The numerous possible reasons for divorce-for-cause in the 1931 laws were whittled to one, having been forced into the marriage against one's will. Otherwise, divorce was to be by mutual consent. In the People's Republic of China "mutual consent" has come to mean being required to go through efforts at reconciliation by members of one's neighborhood and/or workplace committees. Only if these efforts fail is there a court hearing. Determination of responsibilities for any child support is required before the divorce can be made final. These requirements help to explain the still-low divorce rate.

Bride-wealth, dowry, and any other form of marriage payment were not dealt with effectively by the 1931 laws, but they were sternly forbidden in the 1950 and 1980 ones. Their elimination should have made it easier for the less well off to marry. Yet in 1987 most brides in rural areas were still expected to bring some household gear with them. The 1950 incest rules, interestingly, were far stricter than the 1931 laws. The 1931 laws excluded patrilateral kin, unless the common ancestor was at least five generations back. That replaced the former prohibition of anyone bearing the same clan name no matter how remote the link. The 1950 law extended the five-generation prohibition to the matrilateral kin as well. Though this was modified in 1980 to prohibit marriages only to those whose common ancestor was not at least three generations back, clearly the Chinese Communists felt that kinship ties must be made less all-encompassing in people's lives. They were reasoning like the early leaders of the Christian church who had established strict exogamy-requiring rules to break the power of lineage groups. Both to weaken kinship linkages (matrilateral parallel- or cross-cousin marriages having probably been common) and to uphold the principle of equal treatment of both sexes, people were required to marry outside the circle of close kin on both their parents' sides.

The 1950 and even the 1980 laws have almost forced the continuance of village exogamy in rural areas. Yet there are great disadvantages in being a newcomer spouse in a village. One has no one to turn to in case of difficulty, except the village's governing body. However, if it is a one-lineage village, like many in China, that group may be so full of the local spouse's kin that the newcomer spouse can scarcely win a sympathetic hearing. A uxorilocally married man would be no better off in his wife's clan's village than a newcomer wife would be in her husband's clan's village. Therefore, the Communists have tended to try to encourage finding a partner in the same village. Because most newcomer spouses are wives, this is primarily intended to improve a wife's position. Drawing back to prohibiting only a first-cousin marriage in 1980 may have been meant in part to make village endogamy a little easier.

The desirability of providing a new supply of potential marriage partners for village young people may have been in Mao Zedong's mind in the 1960s, when he called on middle-school (mid-teens) graduates from towns and cities to go "down to the country" and settle there for life. He may have hoped that these young people would become spouses to the rising village generation, with the equalizing factor of greater education to make up for their lack of kinfolk to support them in the village. If that were so, it did not work out that way. Few married locally, for village families tended to leave them to themselves. Some married each other. But, in the long run, few stayed unless they could find no way to get back to their birthplace. The city of their birth and youth was more attractive, even if they found no jobs on their return and had to use their own ingenuity to make a place for themselves in the informal economy. From the villagers' standpoint, their departure was preferable to their staying. Villagers wished to maintain links with neighboring villages through their marriages. They had been used to marrying within the group of villages that shared the same trading center, for they wanted and needed cooperation with people from those other villages. Now that the familiar trading center had taken on more political functions, the desire to marry within the circle of those who relied on it was even stronger. The new incest rules made that more difficult, but not impossible. Besides, every marriage with someone in a nearby village that worked out well made it easier to arrange for another one there. Marrying a newcomer from a distant town promised no such future opportunity.

Another significant provision of the 1950 and 1980 marriage laws, one that was also included in the Soviet Union's 1968 legislation, is that a man may not request a divorce from his wife either when she is pregnant or during the first year of the infant's life. Under the 1950 law, if there were a divorce, each former spouse was to receive ½ of the household gear, savings, and other items acquired during the marriage. The wife also recovered all of what she brought into the marriage, which may have been a backhanded recognition of the continuance of dowry. But what the husband brought in went into the common property to be divided equally, which may have been an unsubtle discouragement to husbands' inclinations to divorce. Thus the 1950 law differed from the rules established in the Soviet Union, in which both spouses recover whatever they brought in and then the remainder is divided. The 1980 law states that property division is to be by agreement between the parties, with the court decreeing an equitable division if they cannot agree.

The effort to equalize the spouses' position is carried into explicit provision in both the 1950 and the 1980 laws that the wife may keep her maiden name, as many do. It also appears in the provision in both laws that neither spouse can force the other's choice of residence or work. Few have been required to take positions in different locations since the establishment in the 1950s of what amounts to a job-assignment system for all. Still, the need to use scarce talent to best advantage (and an ideological commitment to demonstrating that public good must come before private preferences) has led to some highly educated spouses being separated. For

such couples, and for many others too, supportive services have been necessary for a dual-career, or at least a two-job, family. Usually these services
have been provided by either neighborhood or workplace, though a resident
older family member may also undertake them.

As Deborah Davis-Friedmann noted in *Contemporary China* for 1976–
77, the three-generation stem family in an urban area tends to mean the
grandparents serve as built-in housekeepers and baby-tenders. The ages at
which men and women are encouraged to marry—28 and 25, respectively—
are approximately half the ages at which men and women now expect to
begin easing off of heavy labor in the villages, or to retire on pensions from
jobs in the towns and cities. Thus the newly retired would become available
for housekeeping and baby-tending as their offspring marry, if the recommended marriage-ages are followed. The successive constitutions of the
People's Republic of China have placed the first responsibility for the support
of parents on their children, and vice versa. The three-generation household
provides a means of doing that without requiring vast capital investments
in new housing, at a time when capital investment is wanted in transportation, industry, and agriculture.

Late marriage makes it easier to implement parental noninterference in
marriage choices. Men and women in their 20s, with the opportunities to
meet each other that are provided by neighborhood and workplace activities,
are in a position to choose their own partners as household-bound young
girls, in particular, could never do before. Late marriage is also part of the
Chinese Communist leaders' efforts to drive down birth rates, like the 1980
marriage law's provision that family planning is the responsibility of both
partners. After 1977 many incentives began to be given for having only one
child. If the Chinese Communists were to be entirely successful in promoting
one-child families, the population would be only slightly more than 1 billion
by A.D. 2000, and would decrease to about 600 million by 2050. That is
unlikely. But with economists arguing that population should be brought
down to 700 million or even fewer, the leaders have reason to continue
encouraging the one-child family. However, by 1987 the drive was easing,
as concerns rose over the psychological dynamics of a society composed of
one-child families.

The Chinese Communist leaders have actively campaigned against the
traditional preference for sons, as part of the drive for small families. They
have reason for concern. When a major steel factory experimented with
offering fetal sex identification to its workers in 1975, 1 in 53 males were
aborted but 29 of 46 females were. The experiment was promptly ended
because it proved to be so dangerously discriminatory. If son-preference is
managed despite the regime's efforts to avert it, the sex ratios of future
censuses may show even greater disparities than the 108 males per 100
females of the 1953 census. At that time the United States ratio was nearly

even, 99 males per 100 females. The 1982 census in the People's Republic still showed 106 males per 100 females.

Among pastoral Central Asian Muslim peoples on the Chinese side of the border with the Soviet Union, the task of implementing the 1950 marriage law was even more difficult than with ethnic Chinese. Muslim law requires mahr or dower, but mahr was outlawed with all other marriage payments. Moreover, traditional incest rules forbade far fewer kin than the 1950 law, and even the 1980 law does not allow first-cousin marriages. Polygyny was also much more common in Muslim areas than elsewhere in China. Among Tibetans, used to polyandrous marriages (and like the Muslims, largely pastoral), the new law seemed an unwarrantable interference in a system that had long kept population down to manageable levels in a harsh environment. Still, the incest rules were actually more lenient than the traditional Tibetan rules, and so did not actively clash with them. The traditional rules excluded descendants of less than a sixth-generation ancestor on the maternal side, and descendants of less than an eighth-generation ancestor on the paternal side. Among the still-pastoral Khalka Mongols changes since the 1920s had prepared them for the 1950 marriage law. For all practical purposes, elopement with a chosen spouse had replaced parental arrangement. Wives were more nearly equal with husbands, and polygyny had lessened. But among the Khalka Mongols, among the more settled agricultural Dagor and Chahar Mongols, and among many of the agricultural minority peoples of the southern borders of China the 1950 incest rules greatly restricted previous freedom to marry close cousins (though usually only on the mother's side). The rules against marriage payments were also hard to accept. For Khalka Mongols and many of the southern border peoples, prohibiting marriage payments was harder to live with than prohibiting parental arrangement of marriages. Like their Southeast Asian neighbors, the southern border peoples already tended to assume parental acceptance of offspring's choice, rather than offspring's acceptance of parental choice. Still, the 1950 marriage law may have influenced the government's willingness to set up autonomous areas for China's minority peoples during the 1950s. In areas defined as autonomous the law's implementation could be tempered in accord with local custom, without seeming to sabotage its application to the 94% who are ethnically Chinese. Even though the 1980 law was intended to be more uniformly applied to all than the 1950 one had been in practice, its framers acknowledged that "patience and guidance" would be required in applying it in the minority regions.

In Korea, too, the post–1945 period meant changes. When Japanese rule ended, 35 years of local application of Japan's 1898 civil code ended too. The Japanese had already broken the power of the Korean clan system by their 1912 code for Korea, which recognized legal bonds only within the household of the spouses, their children, and any of their parents or siblings who lived with them. After 1945 both south and north, under their differing governments, recognized marriage as the spouses' rather than the parents' choice. Both also raised marriage-ages from the 15 for women and 17 for men enforced by the Japanese to 20 for both, with special provision for those under 20 if granted appropriate permission by authorities (north) or parents (south). But neither tried to restore old incest rules, which the Japanese had limited to all first cousins. The go-between disappeared more slowly in the south than in the Communist north. Actual marriage-ages gradually continued to rise, as they had begun to do in the 1920s when women began being able to work and earn outside the home. However, much as in China and Japan, parental acceptance of an offspring's choice is usually still regarded as important, since a disapproving parent can do much to undermine a marriage. Some parental arrangement still takes place, at least in rural areas in the south. Divorce rates remain low, although divorce is available by mutual consent. In southern Korea, divorces are handled somewhat as in the post–1946 Japanese system, which offers but does not require reconciliation efforts. In the north the system is more like that in mainland China, which does require such efforts.

Overall, parental arrangement of marriages is by no means a vanished phenomenon in eastern Asia. However, it is largely limited to rural areas. In urban centers young people have found ways of making their own arrangements, even if, as in Japan, south Korea, and Taiwan, they still actively seek parental approval. In mainland China and north Korea they are less concerned about parental approval, but they are still reluctant to see parental disapproval. In India the situation is quite different. Parental arrangement of marriages is still very much the norm, although the more modernly educated usually enable the offspring to meet the proposed partner and register acceptance or refusal.

In most of the lands looked at in this chapter thus far, other than Algeria and Libya, Europeans were present as advisers rather than as rulers. But the British ruled most of India directly for well over a century, and in some parts almost two centuries. During their reign they introduced far-reaching changes.

Some Indians have suggested that the British rulers' use of ancient Hindu texts, in trying to work with questions of marriage and inheritance in the courts, may have cut short a gradual drift toward greater recognition of women's property rights. Some kinds of property a woman brought into marriage with her had been acknowledged as rightly descending as dowry to her daughters. That did not include her jewelry and personal gear, however. These were often symbolically taken from her for distribution to the women of her husband's household, and replaced by other jewelry and gear in token of her change to a new family. However, the clothing she brought was always left to her. As in 15th-century northern Italy, recognition of the role a woman's dowry played in her daughters' dowries could have begun preparing the way for the principle of equal partible inheritance to be established, as it finally was in Italy in the 19th century.

It is at least equally possible, however, that the British may have helped to spark indigenously based reform efforts by directing attention to the Vedas, not just to commentaries on them. The Vedas expected only the already mature to marry. They acknowledged maiden's-choice as legitimate, as well as father's-choice. In other ways, too, they differed widely from then-current practice in India. This had not bothered Hindus, who saw commentaries as later corrections, needed because of initial errors. However, they found that the British regarded the "original" as fundamental, and commentaries as relatively ephemeral adaptations to changing circumstances. Some Hindus began to take the same view. The Vedas' nonmention of *sati*, the self-immolation of a high-caste widow on her husband's funeral pyre, was used by some Indians to support the British when the British outlawed the practice in 1829. Although supporters of child marriage as a guarantee of purity could point to many commentaries, its opponents could point to the Vedas' nonmention of it in return.

The British greatly weakened clans in India by introducing private individual landholding in place of previous modes of group landholding and special rights. This paralleled Japanese limitation on legally recognized family obligations in Korea, which largely broke the clans' power there, and the Chinese Communist communalization of land, which sought to end the power of the strong Chinese clans. In the 19th century British introduction of new forms of transport (the railroad and the steamship) and communication (the telegraph and the public mail service) facilitated both commercialization and centralization, which then made other changes possible in marriage and family life. The censuses the British took were a first step toward public registration of births, marriages, and deaths, which only became an even partial reality in the 20th century for the vast populations of India and China. However, during the 19th century, the British also acted to affect the marriage system in other and more direct ways. They specifically legalized the remarriage of widows for all in 1855. (In the higher castes, the only groups that actually forbade it anyway, few took advantage of the permission.) The British declared child marriage illegal in 1860, with little success. Having realized from the 1921 census that 39% of women were married by age 10, they proclaimed minimum marriage ages of 14 for women and 18 for men in 1929. They also refused to register a marriage until the legal ages were reached. Yet the 1941 census still showed that 17% of women had been married by age 10. With *average* marriage-ages in the north still 14 and 18—they were 20 to 22 for women and 25 to 27 for men by then in the south, with its somewhat different marriage patterns—clearly a number were still being wed at earlier ages. In 1961 it was estimated that almost 2 million boys and more than 4 million girls—perhaps $1/10$ of the children aged 10 to 14—were being married before they reached 14.

The British recognized civil marriage as legal in 1872. They thereby legalized marriage between members of different caste groups, or even different religious groups, who previously could not have married. They also established monogamy as a requirement for those who used the civil form of marriage. Both Hindus and Muslims accepted polygyny, although it was rarer among most Hindu caste groups than among Muslims. A 1969 sampling showed only seven in 1,000 Hindu men and nine in 1,000 Muslim men having more than one wife. About seven Hindu households were polygynous for every three Muslim households that were polygynous.

In 1874 the British recognized a Hindu woman's right to manage any property she took into a marriage (rather than her husband's managing it) and any property she might receive while married, either by inheritance or through earnings outside the home. In 1937 they enacted a new inheritance law, entitling a widow to receive as much of a share of her husband's property as each of her sons, and to require that it be divided so that she could take that share and leave the household if she wished. This eased the way for a higher-caste widow to remarry. Widows already freely remarried in the lower castes, having little or no property to try to carry out of a deceased husband's household over his kin's objections. Among those groups such a marriage was regarded as being fully as much a marriage as her first. Among higher castes, however, a widow was still formally regarded as her first husband's wife, in every way, even if she and a man of her caste level dared to defy Hindu law and marry. The British widow-remarriage act of 1855 did not truly take effect among the higher castes until after the 1937 widows' property act, which enabled widows to take their share of property and use the civil marriage act of 1872 to rewed.

In 1946 the last British governor-general signed into law a statute on Hindu marriage passed by the already all-Indian legislature. The new law no longer limited registrable marriages to those that conformed to the wide-reaching incest rules followed in northern India (though not in the south). Now patrilateral second cousins and matrilateral first cousins could marry, among groups that had previously avoided such marriages. In 1948 the newly independent government of India weakened extended families by eliminating the last remaining legal recognition of impartible joint family holdings. Current holders were regarded in law as having already theoretically divided the family property into shares that they could pass on at their deaths to descendants, rather than only those still alive sharing in the division when it finally came about. In 1954–55, after long and heated debate, a general codification of marriage rules for Hindus and others was enacted. It declared 15 the minimum marriage-age for Hindu women, as already enacted in 1939 for Muslims in India. In 1936 the members of the small and highly educated Parsi group, descendants of Zorastrians who had moved to India from Persia during the first centuries of the Christian era, had been recognized as having the right to marry without parental consent at 21, or with parental consent at earlier ages. The 1954–55 code made 18 the minimum marriage-age for Hindu men. It also established monogamy as the rule for all Hindu marriages. The minimum marriage-ages for civil marriage were to be 18 for women and 20 for men. Christian marriages were to be governed by current English law. Formal alterations in the governmentally prescribed ground rules for marriage were rounded out by two more laws. In 1956 Hindu women were entitled to an equal share with their brothers in the inheritance of each of their parents' property. This gave sons a share in mothers' property, as well as giving daughters a share in fathers' property. In 1960 dowry was prohibited, though to little practical avail. It was reported in 1968 that in Kerala, 75% of one sample still gave and took dowry, and 51% claimed not even to have known about the law.

The 1954–55 code for the first time admitted the possibility of legal divorce and remarriage for all Hindus. Muslims and Christians already recognized divorce and annulment, but not even annulment had been traditionally available to Hindus. If the first wife proved barren, a man could formally take another, before 1954, if he could afford the ceremonial costs. He could also formally take another wife if the first proved impossible to live with because of something, such as a hereditary disease, that did not show up until she had already been transferred into his parents' household. But a woman could do nothing comparable. In practice, people found ways of getting out of impossible situations. A woman might return to her parental home for a visit that lasted the rest of her life. Among the lower castes, less concerned for the maintenance of a status of ritual purity they did not have anyway, she might even move into the household of another man as if she were his wife, though without any formal marriage ceremony. A man might take such a woman into his home, or visit her in hers if her male relatives raised no objections.

In 1937 the princely state of Baroda became the first region in India to recognize divorce and remarriage as legally permissible for Hindus. The Baroda experiment prepared the way for the 1954–55 marriage acts to provide for mutual-consent divorces for all formally registered Hindu marriages, and for a series of causes sufficient for divorce for those Hindu marriages that (for whatever reason) had never been formally registered. The 1954–55 provisions were supplemented in 1964 to permit divorce for Hindus after two years of separate residence (cut to one year in 1970). In practice, members of lower socioeconomic groups—which usually means lower castes—would find it easier to divorce and remarry. In those groups both spouses were always apt to work outside the household out of sheer necessity. Members of higher socioeconomic groups—usually higher castes—would find it harder, for women generally had not worked outside the household. Consequently a woman would have to find means of support before she could seek a divorce, while a man would have to be prepared to continue supporting his former wife if he wanted a divorce.

None of the reform legislation of either the British government or the government of independent India touched the authority of the Hindu family to arrange its members' marriages. Only in 1976 was there a first faint hint of legal recognition of the principle that the parties themselves should agree to the marriage. In that year a new law provided that a marriage could be annulled if one party had been mentally unable to give consent. This was not to be treated as a divorce from a valid marriage, but as a declaration that the marriage had not been valid in the first place. (The bridegroom who turns out to be insane, which is why his family would accept a smaller dowry and/or give a larger amount of bride-wealth than usual, is a stock figure in popular oral tradition in India.) Letting a marriage be annulled because one party was incapable of giving consent, if asked, is far from enacting a law which recognizes that the spouses, not the parents, are the ones to make the marriage. When the Chinese eliminated parental consent in 1931, the law had only limited effect at first. The Japanese did not enact such legislation until 1946. In the 1980s in the Middle East neither relatively modern Egypt nor relatively unmodern Oman required a woman's consent for her first marriage, which, by Muslim law, is arranged by her father or guardian. But proponents of reform (or revolution, as their opponents more correctly claim) regard the 1976 law as the entering wedge in India for a recognition in law and eventually in practice that spouses should choose each other, rather than be chosen for each other by someone else.

In an economy still largely based on subsistence agriculture, the affinal network remains vitally important in rural life. As K. Ishwaran noted in George Kurian's collection *The Family in India* (1974), a study in a south Indian village showed that the average farming family (whether nuclear or extended) relied on consanguine or affine kin for about 20% of the labor power needed during the year, yet still had to hire 10% to 20% of its labor power. Inheritance of cultivation rights remains important too. So does the desire of women's parents for bride-wealth, which repays them for the loss of a daughter's labor power. Even though its equivalent must be paid out to bring in a daughter-in-law, she is seen as an investment because she can give birth to sons. All these considerations combine to make parental arrangement of marriages likely to continue for a long time. The wish to maintain, or even improve, family status through governing sons' and daughters' marriages also remains high, in a society still largely based in practice on caste. The caste system lost all legal support when the new constitution went into effect in 1950. The possession of a university degree can make someone of low rank into an "honorary Brahmin," acceptable to the most modern-minded among the upper castes as a friend. But few in those upper castes would actually arrange a son's or daughter's marriage with such a person. Concern for caste standing also makes the continuance of parental arrangement likely among most town- and city-dwellers, even though they are part of the commercial economy. One sample of urban fathers in Kerala reported on by George Kurian in *The Family in India* showed 76% still preferring parental arrangement with consultation of the child, 17% accepting the offspring's choice if parents were consulted, and 6% still thinking in terms of parental arrangement without consulting children. Only 1% accepted the idea of partner self-selection in full.

The matrimonial advertisements regularly found in most newspapers, seeking "well-placed Smartha nonbharadhwaja bridegroom for good-looking Vathina graduate girl 27 158 cm. subsects no bar," or "suitable Punjabi Brahmin matches Manglik girl 19 convent educated tall homely [i.e., home-loving] beautiful and boy 21 well settled own flat respectable family," attest to that. These advertisements are India's version of the Japanese professional go-between. One could feel reasonably sure that the not-so-young Vathina graduate's parents would give a sizable dowry with her to attract the acceptable Smartha bridegroom, while the Manglik family would hope for a rather equal exchange of marriage-gifts with a family who also had a son and daughter they wished to wed. Education and occupation have become important symbols of rank. But marriage-level also remains important in the eyes of many. The emotional conflict can be almost unbearable, for a Brahmin family whose son or daughter returns from abroad with a Ph.D. and also a Ph.D. spouse (born into an untouchable family), met and married while overseas. Even if an educated untouchable wife has brought a long-desired first grandson into her husband's family, the welter of emotions surrounding the child can be tremendous.

The importance of marriage-level as a status symbol is a factor in maintaining high kin endogamy in the south, where kin endogamy has traditionally been favored. One sample of 6,945 marriages in 39 villages in the province of Andhra, reported by S. K. Basu to the Council of Scientific and Industrial Research in New Delhi and mentioned by Kurian, displayed more than 40% uncle-niece or matrilateral cross-cousin marriages. One in five is a very common proportion of close-kin marriages in the south. High proportions of kin endogamy are also found among urban untouchables. Even in the relative anonymity of an urban setting, those outside their group are not willing to accept marriages with them.

Another 19th-century British reform effort was a general attack on female infanticide. This campaign affected marriage patterns by making more brides available, which in turn made raising marriage-ages easier. It eroded polyandrous practices as well. The British also worked to alter specific marriage patterns in order to lessen the likelihood of female infanticide. In Gujarat, for example, one prosperous peasant caste group openly practiced female infanticide in the 1840s, to avoid having to give too many dowries and/or having to accept men of lower status for their daughters. At the same time they accepted daughters of a slightly lower status group as wives, with high dowries that contributed to their prosperity. The British encouraged the formation of "marriage circles," each made up of lineages of that group in several villages, so that daughters could be exchanged among the lineages of a circle on a basis of equality of status. The British then enforced the fines levied by each circle's governing council on any members who did not marry within the circle. A circle only had to cover a few neighboring villages. Lack of transport facilities limited the distance it was reasonable to expect a bride to move to about five miles. According to Samitri Shahani in *The Family in India*, five miles was still the practical limit for marriage-arranging of many peasants in a Maharashtra village in 1967. However, upper-caste members who were seeking proper status-reinforcing spouses brought (or sent) most of their daughters-in-law (or daughters) over distances of at least fifteen miles. A fairly large number of peasants now found spouses for their offspring between five and fifteen miles away, which corresponds roughly to ten-mile limits for pre-1850 Germany and for Malaya in the 1930s.

Even with all the reforms in India's marriage systems that the British consciously initiated, the British facilitation of commercialization and centralization has had and will have the greatest effects on marriage patterns in the long run. The introduction of a market economy, in which free competition rather than the ruler's favor determines who may trade where and in what, moves all social and economic relationships toward recognition of the individual. That in turn begins nudging the society toward self-arranged rather than family-arranged marriages. The introduction of land-holding rules that allow the partition and the sale or purchase of what had previously been held in trust as lineage land furthers those tendencies. In a patrilineally organized group this is upsetting. Husbands begin to wish to establish conjugal funds with wives for the benefit of their own children. They cease to be willing to see what they acquire go to brothers, nephews, or cousins, now that they no longer need their male kin's close economic cooperation simply to survive. But in a matrilineal system this is not merely upsetting, it is devastating. A matrilineal extended-family household divides into group of brothers, sisters, and sisters' children, not into husband-wife-children units like the patrilineal one. Conjugal relations play no part in the division, to the distress of both husbands and wives. Both spouses see husband-father's earnings and property going to someone other than his own children, whom he has helped to raise.

As long as the Nayar men of central Kerala still led a soldierly life, the visiting-husband form of marriage and the matrilineal inheritance system could work together well. But once the British disbanded their military units in 1792, Nayar men began to ask for division of their matrilineal units so that all of them could be heads of households. They also began to obtain cash incomes, either from the government positions they were beginning to fill or through the crops they were marketing. Then they started to seek ways to share their earnings with their wives, whom they now gravitated toward marrying monogamously, visiting only one wife, who in turn accepted only one husband as visitor. By 1850 the central Nayar had informally accepted the idea that if a man's heirs agreed, he could make gifts to his wife and children while he lived, but he could not bequeath them anything. However, only in the course of the 1920s and 1930s were laws enacted to enable a man in a matrilineal group to give half his earnings to his wife and children and to bequeath to them any land he himself acquired (though no share in his matrilineage's land). Earlier legislative efforts in the 1890s were only partly successful, from Nayar husbands' point of view. Not until 1958 did a new law allow a man in a matrilineal group to pass on all his property to his wife and children, and to share his earnings only with them. A Nayar woman's own children would, in any case, have been the recipients of her personal property, and she had not had rights in land until the 1956 law entitling daughters and sons to equal shares in property. The nuclear conjugal family had effectively won out among the Nayar, now part of the commercialized market economy.

Among the patrilineal Nambudri former overlords of the Nayar, the nuclear family also began to appear. After 16 years of agitation with British officials and Indian advisory council members, who were fearful at first of provoking disturbances by acceptance of the change, Nambudri men succeeded in 1933 in obtaining the legal right for all Nambudri men to marry, not just oldest sons. The matrilineal Tiyyar tenants of the Nambudri used the same property laws as the Nayar from the 1890s on, with similar effects. However, they tended to find it harder to maintain a lasting marriage because they were economically less well off. In northern Kerala, also, economic and legal changes have turned matrilineal joint families into single nuclear families, which the new inheritance laws are pushing toward bilaterality. The weakening of the power of lineages, as royally granted monopolies gave way to open competition, has meant a similar shift among the matrilineal merchant Muslim Mappilla. Only after 1950 was a law enacted that allowed a father to continue to regard his children by a divorced wife as being among his heirs. For the Mappilla that may be about equivalent to the stage reached by the central Nayar a century before. For them, as for the matrilineal Muslim Minangkabau of Sumatra in Indonesia, the introduction of a free market economy was leading to a substitution of spouse-children ties for matrilineal ones.

For the Minangkabau, and other matrilineal groups in Indonesia, the wish of fathers to bequeath to children had not yet been formally recognized in the 1980s. Still, men were permitted in 1907 to sell lineage property, and their right to give money and movables to their children was recognized. A 1960 ruling that women have inheritance rights from parents may become an entering wedge for matrilineal husbands to bequeath to their own children in Indonesia, as the 1956 law in India was there. On Truk in the Pacific, too, the introduction of commercial opportunity through copra-growing has meant the breakdown of matrilineal matrilocal life in favor of the nuclear family.

Lineage patterns, and therefore marriage choices, have been changed in other ways as well, by the actions of colonial rulers. In the Gilberts (Kiributu) the 1910 colonial administration prohibited multifamily dwellings, in an effort to limit the spread of contagious diseases. This effectively forced a nuclear form on an ambilineal group. The government then proceeded in 1922 to register all land claims. As among the Maori of New Zealand, so in the Gilberts, registration encouraged individuals to keep up ties with as many as possible of their eight great-grandparental lines, rather than concentrate on only two or three at most. Now they could point to a written document as proof of their belonging, rather than having to rely on people's memory of their parents' or grandparents' participation in work and ceremonial occasions. In the calculations made as people worked out marriage arrangements, such changes could not fail to have some influence.

On Sri Lanka the arrival of Europeans was contemporary with far-reaching changes in the dowry and inheritance system of the Vellalar Tamils. They had used a partly duolineal, partly bilateral system, in which a daughter inherited a mother's dowry-land, a son inherited the land brought into the marriage by his father as a gift from his own parents, and all children inherited what the parents acquired during marriage and had not yet given to them at their marriages. They changed to a system of dowry (including land) from both parents to a daughter at marriage, and either an inheritance from both parents to a son at their deaths or a gift to him when they voluntarily chose to give it (in return for a corresponding share in their maintenance, like the early Norse father). These changes effectively turned a largely duolineal system into a fully bilateral one. They also required careful bookkeeping to keep properties straight when widows or widowers remarried, as both did. The Vellalar Tamils do not seem to have been directly influenced by the 16th-century Portuguese or their 17th-century Dutch and 18th-century British successors on the island. Yet it is also possible that the establishment first of Portuguese and then of Dutch and British rule on the island meant that European patterns of equal partible inheritance became known, and had some indirect influence.

It is not easy to see a European influence on the gradual shifts from matrilineality toward patrilineality observed in the 1970s in the hills of northwest Thailand, unless the greater commercialization of the country's life is assumed to have been primarily responsible for the shift. It is easier to see an indirect British influence in the introduction of dowry in place of bride-wealth among Burmese who became lower-level officials in the British government in Burma. The security of such a post was attractive enough to make a woman's parents willing to give her what would be her share of their property anyway, to gain a husband for her who held such a position. Burmese already practiced bilaterality and neolocality, except for expecting early residence with the bride's parents. They also practiced what amounted to an informal near-ultimogeniture, in that the last one to marry would probably remain with the parents until their deaths. They willingly listened to their offsprings' suggestions to parents concerning whom they would like to marry. They were also accepting toward divorce, remarriage of both widows and widowers, and a single life in celibacy. Consequently it is hard to see much British influence on the data reported by P. M. Hauser and E. M. Kitagawa in Joseph J. Spengler and O. D. Duncan's collection *Demographic Analysis* (1956). In a four-town sample in Burma in 1952 the median age for women's first marriages was just over 18, with 8% marrying at 14 or younger and 6% at over 25. This was in a total population in which the median age for all living women was just over 22 and for all living men, just under 24. In the United States in 1950 the median ages for all living women and men were just over and just under 30, respectively. However, only 75% of the women in the sample in Burma who were 20 and over had married, compared with 88% of women 20 and over in the United States in 1950 who had married.

The nonuniversality of marriage by age 20 or so in the Burma of 1952 contrasts sharply with the virtual universality of marriage by that age for women in most of Africa south of the Sahara at that time. By the end of the 1950s, as Europeans began to give up rule in the region—or in a few cases (but not in South Africa) to accommodate themselves to becoming simply citizens alongside other citizens in one-person, one-vote elective governmental systems—all of the new states-to-be had introduced monogamous civil statutory marriage as an option. Independent Liberia had already done so in the 19th century. Independent Ethiopia did not do so until the 1970s. Statutory civil marriage took its place in African states alongside customary and usually polygynous forms. Provisions were made for recognizing the spouses' property in a civil marriage as a conjugal fund for themselves and their children. The spouses and their offspring, rather than the spouses' other kin, would be entitled to that conjugal fund in case of death or divorce.

Not every woman who marries in the civil statutory form fears a charge of witchcraft from a husband's kin if they divorce. But if his kin accuse her of having used witchcraft to lure him into that strange form of marriage, away from his obligations to his kin, that would probably make it hard for her to find another husband. Such a situation was reported for Ghana by C W. Hobart, in George Kurian's collection *Cross-Cultural Perspectives on Mate Selection and Marriage* (1979). Those who enter statutory civil marriage have rejected a system in which marriages ultimately must have the support of kin, even though courting customs in many groups might allow much personal initiative in selecting a spouse. In its place they have entered one that recognizes only the spouses' interest in a marriage. A woman divorced after a statutory civil marriage usually receives little help from her own kin in finding a new husband. By entering such a marriage she has proclaimed that she intends her property to go to her husband and children. She has probably also done less to aid her kinfolk than they would wish, in terms of gifts, invitations to nephews or nieces to live with her while in school in the town, and the like. In their eyes she has effectively refused her own side of the reciprocal obligations of kin. So has her former husband, of course. But witchcraft in Africa, as in the Europe of the 16th and 17th centuries, has tended to be seen as something that a woman uses. As a result any counteraccusation against her former husband of having bewitched her into a statutory civil marriage would probably be given little heed even if it were made.

Women in modern statutory marriages in Africa are still as rare as those in India who have used civil marriage rather than religious ceremonies. They do exist, but they are most apt to be found among two groups: the well educated who have managed to combine career and marriage (through the use of household help, as the Rapoports point out for England) and those who make a career of wifery and motherhood, either with a salaried government man or with a successful businessman. They lose more prestige than do their husbands if there is a divorce. Yet in many African lands statutory civil marriage and divorce rules tend to make it easier for men to obtain a divorce than for women. That is because that was still the situation in the European ruling country when the European administration established the local statutory marriage code, which often has not been thoroughly revised since independence in the 1960s.

European rule brought many changes, some intentional and others not. Some of those changes have encouraged the replacement of polygynous systems with monogamous ones. Others have made divorce more available to those who previously could not easily obtain it, but probably less available to those who could easily obtain it before. The overarching tendency has been toward an equalization of the previously unequal, as in the raising of women's and the lowering of men's average ages at first marriage. The pressure of the equalization tendencies appears also to be modifying all kinship systems other than the already-bilateral in the direction of bilaterality. Patrilineality remains attractive to many, and matrilineality to some. But recognition of a conjugal fund to which one's children are entitled necessarily will weaken both, as that idea spreads.

After an initial attempt to oppose the payment of bride-wealth as too much like purchasing a slave, European administrations in Africa came to accept it. But they did succeed in establishing the expectation by about 1950 that some kind of judicial action was needed for a divorce to be effective. Divorce ceased to be just a privately arranged matter. This change tended to protect women's interests more than men's. Most women lived in patrilineal systems, in which previously they had not been as free to initiate a wanted divorce (or to resist an unwanted one) as in the matrilineal systems or even in the bilateral or duolineal ones. Now a woman's kin could no longer use bride-wealth either to prevent a divorce the spouses wanted, by refusing to return the bride-wealth, or to effect a divorce against the spouses' wishes by returning it. The idea that marriage was the spouses' affair rather than their families' was thereby introduced. This was a novel idea to most Africans.

Polygyny was already declining in Africa by the 1950s. The decline owed more to the ability of young men in gradually commercializing economies to earn cash to use for bride-wealth (instead of waiting for their turn at use of lineage wealth or waiting to inherit wives from older male kin) than it owed to any Christian preaching. Wage labor for European-run enterprises, or the sale of crops or animals or other goods and services to Europeans, enabled men's first-marriage ages to decrease. Opportunities for schooling increased men's opportunities to earn. Opportunities for schooling and earning also raised first-marriage ages for women in most regions. They no longer had to lean on kinsmen or on husbands to provide services like field-clearing, which they might need to practice the hoe agriculture that had previously been their mainstay, except in the purely pastoral-herding or hunting-gathering societies in which dairying or gathering formed their main work. They therefore no longer needed to accept marriages arranged for them by kinsmen who wanted bride-wealth, for alternative modes of livelihood were becoming available to them. As marriage-ages for women and men approached each other, polygyny became harder to maintain.

European rulers hastened commercialization by introducing taxes that had to be paid in money, not in goods. They also set up a governing apparatus whose officials could not be persuaded to take goods in substitution for money, whether those officials were Europeans or Africans who had been taught by Europeans. All over Africa this forced people either to find a crop they could sell for cash or to go to work in European-run mines, plantations, shops, and offices. They were thereby hauled willy-nilly into a life oriented at least partly toward commerce. But that this would itself change marriage-ages, widen choices, or lessen polygyny was far from European rulers' minds. Yet among the Zande, for example, the sister-exchange common in the 19th century increasingly began to be replaced by bride-wealth payments in the 20th century. The new system gave more choice to potential grooms among potential brides. It also gave more opportunity for brides or their kinsmen to reject potential grooms.

The effectiveness of European-established governments in maintaining order meant that lineages were no longer the primary protectors from theft or assault. Moreover European administrators in most regions instituted land-tenure forms that recognized individual holdings, and treated lineage holdings as divisible property. That meant a gradual, though sometimes painful, turn toward single-family rather than extended-family forms, although these single families might still be polygynous. The movement of the Bena in Tanganyika (Tanzania) from matrilinealocality to patrilineal-ocality between 1850 and 1950 has already been noted in Chapter 5. All over sub-Saharan Africa movements toward patrilineality or toward bilateral nuclearity (like that of the Nayar of Kerala) have affected not only matrilineal groups, such as the Tonga and others of Zambia or the Ashanti and others of Ghana, but also patrilineal groups, such as the Kikuyu of Kenya, and duolineal groups, like the Yako of Nigeria.

The Plateau Tonga of Zambia clearly illustrate the tendency of matrilineal systems to move toward more patrilineal forms, urged by several new factors. After 1920, cash cropping for the market of the nearby mines provided sources of wealth other than using kinship ties. Growth in population and the maintenance of order by central government made it no longer feasible to move to another area to seek new crop land. Therefore, establishing the personal right to raise crops in a particular area became increasingly important.

In the late 1940s the Tonga lived in neighborhoods of four hundred to six hundred persons. Each neighborhood consisted of a number of hamlets, made up of extended-family households. A couple would move out of a hamlet to establish their own homestead, but only after the husband had finished paying bride-wealth to both the wife's father and the wife's mother's kinsmen. He had to complete the payment of his own bride-wealth before he could receive bride-wealth for any daughters he might have with that wife. It was uncommon for a Tonga man to have more than two wives. If he did, they could never be born of the same mother, although they might be otherwise related to each other. But it was not uncommon for him to have experienced divorce. About 31% of all ever-married men and 26% of all ever-married women had experienced divorces. It was also not uncommon—44%—for a Tonga man to be at least ten years older than a wife.

A Tonga wife's brothers resented her husband's putting income either into savings or into movable wealth. They could then be transmitted to members of his own kin group, like his sisters and their children, rather than remaining available for division among his own children's kinfolk (through their mother) at his death. A husband's sisters similarly resented his establishing a savings account or acquiring movable property because these items might go to his children instead of to theirs. By 1945 cash-cropping led to an insistence (accepted in principle and increasingly in practice by central government officials) that crop land should be inherited by the younger generation of those actually residing in an extended-family household, rather than continue to be periodically redistributed by the matrilineal clan. By the 1950s land was even salable. It was no longer a common good.

Cash-cropping was accompanied by an introduction of plow rather than hoe agriculture. This change let a husband claim more of what his wife might raise because now he plowed the field for her. By the 1940s he was increasingly taking all the surplus above the household's needs for sale, and keeping the proceeds. She was no longer able to sell at least some of that surplus herself, and keep the proceeds. A number of men in the 1940s were still opposing automatic inheritance of crop land by their sons, as likely to make sons desire the early death of fathers. However, resistance to the idea was declining visibly, in just one generation of experience with plow agriculture and cash crops.

Cross-cousin marriages of both types, which accounted for more than 20% of all existing men's marriages in 1950, were declining. Scarcely 7% of marriages contracted in one group of villages between 1946 and 1950 involved cross-cousins. Fully 60% involved no kinship affiliation, despite a long-standing custom of preferring that a man marry into a matrilineal group from which other men of his own matrilineal group had taken wives. Patrilateral parallel-cousin marriages had never been accepted. Usually clusterings of marriages within sets of matrilineal groups tended to coincide with cattle-keeping practice. The Tonga were accustomed to mutually lending and borrowing cattle among men of several contiguous neighborhoods, as insurance against both drought and epidemic. They also recognized a kind of peace-circle within each cattle-keeping and wife-seeking group. However, wife-seeking as a peace-keeping device became less significant, once a central government took over peace-keeping responsibility. It is hard to say how that in turn might have influenced residential choices. By 1950, 40% of adult men lived near their father's matrilineal kinsmen, and just over ⅓ lived near their own matrilineal kinsmen. As central government peace-keeping increased in effectiveness, men's former use of rituals to establish a brotherhood pact with someone in a distant neighborhood, to facilitate safe travel, diminished too.

For the Tonga the move from shifting subsistence-cultivation to more settled cash-cropping and cattle-raising only began when the copper mines were opened in the late 1920s, providing a market for the food they could raise. By the 1950s the resulting changes had brought recognition of a father's right to keep his children after a divorce, even after his bride-wealth had been repaid. If he was willing to provide for them, they could live and work with him and his next wife, while his former wife remarried someone else. Ultimately the children were still regarded as part of their mother's matrilineage. But in practical terms they were increasingly linked to their father too. Bride-wealth had also increased, which helps to explain the frequency of divorce. A woman's male kin would wish to collect another bride-wealth for her (even though they had to return at least part of the initial one), if the current level of bride-wealth was higher than the level at her earlier marriage. Women were beginning to welcome the birth of sons more than that of daughters in the 1950s. A son was likelier than a daughter to be able to support them as they grew old, in view of wives' decreasing control over the crops they planted. Men's first-marriage age had decreased to about 25. Men were making their own arrangements even for their first marriage, now that they did not have to use lineage wealth, but could earn their own bride-wealth by working in the mines or by selling food to people in the mining district. The kinds of arguments that had begun to lead to change among the Nayar by 1850 were surfacing, arguments between spouses (over how much husbands gave their sisters) as well as between siblings (about how much brothers gave their wives). In short, the matrilineal era was drawing to a close.

Among the Yako, fathers started keeping bride-wealth payments for themselves in the 1930s, instead of sharing them with matrilineal kin. Sons also began to claim their deceased fathers' personal possessions, instead of yielding them to the father's matrilineage. These changes were significant in the duolineal system of the Yako. Land had customarily gone patrilineally, but livestock, crops, money, and shares in the raffia-palm clumps in the swamps (from which money had been earned for centuries) had previously gone matrilineally. Clearly the movement in the 1930s was away from matrilineality. It might have taken place without British presence. However, British courts tended to favor parent-child ties over sibling ties, even when trying to apply local customary law. Yako men made full use of that.

In Kenya the experiences of people in a Kikuyu village 20 miles from Nairobi are described by the Whitings, in Alice Rossi and others' collection *The Family* (1978). The first Christian mission school opened there in 1911. Sons (and daughters) of the village soon began moving to Nairobi, in search of a securer and more varied life than that of the increasingly crowded village. As the years passed the village women increasingly came to prefer monogamy to the traditional polygyny. This was not from conversion to Christianity, but because monogamy assured a woman of her husband's undivided effort to provide for her and her children. It would also assure her that his land holdings would be used for her and her children alone. As a result of changes in landholding rules introduced by the British, land is no longer "just there." It is individually held, heritable, and salable.

In more recent decades the desire to work in town for wages and to send children to school to improve their future chances has strengthened the Kikuyu preference for monogamy. In a school-conscious society, monogamy seems less costly to a man and less friction-causing to a woman than polygyny. As a result three-room homes (with one room for wife and husband, one for all but the youngest children, and one for waking-hours activities) have replaced the previous one-room huts (with husband in one and each wife and her children in a separate one) in the villages. Fathers, therefore, tend to do more child-raising tasks than before, with all that that can mean for both the daughters and the sons. Schooling makes children an expense rather than a chore-performing asset. However, it is also a substitute, both for giving bride-wealth on a son's behalf and for feeling that early marriage is required for a daughter's well-being.

Some Kikuyu husbands now try to combine work in Nairobi with a village home that they visit on weekends. But their wives fear losing their attention and support because of the long separations. Other women move into town with their husbands, but they lose the food raised on the land. There are also the city's dangers for the children, from being hurt in traffic to being drawn toward illicit activities. In addition, a wife often feels that she should work to support her children, as she would in the village; but if she takes a job, she needs to find someone reliable to take care of the children and do part of the household work. Such a person is not always easy to find in a strange place.

Whether in Kenya or elsewhere, wives in traditional marriages who follow their husbands to a city have effectively lost traditional kin-network supports, unless and until related couples come into their neighborhood. They lack the mutual-aid network of women in the villages, or in a traditionally organized urban household like those still found among the Yoruba of Ibadan in Nigeria. The Yoruba household may encompass up to three hundred persons in a multiroom compound, with separate sleeping rooms for each man and for each of his wives (with her children). In such a large household there is always someone to help out in child-tending, cooking, and other tasks. However, even in a town, a traditionally married woman can still call on any kin who are within reach. A woman who marries in the modern statutory civil way cannot. Neither spouse in such a marriage can call on kin. By choosing the statutory civil marriage they have established a conjugal fund, and the members of their lineages are unlikely to aid someone who has thus removed his or her property from traditional lineage-group controls.

As centralization and commercialization have taken root in the lands of the Middle East, Asia, and Africa, then, the concepts of the conjugal fund and mutual partner-choice have begun to find acceptance in varying degrees. Both women's and men's marriage-ages in all these lands have begun to move toward the early to middle 20s, approaching the ages found now in Europe and in the transoceanic regions settled by Europeans. However, many of the patterns of the past continue to have influence.

CHAPTER 12

Marriage in Industrial-Commercial Societies: The Western Hemisphere and the Pacific

In this chapter we will look at the experiences of the peoples of the Americas, Australia, and New Zealand. European settlers established European-style social, economic, and political institutions in these regions between the 16th and 19th centuries A.D. However, they also had to adjust to the indigenous peoples, who in turn had to adjust to them. As a result patterns that had been developed in Europe might be considerably modified in these new lands.

The experience of most of sub-Saharan Africa with European rule was brief, less than a century on paper and often less than half a century on the ground. The only exceptions were in the southernmost parts of the continent, where the Portuguese arrived in the late 15th century, and the ancestors of South Africa's Boers came from the Netherlands in the 17th century. The experience of Latin America was quite different.

In the 1490s Spanish rule was established in the Caribbean, and the Portuguese began to explore Brazil. Three centuries of Spanish and Portuguese rule followed, from the conquest of Mexico and Peru by Spain in the first decades of the 16th century until the 1820s. Then local governments were established in Brazil and almost all of the former Spanish empire. Spain retained Cuba, Puerto Rico, and the Philippines, which had been governed through Mexico until Mexican independence was achieved, but lost them in 1898.

Many indigenous Central and South American people, including almost all the Caribbean islanders, died of European-brought diseases to which they had no immunity. Therefore, the Spanish and Portuguese conquerors soon began bringing slaves from Africa to work in their mines and plantations. This led to an eventual complexity of racial intermingling that the Spaniards tried to classify carefully into categories of European-and-African, European-and-Indian, European-and-African-and-Indian, and African-and-Indian. They even subdivided the mixtures involving Europeans in terms of

how much ancestry was European. They also distinguished between indigenous nobility and other indigenous people, at least in Mexico, where the
privileges of the Aztec nobility were formally and legally acknowledged.
The Portuguese were somewhat more casual about all ancestries other than
pure European. One is inescapably reminded of the distinction among Europeans, Coloreds, Indians, and Bantu in South Africa. However, after 1948
the South Africa government erected legal barriers to marriage or even to
intercourse without marriage between Europeans and non-Europeans, in
the name of separate development, far more thoroughly than Portuguese or
Spaniards ever did. Though those barriers were removed in 1985, classification of the population by race continued.

An initial lack of Spanish or Portuguese women led to some formal Spanish marriages to Aztec and Inca aristocratic wives. It also led to more
informal liaisons between Spaniards or Portuguese and local women (and
later African slave women). As European women began to arrive in the
course of the 16th century, a different pattern soon emerged both on the
mainland and in the Caribbean islands, some of which the British and French
took from the Spaniards in the 17th and 18th centuries. The European-
born elite ranked first. Then came the *creoles*, or *criollos*, those born locally
of European ancestry. However, the Spanish government in particular never
favored the creoles in making official appointments. Spain's rulers feared
they might be less loyal than officials who still had relatives as close as
siblings or even parents in Spain. Then came the Aztec nobility, as a special
case in Mexico. Then came those of European-mixture ancestry. Then came
the Indians. Last came the Africans and those of mixed African-Indian
ancestry. Their status at the bottom of the socioeconomic system was largely
differentiated by whether they were slave or free, until the end of slavery.
The French Revolution of 1789 ended slavery in France's few Caribbean
islands. Independence ended it in most of the Spanish territories in the 1820s.
The British abolished it for all their empire in 1833. Independent Brazil was
the last to abolish it in 1888. Not surprisingly, the European family patterns
brought by the conquerors survived best where there were the fewest Indians
and/or the fewest African slaves, as in northern Mexico or in Argentina and
Chile. Those patterns flourished least successfully where Europeans remained always in a distinct minority.

The underlying basis for the patterns brought by 16th-century Spanish
and Portuguese conquerors was the Mediterranean concept of honor, as
understood from Portugal and Morocco to Greece, Turkey, Lebanon, Iran,
and beyond. As noted in Chapter 9, honor included providing for one's
wife and children (if a man), maintaining proper links with other kin, and
being fair in one's dealings with all one's kin, both consanguine and affine.
For men it required maintaining their own honor against attack and seizing
honor from others, in the pattern often called *machismo*. For women it
required maintaining their own honor against attack, above all their chastity

and their reputation for chastity, in the pattern often called *marianismo*. In the Mediterranean Muslim world, where even first cousins could marry, that meant a woman was extremely limited in movement. Even being seen with a male first cousin could compromise her. But in the Mediterranean Christian world, where incest rules forbade marriage to first and second cousins, she could move uncompromised within a far larger circle of kin. Moreover, since Gothic times in Spain, a woman had been recognized as fully competent when widowed, fully able to manage both her own and her husband's property on their children's behalf until her own death. In Spain and Portugal her children received her surname as well as their father's. In addition, once a woman was married, she did not need to fear a change in status through divorce in any of the Roman Catholic lands.

Latin American independence leaders feared to give women the vote lest they prove too reactionary, too loyal to the church that protected their status (through refusing to accept divorce) to allow such innovations as public rather than church schools. But not only women opposed divorce. When Uruguay enacted divorce legislation early in the 20th century, it was as socially revolutionary as when Italy did so in 1971. When a new and socialist-minded governor tried to introduce civil marriage and divorce by mutual consent in the Mexican state of Yucatan after 1915, and then in 1923 added provisions for unilateral "postcard divorce" like the Soviet Union's, a local revolution threw him out in 1924. As recently as 1954, when the popular Juan Perón tried to introduce divorce in Argentina (after having enabled women to vote and to be paid equally with men for the same work), the opposition was so strong that he was thrown out of office in 1955 by the first of the military juntas which held the real power in Argentina from then to 1983. Colombia only allowed civil divorce (and only for civil marriage) in 1973, Brazil in 1977, Argentina in 1987. It is no accident that the few remaining states that did not recognize divorce in 1987, other than Ireland, were all former Spanish colonies: the Philippines, Chile, and Paraguay. Only annulments were available to their people, under the Roman Catholic rules still followed within their borders, even for the Muslims of the southern Philippines.

Unhappy marriages are continued rather than dissolved in lands where divorce is not allowed. Unhappy husbands take mistresses, generally from a lower level in the social hierarchy of color-groups in Latin America. Many women at all levels below the elite see little value in tying themselves for life to a man of their own level or lower. Nonelite men are often unable to find steady employment. Nonelite women may therefore prefer, for practical economic reasons, to live with men in informal consensual unions, almost like the legal concubinage of ancient Rome. A nonelite woman may choose to live with a man who would be "worth marrying," if he could obtain a steady job. She would then be willing to marry him, as he would her. Marriage would legitimize their children, enabling them to inherit legally whatever little the parents might have, as well as to enjoy the preferable social status of legitimacy. But until he would be a support rather than a burden to her, she would not be apt to care to marry him. A nonelite woman may also choose to live with a higher-status man as his mistress, in return for the economic support she could expect for herself and their children as long as he felt sure of her fidelity. But the unhappy wives whose unhappy husbands take those mistresses see social and legal acceptance of divorce as a threat to their positions. They therefore strive to keep divorce almost unused, even where it is legally available in Latin America. They have been quite successful. Divorce remains rare among most European-ancestry elite members in most of those Latin American countries that allow it.

To maintain the system of lifelong indissoluble marriage, women continue to accept the role of suffering wife and mother, suffering but self-controlled, and therefore morally superior. They then contrast their self-control with men's immaturity and impulsiveness. They see this as a necessary prop to the maintenance of their rights (as wives and widows) to retain whatever property they bring into marriage. Indeed, they feel some pity for the North American woman, who in some areas still suffers under legal disabilities imposed on Anglo-Saxon women by the Norman conquerors. The veneration of the Virgin Mary, very popular in Roman Catholic Mediterranean countries, has led to the nickname of marianismo for this counterpart to machismo. Marianismo may be stronger in Latin America than in the Christian Mediterranean world because of the existence of far greater social differences, and the consequent concern for social standing.

In Latin America, as in Hindu India, concern for a social standing primarily based on ancestry tends to be expressed in great concern for women's chastity, as a sign of higher status. As in Hindu India, so in Latin America, a woman's expression of that chastity is redefined as one moves down the social scale. At higher levels in Latin America it means being a formal wife, and of course a faithful one. At lower levels it means not betraying one's partner in a consensual union, whether he is an eventual possible husband at a similar level or a married man at a higher level, unless she is first cast off by him. The associated desire to ensure a woman's virginity at marriage— strong at elite levels in both Latin America and Hindu India—leads to early mean first-marriage ages for women. In the 1970s in Mexico, for example, women's mean first-marriage ages ranged only from 17 for the rural woman or the uneducated one to 20 for the urban woman or the one with at least a high-school education.

From the beginning, in colonial Mexico, the introduction of 16th-century Spanish laws on marriage and women's property rights primarily applied to Spaniards, in practice. The Spaniards also applied it to the Aztec nobility, with whom the first Spanish men had briefly intermarried. However, the Aztec nobility used dowry far less often than European or creole Spaniards, about 64% of whose marriages in Mexico between A.D. 1600 and 1800 involved dowry.

By 16th-century Spanish law as applied in Mexico, a woman retained both her dowry and any dower for herself and her heirs. She also succeeded to a deceased husband's property, unless it were entailed. During her marriage a woman needed her husband's permission for legal transactions, unless she could show that his objections were unreasonable. A woman could not marry without her parents' prior agreement until 25. After 1776 both sons and daughters could be disinherited at any age for contracting a marriage that their parents disapproved. This law was intended to discourage the fully European from marrying persons of mixed ancestry. Though it was formally swept away at independence almost 50 years later, it remained an informal reality. But among Indians and mixed-bloods customary patterns of bride-wealth and neighborhood endogamy resembling the calpulli land corporations of the Aztec period often persisted. Land rights within these corporations might descend to children either patrilineally or bilaterally. There were only a few Africans in the colonial population of Mexico. There were also a handful of Chinese, from the Chinese trading settlement the Spaniards found on the shores of Manila Bay when they took over the Philippines half a century after conquering Mexico and Peru.

The local population in Mexico quickly began making use of godparenthood, especially the aspect of co-godparenthood or spiritual kinship between parents and godparents. Godparenthood, as shown in Chapters 8 and 9, can be useful to people in a disadvantaged social, economic, or political condition. The Indians in Mexico used it to establish ties to the ruling Spaniards, seeking protection or even advancement. In later years they also used it to establish ties to mixed-bloods who achieved some authority. In addition, they used it from the outset to strengthen kinship or neighborhood ties. A pair of parents might even seek to achieve all of these goals, with different children. In northern Mexico the owner of the great ranch or hacienda was often godfather to at least one child of each of his tenants. In Yucatan the parents of the spouse to whose home the other came for the first years of marriage (which might be either the husband's or the wife's) were always godparents to the first child. Farther south, in Guatemala, it was common for an Indian couple to ask a mixed-blood or a Spaniard to be godparent to their child. The two groups who were least likely to seek godparents outside their own community were the Spanish (or Portuguese) rulers and those who had the least contact with them. The more contact with other groups of higher status a group had, the likelier its members were to seek godparents from that group. They hoped that link would improve their offspring's chances in life, which would serve their own interests as well in the long run.

Spanish widows were required to remarry in early colonial Mexico because of a shortage of Spanish women, but in the next two centuries the
situation changed. S. M. Arrom observed in the *Journal of Family History*
for 1978 that in 1828, after independence, with 55% women and 45% men
among those over age 25 in Mexico City, ⅓ of the women in both a mostly
Spanish and a half-Indian, part-mixed section were either unmarried or
widowed without children. Yet in the whole city only 2% of the unmarried
Spanish women lived in convents rather than at home. Clearly the convent
was no longer the sole effective alternative to life with a husband. Conven-
tional limits on moving outside the family circle probably had much to do
with the number of unwed Spanish women. However, among the Indians
and mixed-bloods—who were assumed by the record-keepers to be married
if they had children, but may not always have been—the unavailability of
candidates probably came from a lack of urban jobs for men.

Throughout Latin America the Spanish and Portuguese conquerors encouraged economic activity for local women, using them in household service, buying food and cloth from them in marketplaces, training them as
seamstresses and embroiderers, and in other ways giving them opportunity
to earn a living in the towns. But consciously or unconsciously the new
rulers seem to have felt it dangerous to enable large numbers of local men
to live in anything but a dependent, hand-to-mouth fashion in the towns
and cities. Both Europeans and creoles tended to keep Indian men at uncertain day-laborer jobs, rather than hiring them if they aspired to become
skilled artisans. Even mestizos (European-Indian mixed-bloods) had some
difficulty in obtaining work as artisans from the ruling European and creole
elite. Consequently fewer local men than local women could survive for
long inside the town. Moreover, local men would not look like promising
husband-candidates to concerned families. In 20th-century Lima, Peru,
women who came in as domestic servants from the country still found more
opportunity than did men who came in from the country. Women in domestic service could learn skills like sewing and embroidery, which they
could continue to use after finding a husband or entering a consensual union.
They could earn enough by their new skills to put their children through
secondary school, so the children could find salaried positions instead of
being domestic servants or day-laborers. However, rural men still found it
hard to obtain any job in which they might learn salable skills.

Much the same turn to godparenthood, combined with retention of traditional relationships among indigenous people, became visible in the Philippines when it was ruled from Mexico. A similar exclusiveness among
those of European ancestry also appeared. These patterns continued even
after the Spaniards were turned out of the country as rulers, and the United
States took Spain's place from 1898 to 1946. Much the same marianismo-
machismo pattern entered the Philippines with the Spaniards, and with much
the same result. Many consensual unions were formed but were not for-

malized as marriages. Some could not be formalized because of the man's existing marriage to a woman of his own higher social level. However, there was one major difference. The indigenous Filipinos had used patterns like those of many Southeast Asians and Pacific Islanders, leaving much of the initiative to young people in finding their own marital partners even though the parents made the final arrangements. The indigenous Filipinos continued to use those customs. But in much of Spanish and Portuguese America preconquest patterns had relied on parental selection. Among the indigenous peoples of Central and South America that reliance on parental choice continued to prevail.

In Inca Peru the conquering Spaniards forced polygynists to take one wife and leave the rest. However, they allowed all existing nonpolygynous marriages to stand, even the sibling marriages. They reserved the application of the church's incest rules to the next generation. Only as the 16th century ended did the sex ratio among Spaniards decline toward equality, from an early ten men per woman. Thus Spanish men could not reasonably be expected to marry Spanish women until after 1600. Thereafter social patterns much like those in Mexico came into being, and persisted after independence.

In 19th-century Peru, as well as elsewhere, women benefited somewhat from the throwing off of Spanish rule. They retained their former rights to hold and manage property and to transact business. Their right to education was recognized, though not a right to vote. However, women also usually continued to experience whatever restrictions there had been on their freedom to carry on business and property transactions while their husbands were alive. Argentina was among the first to lift those restrictions, in 1926.

Spanish hacienda-holders in Peru continued to encourage the continuance of ayllu patterns of local endogamy as long as the haciendas existed because then they would not lose their laborers. Land reform in 1947 resulted in the breaking up of the haciendas. Yet little change took place in marriage patterns. The plots of land sold to the peasants were too small to support a family. The peasants therefore still had to work for wages for others to survive. Peasants continued to look for a marriage partner who came from nearby because then that partner's kin would be more readily available for help, if wanted.

The shortage of Spanish women which led to a requirement that Spanish widows remarry in early colonial Mexico had a counterpart in Brazil. The small number of marriages in the Portuguese colonial community led in 1732 to a prohibition on Portuguese women leaving Brazil without royal permission, as A.J.R. Russell-Wood points out in Asuncion Lavrin's collection *Latin American Women: Historical Perspectives* (1978). However, the small number of marriages among the Portuguese resulted from an artificial rather than a real shortage of women. Portuguese elite families preferred to give full dowry for only one daughter. Only one son could wed in turn, if all of the elite families were using the same strategy. And almost all did, because the laws of equal partible inheritance left each married couple hard pressed to find full dowry for more than one daughter. That was why convents began to be established in 1677, so that Portuguese parents could honorably place unmarried daughters in them. Between 1677 and 1800, 77% of the daughters of elite families in Bahia entered convents, 9% died before age 20, and only 14% married. Such an outcome ran counter to the royal preference for many Portuguese-to-Portuguese marriages. That was why the 18th-century Portuguese royal court tried to force Portuguese men to take Portuguese wives, by limiting official appointments to those thus married. But prudent family calculation ran counter to royal policy.

It becomes more understandable that 77% of Bahia elite daughters were in convents between 1677 and 1800 when it is realized that more than ½ the children in another 17th-century Brazilian Portuguese community, Vila Rica, were in families with 13 to 17 children. Those Portuguese who did marry were prolific. Many elite families could have had five or more non-marrying daughters per marrying daughter. The large numbers of slaves on Brazilian plantations helped to make unmarried Portuguese men willing to remain unwed. In most of Latin America other than the West Indies there were few slaves. However, in Brazil both unmarried and married men often had illegitimate offspring with slaves, freed women, and mixed-bloods. This could lead to uncomfortable surprises. Portuguese widows, like Spanish widows, were entitled to manage the entire conjugal estate. When a widow came to manage her husband's property, she often found that he had specified what was to go to his illegitimate offspring.

Formal marriage was less common in Brazil than in Portugal both before and after independence, in 1822. Formal marriage continued to be less common in Brazil than in Portugal after the replacement of the initial Brazilian constitutional monarchy by a republic, in 1889. Female-headed households were numerous. In one town 45% of all households were female-headed in 1804. Almost all the female heads were non-European. The average proportion of female-headed households in the cities of Brazil in 1838 was 40%, and ⅓ of all households in the entire country were female-headed. In 1850 the Brazilian state recognized a woman's right to continue as sole owner of her own business after marriage. Her husband would no longer automatically gain a share in it. The Brazilian government also reaffirmed an unmarried woman's right to manage her own property, and allowed a married woman to open a business with her husband's permission. But neither then nor since, in Brazil or elsewhere in Latin America, has it been assumed that any marriage would take place without consent of family.

The laws of Latin America have upheld the ultimate interest of spouses in their own marriage since the conquerors brought the 1563 rulings of the Roman Catholic Church to their new holdings, requiring the consent of both bride and bridegroom and limiting parental power to disinheritance.

Yet, in practice, marriage still normally involves some consultation between parent and offspring. When consensual unions are regularized, parents may be indicating to offspring that they wish to marry. They can expect the children to agree. Legitimization will enhance the children's social standing, as well as ensure any inheritance they might expect. But more often it is children's marriages for which parents take responsibility. Where offspring still depend on family ties for future livelihood, the degree of parental control over children's marriages tends to be greatest. That means the top of the socioeconomic scale (the Spaniards and Portuguese), or the Indians toward the bottom. They, not mixed-bloods, are the ones who have the land, whether in the Indians' small fields or in the still-great holdings of some of the descendants of the conquerors. But where there is more commercial activity, less parental influence may be felt.

The prevalence of consensual unions in much of Latin America, not only in the Caribbean area where they have been most studied, forces a recognition that formal marriage may make little economic sense to a man and a woman. If he has little opportunity for steady and well-paying work, and especially if she has more chance for it than he has, she may see a husband as a burden. If she has the legal right to manage her own property as a single woman, rather than being regarded as a legal minor while single, she may hesitate to give a husband access to what she has. If besides all that the economy in which both he and she are seeking work is one in which the controlling group sees itself as profiting from cheap labor, then both of them are apt to feel that the responsibilities of formal marriage are too risky to accept. That is especially likely if the controlling group also sees itself as absolutely socially distinct from the ones who provide the cheap labor, like the European-descended elite who still run the economies (though not always the governments) of most Caribbean or Latin American states. For that elite the descendants of slaves in the islands and of both Indians and slaves on the mainland form such a socially separate source of cheap labor. This is quite unlike the situation among elite Chinese on Taiwan, who hire fellow-Chinese at relatively low wages. They do not object to a farm tenant's or factory worker's brilliant scholarship-winning son making a landlord's or factory manager's daughter the wife of a respected university professor. But in the Caribbean islands and on the Latin American mainland, color still counts, despite all efforts to diminish its effect.

The salaried and professional elite in the Caribbean islands generally marry in their 20s. Below that level, consensual unions increase in frequency as one goes down the socioeconomic scale. Only as a woman becomes secure enough to feel that she need not depend on a man's earnings will the status symbol of marriage become important to her. Often she only reaches that level through receiving assistance from her own children as they go to work. Only as a man reaches a level of nondependence on a woman's earnings will he consider it acceptable to marry. He does not wish to seem like a kept man, which would derogate his manliness in both his own and other people's eyes. Yet that level may be harder for him than for her to achieve. He cannot usually count on children to aid him as much as she can, having given less than their mother to their support.

A woman, and a man, may prefer marriage for status reasons. But until each one feels reasonably sure of steady income, neither one is apt to enter it. That was the social reality against which Castro and his followers were fighting when they came to power in Cuba at the end of the 1950s. Their break with United States sugar interests made little economic sense from the standpoint of national income. Their resulting political break with the United States government forced a very different set of international alliances on them. But in the everyday life of a great many nonelite Cubans the change meant the end of the hand-to-mouth uncertainty of seasonal day-labor. The new regime at least made an effort to put everyone at steady work. This made Castro's revolution one that, in its way, freed them to choose to marry when and whom they would, as much as the breaking of clan power through the communalization of land in the People's Republic of China freed young Chinese in the same fundamental way.

The experience of the conquered in Latin America is in sharp contrast to that of the Maori in New Zealand, who have not been thrust into the bottom level of the society. The Maori kept much of their land, through mutual (though not entirely uncoerced) agreement with the British settlers. They kept their customary forms of marriage and divorce as well. They still keep their personal independence by often using those customary forms without resort to governmental registration. This may be confusing to government officials, but it has become accepted as a reality of Maori life. Once a Maori man's and woman's intention to marry has been accepted by representatives of the two kin groups in which the intending spouses currently reside, they are married. For the 50% or more of Maori who live in urban areas that generally means the *hapu* or lineage group in which their parents currently live or last resided. However, it may mean the hapu in which one of their parents currently lives or last resided, if the parents had divorced. The pair will be apt to choose which hapu to claim in accord with their own calculations of what affiliations may be most helpful in the future, at least as much as out of their affection for that parent. (When written records were introduced, Maori began to use them as well as participation in ritual and work activities to bolster claims to hapu membership.) If a married couple quarrel, the two hapu to which they initially announced their intent to marry try to reconcile them. If the reconciliation efforts fail, then they are free to seek new partners. The whole process of consultation and agreement between the appropriate hapu representatives will then take place again.

The situation of the conquered in Latin America perhaps resembles somewhat more the situation of the Australian Aborigines. They still faced enough discrimination in 1982 to seek worldwide visibility by staging a protest demonstration at the Commonwealth Games. In Victoria and New South Wales they had ceased to be wards of the state by 1910, but only recently had they been freed from that status (e.g., having to obtain official permission to marry) in the other four Australian states.

Consensual unions are fairly common among the Aborigines, as well as among the low-paid casual-laborer whites whose economic status most Aborigines share for lack of education and social acceptance. Much as among nonwhites in Latin America, consensual unions among Aborigines involve no formalities. Approximately ⅓ of firstborn infants among the Aborigines are born before the mother enters a formal registered marriage, either with the father or with someone else. In the continuing extended-family household form still favored by most Aborigines, such a child belongs to its mother's natal family, unless her later husband accepts it. In 1975 about 7% of all Australian families were below the poverty line, including three of every eight fatherless families, one of every six motherless families, and one in twenty-five of all two-parent families. Clearly, with fatherless families almost 9% of the population, far more than Aborigines were experiencing poverty or fatherlessness, or both. Most Aborigine families were not fatherless, and Aborigines were less than 2% of the population as a whole.

Though Aborigines are few in number, they have a disproportionate share of the 8% of infants born outside of marriage. They do not regard pregnancy as necessitating a formal registered marriage, as do most white Australians. In 1909–10, one in four white Australian marriages produced an infant within seven months. That figure went down to one in six in 1936–40 but was back up to one in five by 1966, according to Jerzy Krupinski in *The Family in Australia* (1978, 2d edition).

Nineteeth- and 20th-century European immigrants to Australia brought the courting patterns of their homelands. Before World War II, that meant English, Irish, Scots, or Welsh patterns. After World War II, it began to mean patterns from the continent, from the Netherlands and Germany to Poland, Yugoslavia, Italy, and Greece. However, all Australian settlers may have been influenced by the experience of Australia's first years of settlement. Australia was a colony for convicts from 1788 to 1793, and convicts continued to be sent there for almost half a century after free settlers began to come. Years of conflict followed between settlers and freed convicts who had finished their terms. The free settlers, who far outnumbered the "emancipists" (as freed convicts were called by the 1840s), rejected emancipist efforts to join the free community. Some emancipists reacted by turning "bushranger" and attacking those who had rejected them. Those years left a mild strain of something almost like marianismo-machismo in Australian life, which has affected both courtship patterns and the experience of the already-married.

The percentage of those over 15 currently married in Australia rose from 53% of men and 55% of women in 1921 to 64% of men and 62% of women in 1976. (The sex ratio shifted from a slight surplus of males to a slight surplus of females between those years.) Rural residents were the least married in earlier years but became the most married by the 1960s. Far more women (41% by 1977) now work outside the home after marriage than did so before World War II. More than ½ of those working have children under 15. However, nonworking wives have suffered more than working wives from the 20th-century rise in the percentage of deserting husbands.

Once Australia achieved Dominion status, in 1901, the British divorce act of 1858 no longer applied. Each of the six states therefore enacted its own laws. To end resulting confusion, in 1959 the federal government enacted a Matrimonial Causes Act, which took effect in 1961. The act recognized 14 causes for divorce. However, five years' separation (one of the causes) did not seem different enough from simple desertion for many to make use of it. The number of deserted wives per 1,000 total population multiplied from 1.3 to 4.7 between 1961 and 1976. That was a strong factor in the decision to change the divorce law in 1976 to make "irretrievable breakdown of marriage" the single cause for which divorce could be sought, with breakdown to be established by 12 months of separation. Men under 24 and women under 20 formed a disproportionate share of the divorcing population during 1976, showing the fragility of youthful marriages. Part of the rise in both desertions and divorces in the years leading up to 1976 undoubtedly reflected an increase in the number of youthful brides and grooms. Clearly maturity at time of choice improves stability in a self-selecting system of marriage arrangement.

The settlement of Canada by French colonists was very different from the first settlement of Australia by convicts. The French settlers came as full families to make a new life on the banks of the Atlantic and the St. Lawrence. They brought with them the injunction to be fruitful and multiply. They obeyed it by averaging about five children per marriage (including those ended by the early death of one partner) from 1650 through 1950.

The British took over in Canada during the 18th century, forcing most of the French in Nova Scotia to leave for the Louisiana Territory and elsewhere. The British then encouraged migration from the crowded Scottish highlands, peopled by Roman Catholics who also tended to have large families. The French in the St. Lawrence region felt increasingly closed in by the English, Irish, and Scottish migration to the east and west of them. They developed marriage-and-inheritance patterns like some in France, in which one heir remained with the parents, bringing in his wife. Yet in the New World the rest could marry too, and take up land in new settlements either in Quebec Province or (after the railroads came) in the western plains beyond Ontario. The heir tended to marry a third or fourth cousin because a kinswoman would already know his mother and find it easier to work with her. In one sample of late-19th- and early-20th-century French Canadian heir-marriages, 90% were of this type. Nonheirs married kin less often (only about one in six in the same sample), according to K. Ishwaran in *Canadian Families* (1980). However, French Canadians did not tend to marry early, according to a study of the 1871 Canadian census by L. Tepperman in *Canadian Review of Sociology and Anthropology* for 1974. The 1871 census showed that women among the French (then 36% of the population) and Irish (then 22%) first married at 23.9 years. Scottish women (Scots being 14%) married at 27.6, English (19%) at 22.6, and German (6%) at 22.0. Most of the other 3% were Eskimo (Inuit) or Indian.

All of the immigrant groups who first followed the early French settlers to Canada continued to follow their own courting and marriage patterns. So did those who came in later and smaller waves of immigration in the 20th century, whether from China, Japan, and India, or from Greece, Poland, Italy, Russia, or the Netherlands. Ethnic homogamy persists even yet. Each ethnic group actively encourages its young people to date only fellow-whoever. However, in the metropolitan centers and among university graduates some of that exclusiveness has broken down. So have earlier preferences that married women not work outside the home. In 1972, 34% of married women worked outside the home, not greatly less than the 41% of the neighboring United States that year.

Women's mean first-marriage age in Canada rose somewhat after 1871, reaching a peak of 25.5 in 1921. Men's mean first-marriage age that year was 29.9. Women's mean first-marriage age declined again to a low of 20.8 in 1970, when men's was 23.7. Women's mean first-marriage age then began to rise again, reaching 22.6 by 1972, to 24.9 for men. As S. E. Palmer indicated in George Kurian's collection *Cross-Cultural Perspectives on Mate Selection and Marriage* (1979), early marriages multiplied the likelihood of divorce. In her study of divorces in southwest Ontario, which was completed in 1965, 70% of the women and 75% of the men who divorced had married at less than the then median first-marriage ages, 21.2 for women and 23.7 for men. One-third of the divorcing couples had had a child within seven months of marriage. Canada liberalized its divorce laws in 1967 to recognize three years of separation, as well as adultery, cruelty, and desertion, as cause for divorce. J. F. Peters, in the Kurian collection, found that 43% of the women and 13% of the men who divorced in 1973 had married when they were less than 20. In 1973, 28% of brides and 8% of grooms were under 20. Urban dwellers divorced almost five times as often as farm residents and more than twice as often as those in villages and small towns. But many divorced people rewed; 8.6% of 1973's brides and 9.5% of its grooms were remarrying after a divorce. From 1950 to 1964, according to Benjamin Schlesinger in the Kurian collection, only 3.6% of brides had been divorced and only 3.8% of grooms. The percentage of brides that had been widowed was 4.9% and of grooms, 4.6%. Both widowed and divorced preferred single or widowed persons to divorced persons. In the case of divorced persons, 60% chose singles, and 35% of widowed persons chose other widowed persons. In 13% of all marriages, at least one partner was remarrying. Men remarried sooner than women, whether widowed or divorced. Both men and women remarried soonest when either under 30 or over 70. Widowed men waited longer than divorced men when under 30, but less long when over 30. The reverse was true for women.

For Indians and Inuit it has been hard to adjust to others' occupation of more and more of their territory. They have been pushed to harsher and harsher regions, unless they would take up settled agriculture in place of the familiar hunting-gathering life (with some gardening in the St. Lawrence valley). Where conversion to Christianity has taken place, as among the Kutchin Indians of the Northwest, it has ended any previous use of polygyny. Among previously easily divorcing people like the Kutchin, conversion has also meant fewer formal divorces. Premarital intercourse and childbirth have not lessened correspondingly, though, nor has extramarital intercourse. Among the Kutchin studied in Ishwaran's collection, one in six of the children under 15 had been born to unmarried women, and one in eight to women living apart from their husbands. The Kutchin have changed from an entirely roving to a largely settled life, only making hunting and trapping excursions from the villages they have established near a government agency-post. This makes it easier for unmarried mothers to apply for government child-support benefits. That lessens their inclination to marry even if they have an opportunity because they would then lose the benefits.

The Inuit are adjusting to a settled town life as workers in the new petroleum-based communities in their lands. This has meant even greater changes than those of the 19th or early 20th century, when they settled in their own small villages within a few days' travel of the nearest trading post. Village settlement brought a shift away from concern for spouse and children above all, with somewhat fluid networks intermittently linking nuclear families for hunting purposes. In its place came recognition of the value of joining siblings and their spouses (or other close kin) for purposes like buying and using fishing boats. That tended to heighten families' concern over whom their younger members might marry. It also heightened concern for arranging matters amicably if a divorce took place, so that useful links with the departed spouse and his or her kin could be kept. Town settlement has meant some shift back toward the nuclear family as central, in practical calculations, since town jobs are individually obtained. Yet town life has made maintaining ties with kin even easier because the settlements are larger. Kin may now see a great deal of one another in leisure-time activities. But whether this will produce more kin endogamy is still uncertain, for there are also more nonkin to choose from in the towns than there were in the villages.

In New Zealand, in Australia, in Canada, and also in the United States a majority population of European ancestry has had to work with a much smaller set of indigenous peoples. These have perhaps been most successfully included in national life in New Zealand. Because the Maori were already sedentary cultivators when the European settlers came, they could be brought into a commercializing economy more easily than the hunter-gatherers of Australia and North America.

In Australia, Canada, and the United States the European-descended population has had to work with variety among its own members as well. This has been particularly true in Canada, after the British conquest made the French settlers' descendants feel surrounded. It was also truer in the United States than in Australia, unless one thinks of convict versus free settler as parallel to an ethnic difference. Certainly the emancipists were discriminated against in the 19th century, as non-English ethnics complained of being discriminated against in Canada and the United States in the 20th century. Diversity of ethnic settlement in the United States began in the colonial era, with Dutch, Germans, and others, but Australia did not receive continental Europeans until the post–World War II influx from all over the war-devastated continent.

Only the early United States had a sizable African slave population, however. Today only the United States population includes millions of descendants of Africans, now far more numerous than the descendants of the Indians of the colonial and early national periods. And only in the past few decades have Spanish-speaking newcomers from Puerto Rico and Cuba made many Americans aware that the United States has its own partial equivalent to the French of Quebec, in the Spanish speakers whose ancestors were already in the Southwest when it was part of Mexico, before the 1840s.

Patrick Festy has compared Australia, Canada, New Zealand, and the United States in an article in *Population Studies* for 1973. Mean first-marriage ages declined in all of these countries between 1900 and 1970. They also showed fairly high levels of marriage by age 50 for both sexes. At least 84% of both sexes married by age 50, between 1875 and 1970, in both Canada and the United States. At least 84% of women in Australia and New Zealand married by age 50 during that time too. The percentage of men who married by age 50 in Australia and New Zealand only went below 84% (and never below 72%) between 1875 and 1930. (See Table 30.) That was still a period of settlement and consolidation in which men far outnumbered women, much as women had been scarce in the 17th century in the future United States.

Mean first-marriage ages declined farthest in the 20th-century United States, from 27.5 for men born in 1881–85 to 23.7 for those born in 1936–40, and from 23.6 for women born in 1886–90 to 21.6 for those born in 1941–45. Canadian ages went from 28.1 to 24.8 for men, but only from 23.9 to 22.5 for women. Australian ages went from 28.6 to 25.6 for men and from 25.3 to 21.9 for women, and New Zealand ages went from 29.5 to 25.3 for men and from 25.5 to 22.2 for women. (See Table 31.) All of these were one to three years lower than the ages then prevalent in western Europe.

In all four nations marriage rates faithfully reflected economic upturns and downturns at intervals of a year or so. They also remained higher than in western Europe, even during the depression of the 1930s. Clearly these lands of relatively new settlement still seemed more promising to their residents than the longer-settled lands of Europe did to Europeans. From the beginning these new lands seemed promising enough so that neither dowry nor other marriage payments played much part in their European settlers' marriage patterns. All that was expected in most cases was that a bride would have some household gear. Those items might be given by friends as much as by family, in connection with prewedding festivities.

From early colonial days in the future United States, colonists' marriage-ages were about 21 for women and 22 for men. That was half a decade earlier than in western Europe. The colonists brought their courtship patterns with them. At least among Puritans that meant the companionship expected in marriage required the two to become well acquainted before agreeing to marry. It also meant that they should have their families' approval. In the cold winters of New England the Puritans accepted bundling, with a bundling-board down the center of the bed to be sure that conversations under the quilts did not become too intimate.

By 1774 more women over 15 were married in Connecticut (79%) than in French Canada in 1681 (76%). Only 3% of women and only 1% of men under 20 were already married in the Connecticut of 1774, however. By contrast, in the United States of 1965, 25% of all grooms in first marriages and almost 50% of all brides had not yet reached 20.

The shortage of women in a frontier society meant that widows as well as widowers remarried. That was true most often for those under 30 and least often for those over 50. In 17th-century Plymouth, Massachusetts, more than ½ of all possible remarriages took place. English law continued to apply with regard to widows' recovery of their own real property, and their use of ⅓ of their husbands' real property either for life or until they remarried. Widowers also continued to be able to use all of their wives' property for life, if there were children. By the 18th century the wish of second husbands in New England to be reassured that they would not be responsible for any debts from a widow's first marriage led to the "smock marriage," in which the widow-bride symbolized her freedom from debt by dressing only in a smock.

Sometimes a remarrying colonial New England bride had actually been divorced from her first husband. The Puritans saw marriage as a contract intended to be for life, but they did not regard it as a holy sacrament. They admitted that under sufficiently painful circumstances, even lifelong contracts could and should be broken. They therefore allowed divorce with right of remarriage for adultery or desertion, to both women and men. They also allowed divorce for repeated physical abuse or nonsupport. However, the southern colonies had no provision for divorce, although occasionally an annulment was obtained. Marriages in the South tended to be arranged with more parental initiative and less partner initiative than in the North, especially among the great landed plantation families. The presence of slaves also meant that some white husbands supplemented formal monogamy with slave concubines. Among the slaves men outnumbered women until the 1840s, having been brought over in greater numbers while the slave trade lasted. The clandestine slave trade only ended in the 1850s, although it had been illegal for several decades.

Canny colonial New England merchants like those of 18th-century Salem often married cousins for political support. Their artisan fellow-townsmen also often chose cousins, for economic purposes. As noted at the opening of Chapter 2, southern planters later used cousin-marriage. They wanted to reunite properties divided by partible inheritance patterns, once primogeniture and entail had been swept away in the enthusiasm of the revolutionary era for eliminating every trace of privilege by birth—among whites. Yet in a parallel to early medieval European serfs' use of church rules against incest to seek more freedom of action by marrying someone from another manor, the slaves of those southern planters avoided first-cousin and even second-cousin marriages. Not only did they want some opportunity to play off their respective masters. By their marriage choices they strove to ensure that wherever they might be sent, they might have a chance of finding someone who was kin (at least by marriage) to someone they knew, if not actually to themselves. They wanted the widest kin network possible, in case of sale to another plantation, another country, or another state.

In Massachusetts, where slaves were few and some blacks were already free, whites were forbidden in 1705 either to marry blacks or to have intercourse with them. In 1786 whites were also forbidden to marry Indians. Both laws were repealed in 1843, as abolitionists protested that such laws perpetuated attitudes of superiority and inferiority. Miscegenation laws against black-white intermarriage persisted far longer in southern states. The last such laws were not struck down until the Supreme Court ruled them unconstitutional in 1967. But attitudes persisted even after laws changed. Some of the prejudice against the many southeast Europeans who came to the United States between 1880 and 1925 was that of Protestant versus Roman Catholic (or Orthodox, whose differences from Roman Catholics were little understood by most Protestants). But some of that prejudice was one of light skin versus darker skin. Darker skin hinted at Africanness. It thus suggested slave status, which was unconsciously taken to mean some kind of natural inferiority.

As long as most young people stayed at home with parents until they married, their parents could influence their courtship. When they began to be lodgers and boarders in the homes of others while they worked and earned in a new town (or even lived in dormitories like those of some early 19th-century textile mills), the keepers of those rooming houses and boarding houses did not hesitate to act as surrogate parents to them. It made little difference whether they worked and earned outside the home, like almost all young non-farm men and many young non-farm women, or whether they worked as part of a household team, like farm youths or the offspring of shopkeepers who lived above their business places. In Massachusetts in 1885, 78% of unmarried 20- to 29-year-olds lived with parents in smaller towns (86% in larger towns). There were fewer still at home in smaller towns because more had left to work elsewhere. That helps to explain why more than ½ of rural marriages in Massachusetts in 1885 were with someone from outside the local community, but only ¼ of urban marriages were with someone from another place.

For young people in the 19th-century United States the transitions of leaving school, entering work, and marrying were far from simultaneous. Those who went to work earlier might use their potentially self-supporting status to win parental acceptance of early marriage. Working-class members married earlier than salaried-class members, then as now. Those who went to work earlier might also be urged to put off marriage a bit. In late 19th-century Philadelphia middle children married latest, rather than firstborn or lastborn, possibly because they were asked to keep on "helping out" until the youngest began to earn. A few wives did work, especially as they and their husbands aged and the children left home. (However, fewer than 40% of 19th-century United States women experienced a marriage that lasted through their children's marriage and departure.) Some wives worked in late 19th-century Massachusetts, for example. But more of the 32% of Massachusetts-born women who were working in that state in 1885 were single women or widows. Fewer women worked among the Massachusetts-born than in any foreign-born group in the state. French Canadian immigrants there had the highest percentage of women working, at 48%, or triple the national percentage. But usually daughters rather than wives went out to work.

Only as rooming houses faded from the scene in the 1920s and 1930s could young people control their own courtship entirely. Rooming houses were replaced by apartments in which two to four young persons lived as they started to work. As time went on more and more young people even began to live alone. In college dormitories the shift in the 1960s from the parental housemother (often widowed) to the more sibling-like head resident marked a corresponding change. Until then salaried middle-class and professional parents had seen the college residential system as a last bastion of socioeconomic endogamy, if not of ethnic and religious endogamy. Sorority and fraternity lodges tend to promote ethnic and religious endogamy too.

Many working-class wage worker parents continued to expect their off-spring to remain at home until they married, however. They could then contribute toward family expenses, in return for what they received when they were young. Their dating partners and other companions would also remain under the parents' watchful eye.

As schooling increased to include at least part of high school for most people, and as apartments replaced rooming houses, the three major transitions of leaving school, starting to work, and marrying (and the subsequent fourth transition of having the first child) tended to come closer and closer together, until the end of the 1950s. This was especially true for the native-born. Since then, however, they have begun to spread apart again, slowly during the 1960s and more rapidly after 1970. The movement from home to apartment for young working people was paralleled by college students who sought to avoid having to live in dormitories. The two groups used the same set of arguments. Both declared that they would learn to budget time and money better, and be more prepared for home responsibilities, if they had lived on their own in that way.

Americans have been a marrying people. First-marriage ages for women rose only slightly during the 19th century. The median (not the mean) was 22 in 1890. First-marriage ages for men rose slightly more, reaching 26 in 1890. Thereafter those median first-marriage ages declined. In 1956 they reached a low for women at 20.1, and in 1959 they reached a low for men at 22.5. In 1960 only 10.5% of women and 20.8% of men aged 25 to 29 had not married. In 1970 those figures were 10.5% for women and 19.1% for men. In 1978 they had risen to 18% for women (28.1% in 1986) and 27.8% for men (41.4% in 1986). Women in the 20 to 24 age group experienced greater change. In 1960, 28.4% of them were unmarried. That rose to 35.8% in 1970, 47.6% in 1978, and 50.2% in 1980. By 1985 it had reached 58.5%, but then it began (slightly) to decline again. Yet it should be remembered that in 1890, 52% of women aged 20 to 24 had not yet married. That figure declined slowly for the next half-century, reaching 48% in 1940. Only then did it fall sharply. For men aged 20 to 24 the percentage of those still unmarried was 81% in 1890, 71% in 1940, 53.1% in 1960, 54.7% in 1970, 65.8% in 1978, and 71% (as in 1940) in 1983. By 1985 it rose to 75.6% but then began (very slightly) to decline. Nevertheless, men's median age at first marriage only moved from 22.8 in 1960 to 23.2 in 1970, 24.6 in 1980, and 25.5 in 1985 (still lower than in 1890), and women's median age moved from 20.3 to 20.8, 22.1, and 23.3.

During the 1960s a 10% surplus of women over men in the 18 to 27 age bracket (in which most first marriages take place) doubtless had some effect on the change for women between 1960 and 1970. That ratio began to reverse in the 1970s. By 1990 there will be 5% more men than women in that age bracket. Young people of both sexes have also been stretching out their transitions again, marrying only after leaving school and working for some time. Both the change in the sex ratio and the trend to marry some time after finishing school and going to work help to explain the apparent peak in 1985 in men and women not yet married at 24. The rising use of self-described selective dating services in the 1970s and 1980s may parallel the rise of the professional matchmaker in contemporary Japan, as both the young and the less-young seek compatible partners in a mobile urbanized society.

Since 1945 young people in the northeast United States, like young people in most of Europe, have thought of the appropriate age for marriage as the middle 20s. That was far later than in the South before 1970, where the favored ages were 18 to 21. However, since the mid–1970s young people in parts of the country other than the Northeast have moved toward marrying in the middle or even late 20s. Much like young Europeans, they appear to prefer having time to gain postschooling experience and learn to adjust to others as an adult before marrying. They appear to be reproducing the western European marriage pattern, which by the 16th century took young people out of their natal homes into others' homes. This broadened their experience and gave them practice in adjusting to the habits and wishes of others who were not part of their natal family. Only then did they enter betrothal and marriage, generally at least ten years after they left home.

Yet Americans have remained a marrying and a parenting people. Although individual couples were having fewer children by 1980, as high a percentage of couples as ever were having them. The 1980 census showed single-person households as 23% of all households. Only 61% of all households included a married couple, rather than almost 74% as in 1960 or 70% as in 1970. Lower death rates enabled more to live beyond the child-bearing and child-rearing years. Better health and pension programs enabled them to live independently, rather than move in with offspring. Fewer than ½ of the couples who married in 1900 could expect both partners to live to see all the children married. However, those who married in 1960 could expect to be together for at least 12 years after the last child married. That figure has continued rising gradually ever since. All this helps to explain how it is that average household size diminished only from five to four between 1882 and 1932, but plummeted to 2.7 by 1982 (2.69 in 1985). Nonetheless, marriage rates per 1,000 persons only went below 8 per year in 1932, unlike the situation in a number of European countries.

The low point of 1932 meant delay, more than complete foregoing. For the sons of those who lost more than ⅓ of their income between 1929 and 1934, it meant about two years' delay in marriage. (Somewhat similarly, unmarried men in late-19th-century Philadelphia who neither set aside savings nor obtained property during a ten-year span were only half as likely to marry during that period as men who did.) The drop of 1932 was more than made up for by marriage rates of 13 per 1,000 in 1941 and 17 in 1946, as

World War II approached and ended. However, these were aberrations. From 1870 to 1897 the rate hovered around eight to nine. It climbed toward ten by 1905 and stayed there until 1920. Then it declined again, really falling in the 1930s but shooting upward in the World War II era. By 1950 it was back to around ten again. By 1958 to 1962, when those born in the depression and the war years were marrying, it was down to the 1870–97 level again. In 1970 it was back to around ten. It fluctuated down toward nine till 1975, but by the 1980s it was once more about ten.

Only one in 20 men and one in 18 women had never married by age 65 in 1984. In 1960, 8% of women had never married at age 55. By the 1970s that had fallen below 6%. The total number of men never married at age 55 declined at about the same rate. True, only about 84 of every 100 men aged 45 to 54 were currently living with a wife in 1984. In 1930 that figure had been 89. But it had been only 82 in 1870 because of high mortality rates. In 1984 it was from having been divorced about as often as having been widowed or never having married at all.

The New England Puritans recognized that women as well as men might be justified in wanting to end a marriage and remarry before the original spouse's death. Ever since, Americans have tended to regard divorces—or in the case of contemporary Roman Catholics, annulments for an impediment that made a valid marriage impossible—as preferable to agonizing strains. Becoming free to seek another partner seemed better than trying to cope with too-great divergence between actual behavior and reasonable expectations for behavior between spouses, toward other family members, and in the community. However, only in the 1970s did most states in the United States move from granting divorce only for specific cause (like adultery, nonsupport, desertion, or cruelty) to letting divorce be granted for "irretrievable breakdown of marriage" (to quote the Australian law of 1976), and to accepting a specified period of separation as proof of the breakdown. By then the divorce rate was already rising from the rather steady level of 1950 to 1965. That level had been about one divorce for every 100 existing marriages, or one for every 400 persons of all ages.

Most people expect those who share similar backgrounds and/or current socioeconomic standing to be most likely to have similar enough expectations to avert undue strain. That has made looking for someone of similar ethnic or religious background or current socioeconomic standing second in importance only to simple propinquity (being in the same community and therefore in a position to meet and come to know each other) in American courtship and marriage patterns. Since New England Puritan parents permitted bundling to their courting offspring, Americans have assumed that the future partners are the ones to take the first initiative. Yet parents also still try to influence whom their offspring meet by encouraging this or that after-school activity, this or that young people's group, this or that summer or full-time job, this or that college, insofar as choices are available. For those low on the socioeconomic scale, choices of jobs—not of colleges, which are not even on the horizon—are likely to be few.

As F. Ivan Nye pointed out in *Role Structure and Analysis of the Family* (1976), spouses in the United States have long been expected to ensure that either or both of them are satisfactorily fulfilling many roles—provider, housekeeper, child-tender (protector), child-socializer (instructor), partner in intercourse, sharer in recreation (including re-creation through religion), and maintainer of whatever contact with the kin of both spouses is agreed on as desirable. That is enough to occupy anyone fully. Moreover, since 1955, what Nye calls the therapeutic function, or listening with nonjudgmental sympathy while offering constructive suggestions, has been added to the list. Nye comments that in his survey of Yakima County in Washington, whose people are reasonably representative of the general United States population, those who see their spouses as best performing the therapeutic role also indicate the greatest satisfaction with their marriages. Yet it is the role both partners find least satisfaction in playing. All these expectations make it easier to understand both the rise in the divorce rate and the more recent wish to wait until maturity to marry, and to find a maturer partner as well.

Former expectations that the wife would be the housekeeper and the husband the provider had clearly given way by the bicentennial year of 1976. Those expectations were already being questioned by most of the authors of utopian articles and books published in this country from 1888 to 1900, according to Kenneth M. Roemer in *American Studies* for 1972. Most of these authors were men. Most of them constructed their utopias so that women's and children's economic security was not provided for by husbands and fathers, but in some other way. Their vision was beginning to take form by 1976. In that year 45% of all wives were working (three in eight of those with children under 6, slightly more than ½ of those with children 6 to 17, and fully ⅔ of those with no children under 18). By 1985, 54.2% of all wives were working, including more than ½ of those with children under 6, more than ⅔ of those with children 6 to 17, but, interestingly, just under ½ of those with no children under 18. Perhaps having children to provide for had become one of the stronger reasons for a wife to work. Obviously there is great need for adjustments like those the Rapoports suggest for dual-career or two-earner families in England. By the 1980s Rosanna Hertz noted in *More Equal Than Others* (1986) that household helpers were apt to be earning very little compared with those who employed them, and wondered what that meant within those helpers' families. Adjustments of all kinds came hard for those brought up with other expectations, even though by 1985 fewer than ½ of all men and women continued to believe that it was preferable for the husband to be the sole earner. Adjustment may have been especially hard among the children of those who had experienced the 1930s depression as children and young people. As parents, the depression's sons and daughters had responded by trying to gratify every childhood wish for their own offspring. This did not prepare those offspring well for making adjustments in married life. It is part of what underlies the steep rise in divorce rates that began after 1965.

Divorce rates in the United States rose from about one for every 3,700 persons in 1867 to about one for every 1,350 in 1900. Most of that rise came in the 1890s. The divorce rate was still only about one for every 400 persons in 1950, although it had been close to one for every 250 in 1945– 46 as many too-hasty wartime marriages were dissolved. The divorce rate had only been about one in 800 in 1932, and one in 600 in 1935. Those were depression years, when both public and private relief programs tended to favor the married over the unwed. Moreover, marriage rates were also low. The divorce rate stayed at around one for every 400 persons until about 1965. But then it moved up to one for every 300 persons in 1970, when there was one divorce for every five marriages entered. It rose to one for every 200 persons by 1980 (almost one divorce for every two weddings), peaked in 1981–82, and then began a slight downturn. There had been one divorce for every 32 weddings in 1870, one for every 13 in 1900, and one for every six in 1930, as Hugh Carter and Paul Glick show in their comprehensive survey *Marriage and Divorce* (1976, revised edition). Most of the statistics in this section on the United States are taken from that survey, from the collection *Transitions* (1978) edited by Tamara Hareven, from the 1980 census, from the October 1983 *Population Bulletin* survey of the American family by Arland Thornton and Deborah Freedman, and from the 1986 *Statistical Abstract of the United States*.

Economic necessity played a diminishing role in keeping couples together from the 19th century on, particularly after World War II. S. J. Bahr noted in the special issue of *Journal of Marriage and Family* for 1979 (edited by F. Ivan Nye and G. McDonald) that white recipients of welfare were likelier to divorce than white nonrecipients, but divorce rates for blacks were not affected by whether or not they were receiving welfare. Bahr suggested that welfare might be enabling battered wives, and other highly dissatisfied wives, to leave husbands whose ill-treatment or nonsupport they might otherwise have endured. Those at the lowest income level divorced most often. Economic pressures undoubtedly exacerbated marital strains for them, but they may also have married too early to be ready to cope with those strains. Both men and women who divorced after World War II had usually married before rather than after 20. Moreover, unrealistic expectations of personal satisfaction had risen at all socioeconomic levels, as marriages came earlier and earlier. All these factors help to explain the increasing divorce rate. Strains from discrimination against those not of European ancestry were hard on marriages too. Those of other ancestries showed 150% as many divorces in 1970 as those of European descent at the same educational level, which largely sorts out the effects of poverty. Yet they have also tended to be strongly attached to church membership, and therefore were apt to be counseled against divorce.

Divorce tended to come earlier in a marriage as the 20th century unfolded, at least on the basis of the 22 states that furnished divorce statistics before 1967. By 1957 divorce came most often in the second year of marriage, rather than in the fourth as in 1887 to 1906. Those who married youngest divorced most often. In 1980, ½ of the divorces involved women who had first married at 18 or younger. Those women who remarried in 1980 after a divorce tended to have married for the first time when they were about two years younger than those women who were marrying for the first time in 1980. Those who entered marriage already pregnant were also at a high rate of risk. Men with the highest education (undergraduate or graduate degree) and women with an undergraduate degree divorced least between 1960 and 1975. Women with graduate degrees divorced more often than those with high-school education. They may have found it too stressful to be expected to play the housekeeper but not the provider role. Only one in eight women born in 1910–14 could expect to see a first marriage end in divorce. Almost one in three of those born in 1940–44 could, and almost two in five (one in three of men) of those born in 1945–49. The highest divorce rates have always been in the western states. In the 1960s divorce rates in the West were about four times those in the lowest-divorcing northeast states, which were also the latest-marrying and had the lowest marriage rates. The early-marrying South had the next highest rate of divorces after the West, and the north central states had the next lowest rate after the Northeast.

In 1979 it was estimated that ½ the infants born that year would lose a parent through divorce by age 18, and another ¼ would either go through a second parental divorce or lose a parent through death by age 18. However, by 1984 it was estimated that no more than 40% of infants born in 1983 would lose a parent by divorce, in view of the new downturn in the divorce rate. Yet it should be remembered that in 1900, fully ½ of all nuclear families could expect to lose at least one parent or child by death, not one in eleven as in 1976. Two-thirds of all marriages ended in death before 40 years had passed, in 1900. But only slightly more than ⅓ ended that soon because of death, in 1976. As a result 40% of marriages were lasting more than 40 years, rather than 29% as in 1900. In 1860 there was scarcely one divorce for every 800 existing marriages, but one in 36 marriages ended in death. In 1956, before the divorce rate began to climb but with death rates about like those in 1980, one in 100 existing marriages ended in divorce, but the number ending in death reached a new low, one in 57. By 1972 the number of existing marriages ending in divorce and in death were the same, one in 53. In 1982 the number ending in death was down to one in 56 again. The number ending in divorce stood at one in 45, after peaking at one in 43 in 1981.

Remarriages among the older widowed have increased in recent years. The median age for widowed persons remarrying in 1973 was 59.5 for women and 64.7 for men. As in Canada, so in the United States, the widowed prefer the widowed (or previously unmarried, even at the older ages). However, the divorced gravitate toward other divorced persons much more than in Canada. In the years 1921–23 about one of every 100 divorced or widowed women remarried in each year. By 1972–74 one in every 65 were doing so, in a total divorced and widowed population over three times as large as in 1921–23. There were three divorces to every two remarriages (mainly divorced women) in 1972–74, rather than five divorces to every 6 remarriages as in 1921–23. A higher percentage of the 1921–23 remarriages involved widows than in 1972–74, though the divorced remarried in considerable numbers too. By 1975, ½ of the divorced of both sexes were remarrying by the third year, and more than four out of five by the fifteenth year. Eventually, five in six men and three in four women were remarrying, slightly more than for the widowed of each sex. The highest percentage of remarriages for both widowed and divorced was of those under 30. Mean age at second marriage was 25 for women and 30 for men. However, older men and women were also remarrying. So were those who had divorced a second time. The divorced who entered second marriages ended by divorcing again about 40% of the time. Just under 6% of all marriages in the United States in 1975 were the third or more for at least one partner (widowed and divorced both included). Just under 20% were the second for at least one partner, and just under 75% were the first for both, according to Leslie A. Westoff in *The Second Time Around* (1977).

Divorce leaves bitterness in ways that being widowed usually does not. Both partners may feel bitterness, though one may feel it more than the other. A widowed person tends to idealize the deceased partner (often to the discomfiture of a second spouse). A divorced person tends to downgrade the departed one. However, the degree of trauma may not be much different. It may only be differently expressed because of differing circumstances. Child psychologists have found that it takes about five years for a child to come to terms with either parental divorce or a parent's death well enough neither to idealize nor to downgrade the parent(s) or the self.

The consensual unions of the poor, whether among Australian whites or Caribbean blacks, show that if a marriage pairs two who are not seen as equally important contributors, the blood-kin ties of mother and child tend to outweigh any formally marital or informally consensual ties. So do the sibling bonds of children of the same mother. For a lasting marriage, each partner must make a unique contribution whose worth the other partner recognizes and appreciates. The more than 100,000 couples over 65 in the

United States who lived together unmarried in 1980, so as not to lose part of their benefits from Social Security, help to bring home that point. Yet they are a small minority among the 1.5 million unmarried co-residing couples, 2% of all United States households, listed in the 1980 census. That was three times the number so listed in 1970. The number of co-residing unmarried couples rose to 2.2 million out of 86.8 million households by 1985, or one in 25 couples. Most of these were pairings of relatively affluent individuals, or else couples who were using co-residence as the final phase of deciding whether to marry.

The recent wave in the United States of searching for ancestral roots, with the strengthened sense of bonds to blood-kin that it represents, is a natural response to the recently increased frequency of divorce. Where husband-wife ties are seen throughout a society as lasting and mutually supportive, blood-kin ties mean less than where the durability and/or mutual support-iveness of marital ties may seem less fully guaranteed. Those who tradi-tionally sought to ensure strong blood-kin ties took care to enmesh married couples in extended-family households. Even where (as in China or India) the marriage was expected to last for life, extended-family household mem-bers continually drew the partners' attention away from each other as much as possible. Somewhere between two extremes—consensual unions of un-certain duration, or acceptance of blood-kin's right to minimize the devel-opment of close relationships between the partners to a marriage intended to last for life—lies the middle ground Americans have been seeking since the first colonies were planted in Virginia and New England.

Ethnic groups in the United States include people from almost every country in the world. Ethnicity stands for a sense of shared uniqueness that seeks recognition. It contrasts with minority status, which suggests a sense of repression that leads group members to want access to power they per-ceive themselves as denied by systematic policy. Members of a group may act as ethnics at some times, and as members of a minority at others. All of the immigrant ethnic groups—English, too (though they seldom think of themselves as an ethnic group), as well as Polish, Chinese, Arab, Hispanic, the longest-resident American Indian, and African or black, to list only a few—brought with them from the Old World their own patterns of mar-riage-arranging, and patterns of recognizing who could marry (or remarry) and who could not. Yet the ideal of the marriage of companions who choose each other, with only minimal (if any) prior consultation of parents, has taken root in every group. Its acceptance met with some initial difficulty among those who did not already see parents as consultants rather than arrangers before they came to the United States. It took time and effort to make the new idea seem reasonable to those who still saw the parents as the initiators of marriage arrangements, who at most would consult the child only after having first discussed the matter with the parents of the proposed partner.

Most newly arrived ethnic groups have undergone discrimination for a time. This experience usually strengthened ethnic-group endogamy, both by denying access to other groups' members and by making the group wish to assert its ability to live without needing to intermingle—at least not beyond the workplace and participation in relatively anonymous community or public activities. For people of European ancestry, barriers to intermarriage across ethnic boundaries were largely breaking down by the 1970s. That included the English, though they were usually the ones to discriminate rather than be discriminated against. However, interracial marriages remained relatively few.

Fewer than one in five marriages of members of most small, but physically distinctive groups like Chinese were interracial. These married outside their own groups most often. Fewer than one in 100 marriages were interracial for blacks, who almost always married each other. Fewer than one in 500 involving someone of European ancestry also involved someone of Asian, African, or American Indian ancestry. European-ancestry men entered such marriages more often, though European-ancestry women married their socioeconomic equals or superiors from other groups. This compares with more than ½ of those of both sexes of Polish descent marrying non-Poles by the 1970s. By then more than ½ the Japanese and those second-generation Puerto Ricans who lived outside New York State were marrying out of their ethnic group, although the Puerto Ricans might be marrying other Hispanics.

Every group's members have modified their patterns in accord with experience. Most North American Indians developed patterns that did not use bride-wealth, bride-service, or gift-exchange. They had not moved far enough into an agriculture-based economy to want to do so, before the Europeans came. Most Hispanics in the southwest United States followed the injunctions of the Roman Catholic Church. So did Hispanics who came to the eastern United States from Puerto Rico after 1950 and Cuba after 1958. Among Hispanics some were descended entirely from the conquerors; but most in the Southwest also descended in part from American Indians, and many from the Caribbean had some African ancestry. Blacks had to try to fit their lives around the harsh realities of slavery, and then had to contend with continuing discrimination even after slavery was gone. These three groups, which will be given more extended treatment, lived under special handicaps that most others did not.

Europeans' arrival on the East Coast gradually pushed many eastern American Indians westward toward the central plains. Most eastern Indians were monogamous, matrilineal, and accepting toward divorce. The Indians of the plains were largely polygynous and less frequently matrilineal, but they, too, were accepting toward divorce. By the time the eastern Indians began moving westward, the plains Indians were hunting buffalo with the horses that the Spaniards had introduced. In the extreme Southwest the local Indians were cultivators, matrilineal, often monogamous, and accepting toward divorce. The smaller peoples of the Pacific Coast were initially polygynous and easily divorcing. Some were patrilineal, some matrilineal. To the south, they accepted Roman Catholicism, Spanish-based marriage patterns, and the Spanish language. To the north, some managed to keep portions of their former lands by treaty. Some died out, and some were absorbed through intermarrying, mainly with other Indians.

Whether in a California Roman Catholic mission or a Congregationalist one in upstate New York, Christian instruction emphasized the nuclear family above all other kinship ties. This damaged the many matrilineal systems more than the fewer patrilineal and the still fewer bilateral and duolineal ones, even though missionaries emphasized the formalizing of marriages as an intended counterstabilizer. Government efforts to keep peace by providing Indians with goods or money, through trading posts on reservations, weakened the importance of both blood-kinship and marital ties. The Kutchin in Canada were among the many who learned that through experience. Those who stayed on the reservation became government dependents, in effect. Those who left the reservation to seek jobs in towns, nearby or distant, faced both discrimination from non-Indians and isolation from most of their fellow-tribe members. Even if they had learned standard English in a reservation school, discrimination singled them out and limited their access to jobs. Consequently both those on and those off the reservation found themselves poorly situated for marriage. Nonetheless, formal marriage remains almost universal (at least once in one's lifetime) among the members of the tribes. But both formal and informal withdrawal from marriage and both formal and informal entry into new pairings have tended to be more common among American Indians than in most segments of the United States population.

Among Hispanics, both those in the Southwest, who are often partly Indian, and those from the Caribbean, who are often partly descended from Africans, the incest and antidivorce laws of the Roman Catholic Church generally prevail. The patterns of marianismo and machismo are also familiar. Those factors, and the discrimination often faced by people who do not use English in a way regarded as correct by the ruling majority, are all elements in the occurrence of consensual unions. These were once relatively frequent among Puerto Ricans. After Puerto Rico was taken over from Spain, in 1898, 35% of Puerto Ricans responded to the first United States census-takers that they were in such unions. By 1950 that was down to 25%. By 1960 it was 13.5%, and in 1970 it was only 6.5%. However, another 18.5% of island households in 1970 included a mother and children but had no resident husband or consort. The 1980 census, in which no question about consensual unions was asked, showed 18.9% of households including mother and children but no father resident. Increased religious instruction by an expanded clergy has lessened the social acceptability of consensual unions. Some kinds of public benefits, like widows' pensions, are available only to the married, which makes formal marriage more attractive. Above all, an improvement in economic conditions makes marriage appear more feasible. Formal marriage is seen as important for improved social standing, which economic advance makes more attainable. All of these factors have contributed to the decline in consensual unions among Puerto Ricans, both in the island and on the mainland of the United States. On the mainland even more Puerto Rican households were reported in 1970 as mother-children families than on the island; 28% of first-generation and 26% of second-generation Puerto Rican households did not include a husband or consort. That probably stemmed from the relatively poor economic status of Puerto Rican households on the mainland, with its higher average incomes, even though in absolute figures they received more than did households on the island. How many mother-children households in either place might become consensual-union or eventually married-couple households would be hard to say. But on the basis of other Caribbean experience at least some and perhaps most eventually would.

In the Southwest, in 1970, almost 78% of Spanish-surnamed women aged 35 to 44 had a husband present. Almost 7% had a husband who was currently absent. Almost 7% were single, just over 3% were widowed, and 6% were divorced. Of women aged 25 to 64, 12% headed households with children. Most of those women were divorced or widowed. This was more than the 9% among those of European ancestry, although far fewer than the 30% among those of African ancestry in that year. The 30% figure was even higher than the figure for Puerto Rican households at that time. It had risen by 9% from the 21% of 1960. It almost doubled in the next 14 years. By 1984 fully 55.9% of black households with children under 18 were headed by women, compared with 17.4% of all nonblack households. The 1980 census showed 19% of all Spanish-surname households in the 50 states including mother and children but no father.

This recent steep rise in mother-headed black families is a measure of black men's insecurity in American economic and social life. In Latin America the Spanish and Portuguese conquerors gave Indian women livelihood opportunities in the cities, but not Indian men. They did not fear an uprising from Indian women, but at least unconsciously they feared one from Indian men. Similarly, black women in the United States have always found it easier to earn a living than have black men, with all that that implies for the likelihood of consensual unions, divorce, and mother-headed households. Yet from the beginning, slaves brought from Africa did all they could to reestablish stable family life within the severe limits placed on them. They made fictional brothers, sisters, aunts, and uncles of their shipmates. They followed incest rules about not marrying these fictive kin, once in their new places of servitude. They used truncated versions of African marriage ceremonies, with masters' listing of their pairings as a supplement, until conversion to Christianity brought Christian marriage rites. They followed courtship patterns (as much as they were allowed to) that mingled personal initiative and consultation with older advisers among fellow-slaves. Eventually these older advisers could be parents, aunts, and uncles.

Similar courtship patterns continued among freed blacks, for the few fortunate enough to be given freedom. Even if paid for, freedom was a gift. No law obliged a master to allow a slave to buy freedom through earnings that by law were the master's anyway. Nor did any law oblige a master to let a freed spouse buy a spouse still in slavery. When that was done, it was still a gift, a favor. It was not a business transaction between equals, even if money did change hands.

Only among the freed was marriage legally registrable. No slave was legally married, no matter how long he or she remained faithful to a spouse. The continuance of patterns found in much of sub-Saharan Africa, which accepted a trial period during which a child or two was born as a prelude to finalization of marriage, seemed to slave owners a positive proof of moral depravity. They believed that such patterns made it a mockery to talk of marriage as meaningful to Africans. But to the slaves themselves, marriage mattered. In 1864–65, in Mississippi, when emancipation brought opportunity to register marriages (including noncurrent marriages, in order to legitimize offspring), 35% of those who registered reported marriages that had been ended by sale, either of themselves or of the spouse, 41% reported marriages ended by death, and 9% reported marriages that had ended for other reasons. Altogether, 71% reported noncurrent marriages, some of them reporting more than one. More than ½ of the marriages ended by sale had lasted for less than 5 years, but 40% had lasted for 5 to 14 years, and 6% had lasted for 15 or more years. Almost 20% of the marriages reported by those 50 or over had been broken by sale after 15 or more years. The figures were even higher for Arkansas, whose plantation owners regularly sold slaves to labor-needing planters farther south in the heart of the cane and cotton belt.

After emancipation the effort to achieve stable married life continued, as Herbert Gutman makes clear in *The Black Family in Slavery and Freedom, 1750–1925* (1976). In 1880 rural southern blacks showed the same proportion as whites of families with husband and/or father present, more than four in five. In the nation as a whole, blacks showed the same proportion of such families as their occupational counterparts in the lower to lower-middle levels of the economy, more than four in five. Freed blacks and their free-born descendants had shown a similarly high proportion of two-parent families throughout the period from 1800 to 1865. In Manhattan in 1905 and 1925 approximately the same proportion of four in five black families with husband and/or father present still prevailed. In 1960 that proportion was still present among blacks in the nation at large. But in the meantime, between 1905 and 1960, the proportion of families with husband and/or father present among whites had climbed to 94%, reflecting their more favorable economic and social position.

What destabilized black marriages was less the slave experience than the agricultural depression of the 1920s, followed by the general depression of the 1930s and then the mechanization of southern agriculture after World War II. Agricultural mechanization spelled the end of the share-cropping by which many black families had continued to live since 1865. It drove millions from the rural South into the cities, in an exodus joined by four times as many whites as blacks. The whites headed for both nearby and distant cities. The blacks headed almost entirely for the North, seeking to get away from segregation laws that were not swept away until the civil rights legislation of the 1960s. But in the cities lack of skills meant low-paying jobs or none, for both women and men. Still, whites found it less difficult than did blacks to make their way into the new urban situation. Whites were accepted. Blacks, all too often, were not.

Half of United States blacks, like more than ½ of whites, were already in towns or cities by 1940. By 1965 four out of five blacks were urban, with twice as high an unemployment rate as whites, and three times as high a rate of subemployment at low wages on sporadic jobs. Matched for income, blacks in 1960 were almost on a level with their white counterparts above the poverty line in terms of family life. The husband and/or father was present in 93% of black families and 97% of white families. But below that line, where a far higher percentage of blacks than of whites was found, only 64% of black families held together well enough in 1960 to have the husband and/or father present. Among white families below the poverty line in 1960, 78% had the husband and/or father present.

By the end of the 1960s a full ⅓ of all nonwhite households were woman-headed. Yet only one in five of the households in the nation as a whole were woman-headed. That included one-person households, of which there were almost 20% in the nation at large. About ½ of the woman-headed households were woman-headed families, 11% of all families of two or more. The others were one-person households. More white families than black families were headed by women, numerically speaking. But in percentages that was reversed. The 30% woman-headed black families included 6% who had never married, but who presumably had had some form of consensual union, however brief, at some time; 7.5% had been widowed, and 16.5% had been separated or divorced. Although 60% of the black women family heads worked full time, and some received supplemental welfare benefits because of their low income, 60% also were still below the poverty line. By 1984 those figures had changed to 28.1% never-married, 2.7% widowed, and 25.1% separated or divorced. Unquestionably this reflected the difficulty young black men still had in finding steady jobs.

These figures help to explain why at least 14% of black men were reaching midlife in the 1970s without marrying. Black women have consequently had a hard time finding husbands, given the racial endogamy of current American life. These figures also help to explain why about one in five of blacks aged 35 to 44 had been divorced in 1970, to about one in six of whites. That was true even though black men had divorced less often than white men, if their 1970 income level was below $7,000 per year or if they had not finished high school. Black women had divorced more often than white women, if their 1970 income level was below $5,000 per year or if they had completed less than five years of elementary school. The annual divorce rate among blacks rose by 75% from 1960 to 1970, according to Robert Staples in Charles H. Mindel and Robert W. Habenstein's collection *Ethnic Families in America* (1976). That must be compared with a 40% rise for the population as a whole. By 1980, of men aged 15 to 54 who had ever married, 32% of American Indians, 25% of blacks, 23% of whites, 18% of Asian Americans, and 11% of Spanish-surnamed had been divorced.

In view of the steep rise in both divorce and woman-headed families after 1960, it is not surprising that by 1975, only 45% of all black children under 18 were with the two parents they were born to. That was much lower than the proportions of 73% for the white population and 69% for the popu- lation as a whole. Still, 69% were currently with two parents because a parent had remarried. By 1984 that had fallen to only 41%, compared with 81% for whites or 70% for Spanish-surnamed. Blacks as a group (regardless of educational level), like the less educated as a group (regardless of color), experience irregular timing of major life events. Starting to work, marrying, and having a first child come in fairly predictable succession at predictable age-levels for whites, on the one hand, or those with at least high-school education, on the other. Those life events have been less predictable for blacks than for whites. They have also been less predictable for those with less than a high-school education than for those with that much or more schooling. Graham B. Spanier and Paul Glick suggest in the *Journal of Family History* for 1980 that this is because blacks, like the less educated, have less control over the choices they can make. Ever since their ancestors were brought without their own consent as slaves, that has been true.

Lillian Rubin hypothesizes in *Worlds of Pain* (1976) that feeling a lack of control over one's life is one of the strains that leads to divorce. That hypothesis seems well confirmed by comparing divorce rates for low-income and high-income brackets, and by comparing divorce rates for those with less and more education. If it needs more confirmation, that would surely seem provided by both the marital instability and the high percentage of women and men who marry late or not at all, among the indigenous people of the Americas and the descendants of the slaves brought to the New World.

If anything is suggested by the historical development of marriage systems in the Western Hemisphere and the Pacific basin, during the centuries since European settlers started to arrive, it is that marriage and family life are inevitably deeply affected by the larger social, economic, and political conditions under which individuals and families live. Before commercialization and centralization began to dominate in human economic and political life, the awesome forces of nature effectively required individuals to accept parents' and lineage elders' control over their inclinations. As commercialization and centralization spread, individuals could become freer from family controls. Other institutions besides a lineage now provided them with livelihood and protection. However, they became subject to the impacts of impersonal market forces and governmental regulations. Those impacts could affect them as much and as negatively as famine, fire, epidemic, or flood. Yet, on a more hopeful note, the experience of the Western Hemisphere and the Pacific basin also suggests that in a positive environment, individuals can learn to combine blood-kin ties, marital ties, and ties beyond the family circle in a satisfying way.

CONCLUSION

Chapter 1 Revisited

Marriage *is* an alliance before it is anything else. It is an alliance between the two who are marrying. It is an alliance between families who become more closely linked, even if they were already linked by friendship or kinship, because now a member of one is marrying a member of the other. It is also an alliance among all the individuals involved and the larger social system—the larger family, in a metaphor. That metaphor ought to be clearly seen as just a metaphor, however, whether the larger family is thought of as the band, village, or neighborhood (at the immediate operating level); the language group, religious group, or body of people under one government (at a larger operating level); or humanity as a whole (at the largest operating level of all).

Marriage is the means by which the larger social system recognizes not only the mother, but also the father of the children whom the mother bears. Marriage acknowledges each as the other's partner in bringing children into the world and raising them. Marriage is also the means by which the larger social system seeks to control the expression of the powerful instincts of sexual attraction. Marriage is meant to prevent that attraction from so monopolizing the attention of specific pairs of individuals that it effectively withdraws them from social responsibilities. But it is also meant to prevent that attraction from leading to disruptive levels of competition among individuals for opportunity to express it. Through marriage both the larger social system and the family remind the ones who marry that they cannot live in total isolation. Marriage reminds the married that they must ally themselves with others, not just with each other, in order to live fully, productively, and satisfyingly.

Each of the three major aspects of marriage as an alliance—the couple, the family, the larger social system—tends to be stressed more in one kind of situation than in another. Marriage as an alliance of families was stressed most in those societies that operated primarily or entirely at the level of the face-to-face community, rather than at the level of at least a minimal order-keeping and tax-collecting state. Whether hunting-gathering band, crop-raising community, or group of herders, such societies felt a need to ensure that in time of drought or blight or animal-killing disease, every household had links with other households in areas far enough away not to be affected. Each household wanted to be able to turn to daughters or sons already in households in other areas. It made sense, from the standpoint of both individual and family, for families to do much, most, or even all of the arranging, when all aspects of life were primarily lived within the family.

As small states and then larger ones came into being, those whom one knew beyond one's family ceased to be simply other families. To be a family member ceased to be virtually the only set of roles anyone could play. One's family—one's fully extended family, the whole of one's recognized kin—and the similarly fully extended families of others ceased to be the only institutions one knew. There were the state, its courts, its military and police forces, and usually a religious establishment. One could think in terms of interplay between those other institutions and one's family, those institutions and other families, and even those institutions and one's self as somehow distinguishable from one's family.

The ancient Athenians were at that stage when they said a sonless household head could adopt an heir, rather than know his property would be divided among his kin. The Athenians worked out their thoughts and feelings about antagonisms between private and public concerns, antagonisms between generations, and antagonisms between spouses in the great tragedies of *Antigone*, the *Oedipus* plays, and *Medea*. Other societies have recognized that stage too. But they have been apt to mask it with metaphor, calling the ruler the father of his people, like the ancient Chinese. Few other societies have faced it as squarely as the ancient Athenians.

The Athenians had no ruler. They made no pretense that the state was the family writ large, as did the French when they put fraternity into their revolutionary slogan in 1789, along with liberty and equality. Liberty and equality are both also sought in families, as shown by the worldwide gravitation toward equal partible inheritance (and away from living in an extended co-resident family) whenever economic circumstances permit. But the Athenians knew that there was a difference between family and state. One was personal and one was impersonal in its view of individuals. Individuals-in-families were also individuals-in-states. Yet being an individual was different in those two contexts. That meant that the individual was not defined in full by either membership. The individual must be a third entity, besides the family and the state.

For the Athenians the state ought to regulate the marriages of families. The state had an interest in marriages because it had an interest in who were citizens and could actively participate in government, being descended from citizens. That meant that the marriages of citizens were no longer the concern only of families. The codes of Hammurabi and of other early rulers had set forth ground rules like monogamy, incest prohibitions, and tests of eligibility to marry. These earlier codes had treated marriage contracts as contracts, regulating both their making and their breaking. However, the makers of these earlier codes did not take the same kind of interest in marriage as the Athenian code-makers because they did not see a citizen-noncitizen distinction. They saw a subject-nonsubject one and a free-slave one instead. Therefore, they did not prescribe who must be married, as the Athenian code prescribed a kinsman for a brotherless daughter of a citizen.

Marriage was not just a private affair of the families in ancient Athens, any more than it was in imperial China during the centuries when an official was expected to declare a marriage ended because one partner had been convicted of a crime, whether or not the divorce was requested by the other partner or by the family of either partner. The larger society had an interest in marriage too, not just the partners' families. Yet so did the individual, the actual partner to the other actual partner in the marriage. The individual always had an interest, whether the marriage was an exclusive monogamous one or a limitedly more inclusive form of polyandry or polygyny (or of both polyandry and polygyny, like the Nayar of central Kerala in India).

The ancient Athenians looked at Medea and Jason and saw only tragedy in partner choosing partner without even consulting family, let alone waiting for family to suggest. The ancient Hebrews saw the possibility of tragedy there too, when they looked at David and Bathsheba. Yet they also saw the possibility of good—the wise king Solomon, the builder of the Temple—coming forth from it. They did not see the state as family writ large, despite a sense of being Israel's descendants. Nor did they see either state or family as having final authority over those who were in them, as most of their contemporaries did. Instead, they saw that sometimes individuals must go against both state and family to play the prophet, because individuals are defined by more than just their membership in those two groupings. Human beings are defined by being human, which is the largest of all social group-ings. The members of humanity are defined by their distinctiveness as much as by their similarity to one another. They enjoy greater individual unique-ness than any other form of life, as far as human beings know, for they remain capable of learning and changing throughout life. One cannot teach old dogs new tricks, but old humans may learn to think new thoughts and do new things to the very ends of their long lives. Modern biologists refer to that capacity as juvenility. The ancient Hebrews described it in Genesis 1 by saying that men and women are images of God. Others (like Confucius, when he said that by nature people are pretty much alike, but by nurture they become different) have described it in other ways, less conducive to seeing individuals as more than simply members of social units.

When heirs of ancient Athens joined with heirs of ancient Israel in the early Christian church, they eventually concluded that marriage was pri-

marily the relationship of the two partners. Their descendants sought at
Trent in 1563 to make that clear once and for all, by denying families the
right to divide partners who had stated their intent to marry before a proper
witness and whose intent had then been properly recorded. The proper
witness was defined as an ordained priest, and the proper recording was
defined as being recorded in God's eyes through the marriage ceremony
conducted by the priest. Being recorded in other human beings' eyes through
registration in the parish book was only an acknowledgment of what had
happened, although that, too, was expected of the priest who witnessed the
couple's vows to each other before God. The past four hundred years have
seen the coming to fruition of that recognition of marriage as primarily the
partners' concern, first in the Christian culture-sphere and more recently
beyond it.

Much more can be said about how potential partners may be identified,
or about considerations of maintenance or improvement of position in
choosing partners. Much more can be said about roles played by spouses,
or about strains that are felt in those roles, particularly in the therapeutic
role. Much more can be said about ongoing tensions between marital ties
and blood ties, or about ongoing tensions between marital ties and social
ties other than those of family, such as those with friends and workmates.
But perhaps enough has been said already to indicate how dangerous it is
to concentrate on the leopard alone (the marital system alone?) without
looking at the terrain (the economy?), the wind direction (the political
system?), and the other indications of what is going on around both oneself
as observer and what is being observed. The 1979 Nobel economics prize-
winner, Theodore Schultz, has used national income statistics to suggest
that monogamy is more productive than the polygyny and polyandry found
in poorer societies, despite the evidence from anthropologists that both
polygyny and polyandry increase a household's productivity where available
resources and technology are limited. National income statistics do not take
resource bases or current levels of technology into account. What one has
learned to look for is what one sees, until one is surprised, and learns that
one must look for something else as well.

Jonathan Gathorne-Hardy, in *Marriage, Love, Sex, and Divorce* (1982),
suggests that ancient Athens brought the concept of guilt into the Western
world, and thus into the modern world. He also suggests that Christianity
brought the concepts of lifelong marriage and of forgiveness. He further
suggests that the present generation is applying that concept of forgiveness
to those who do not live by the concept of lifelong indissoluble marriage
as the only permissible expression of sexuality for noncelibates, by being
more accepting toward other concepts and their expressions as long as they
do not appear to do irreparable harm to either children or adults.

The modern United States has come to a point at which stressing the
individual, as partner to the multiple alliance involved in marriage, is reach-

ing some kind of limit. Stressing both the family and the larger social grouping as partners to the marriage alliance have reached limits of some kind in other times and places. Stressing the family may have reached a limit among Hindus, when they reached the point of making marriages between children. Stressing the state may have reached a limit in the Nazi years in Germany between 1933 and 1945, when youths and maidens were brought together by the state to produce children for the fatherland. Yet no one can live through family alone, or through state alone, in today's interdependent world. The individuals who are at the core of the marriage, the two partners, must be mature enough to balance claims from each other, from the children who may be born, from their own natal families, and from the larger society. Only as they achieve such maturity can they choose each other well enough, and adjust to each other well enough as the years pass, to make the concepts of forgiveness and of lifelong marriage intertwine successfully. We may not only be learning to be more accepting of those who find that concepts other than indissoluble marriage seem more suited to their current circumstances, as Gathorne-Hardy suggests. We may also be learning how to apply forgiveness—expressed in finding mutually satisfactory ways to adjust to each other and to others—within a marriage, so as to make it more feasible to stay together for as many years as modern life expectancies make modern marriage mean.

In a world in which not only interdependence but also geographic and social mobility are increasingly real, relationships of choice (like marriage) tend to be stressed more than relationships of birth, which blend elements of chance and necessity. That is because people are more conscious of always having to make choices than they were when life seemed to be an ever-repeating cycle, tied inescapably to the seasons of the year. The ancient Athenian view of life focused on repetition of patterns, like the Confucian and the Hindu views, and stressed the need to accept the decree of Fate as unopposable. The ancient Hebrews saw the possibility of real change, looking at Jacob, wrestler with God, as their progenitor. Modern views around the world draw on both Athenian and Hebrew insights into the relations among chance, necessity, and choice, even while blending them with other understandings too.

Marriage has always been and always will be a multiple alliance. It will continue to be an alliance between the partners. It will continue to be an alliance between their families. Even if the partners' families played no specific part in their initial selection of each other, the families will still become linked through the partners' relationship, particularly if there are children. Marriage will also continue to be an alliance between the partners (and their families) and the larger society, to which all belong. Those realities remain. But how all the various participants in that multiple alliance relate to one another can change, has changed, and undoubtedly will continue to change as circumstances change. The capacity to change is what has made us human, from the initial disappearance of the estrous cycle, which made marriage rather than consortship a possibility, on through the various social responses that human beings have always made to changing economic and other circumstances. If we can recognize pressures that have led to what we do not see as good and worth preserving, we can hope to see how we might lift those pressures. We can strive for a better balance among the different partners to that multiple alliance known as marriage, better because providing enough satisfactions to outweigh frustrations for all concerned. We can also move toward a better balance in seeing what is in the realm of choice, what is in the realm of chance, and what is in the realm of unavoidable necessity.

Will Durant once said, "Civilization is a stream with banks. The stream is sometimes filled with blood from people killing, stealing, shooting, doing the things historians usually record; while on the banks, unnoticed, people build homes, make love, raise children, sing songs, write poetry, and even whittle statues." This book looks at what has been happening on the banks. It, too, has involved some pain and bloodshed. But we may find more cause for hope if we look at both the banks and the stream than if we look only where the water's redness draws the eye.

Appendix: Tables

————————————————————————————————————Table 1

Sex Roles in Agriculture and Plurality of Marriage

	No agriculture	Female farming	Male farming	Equal partici- pation	Total
Monogamy	16 (8.6%)	19 (8.2%)	57 (28.4%)	38 (18.5%)	130
Limited polygyny	98 (52.7%)	65 (28.0%)	82 (40.8%)	82 (40.0%)	327
General polygyny	72 (38.7%)	148 (63.8%)	62 (30.8%)	85 (41.5%)	367
Total	186	232	201	205	824

x^2 = 81.27 (df=6)
p< 0.001

Total of table	824
N.I. on agriculture	33
N.I. on plurality of marriage	6
Total	863

The data in this table can be reorganized as follows:

	Monogamy	Limited polygyny	General polygyny	Total
No agriculture	16 (12%)	98 (29%)	72 (20%)	186 (22%)
Female farming	19 (15%)	65 (21%)	148 (40%)	232 (29%)
Male farming	57 (44%)	82 (25%)	62 (17%)	201 (24%)
Equal participation	38 (29%)	82 (25%)	85 (23%)	205 (25%)
Total	130 (100%)	327 (100%)	367 (100%)	824 (100%)

Table 2

Sex Roles in Agriculture and Marriage Transactions

	No agriculture	Female farming	Male farming	Equal partici- pation	Total
Bridewealth	51 (27.1%)	135 (58.4%)	85 (41.7%)	116 (56.6%)	387
Bride service	30 (16.0%)	27 (11.7%)	16 (7.8%)	19 (9.3%)	92
Gift exchange and sister exchange	33 (17.6%)	20 (8.7%)	10 (4.9%)	15 (7.3%)	78
Dowry	2 (1.1%)	0 (0.0%)	15 (7.4%)	7 (3.4%)	24
No payment taken	72 (38.3%)	49 (21.2%)	78 (38.2%)	48 (23.4%)	247
Total	188	231	204	205	828

$x^2 = 93.93$ (df=12)
p< 0.001

Total of table	828
N.I. on agriculture	33
N.I. on marriage transactions	2
Total	863

Jack Goody, ed., PRODUCTION AND REPRODUCTION, Table 19, page 130. Copyrighted 1976 by Cambridge University Press. Reproduced by permission of Cambridge University Press.

The data in this table can be reorganized as follows:

	Bride- wealth	Bride service	Gift/sister exchange	Dowry	No pay- ment taken	Total
No agriculture	51 (13%)	30 (33%)	33 (42%)	2 (8%)	72 (29%)	188 (22%)
Female farming	135 (35%)	27 (30%)	20 (26%)	0 (0%)	49 (20%)	231 (29%)
Male farming	85 (22%)	16 (17%)	10 (13%)	15 (62%)	78 (31%)	204 (24%)
Equal participation	116 (30%)	19 (20%)	15 (19%)	7 (30%)	48 (20%)	205 (25%)
Total	387 (100%)	92 (100%)	78 (100%)	24 (100%)	247 (100%)	828 (100%)

Table 3

Cross-Cultural Data on Sex Division of Labor (by Subsistence Activity) and Type of Social Organization (by Descent Group and Residence)

| Sex Division of Labor | Type of Social Organization | | | | | | | | | TOTAL |
| | No Descent Group | | | | Matrilineal | | | Patrilineal | Mat. & Pat. | |
	Neo-local	Bi-local	Patri-local	Matri-local	Matri-local	Avuncu-local	Patri-local	Patri-local	Patri-local	
Agriculture with cattle										
Men do most	11	6	6	1	1	0	1	34	1	61
Both do	6	2	9	3	4	1	0	40	2	67
Women do most	0	0	0	1	0	0	1	12	2	16
TOTAL	17	8	15	5	5	1	2	86	5	144
Animal husbandry										
Men do most	0	0	2	0	0	0	1	14	0	17
Both do	1	0	2	0	0	1	0	10	1	15
Women do most	0	0	0	0	0	0	0	0	0	0
TOTAL	1	0	4	0	0	1	1	24	1	32
Agriculture without cattle										
Men do most	3	5	13	2	6	0	1	5	0	35
Both do	0	2	0	4	5	10	1	27	2	51
Women do most	2	4	9	4	5	2	1	14	2	43
TOTAL	5	11	22	10	16	12	3	46	4	129
Fishing										
Men do most	1	4	11	0	2	0	1	3	1	23
Both do	0	1	0	2	0	0	1	2	0	6
Women do most	0	0	1	0	0	0	0	0	0	1
TOTAL	1	5	12	2	2	0	2	5	1	30
Hunting and gathering										
Men do most	0	1	7	3	0	0	0	2	0	13
Both do	1	8	10	6	1	0	1	6	6	39
Women do most	0	0	0	0	0	0	0	0	0	0
TOTAL	1	9	17	9	1	0	1	8	6	52
TOTAL	25	33	70	26	24	14	9	169	17	387

Reprinted from Table 4, page 183, Roy G. D'Andrade, "Sex Differences and Cultural Institutions," in THE DEVELOPMENT OF SEX DIFFERENCES, edited by Eleanor E. Maccoby, with the permission of the publishers, Stanford University Press. © 1966 by the Board of Trustees of the Leland Stanford Junior University.

315

Table 4

Descent and Types of Subsistence

Subsistence Type	Descent System									
	Patrilineal		Bilateral		Matrilineal		Duolineal		Total	
	No.	%	No.	%	No.	%	No.	%	No.	%
Plough agriculture	69	28	38	19	9	11	1	4	117	21
African horticulture	32	13	3	2	5	6	6	21	46	8
Dominant horticulture	66	27	68	33	47	56	7	25	188	33
Other horticulture	11	4	15	7	5	6	2	7	33	6
Pastoralists	51	21	8	4	3	4	4	14	66	12
New World pastoralists	0	0	11	5	2	2	0	0	13	2
Extractive	19	8	61	30	13	16	8	29	101	18
Total	248	101	204	100	84	101	28	100	564	100

David Aberle, "Matrilineal Descent in Cross-Cultural Perspective," Table 17-4, page 677, in David M. Schneider and Kathleen Gough, eds., MATRILINEAL KINSHIP, University of California Press. © 1961 The Regents of the University of California.

Table 5

Subsistence Type and Size of Political Unit

Subsistence Type

Size of Unit*	Plough Agriculture		African Horticulture		Dominant Horticulture		Other Horticulture		Pastoral-ists		New World Pastoralists		Extrac-tive		Total	
	No.	%	No.	%	No.	%	No.	%	No.	%	No.	%	No.	%	No.	%
Family level	3	3	1	2	14	8	1	3	1	2	0	0	15	15	35	7
Local communities	12	12	15	33	78	44	24	75	17	27	5	39	74	76	225	43
Peace groups	1	1	1	2	3	2	0	0	7	11	2	15	4	4	18	3
Minimal states	20	20	15	33	53	30	6	19	13	21	6	46	5	5	118	22
Little states	9	9	9	20	17	10	1	3	15	24	0	0	0	0	51	10
States	53	54	5	11	11	6	0	0	10	16	0	0	0	0	79	15
Total	98	99	46	101	176	101	32	100	63	101	13	100	98	100	526	100

* 35 cases of dependent communities omitted; 3 cases of data not available are omitted.

David Aberle, "Matrilineal Descent in Cross-Cultural Perspective," Table 17-5, page 682, in David M. Schneider and Kathleen Gough, eds., MATRILINEAL KINSHIP, University of California Press. © 1961 The Regents of the University of California.

"Peace groups" means that recognized means do exist for settling disputes on an ad hoc basis.

"Minimal states" means a total population of 1,500 to 10,000 people.

"Little states" means a total population of 10,000 to 50,000 people.

Table 6

Subsistence Type and Size of Political Unit, Reduced

Subsistence Type	Plough Agriculture %	African Horticulture %	Dominant Horticulture %	Other Horticulture %	Pastoralists %	New World Pastoralists %	Extractive %	Total %
Family, community, pact	16	37	54	78	40	54	95	53
Minimal states	20	33	30	19	21	46	5	22
Little states, States	63	31	16	3	40	0	0	25
Total	99	101	100	100	101	100	100	100

David Aberle, "Matrilineal Descent in Cross-Cultural Perspective," Table 17-5 (continued), page 683, in David M. Schneider and Kathleen Gough, eds., MATRILINEAL KINSHIP, University of California Press. © 1961 The Regents of the University of California.

"Family, community, pact" combines top three lines in Table 5.
"Little states, States" combines last two lines in Table 5.

318

Descent and Size of Political Unit

Table 7

Size of Unit	Descent Systems									
	Patrilineal		Bilateral		Matrilineal		Duolineal		Total	
	No.	%	No.	%	No.	%	No.	%	No.	%
Family level	13	5	16	8	5	6	1	4	35	6
Community level	75	30	93	46	38	45	19	68	225	40
Peace groups	12	5	6	3	0	0	0	0	18	3
Minimal states	58	24	28	14	27	32	5	18	118	21
Little states	33	13	8	4	9	10	1	4	51	9
States	37	15	36	18	4	5	2	7	79	14
Dependent societies	18	7	16	8	1	1	0	0	35	6
Not ascertained	2	1	1	*	0	0	0	0	3	0
Total	248	100	204	101	84	99	28	101	564	99

*Less than 0.5%

David Aberle, "Matrilineal Descent in Cross-Cultural Perspective," Table 17-6, page 685, in David M. Schneider and Kathleen Gough, eds., MATRILINEAL KINSHIP, University of California Press. © 1961 The Regents of the University of California.

Table 8

Size of Political Unit, Subsistence Type, and Descent

Subsistence Type	Large — Little State and State				Intermediate — Minimal State				Small — Family, Community, Pact				Total
	Pat.	Bilat.	Mat.	Duo.	Pat.	Bilat.	Mat.	Duo.	Pat.	Bilat.	Mat.	Duo.	
Plough agriculture	30	29	2	1	15	1	4	0	9	4	3	0	98
African horticulture	11	1	1	1	9	1	3	2	12	1	1	3	46
Dominant horticulture	9	9	9	1	19	14	17	3	36	35	21	3	176
Other horticulture	0	1	0	0	2	3	1	0	9	11	3	2	32
Pastoralists	20	4	1	0	12	0	1	0	17	3	1	4	63
New World Pastoralists	0	0	0	0	0	5	1	0	0	6	1	0	13
Extractive	0	0	0	0	1	4	0	0	17	55	13	8	98
Total	70	44	13	3	58	28	27	5	100	115	43	20	526

Dependent societies and those not ascertained are omitted.

David Aberle, "Matrilineal Descent in Cross-Cultural Perspective," Table 17-7, page 687, in David M. Schneider and Kathleen Gough, eds., MATRILINEAL KINSHIP, University of California Press. © 1961 The Regents of the University of California.

"Family, community, pact" combines top three lines in Table 7.
"Little states, States" combines last two lines in Table 7.

Table 9

Stratification and Subsistence

Level of Stratification*	Plough Agriculture		African Horticulture		Dominant Horticulture		Other Horticulture		Pastoralists		New World Pastoralists		Extractives		Total	
	No.	%	No.	%	No.	%	No.	%	No.	%	No.	%	No.	%	No.	%
None and age grades	10	9	20	46	96	54	24	75	13	21	7	54	70	69	240	44
Wealth	20	17	3	7	22	12	2	6	21	33	2	15	20	20	90	16
Hereditary aristocracy	17	15	12	27	45	25	5	16	20	32	4	31	11	11	114	21
Complex	68	59	9	20	15	8	1	3	9	14	0	0	1	1	103	19
Total	115	100	44	100	178	99	32	100	63	100	13	100	102	101	347	100

Subsistence Type

*18 cases of data not available omitted.

David Aberle, "Matrilineal Descent in Cross-Cultural Perspective," Table 17-10, page 697, in David M. Schneider and Kathleen Gough, eds., MATRILINEAL KINSHIP, University of California Press. © 1961 The Regents of the University of California.

"Complex" means that there is more than one basis for social stratification.

Table 10

Percentage Distribution of Large and Small Familial Systems by Level of Societal Complexity, Based on Ethnographic Atlas

PREVALENT FORM OF ECONOMIC ORGANIZATION

Size of Familial System	Hunting and Gathering (%)	Incipient Agriculture (%)	Pastoral (%)	Fishing (%)	Extensive Agriculture (%)	Intensive Agriculture (%)	Intensive Agriculture with Irrigation (%)
Large	54	65	71	73	80	80	65
Small	46	35	29	27	20	20	35
No. of cases (N = 1137)* . . .	(180)	(86)	(86)	(118)	(415)	(163)	(89)

*C = .21, C̄ = .27, P<.001; G = .21, P<.001.

R. L. Blumberg and R. Winch, "Societal Complexity and Family Complexity: Evidence for the Curvilinear Hypothesis," Table 10, page 915, in American Journal of Sociology, 1972 (77) 898-920, published by The University of Chicago Press. © 1972 by The University of Chicago.

"Large" means that some form of expanded family is commonest.

"Small" means that nuclear or conjugal family is commonest.

Table 11

Relationship Between Mean Size of Local Community and Familial Complexity: Ethnographic Atlas, Excluding Fishing and Herding Societies

	MEAN SIZE OF LOCAL COMMUNITY*					
FAMILIAL COMPLEXITY	Fewer than 50 Persons (%)	50-99 (%)	100-199 (%)	200-399/ 400-1,000 But No Town of over 5,000 (%)	One or More Town of 5,000-50,000; One or More Cities of over 50,000 (%)
High	39.5	65.3	77.5	78.2	69.0
Low	60.5	34.7	22.5	21.8	31.0
No. of cases (N = 458)†	(86)	(72)	(80)	(133)	(87)

*To eliminate categories with very small frequencies, we have reduced Murdock's categories from eight to five. His categories are: (1) under 50; (2) 50-99; (3) 100-199; (4) 200-399; (5) 400-1,000; (6) 1,000 or more without any town of more than 5,000; (7) having one or more towns in range 5,000-50,000; (8) having one or more cities of 50,000 or more. Note that the first five categories are classified with respect to mean size of community; category 6 introduces the additional criterion of maximum size of city. Finally, in categories 7 and 8 there is no mention of average size of community but merely size of largest city. Thus, although these categories are relevant to our purpose, they are not unidimensional.

†C = .29, C̄ = .41, P< .001; G = .30, P < .001.

R. L. Blumberg and R. Winch, "Societal Complexity and Family Complexity: Evidence for the Curvilinear Hypothesis," Table 2, page 908, in American Journal of Sociology, 1972 (77) 898-920, published by The University of Chicago Press. © 1972 by The University of Chicago.

"High" means that some form of expanded family is commonest.

"Low" means that nuclear or conjugal family is commonest.

323

Table 12

Relationship Between Permanence of Settlement and Familial Complexity

FAMILIAL COMPLEXITY	PERMANENCE OF SETTLEMENT	
	Nomadic (%)	Nonnomadic (%)
High	53.5	75.1
Low	46.5	24.9
No. of cases (N = 909)†	(157)	(752)

*We need not have been so hasty in believing that permanence of settlement would fail to discriminate medium-and higher-complexity societies sufficiently to show the curvilinear relationship with familial complexity. For our categories of permanence (nomadic or seminomadic, semisedentary, neighborhoods or hamlets, and compact or complex permanent settlements), the percentages of high complexity are: 54%, 71%, 80%, and 73%. Although not spectacular, the distribution does show an inflected curve.

†C = .18, $\overline{C}$ = .25, $\overline{P}$ < .001; C = .45, P < .001.

R. L. Blumberg and R. R. Winch, "Societal Complexity and Family Complexity: Evidence for the Curvilinear Hypothesis," Table 3, page 908, in American Journal of Sociology, 1972 (77) 898-920, published by The University of Chicago Press. © 1972 by The University of Chicago.

"High" means that some form of expanded family is commonest.

"Low" means that nuclear or conjugal family is commonest.

Relationship Between Stratification and Familial Complexity

Table 13

FAMILIAL COMPLEXITY	STRATIFICATION			
	Absent among Freemen (%)	Wealth and Elite Distinctions (%)	Hereditary Aristocracy (%)	Social Classes (%)
High	66.4	71.4	79.1	66.7
Low	33.6	28.6	20.9	33.3
No. of cases (N = 851)*	(443)	(154)	(182)	(72)

* C = .11, C̄ = .16, P < .05. G = .14, P < .05.

R. L. Blumberg and R. Winch, "Societal Complexity and Family Complexity: Evidence for the Curvilinear Hypothesis," Table 4, page 909, in American Journal of Sociology, 1972 (77) 898-920, published by The University of Chicago Press. Ⓒ 1972 by The University of Chicago.

"High" means that some form of expanded family is commonest.

"Low" means that nuclear or conjugal family is commonest.

Relationship Between Political Complexity and Familial Complexity ———— **Table 14**

| | POLITICAL COMPLEXITY | | | |
| | (Levels of Jurisdictional Hierarchy beyond the Local Community) | | | |
FAMILIAL COMPLEXITY	No Levels (%)	One Level (%)	Two Levels (%)	Three or Four levels (%)
High	59.0	82.5	83.3	74.1
Low	41.0	17.5	16.7	25.9
No. of cases (N = 883)*	(398)	(274)	(126)	(85)

* C = .24, C̄ = .34, P < .001; G = .38, P < .001.

R. L. Blumberg and R. Winch, "Societal Complexity and Family Complexity: Evidence for the Curvilinear Hypothesis," Table 5, page 909, in American Journal of Sociology, 1972 (77) 898-920, published by The University of Chicago Press. ©️ 1972 by The University of Chicago Press.

"High" means that some form of expanded family is commonest.

"Low" means that nuclear or conjugal family is commonest.

Table 15

Percentage of Societies in Six World Regions* with Major Types of Subsistence Economy

	Region						
Economy	A	C	E	I	N	S	World
Gathering	1	0	4	7	24	14	8
Hunting	1	0	1	2	23	14	8
Fishing	3	1	8	10	31	11	12
Animal husbandry	5	23	13	0	0	1	5
Agriculture	90	76	74	81	22	66	66
Total	100	100	100	100	100	100	100
Number of Societies	238	96	94	127	219	89	863

*A = Africa (sub-Saharan); C = Circum-Mediterranean; E = East Eurasia; I = Insular Pacific; N = North America; S = South America and Central America.

R. L. and R. H. Munroe, "Perspectives Suggested by Anthropological Data," Table 7-1, page 257, in H. C. Triandis, ed., HANDBOOK OF CROSS-CULTURAL PSYCHOLOGY (1980), Volume I, PERSPECTIVES, H. C. Triandis and W. W. Lambert, eds. Reprinted by permission of the authors and Allyn and Bacon.

————————————————————————————Table 16
Percentage of Societies in Six World Regions* with Major Types of Marriage

Marriage Type	Region						
	A	C	E	I	N	S	World
Monogamy	1	38	22	24	14	20	16
Limited Polygyny	14	26	62	52	49	55	39
General Polygyny	85	36	13	23	37	25	45
Polyandry	0	0	3	1	0	0	0
Total	100	100	100	100	100	100	100
Number of Societies	238	95	93	124	216	88	854

*A = Africa (Sub-Saharan); C = Circum-Mediterranean; E = East Eurasia; I = Insular Pacific; N = North America; S = South America and Central America.

R. L. and R. H. Munroe, "Perspectives Suggested by Anthropological Data," Table 7-2, page 257, in H. C. Triandis, ed., HANDBOOK OF CROSS-CULTURAL PSYCHOLOGY (1980), Volume I, PERSPECTIVES, H. C. Triandis and W. W. Lambert, eds. Reprinted by permission of the authors and Allyn and Bacon.

Table 17

Percentage of Societies in Six World Regions* with Major Types of Postmarital Residence Patterns[a]

Residence Pattern[a]	Region						
	A	C	E	I	N	S	World
Avunculocal[b]	10	2	0	3	3	2	4
Ambilocal[c]	1	4	3	12	14	10	7
Matrilocal & Uxorilocal[d]	2	0	12	14	21	38	13
Neolocal[e]	2	13	2	2	5	9	5
Natolocal[f]	0	1	1	4	0	0	1
Patrilocal & Virilocal[g]	82	80	82	63	57	41	69
Other	3	0	0	2	0	0	1
Total	100	100	100	100	100	100	100
Number of Societies	237	96	94	126	218	88	859

[a] prevailing profile of marital residence--initial periods and minor patterns not counted.

[b] with or near the maternal uncle or other male matrilineal kinsmen of husband.

[c] optional with or near the parents of either husband or wife.

[d] with or near the female matrilineal kinsmen of the wife both when these kinsmen live as aggregated units and when these kinsmen are not so aggregated.

[e] apart from the relatives of both spouses.

[f] both spouses remain in natal households, with no common household established by married couple.

[g] with or near the male patrilineal kinsmen of the husband both when these kinsmen live as aggregated units and when these kinsmen are not so aggregated.

*A = Africa (sub-Saharan); C = Circum-Mediterranean; E = East Eurasia; I = Insular Pacific, N = North America; S = South America and Central America.

R. H. and R. L. Munroe, "Perspectives Suggested by Anthropological Data," Table 7-3, page 258, in H. C. Triandis, ed., HANDBOOK OF CROSS-CULTURAL PSYCHOLOGY (1980), Volume I, PERSPECTIVES, H. C. Triandis and W. W. Lambert, eds. Reprinted by permission of the authors and Allyn and Bacon.

Percentage of Societies in Six World Regions* with Social Stratification

————————————————————————————— Table 18

				Region			
Social Stratification	A	C	E	I	N	S	World
Present[a]	38	65	49	34	14	12	32
By Wealth[b]	14	16	31	21	26	10	20
Absent[c]	48	19	20	45	60	78	48
Total	100	100	100	100	100	100	100
Number of Societies	216	88	89	127	211	87	818

[a] complex occupational, dual, or elite stratification present.

[b] distinction based on present possession of property but not crystallized into distinct and hereditary social classes.

[c] absence of significant class distinctions, although stratification by individual skill, valor, piety, or wisdom may be present.

*A = Africa (sub-Saharan); C = Circum-Mediterranean; E = East Eurasia; I = Insular Pacific; N = North America; S = South America and Central America.

R. H. and R. L. Munroe, "Perspectives Suggested by Anthropological Data," Table 7-4, page 258, in H. C. Triandis, ed., HANDBOOK OF CROSS-CULTURAL PSYCHOLOGY (1980), Volume I, PERSPECTIVES, H. C. Triandis and W. W. Lambert, eds. Reprinted by permission of the authors and Allyn and Bacon.

——Table 19
Diverging Devolution by Continent

	Eurasia and Circum-Mediterranean	Africa	America	Pacific	Total
Diverging devolution:					
Present	84	12	32	32	160
Absent	75	178	58	44	355
No individual property rights or no rule of transmission	2	3	70	2	77
	161	193	160	78	592
		Total of table			592
		No information (N.I.) on devolution			271
					863

Jack Goody, ed., PRODUCTION AND REPRODUCTION, Table 1, page 12. Copyrighted
1976 by Cambridge University Press. Reproduced by permission of Cambridge
University Press.

Of the 271 societies on which no information was available
        29 were in Eurasia and Circum-Mediterranean
        45 were in Africa
       148 were in the two Americas
        49 were in the Pacific Islands.

Table 20

The Relationship of Preferential Marriage to Descent

Rules Governing Cousin Marriage	Matri-lineal Descent	Double Descent	Patri-lineal Descent	Bilateral Descent	Totals
Preferential marriage with a parallel cousin	0	0	12	0	12
Cross-cousin marriage with patrilateral preference	8	5	2	1	16
Cross-cousin marriage with matrilateral preference	7	5	34	3	49
Symmetrical cross-cousin marriage	21	4	45	18	88
Marriage permitted with any first cousin	2	0	13	30	45
Marriage not approved with any first cousin	33	14	109	121	277
No data available on cousin marriage	13	1	32	31	77
Totals	84	29	247	204	564

George P. Murdock, "World Ethnographic Sample," Table 3, page 687. Reproduced by permission of the American Anthropological Association from American Anthropologist, 59:4 (1957) 664-687. Not for further reproduction.

Totals for societies on which information was available: matrilineal descent 71, double descent 28, patrilineal descent 215, bilateral descent 173, total 487.

Murdock considers patrilateral parallel-cousin marriage, but not matrilateral parallel-cousin marriage.

_____Table 21

Marriage Transactions and Continent

	Bride-wealth	Bride-service	Dowry	Gift exchange	Sister exchange	Transactions absent or token
Circum-Med.	65 (68%)	1 (1%)	13 (14%)	3 (3%)	0	14 (15%)
East Eurasia	53 (56%)	5 (5%)	8 (9%)	2 (2%)	0	26 (28%)
Africa	195 (82%)	19 (8%)	0	1	10 (4%)	13 (5%)
Insular Pacific	47 (38%)	6 (4%)	2 (1%)	20 (16%)	15 (12%)	37 (29%)
North America	40 (18%)	28 (13%)	0	28 (13%)	0	122 (56%)
South America	7 (8%)	36 (42%)	0	1 (1%)	2 (2%)	41 (48%)
Total	407	95	23	55	27	253

N.B. Codes: horizontal, col. 1 = Continent
            vertical, col. 12 = Mode of marriage

The table is derived from the Ethnographic Atlas (1967).

Table 22

The Continental Distribution of Prohibited and Permitted Marriage to Cousins (Percentages)

	Cousin marriage prohibited	Permitted marriage to		
		FZD	FBD	MBD
Africa	65.2(134)	27	3.6	25
Eurasia	37.5 (60)	52.5	17.5	50.5
Pacific	70.5 (8?)	22.7	6.5	20.3
N. America	82.7(167)	13.4	2.4	13.9
S. America	37 (27)	55	11	56.4
All	62.5(475)			

n = 673. The table is derived from the Ethnographic Atlas (1967).

Jack Goody and S. J. Tambiah, eds., BRIDEWEALTH AND DOWRY IN AFRICA AND EURASIA, Table 4, page 32. Copyrighted 1973 by Cambridge University Press. Reproduced by permission of Cambridge University Press.

"FZD" means father's sister's daughter.
"FBD" means father's brother's daughter.
"MBD" means mother's brother's daughter.

No mention is made of marriage to mother's sister's daughter.

Relatively few societies which allow one type of cross-cousin marriage will then absolutely prohibit the other type.

Table 23

Marriage Transactions and Kin Groups

	Bride-wealth	Bride-service	Dowry	Gift-exchange	Sister-exchange	Transactions absent or token
Patrilineal	288 (72%)	25 (6%)	8 (2%)	12 (3%)	19 (5%)	49 (12%)
Matrilineal	44 (37%)	17 (14%)	1 (1%)	6 (5%)	2 (2%)	50 (42%)
Double	14 (52%)	1 (4%)	1 (4%)	5 (19%)	4 (15%)	2 (7%)
Bilateral	60 (19%)	52 (17%)	13 (4%)	32 (10%)	2 (1%)	150 (49%)
Total	406	95	23	55	27	251

N.B. Codes: horizontal: derived from cols. 20, 22 = Descent
vertical: col. 12 = Mode of marriage

Jack Goody and S. J. Tambiah, eds., BRIDEWEALTH AND DOWRY IN AFRICA AND EURASIA,
Table 5, page 50. Copyrighted 1973 by Cambridge University Press. Reproduced
by permission of Cambridge University Press.

The table is derived from the Ethnographic Atlas (1967).

Table 24

Marriage Transactions, Kin Groups and Continent

Marriage Transactions

		Bride-wealth	Bride-service	Dowry	Gift-exchange	Sister-exchange	Token or absent	Total
Africa	Patrilineal	154	10	0	1	8	3	176
	Matrilineal	22	8	0	0	0	7	37
	Double	12	0	0	0	0	0	12
	Bilateral	7	1	0	0	2	3	13
Eurasia	Patrilineal	99	3	7	2	0	14	125
	Matrilineal	7	0	1	1	0	6	15
	Double	2	0	0	0	0	1	3
	Bilateral	10	3	13	2	0	19	47
Insular Pacific	Patrilineal	25	0	1	6	9	2	43
	Matrilineal	10	1	0	3	2	12	28
	Double	0	1	1	5	4	1	12
	Bilateral	12	4	0	6	0	21	43
North* America	Patrilineal	9	6	0	3	0	24	42
	Matrilineal	3	4	0	2	0	24	33
	Bilateral	28	18	0	23	0	74	143
South* America	Patrilineal	1	6	0	0	2	6	15
	Matrilineal	2	4	0	0	0	1	7
	Bilateral	3	26	0	1	0	33	63

*Double descent systems are not recorded for the Americas

Jack Goody and S. J. Tambiah, eds., BRIDEWEALTH AND DOWRY IN AFRICA AND EURASIA, Table 6, page 50. Copyrighted 1973 by Cambridge University Press. Reproduced by permission of Cambridge University Press.

Subtotals and totals in Table 24 are:

	Bride-wealth	Bride-service	Dowry	Gift-exchange	Sister-exchange	Token or absent	Total
Africa	195	19	0	1	10	13	238
Eurasia	118	6	21	5	0	40	190
Insular Pacific	47	6	2	20	15	36	126
North America	40	28	0	28	0	122	218
South America	6	36	0	1	2	40	85
Total	406	95	23	55	27	251	857

Table 25

Marriage Rates per 1,000 Population: Selected Countries, 1965 to 1974

Country	1974	1973	1972	1971	1970	1965
Australia[a]	8.3[b]	8.6	8.8	9.2	9.3	8.3
Austria	6.5	6.6	7.7	6.5	7.1	7.8
Canada		9.0	9.2	8.9	8.8	7.4
Chile[a]				8.6	7.3	7.6
Denmark		6.1	6.2	6.6	7.4	8.8
Egypt		9.4	10.4	10.2	9.8	9.8
Finland	7.5	7.5	7.7	8.2	8.8	7.9
France	7.6	7.7	8.1	7.9	7.8	7.1
Germany (Fed. Rep.)	6.1	6.4	6.7	7.1	7.3	8.3
Ireland[a]	7.3	7.5	7.3	7.3	7.1	5.9
Israel	9.5	9.1	9.5	9.4	9.1	7.9
Italy	7.3	7.6	7.7	7.5	7.4	7.7
Japan[a]	9.2[b]	10.0	10.4	10.5	10.1	9.7
Mexico[a]		8.3	8.1	7.5	7.3	6.9
Netherlands	8.1	8.0	8.8	9.3	9.5	8.8
Norway	6.8	7.0	7.3	7.6	7.6	6.5
Spain	7.6	7.7	7.6	7.5	7.4	7.2
Sweden	5.5	4.7	4.9	4.9	5.4	7.8
Switzerland	6.0	6.2	7.0	7.1	7.5	7.6
United Kingdom[a] (England and Wales)			8.6	8.3	8.5	7.8
United States[c]	10.5[b]	10.9	11.0	10.6	10.6	9.3
U.S.S.R.		10.1	9.4	10.0	9.7	8.7

Source: United Nations, Demographic Yearbook, 1973, table 19; and 1969, table 47. Also, unpublished data from the United Nations.

[a] Data by year of registration rather than year of occurrence.

[b] Provisional.

[c] Official publications of the U.S. National Center for Health Statistics.

Note: Rates are number of legal (recognized) marriages performed and registered per 1,000 population, excluding unions established by mutual consent or by tribal or native customs. For population and territorial inclusions and exclusions, see source.

Hugh Carter and Paul Glick, MARRIAGE AND DIVORCE: A SOCIAL AND ECONOMIC STUDY, revised edition, Table 13-2, page 387. Published by Harvard University Press, 1976. Reprinted by permission.

Table 26

Crude Divorce Rates: Selected Countries, 1932 to 1965

Country	Year[a]											
	1965	1964	1963	1962	1961	1960	1955	1950	1945	1940	1935	1932
Australia[b]	0.8	0.7	0.7	0.7	0.6	0.7	0.7	0.9	1.0	0.5	0.4	0.3
Austria[b]	1.2	1.2	1.1	1.1	1.1	1.1	1.3	1.5	0.7	0.9	0.1	0.1
Canada[b]	0.5	0.5	0.4	0.4	0.4	0.4	0.4	0.4	0.4	0.2	0.1	0.1
Finland[b]	1.0	1.0	0.9	0.9	0.9	0.8	0.9	0.9	1.5	0.4	0.4	0.3
France[b]	0.7	0.7	0.6	0.7	0.7	0.7	0.7	0.9	0.6	0.3	0.5	0.5
Germany (Fed. Rep.)[b]	0.9	1.0	0.9	0.8	0.8	0.8	0.9	1.6	---	---	---	---
Japan[b,c]	0.8	0.8	0.7	0.8	0.7	0.7	0.9	1.0	---	0.7	0.7	0.8
Netherlands[b]	0.5	0.5	0.5	0.5	0.5	0.5	0.5	0.6	0.5	0.3	0.4	0.4
Norway	0.7	0.7	0.7	0.7	0.7	0.7	0.6	0.7	0.6	0.3	0.3	0.3
Sweden	1.2	1.2	1.1	0.8	0.9	0.9	1.2	1.1	1.0	0.6	0.4	0.4
United Kingdom[b] (England and Wales)	0.8	0.7	0.7	0.6	0.5	0.5	0.6	0.7	0.4	0.2	0.1	0.1
United States[d,e]	2.5	2.3	2.3	2.2	2.3	2.2	2.3	2.6	3.5	2.0	1.7	1.3

Source: United Nations, Demographic Yearbook, Vols. 10, 14, 15, 16, and 19.

[a]Rates are the number of final divorce decrees granted under civil law, per 1,000 population.
Annulments and legal separations are excluded, unless otherwise specified.

[b]For population and territorial inclusions and exclusions, see source.

[c]Tabulated by year of registration rather than occurrence.

[d]Data include annulments.

[e]Official publications of National Center for Health Statistics.

Hugh Carter and Paul Glick, MARRIAGE AND DIVORCE: A SOCIAL AND ECONOMIC STUDY, Table 2-4, page 29.
Published by Harvard University Press, 1970. Reprinted by permission.

Table 27

Divorce Rates per 1,000 Population: Selected Countries, 1965 to 1973

Country	1973	1972	1971	1970	1965
Australia	1.2	1.2	1.0	1.0	0.8
Austria	1.3	1.3	1.3	1.4	1.2
Canada	1.7		1.4	1.4	0.5
Denmark	2.5	2.6	2.7	1.9	1.4
Egypt[a]	2.1	2.2	2.1	2.1	2.2
Finland	1.8	1.8	1.6	1.3	1.0
France		0.9	0.9	0.8	0.7
Germany (Fed. Rep.)		1.4	1.3	1.2	0.9
Israel	0.8	0.9	0.8	0.8	0.9
Japan[a]	1.0	1.0	1.0	0.9	0.8
Netherlands	1.3	1.1	0.9	0.8	0.5
Norway	1.2	1.0	1.0	0.9	0.7
Sweden	2.0	1.9	1.7	1.6	1.2
Switzerland	1.3	1.2	1.1	1.0	0.8
United Kingdom (England and Wales)	2.1	2.4	1.5	1.2	0.8
United States[b]	4.4	4.0	3.7	3.5	2.5
U.S.S.R.	2.7	2.6	2.6	2.6	1.6

Source: United Nations, Demographic Yearbook, 1973, table 21; and 1969, table 49.

[a]Data by year of registration rather than year of occurrence.

[b]Official publications of the U.S. National Center for Health Statistics. Data include annulmants.

Note: Rates are number of final decrees granted under civil law per 1,000 population. Annulments and legal separations are excluded unless otherwise specified.

Hugh Carter and Paul Glick, MARRIAGE AND DIVORCE: A SOCIAL AND ECONOMIC STUDY, revised edition, Table 13-5, page 391. Published by Harvard University Press, 1976. Reprinted by permission.

———————————————————————————————Table 28

Children in Divorce Cases: Selected Countries, 1948 to 1963

Country and year	Average number of children[a,b]		Percent of divorces with children
	Per 100 divorces	Per 100 divorces with children	
Australia[c]			
1963	118.7	194.6	61.0
1948	117.1	191.8	61.1
Austria[c]			
1957	94.1	163.0	57.7
1951	89.9	161.5	55.6
Finland			
1957	133.6	198.7	67.2
1950	112.0	176.3	63.5
France[e]			
1951	59.8	120.2	49.7
Germany, Fed. Rep. of[c,e]			
1957	92.7	160.1	57.9
1950	100.0	171.1	58.4
Japan[c,d]			
1962	99.7	171.2	58.3
1951	99.6	169.5	58.8
Netherlands[c]			
1957	122.5	200.2	61.2
1950	118.0	195.5	60.3
Norway[c]			
1957	89.1	156.5	56.9
1950	124.5	180.9	68.8
Sweden			
1950	116.8	173.6	67.3
United Kingdom[c,e] (England and Wales)			
1962	139.2	201.6	69.1
1951	121.5	185.2	65.6
United States[f]			
1962	130.0	214.0	60.2
1953	84.9	186.6	45.5

Table 28—Continued

Source: <u>United Nations Demographic Yearbook</u>, Vol. 10; <u>Vital Statistics of the United States</u>, 1953, Vol. 1; unpublished data in the Division of Vital Statistics from reporting States and for 1960 from a sample of vital records from all of the United States. Unpublished data from the United Nations Statistical Office; Commonwealth Bureau of Census and Statistics, Social Statistics, Australia, No. 23, Divorce.

[a]Definition of "children" varies as listed: Australia--varied from State to State; since 1961 uniform for the entire country (all living children under 21); <u>Austria</u>--total number of children (living and deceased) born of the marriage, irrespective of dependency status; <u>Finland, France, Norway, United Kingdom</u> (1951)--all surviving children of dissolved marriage irrespective of age or dependency status; <u>United Kingdom</u> (1962)--those alive at the date of petition, irrespective of age, including children legitimized by the marriage and adopted children; <u>Japan</u>--children of dissolved marriage under 20 years of age; <u>Federal Republic of Germany, Netherlands, Sweden</u> (1950)--those under 21 years of age irrespective of dependency status; <u>United States</u>--all under 18, including adopted and those from previous marriages (most of the 50 States). Some States use varying definitions: Alabama and Virginia--number of minor children affected; Alaska--number of children under 21 affected; Hawaii--number of minor children; Idaho and Nebraska--number of children affected by decree; Kansas--number of children; Tennessee--number of children under 18 of this marriage.

[b]Rates were computed from divorces with known number of children except for France and United States, where nonreports were comparatively numerous and were distributed in proportion to those reporting.

[c]For territorial and population inclusions and exclusions, and for inclusions of annulments, see <u>United Nations Demographic Yearbook</u>, Vol. 10.

[d]Data by year of registration rather than occurrence.

[e]Total number of children estimated; method used by United Nations for France, Federal Republic of Germany, United Kingdom (1951), and Japan (1962), unlike that of the United States for its calculations, results in a figure slightly lower.

[f]For 1960, based on sample of vital records from each State. For other years, children per 100 divorces based on estimate for entire country; children per 100 divorces with children and percent of divorces with children based on data from reporting States (22 in 1953 and 21 in 1962).

Hugh Carter and Paul Glick, MARRIAGE AND DIVORCE: A SOCIAL AND ECONOMIC STUDY Table 2-8, page 36. Published by Harvard University Press, 1970. Reprinted by permission.

_____Table 29
Divorce Rate per 1,000 Married Couples: Selected Countries, 1935 to 1964

Country and year	Rate	Country and year	Rate	Country and year	Rate
Australia		Germany		Sweden[a]	
1963[a]	3.1	(Fed. Rep. of)		1962[a]	5.0
1960-62[a]	2.8	1963[a]	3.5	1959-61[a]	4.9
1953-55	3.3	1960-62[a]	3.4	1949-51	4.9
1946-48	4.4	1949-51	6.4	1944-46	4.2
Austria		1946-47	6.3	1939-41	2.7
1950-52	6.7	Japan		1934-36	2.3
1938-40	3.8	1962[a]	3.7	United Kingdom	
Canada[a,b]		1959-61[a]	3.7	(England and	
1963[a]	1.9	1954-56	4.4	Wales)[c]	
1960-62[a]	1.7	1949-51	5.3	1960-62[c]	2.1
1955-57	1.7	Netherlands		1950-52	2.8
1950-52	1.7	1962[a]	2.2	1944-46	1.8
1940-42	1.1	1959-61[a]	2.2	1939-41	0.7
Finland		1951-53	2.6	United States	
1962[a]	4.4	1946-48	4.5	1964	10.7
1959-61[a]	4.1	Norway		1963	10.3
1955[a]	4.2	1962[a]	2.9	1962	9.4
1949-51	4.6	1959-61[a]	2.8	1960	9.2
1939-41	2.2	1949-51	3.2	1955	9.3
France		1945-47	3.2	1950	10.3
1961-63[a]	2.9			1945	14.4
1953-55	2.9			1940	8.8
1945-47	4.9			1935	7.8
1935-37	2.3				

Source: United Nations, Demographic Yearbook, Vols. 6, 10, 14, 15, and 16. For population and territorial exclusions and inclusions refer to these volumes. Unpublished data from the United Nations Statistical Office; unpublished data from the Division of Vital Statistics and the Bureau of the Census; Vital Statistics of the United States, Vol. 1, 1959, and Vol. 3, 1962; Yearbook of the Commonwealth of Australia, No. 49 (1963); Statistical Review of England and Wales for the year 1961, Part II.

[a]Rates computed from latest data available in the sources listed. When population figures were not available for the data year, populations for the nearest year were used.

[b]Provisional.

[c]Rate based on estimated 1961 population rounded to the nearest thousand.

Hugh Carter and Paul Glick, MARRIAGE AND DIVORCE: A SOCIAL AND ECONOMIC STUDY, Table 2-5, page 31. Published by Harvard University Press, 1970. Reprinted by permission.

Table 30

Proportions Ever Married at Age 50 (Percentages)

Birth cohorts	Canada		United States		Australia		New Zealand	
	males	females	males	females	males	females	males	females
1826-1830	90.5				72		72	
1831-1835	90.5	89.5			74	96	73.5	96
1836-1840	90.5	89.5			75.5	96	75	95.5
1841-1845	90	89.5	90.5		77	94	76	94.5
1846-1850	89	89	89.5	92.5	77.5	92.5	77.5	93.5
1851-1855	88	88.5	88.5	92	77	91	78.5	92
1856-1860	87	88	88	91.5	77	89	79.5	90
1861-1865	85.5	88.5	88	91	78.5	87	81	88
1866-1870	86.5	88.5	88	91	80	85	82	86
1871-1875	86.5	89	88	90.5	81	84	83	85
1876-1880	86.5	89	88	91	83	84.5	85	85.5
1881-1885	86.5	90	88	91	85	85.5	86	86
1886-1890	86.5	89.5	88	91	85.5	86.5	86	86.5
1891-1895	86	89	88	91	85	86.5	87	87
1896-1900	87	89	88.5	91	86	87	88.5	88
1901-1905	87	89	89	91	88	89	90	89
1906-1910	88.5	89.5	90.5	92	89	90.5	91	90
1911-1915	89.5	90.5	93	94	90.5	92.5	91	92
1916-1920	90	92	93	95	91.5	94	91	94.5
1921-1925	90	93	93	96	92	94	91	95.5
1926-1930	90.5	94	93.5	97	92	95	92	96
1931-1935	91	95	94	98	93	97	94	96
1936-1940	92	95	94	98	94	96	95	95
1941-1945		93.5		96		95		94

Patrick Festy, "Canada, United States, Australia, and New Zealand: Nuptiality Trends," Table A, page 491, in POPULATION STUDIES, Volume 27/3 (1973) 479-492. Reprinted by permission.

Mean Age at First Marriage (in Years, to One Decimal Place)

Table 31

Birth cohorts	Canada		United States		Australia		New Zealand	
	males	females	males	females	males	females	males	females
1881-1885	28.1		27.5		28.6		29.5	
1886-1890	27.5	23.9	27.3	23.6	28.2	25.3	28.5	25.5
1891-1895	27.0	23.8	27.2	23.3	28.0	25.2	28.2	25.3
1896-1900	27.6	24.0	26.9	23.1	28.2	25.3	28.0	25.2
1901-1905	28.1	24.6	27.0	23.2	28.3	25.3	28.0	25.4
1906-1910	27.8	24.9	26.7	23.2	28.3	25.3	28.0	25.5
1911-1915	27.4	24.7	26.0	23.2	27.6	25.0	27.5	25.2
1916-1920	26.5	24.1	25.4	22.7	26.8	24.1	26.8	24.6
1921-1925	25.9	23.3	24.8	22.1	26.0	23.4	26.3	24.1
1926-1930	25.5	23.0	24.5	21.6	25.9	22.9	26.0	23.1
1931-1935	25.1	22.6	24.0	21.4	25.8	22.4	25.6	22.6
1936-1940	24.8	22.3	23.7	21.3	25.6	22.0	25.3	22.3
1941-1943		22.5		21.6		21.9		22.2

Patrick Festy, "Canada, United States, Australia, and New Zealand: Nuptiality Trends," Table B, page 491, in POPULATION STUDIES, Volume 27/3 (1973) 479-492. Reprinted by permission.

Bibliography

FURTHER REFERENCES

Journal of Family History.
Journal of Marriage and Family.
Soliday, Gerald L., and others, eds. *History of the Family and Kinship: A Select International Bibliography.* New York: Kraus Publications, 1980.
United Nations Demographic Yearbook.

BIOLOGY OF SOCIAL FORMS

Amundsen, D. W., and C. J. Diers. Four articles in *Human Biology* on menarche and menopause in ancient Greek and Roman times and in medieval times:
"Menarche: Greek and Roman," 41 (1969), pp. 125–32.
"Menopause: Greek and Roman," 42 (1970), pp. 79–86.
"Menarche: Medieval," 45 (1973), pp. 363–69.
"Menopause: Medieval," 45 (1973), pp. 605–12.
Van Den Berghe, P. L. *Man in Society: A Biosocial View.* New York: Elsevier, 1975.
Bischof, N. "The Biological Foundations of the Incest Taboo," *Social Science Information*, 11 (1972), pp. 7–36.
Daw, S. F. "Puberty in Leipzig, 1727–1749," *Human Biology*, 42 (1970), pp. 87–89.
Forster, Robert, and Orest Ranum, eds. *Biology of Man in History.* Baltimore, Md.: Johns Hopkins University Press, 1975.
Lancaster, Jane B., and others, eds. *Parenting Across the Life Span: Biosocial Dimensions.* New York: A. de Gruyter, 1987.
Mackey, Wade C. "The Adult Male-Child Bond: An Example of Convergent Evolution," *Journal of Anthropological Research*, 32 (1976), pp. 58–73.
Money, John, and Anke Ehrhardt. *Man and Woman, Boy and Girl.* Baltimore, Md.: Johns Hopkins University Press, 1972.
Stukovsky, R. "Family Size and Menarcheal Age in Constanza, Roumania," *Human Biology*, 39 (1967), pp. 277–83.

DEMOGRAPHICS

Barnes, J. A. "Agnatic Taxonomies and Stochastic Variation," *Anthropological Forum*, 3 (1971), pp. 3–12.

Van Den Berghe, P. L. *Age and Sex in Human Societies*. Belmont, Calif.: Wadsworth, 1973.

Churcher, C. S., and W. A. Kenyon. "The Tabor Hill Ossuaries: A Study in Iroquois Demography," *Human Biology*, 22 (1960), pp. 249–73.

Cohen, Joel. "Mortality and Birth Order in Preindustrial Europe," *Demography*, 12 (1975), pp. 35–55.

Dupaquier, J., and others. *Marriage and Remarriage in Populations of the Past*. New York: Academic Press, 1981.

Dyke, Bennett, and W. T. Morrill, eds. *Genealogical Demography*. New York: Academic Press, 1980.

Gaskin, Katherine. "Age at First Marriage in Europe Before 1850: A Summary of Family Reconstitution Data," *Journal of Family History*, 3 (1978), pp. 23–36.

Glass, David, and D.E.C. Eversley, eds. *Population in History*. Chicago: Aldine Publishing, 1965.

Glass, David, and Roger Revelle, eds. *Population and Social Change*. London: Edward Arnold Ltd., 1972.

Goubert, Pierre. "Legitimate Fecundity and Infant Mortality in France During the Eighteenth Century: A Comparison," *Daedalus*, 97 (1968), pp. 593–603.

Halsband, Robert. "New Light on Lady Mary Wortley Montagu's Contribution to Inoculation," *Journal of the History of Medicine*, 8 (1953), pp. 390–405.

Hollingsworth, Thomas H. *Historical Demography*. Ithaca, N.Y.: Cornell University Press, 1969.

Laslett, Peter, ed. *The World We Have Lost*. Cambridge, England: Cambridge University Press, 1965.

Malkin, H. J. "Observations on Social Conditions, Fertility, and Family Survival in the Past," *Proceedings of the Royal Society of Medicine*, 53 (1960), pp. 117–22.

Marcy, Peter. "Factors Affecting the Fecundity and Fertility of Historical Populations: A Review," *Journal of Family History*, 6 (1981), pp. 1309–26.

McEvedy, Colin, and Richard Jones. *Atlas of World Population History*. Harmondsworth, England: Penguin, 1978.

McNeill, William H. *Plagues and Peoples*. Garden City, N.Y.: Doubleday/Anchor, 1976.

Needham, Joseph, and Lu Gwei-djou. "Hygiene and Preventive Medicine in Ancient China," *Journal of the History of Medicine*, 17 (1962), pp. 429–78.

Rotberg, Robert, and Theodore K. Rabb, eds. *Marriage and Fertility*. Princeton, N.J.: Princeton University Press, 1980.

Russell, Josiah Cox. *Late Ancient and Medieval Populations*. Philadelphia: American Philosophical Society, 1958.

Spengler, Joseph J., and O. D. Duncan, eds. *Demographic Analysis: Selected Readings*. Glencoe, Ill.: Free Press, 1956.

Thomlinson, Ralph. *Population Dynamics*. New York: Random House, 1965.

Thompson, Roger. "Seventeenth-century English and Colonial Sex Ratios: A Postscript," *Population Studies*, 28 (1974), pp. 153–65.

Tilly, Charles A., ed. *Historical Studies of Changing Fertility.* Princeton, N.J.: Princeton University Press, 1978.

Westoff, Charles F., and Robert Park, Jr., eds. *Demographic and Social Aspects of Population Growth.* Washington, D.C.: Government Printing Office, 1972.

GENERAL STRUCTURE AND THEORY

Birren, James E., and others. *Developmental Psychology: A Life-Span Approach.* Boston: Houghton Mifflin, 1981.

Blumberg, R. L., and R. Winch. "Societal Complexity and Familial Complexity: Evidence for the Curvilinear Hypothesis," *American Journal of Sociology,* 77 (1972), pp. 898–920.

Buchler, Ira R., and Henry A. Selby. *Kinship and Social Organization.* New York: Macmillan, 1968.

Chapman, Richard A. "Hobbes on the Family," *American Political Science Review,* 69 (1975), pp. 76–90.

Eisenstadt, S. N. "Ritualized Personal Relationships: Some Comparative Hypotheses and Suggestions," *Man,* 56 (1956), pp. 90–95.

Engels, Friedrich. *Origin of the Family.* New York: International Publishers, 1972 reprint.

Erikson, Erik. *Childhood and Society.* New York: W. W. Norton, 1950.

Erikson, Erik. *Life History and the Historical Moment.* New York: W. W. Norton, 1975.

Farber, Bernard. *Conceptions of Kinship.* New York: Elsevier, 1981.

Farber, Bernard. *Family and Kinship in Modern Society.* Glenview, Ill.: Scott, Foresman, 1973.

Foa, U. G., and others. "Cross-cultural Invariance in the Differentiation and Organization of Family Roles," *Journal of Personality and Social Psychology,* 4 (1966), pp. 316–27.

Fox, Robin. *Kinship and Marriage.* Harmondsworth, England: Penguin, 1967.

Freud, Sigmund, trans. by James Strachey. *Totem and Taboo.* London: Routledge and Kegan Paul, 1950.

Fromm, Erich. *The Sane Society.* New York: Rinehart, 1955.

Ginsburg, Herbert, and Sylvia Opper. *Piaget's Theory of Intellectual Development,* 2d ed. Englewood Cliffs, N.J.: Prentice-Hall, 1979.

Goldschmidt, Walter, and E. J. Kunkel. "The Structure of the Peasant Family," *American Anthropologist,* 73 (1971), pp. 1058–76.

Goode, William J. *Social Systems and Family Patterns, A Propositional Inventory.* Indianapolis: Bobbs-Merrill, 1971.

Goode, William J. *World Revolution and Family Patterns.* New York: Free Press, 1971.

Goody, Jack, ed. *Production and Reproduction.* Cambridge, England: Cambridge University Press, 1976.

Goody, Jack, and S. J. Tambiah, eds. *Bridewealth and Dowry in Africa and Eurasia.* Cambridge, England: Cambridge University Press, 1973.

Homans, G. C., and David Schneider. *Marriage, Authority, and Final Causes: A Study of Unilateral Cross-Cousin Marriage.* New York: Free Press, 1955.

Hsu, Francis L. K. *Clan, Caste, and Club.* New York: Van Nostrand, 1963.

Hutter, Mark. *The Changing Family: Comparative Perspectives.* New York: John Wiley and Sons, 1981.

Keesing, Roger M. *Kin Groups and Social Structure.* New York: Holt, Rinehart, and Winston, 1975.

Kephart, William M. *The Family, Society, and the Individual.* Boston: Houghton Mifflin, 1961. Included as a representative example of a standard text that assumed the woman's lack of physiological basis for interest in sexual activity (p. 453).

Kohlberg, Lawrence, and R. Kramer. "Continuities and Discontinuities in Childhood and Adult Moral Development," *Human Development,* 12 (1969), pp. 93–120.

Korn, Francis. *Elementary Structures Reconsidered: Levi-Strauss on Kinship.* Berkeley: University of California Press, 1973.

Laing, Ronald D. *The Politics of the Family and Other Essays.* New York: Pantheon, 1971.

Lasch, Christopher. *Haven in a Heartless World: The Family Besieged.* New York: Basic Books, 1977.

Lomax, A., and N. Berkowitz. "The Evolutionary Taxonomy of Culture," *Science,* 177 (1972), pp. 228–39.

Longabaugh, Richard. "The Structure of Interpersonal Behavior," *Sociometry,* 29 (1966), pp. 441–60.

Malinowski, Bronislaw. *Sex and Repression in Savage Society.* New York: Meridian Books, 1927.

Malinowski, Bronislaw. *The Father in Primitive Psychology.* New York: W. W. Norton, 1927.

Murdock, George P. *Ethnographic Atlas.* Pittsburgh, Pa.: University of Pittsburgh Press, 1967.

Murdock, George P. *Social Structure.* New York: Macmillan, 1965.

Murdock, George P. "World Ethnographic Sample," *American Anthropologist,* 59 (1957), pp. 664–87.

Murdock, George P., and Caterina Provost. "Factors in the Division of Labor by Sex," *Ethnology,* 12 (1973), pp. 203–25.

Murdock, George P., and Caterina Provost. "Measurement of Cultural Complexity," *Ethnology,* 12 (1973), pp. 379–92.

Parsons, Talcott, and Robert Bales. *Family, Socialization, and Interaction Process.* New York: Free Press, 1960.

Pasternak, Burton, and others. "On the Conditions Favoring Extended Family Households," *Journal of Anthropological Research,* 32 (1976), pp. 109–123.

Peterson, G. B. "Family Development and Moral Stage Framework," *Journal of Marriage and Family,* 41 (1979, May), pp. 229–35.

Piaget, Jean. "Intellectual Evolution from Adolescence to Adulthood," *Human Development,* 15 (1972), pp. 1–12.

Piaget, Jean. *Psychology of Intelligence.* London: Routledge and Kegan Paul, 1966.

Piaget, Jean, and Bärbel Inhelder. *Memory and Intelligence.* New York: Basic Books, 1973.

Poster, Mark. *Critical Theory of the Family.* New York: Seabury Press, 1978.

Radcliffe-Brown, A. R. *Structure and Function in Primitive Society, and Other Essays.* New York: Free Press, 1965.

Rivers, William H. R. *Kinship and Social Organization*. London: Athlone Press, 1914.

Sharma, Satya P. "Structural and Functional Characteristics of Lineages in Societies with Unilineal Descent Groups and Centralized Government: A Comparative Exploration," *Journal of Asian and African Studies*, 6 (1971), pp. 226–32.

Smith, Richard M., ed. *Land, Kinship, and Life-Cycle*. Cambridge, England: Cambridge University Press, 1984.

Uzoka, A. F. "The Myth of the Nuclear Family," *American Psychologist*, 34 (1979), pp. 1095–1106.

Zaretsky, Eli. *Capitalism, the Family, and Personal Life*. New York: Harper, 1976.

Zimmerman, Carle. *Family and Civilization*. New York: Harper, 1947.

SPECIFIC TOPICS

Barry, Herbert, Margaret K. Bacon, and I. I. Child. "A Cross-cultural Survey of Some Sex Differences in Socialization," *Journal of Abnormal Social Psychology*, 55 (1957), pp. 327–32.

Barry, Herbert, Lili Josephson, Edith M. Lauer, and Catherine Marshall. "Agents and Techniques for Child Training," *Ethnology*, 16 (1977), pp. 191–230.

Barry, Herbert, and L. M. Paxson. "Infancy and Early Childhood," *Ethnology*, 10 (1971), pp. 466–508.

Booth, A., and J. N. Edwards. "Crowding and Family Relations," *American Sociological Review*, 41 (April, 1976), pp. 308–21.

Boxer, Marilyn J., and Jean Quataert, eds. *Connecting Spheres: Women in the Western World, 1500 to the Present*. Oxford, England: Oxford University Press, 1987.

Bullough, Vern L. *Sexual Variance in Society and History*. New York: John Wiley and Sons, 1976.

Byrne, Pamela R., and Suzanne R. Ontiveros, eds. *Women in the Third World: A Historical Bibliography*. Santa Barbara, Calif.: ABC-Clio Information Services, 1986.

Chodorow, Nancy. *The Reproduction of Mothering: Psychoanalysis and the Sociology of Gender*. Berkeley: University of California Press, 1978.

Foucault, Michel, trans. by Robert Hurley. *History of Sexuality*, volumes I-III. New York: Pantheon, 1978–86.

Fried, Martha N., and Morton H. Fried. *Transitions: Four Rituals in Eight Cultures*. Harmondsworth, England: Penguin, 1980.

Gathorne-Hardy, Jonathan. *Marriage, Love, Sex, and Divorce*. New York: Summit Books, 1982.

Hammond, Dorothy, and Alta Jablow. *Women in Cultures of the World*. Menlo Park, Calif.: Cummings Publishing Co., 1976.

Kirp, David L., Mark G. Yudof, and Marlene Strong Franks. *Gender Justice*. Chicago: University of Chicago Press, 1987.

Lasswell, Harold D. *Psychopathology and Politics*, new edition. Chicago: University of Chicago Press, 1960.

Lerner, Gerda. *The Creation of Patriarchy*. Oxford, England: Oxford University Press, 1986.

Levinson, Daniel. *Seasons of a Man's Life*. New York: Knopf, 1978.

Lewis, Robert A., and Robert E. Salt, eds. *Men in Families*. Beverly Hills, Calif.: Sage Publications, 1985.

Martin, M. Kay, and Barbara Voorhies. *Female of the Species*. New York: Columbia University Press, 1975.

Medick, Hans, and David Warren Sabean, eds. *Interest and Emotion*. Cambridge, England: Cambridge University Press, 1984.

Miller, Jean Baker. *Toward a New Psychology of Women*. New York: Harper and Row, 1976.

Mintz, Sidney W., and Eric Wolf. "An Analysis of Ritual Coparenthood: Compadrazgo," *Southwestern Journal of Anthropology*, 6 (1950), pp. 341–68.

Murdock, George P. "Family Stability in Non-European Cultures," *Annals of the American Academy of Social and Political Science*, 272 (1950), pp. 195–201.

Newman, Graeme. *Comparative Deviance*. New York: Elsevier, 1976.

Noonan, John T. *Contraception: A History of Its Treatment by the Catholic Theologians and Canonists*. Cambridge, Mass.: Harvard University Press, 1966.

Ogburn, William F., and Meyer Nimkoff. *Technology and the Changing Family*. Boston: Houghton Mifflin, 1955.

Rohrbaugh, Joanna Bunker. *Women: Psychology's Puzzle*. New York: Basic Books, 1979.

Rueschemeyer, Marilyn. *Professional Work and Marriage: An East-West Comparison*. New York: St. Martin's, 1985.

Schaef, Anne Wilson. *Women's Reality*. Minneapolis, Minn.: Winston Press, 1981.

Schatzman, Morton. *Soul Murder: Persecution in the Family*. New York: Random House, 1976.

Scott, Joan W. "Gender," *American Historical Review*, 91 (1986), pp. 1053–75.

Simon, Rita J., and Caroline B. Brettell, eds. *International Migration: The Female Experience*. Totowa, N.J.: Rowman and Littlefield, 1986.

Söderberg, Bertil. "An Ethno-Historical Survey of Family Planning," *Ethnos*, 36 (1971), pp. 163–80.

Stearns, Peter N., and Carol Z. Stearns, eds. *The History of Emotion*. New York: Holmes and Meier, 1986.

Tulkin, S. R., and M. J. Konner. "Alternative Conceptions of Intellectual Functioning," *Human Development*, 16 (1973), pp. 33–52.

Weibust, Knut. "Ritual Coparenthood among Peasants," *Ethnologia Scandinavica*, (1972), pp. 101–14.

Whiting, B. B., and J.W.M. Whiting. *Children of Six Cultures: A Psycho-cultural Analysis*. Cambridge, Mass.: Harvard University Press, 1975.

Witkin, H. A., and J. W. Berry. "Psychological Differentiation in Cross-cultural Perspective," *Journal of Cross-cultural Psychology*, 6 (1975), pp. 4–87.

Witkin, H. A., and others. "Social Conformity and Psychological Differentiation," *International Journal of Psychology*, 9 (1974), pp. 11–29.

COLLECTIONS AND COMPARISONS

Anshen, Ruth Nanda, ed. *The Family: Its Functions and Destiny*, revised edition. New York: Harper and Row, 1959.

Becker, Howard, and Reuben Hill, eds. *Family, Marriage, and Parenthood*. Boston: D.C. Heath, 1948.

Bell, Norman W., and Ezra F. Vogel, eds. *Modern Introduction to the Family*, revised edition. Glencoe, Ill.: Free Press, 1968.

Blitsten, Dorothy R., ed. *The World of the Family*. New York: Random House, 1963.

Bohannon, Paul, and John Middleton. *Kinship and Social Organization*. New York: American Museum of Natural History, 1968.

Christensen, Harold T. *Handbook of Marriage and the Family*. Chicago: Rand McNally, 1964.

Cordell, Linda S., and Stephen Beckermann, eds. *The Versatility of Kinship*. New York: Academic Press, 1980.

Goody, Jack, ed. *The Character of Kinship*. Cambridge, England: Cambridge University Press, 1973.

Goody, Jack, ed. *The Developmental Cycle in Domestic Groups*. Cambridge, England: Cambridge University Press, 1958.

Goslin, D. A., ed. *Handbook of Socialization Theory and Research*. Chicago: Rand McNally, 1969.

Hareven, Tamara K., ed. *Themes in the History of the Family*. Worcester, Mass.: American Antiquarian Society, 1978.

Harris, C. C. *Readings in Kinship in Urban Society*. Oxford, England: Pergamon Press, 1970.

Hoffman, M. L., and L. W. Hoffman, eds. *Review of Child Development Research*, vols. 1 and 2. Hartford, Conn.: Russell Sage Foundation, 1964–65.

Hsu, Francis L. K., ed. *Kinship and Culture*. Chicago: Aldine Publishing Co., 1971.

Korbin, Jill E., ed. *Child Abuse and Neglect: Cross-cultural Perspectives*. Berkeley: University of California Press, 1981.

Kurian, George, ed. *Cross-cultural Perspectives on Mate Selection and Marriage*. Westport, Conn.: Greenwood Press, 1979.

Lamb, M. E., ed. *The Role of the Father in Child Development*. New York: John Wiley, 1976.

Maccoby, E. E., ed. *The Development of Sex Differences*. Stanford, Calif.: Stanford University Press, 1966.

Mead, Margaret, ed. *Cultural Patterns and Technical Change*. New York: UNESCO, 1953.

Needham, Rodney, ed. *Right and Left: Essays on Dual Symbolic Classification*. Chicago: University of Chicago Press, 1973.

Netting, Robert C., and others, eds. *Households*. Berkeley: University of California Press, 1984.

Nimkoff, Meyer F., ed. *Comparative Family Systems*. Boston, Mass.: Houghton Mifflin, 1965.

Outhwaite, R. B., ed. *Marriage and Society: Studies in the Social History of Marriage*. New York: St. Martin's, 1981.

Pick, Anne, ed. *Minnesota Symposium on Child Psychology*, vol. 9. Minneapolis: University of Minnesota Press, 1975.

Queen, Stuart, and John B. Adams, eds. *The Family in Various Cultures*. New York: Harper, 1952.

Rabb, Theodore K., and Robert I. Rotberg, eds. *The Family in History*. New York: Harper and Row, 1973.

Reiter, Rayna R., ed. *Toward an Anthropology of Women*. New York: Monthly Review Press, 1975.

Rosaldo, Michelle Z., and Louise Lanphere, eds. *Woman, Culture, and Society*. Stanford, Calif.: Stanford University Press, 1974.

Rosof, Patricia J. F., and William Zeisel, eds. *Trends in History: Family History*. New York: Haworth Press, 1985.

Safilios-Rothschild, Constantina, ed. *Toward a Sociology of Women*. Lexington, Mass.: Xerox College Publishing, 1972.

Schlegel, Alice, ed. *Sexual Stratification: A Cross-cultural View*. New York: Columbia University Press, 1977.

Schneider, David M., and Kathleen Gough, eds. *Matrilineal Kinship*. Berkeley: University of California Press, 1961.

Schultz, Theodore W., ed. *Economics of the Family*. Chicago: University of Chicago Press, 1975.

Shanas, Ethel, and Gordon F. Streit, eds. *Social Structure and the Family: Generational Relations*. Englewood Cliffs, N.J.: Prentice-Hall, 1965.

Shapiro, Harry L., ed. *Man, Culture, and Society*, revised edition. Oxford, England: Oxford University Press, 1971.

Triandis, H. C., ed. *Handbook of Cross-cultural Psychology*, 6 vols. Boston: Allyn and Bacon, 1979–80.

Wachter, Kenneth, and others. *Statistical Studies of Historical Social Structure*. New York: Academic Press, 1978.

Whiting, Beatrice B., ed. *Six Cultures: Studies of Child Rearing*. New York: John Wiley and Sons, 1963.

Whiting, Beatrice B., and others, eds. *Handbook of Cross-cultural Human Development*. New York: Garland Publishing Co., 1981.

Winch, Robert, ed. *Selected Studies in Marriage and the Family*. New York: Holt, Rinehart and Winston, 1974.

Winch, Robert, and Louis Goodman, eds. *Selected Studies in Marriage and the Family*. New York: Holt, Rinehart and Winston, 1968.

Winch, Robert, and Robert McGinnis, eds. *Selected Studies in Marriage and the Family*. New York: Holt, 1953.

Winch, Robert, and others. *Familial Organization*. New York: Free Press, 1977.

PRIMATES

Altmann, S. A., ed. *Japanese Monkeys: A Collection of Translations*. Atlanta, Ga., 1965.

Chevalier-Skolnikoff, S., and F. E. Poirier, eds. *Primate Bio-social Development: Biological, Social, and Ecological Determinants*. New York: Garland Publishing Co., 1977.

Goodall, Jane. *The Chimpanzees of Gombe: Patterns of Behavior*. Cambridge, Mass.: Harvard University Press, 1986.

Hamberg, David A., and Elizabeth McCann, eds. *The Great Apes*. Menlo Park, Calif.: Benjamin/Cummings Publishing Co., 1979.

Kohts, Nadjejeta. "The Handling of Objects by Primates (Apes and Monkeys) in the Light of Anthropogenesis," Fifteenth International Congress of Zoology, 1958, *Proceedings* (1959), pp. 855–57.

Lancaster, J. B. *Primate Behavior and the Emergence of Human Culture*. New York: Holt, Rinehart and Winston, 1975.

Marsh, C. W. "Female Transference and Mate Choice Among Tana River Red Colubus," *Nature*, 281 (1979, October 18), pp. 568–69.

Miyadi, Denzaburo. "On Some New Habits and Their Propagation in Japanese Monkey Groups," Fifteenth International Congress of Zoology, 1958, *Proceedings* (1959), pp. 857–60.

Poirier, F. E., ed. *Primate Socialization*. New York: Random House, 1972.

Rowell, T. E. *The Social Behavior of Monkeys*. Harmondsworth, England: Penguin, 1972.

Simonds, P. E. *The Social Primates*. New York: Harper and Row, 1974.

FROM HOMINID TO NEOLITHIC TIMES

Van Den Berghe, P. L. *Human Family Systems: An Evolutionary View*. New York: Elsevier, 1979.

Gough, Kathleen. "The Origin of the Family," *Journal of Marriage and the Family*, 33 (1971), pp. 760–71.

Hrdy, Sarah B. *The Woman That Never Evolved*. Cambridge, Mass.: Harvard University Press, 1982.

von Koenigswald, G.H.R. *The Evolution of Man*, revised edition. Ann Arbor: University of Michigan Press, 1976.

Wenke, Robert J. *Patterns in Prehistory*. Oxford, England: Oxford University Press, 1980.

Wilson, Peter J. *Man, the Promising Primate*. New Haven: Yale University Press, 1980.

NEW GUINEA

Brown, Paula. "Enemies and Affines," *Ethnology*, 3 (1964), pp. 335–56.

Brown, Paula. "Non-Agnates Among the Patrilineal Chimbu," *Journal of the Polynesian Society*, 71 (1962), pp. 57–69.

Cook, Edwin A. "Converting Non-Agnates to Agnates," *Southwestern Journal of Anthropology*, 26 (1970), pp. 190–96.

Gelber, Marilyn G. *Gender and Society in the New Guinea Highlands*. Boulder, Colo.: Westview Press, 1986.

Glasse, Robert M., and M. J. Meggitt, eds. *Pigs, Pearlshells, and Women: Marriage in the New Guinea Highlands*. Englewood Cliffs, N.J.: Prentice-Hall, 1969.

Glick, Leonard B. "The Role of Choice in Gimi Kinship," *Southwestern Journal of Anthropology*, 23 (1967), pp. 371–82.

Kelly, Raymond C. "Demographic Pressure and Descent Group Structure in the New Guinea Highlands," *Oceania*, 39 (1968), pp. 36–63.

Koentjraningraf. "Bride-Price and Adoption in the Kinship Relations of the Bgu of West Irian," *Ethnology*, 5 (1966), pp. 233–44.

Lane, Barbara S., and Robert B. Lane. "Implicit Double Descent in South Australia and the Northeastern New Hebrides," *Ethnology*, 1 (1962), pp. 46–52.

Mead, Margaret. *Sex and Temperament in Three Primitive Societies*. New York: William Morrow, 1935.

Meggitt, Mervyn J. "Growth and Decline of Agnatic Descent-Groups Among the Mae Enga of the New Guinea Highlands," *Ethnology*, 1 (1962), pp. 158–65.

Salisbury, Richard F. "Descent-Group Theory," *Man*, 64 (1964), pp. 168–71.

Salisbury, Richard F. "Unilineal Descent Groups in the New Guinea Highlands," *Man*, 56 (1956), pp. 2–7.

OCEANIA (INCLUDING MAORI AND AUSTRALIAN ABORIGINES)

Davenport, William. "Nonunilinear Descent and Descent Groups," *American Anthropologist*, 61 (1959), pp. 557–72.

Ember, Melvin. "Kinship Structure and Political Authority in Samoa," *American Anthropologist*, 64 (1962), pp. 964–71.

Ember, Melvin. "The Nonunilinear Descent Groups of Samoa," *American Anthropologist*, 61 (1959), pp. 573–77.

Finney, Ben R. "Notes on Bond-Friendship in Tahiti," *Journal of the Polynesian Society*, 73 (1964), pp. 431–35.

Freeman, Derek. "Kinship and Political Authority in Samoa," *American Anthropologist*, 66 (1964), pages 553–68.

Hagaman, Roberta M. "Divorce, Remarriage, and Fertility in a Micronesian Population," *Micronesica*, 10 (1974), pp. 237–42.

Keesing, Roger M. "Kwaio Fosterage," *American Anthropologist*, 72 (1970), pp. 991–1019.

Keesing, Roger M. "Kwaio Kindreds," *Southwestern Journal of Anthropology*, 22 (1966), pp. 346–53.

Keesing, Roger M. "Shrines, Ancestors, and Cognatic Descent: The Kwaio and The Tallensi," *American Anthropologist*, 72 (1970), pp. 755–75.

Keesing, Roger M. "Step-Kin, In-Laws, and Ethnoscience," *Ethnology*, 7 (1968), pp. 59–70.

Lambert, Bernd. "Ambilineal Descent Groups in the Northern Gilbert Islands," *American Anthropologist*, 68 (1966), pp. 641–64.

Leach, Edmund R. "Nonunilineal Descent," *American Anthropologist*, 64 (1962), pp. 601–4.

Mead, Margaret. "Kinship in the Admiralty Islands," *Anthropological Papers of the American Museum of Natural History*, 34 (1934), pp. 181–358.

Monberg, Torben. "Determinants of Choice in Adoption and Fosterage on Bellona Island," *Ethnology*, 9 (1970), pp. 99–136.

Panoff, Michel. "Patrifiliation as Ideology and Practice in a Matrilineal Society," *Ethnology*, 15 (1976), pp. 175–88.

Sahlins, Marshall. *Islands of History*. Chicago: University of Chicago Press, 1985.

Scheffler, Harold W. "Descent Concepts and Descent Groups: The Maori Case," *Journal of the Polynesian Society*, 73 (1964), pp. 126–33.

Schneider, David M. "Double Descent in Yap," *Journal of the Polynesian Society*, 71 (1962), pp. 1–24.

Sider, K. B. "Affinity and Father-Role," *Southwestern Journal of Anthropology*, 23 (1967), pp. 90–109.

Spoehr, Alexander. "Generational Kinship," *Southwestern Journal of Anthropology*, 5 (1949), pp. 107–16.

Swartz, Marc J. "Situational Determinants of Kinship Terminology," *Southwestern Journal of Anthropology*, 16 (1960), pp. 393–97.

Tiffany, Sharon. "The Cognatic Descent Groups of Contemporary Samoa," *Man*, 10 (1975), pp. 430–47.

Webster, Steven. "Cognatic Descent Groups and the Contemporary Maori: A Preliminary Reassessment," *Journal of the Polynesian Society*, 84 (1975), pp. 121–52.

AFRICA

Anderson, James N. D., ed. *Family Law in Asia and Africa*. London, England: Allen and Unwin, 1968.

Bascom, William R., and Melville J. Herskovits, eds. *Continuity and Change in African Cultures*. Chicago: University of Chicago Press, 1959.

Bledsoe, Caroline. "Women's Marriage Strategies Among the Kpelle of Liberia," *Journal of Anthropological Research*, 32 (1976), pp. 372–89.

Callaway, Barbara J. *Muslim Hausa Women in Nigeria: Tradition and Change*. Syracuse, N.Y.: Syracuse University Press, 1987.

Chock, Phyllis. "Ndembu Kinship," *Southwestern Journal of Anthropology*, 23 (1967), pp. 74–89.

Clignet, Remi. *Many Wives, Many Powers*. Evanston, Ill.: Northwestern University Press, 1970.

Colson, Elizabeth. *Marriage and the Family Among the Plateau Tonga of Northern Rhodesia*. Manchester: Manchester University Press, 1958.

Evans-Pritchard, E. E. *Kinship and Marriage Among the Nuer*. Oxford, England: Clarendon Press, 1951.

Fortes, Meyer. *Time and Social Structure, and Other Essays*. London: Athlone Press, 1970.

Goody, Jack. "The Mother's Brother and the Sister's Son in West Africa," *Journal of the Royal Anthropological Institute*, 89 (1959), pp. 61–88.

Gulliver, P. H. *The Family Herds*. London: Routledge and Kegan Paul, 1955.

Harrell-Bond, Barbara E. *Modern Marriage in Sierra Leone*. The Hague: Mouton, 1975.

Hay, Margaret Jean, and Sharon Stichter, eds. *African Women South of the Sahara*. Harlow, England: Longman, 1984.

Hunter, John M. *The Clans of Nangodi*. East Lansing: Michigan State University International Programs, 1970.

Imadiume, Ifi. *Male Daughters, Female Husbands: Gender and Sex in an African Society*. London: Zed Press, 1987.

Jackson, Kennell. "The Family Entity and Famine among the Nineteenth-Century Akamba of Kenya," *Journal of Family History*, 1 (1976), pp. 193–216.

July, Robert W. *Precolonial Africa: An Economic and Social History*. New York: Scribner, 1975.

Kayongo-Male, Diane, and Philista Onyango. *Sociology of the African Family*. Harlow, England: Longman, 1984.

Krige, Eileen Jensen. "Woman-Marriage, with Special Reference to the Lovedu," *Africa*, 44 (1974), pp. 11–38.

Lloyd, P. C. *Africa in Social Change*. Harmondsworth, England: Penguin, 1967.

Mair, Lucy. *African Marriage and Social Change.* London: Frank Cass, 1969.

Mann, Kristin. *Marrying Well: Marriage, Status, and Social Change Among the Educated Elite in Colonial Lagos.* Cambridge: Cambridge University Press, 1985.

Muller, Jean-Claude. "Ritual Marriage, Symbolic Fatherhood, and Initiation among the Rukuba of Plateau-Benue State in Nigeria," *Man,* 7 (1972), pp. 283–96.

Oboler, Regina Smith. *Women, Power, and Economic Change: The Nandi of Kenya.* Stanford, Calif.: Stanford University Press, 1985.

Oppong, Christine. *Middle Class African Marriage.* London: Allen and Unwin, 1981.

Oppong, Christine, ed. *Marriage, Fertility, and Parenthood in West Africa.* Canberra: Australian National University, Department of Demography, 1976.

Ottenberg, Simon. *Double Descent in an African Society: The Afikpo Village-Group.* Seattle: University of Washington Press, 1968.

Paulme, Denise, ed., trans. by H. M. Wright. *Women of Tropical Africa.* Berkeley: University of California Press, 1963.

Phillips, Arthur, ed. *Survey of African Marriage and Family Life.* Oxford, England: Oxford University Press, 1953.

Radcliffe–Brown, A. R., and Daryll Forde, eds. *African Systems of Kinship and Marriage.* Oxford, England: Oxford University Press, 1950.

Reyna, S. P. "Extending Strategy: Regulation of the Household Dependency Ratio," *Journal of Anthropological Research,* 32 (1976), pp. 182–98.

Richards, Audrey I. *Bemba Marriage and Present Economic Conditions.* Livingstone, Northern Rhodesia: Rhodes-Livingstone Institute, 1940.

Robertson, Claire C., and Martin A. Klein, eds. *Women and Slavery in Africa.* Madison: University of Wisconsin Press, 1984.

Sacks, Karen. *Sisters and Wives.* Urbana: University of Illinois Press, 1979.

Shostak, Marjorie. *Nisa: The Life and Words of a !Kung Woman.* Cambridge, Mass.: Harvard University Press, 1981.

Skinner, Elliott P., ed. *Peoples and Cultures of Africa.* Garden City, N.Y.: Doubleday, 1973.

Stichter, Sharon, and Jane Parpart. *Patriarchy and Class: African Women in the Home and Workforce.* Boulder, Colo.: Westview Press, 1987.

Ukaegbu, Alfred O. "Traditional Marriage Habits and Population Growth," *Africa,* 46 (1976), pp. 390–98.

Wilson, Monica. *For Men and Elders: Change in the Relations of Generations and of Men and Women Among the Nyakyusa-Ndongo People, 1875–1971.* New York: Holmes and Meier, 1978.

ASIA

Anderson, James N. D., ed. *Family Law in Asia and Africa.* London: Allen and Unwin, 1968.

Buxbaum, David C., ed. *Family Law and Customary Law in Asia.* The Hague: Martinus Nijhoff, 1968.

Chipp, Sylvia, and Justin Green, eds. *Asian Women in Transition.* University Park: Pennsylvania State University Press, 1982.

Cho, Lee-Jay, and Kazumasa Kobayashi, eds. *Fertility Transition of the East Asian Populations.* Honolulu: University of Hawaii Press, 1979.

Das, Man Sing, and Panos D. Bardis, eds. *The Family in Asia*. London: Allen and Unwin, 1979.

Devos, George A., and Takao Sofue, eds. *Religion and the Family in East Asia*. Berkeley: University of California Press, 1987.

Hanley, Susan B., and Arthur P. Wolf, eds. *Family and Population in East Asian History*. Stanford, Calif.: Stanford University Press, 1985.

Headley, Lee A., ed. *Suicide in Asia and the Near East*. Berkeley: University of California Press, 1983.

Murphy, Gardner, and Lois Murphy, eds. *Asian Psychology*. New York: Basic Books, 1968.

Smith, Peter C. "Asian Marriage Patterns in Transition," *Journal of Family History*, 5 (1980), pp. 58–96.

Whyte, Robert Orr, and Pauline Whyte. *The Women of Rural Asia*. Boulder, Colo.: Westview Press, 1982.

CHINA (INCLUDING MONGOLS)

Andors, Phyllis. *The Unfinished Liberation of Chinese Women, 1949–1980*. Bloomington: Indiana University Press, 1983.

Baker, Hugh D. R. *Chinese Family and Kinship*. New York: Columbia University Press, 1979.

Barrett, Richard E. "Short-term Trends in Bastardy in Taiwan," *Journal of Family History*, 5 (1980), pp. 293–312.

Buxbaum, David, ed. *Chinese Family Law and Social Change in Historical and Comparative Perspective*. Seattle: University of Washington Press, 1980.

Casterline, John. *The Timing of Marriage: Nuptiality Trends in Taiwan*. Boulder, Colo.: Westview Press, 1987.

Chan, Anita, Richard Madsen, and Jonathan Unger. *Chen Village: The Recent History of a Peasant Community in Mao's China*. Berkeley: University of California Press, 1984.

Cheng, Lucie, and others, compilers. *Women in China: Bibliography of Available English-Language Materials*. Berkeley: Institute of East Asian Studies, University of California, 1984.

Ch'ü, T'ung-tsu, ed. by Jack L. Dull. *Han Social Structure*. Seattle: University of Washington Press, 1972.

Cohen, Myron. *House United, House Divided: The Chinese Family in Taiwan*. New York: Columbia University Press, 1976.

Croll, Elisabeth. *Chinese Women Since Mao*. Armonk, N.Y.: M. E. Sharpe, 1983.

Davis-Friedmann, Deborah. *Long Lives: Chinese Elderly and the Communist Revolution*. Cambridge, Mass.: Harvard University Press, 1983.

Davis-Friedmann, Deborah. "Strategies for Aging: Interdependence Between Generations in the Transition to Socialism," *Contemporary China*, 1 (1976–77), pp. 35–42.

Ebrey, Patricia B., and James L. Watson, eds. *Kinship Organization in Late Imperial China, 1000–1940*. Berkeley: University of California Press, 1986.

Fei, Hsiao-tung. *China's Gentry: Essays on Rural-Urban Relations*. Chicago: University of Chicago Press, 1953.

Gallin, Bernard. "Matrilateral and Affinal Relationships of a Taiwanese Village," *American Anthropologist*, 62 (1960), pp. 632–42.

Gernet, Jacques, trans. by H. M. Wright. *Daily Life in China on the Eve of the Mongol Invasion, 1250–1276.* Stanford, Calif.: Stanford University Press, 1962.

Hemmel, Vibeke, and Pia Sindbjerg. *Woman in Rural China: Policy Towards Women Before and After the Cultural Revolution.* London: Curzon, 1984.

Hsu, Francis L. K. *Under the Ancestors' Shadow: Chinese Culture and Personality.* New York: Columbia University Press, 1948.

Johnson, Kay Ann. *Women, the Family, and Peasant Revolution in China.* Chicago: University of Chicago Press, 1983.

Kessen, William, ed. *Childhood in China.* New Haven, Conn.: Yale University Press, 1975.

Kroeber, Alfred L. "Process in the Chinese Kinship System," *American Anthropologist*, 35 (1933), pp. 151–57.

Levy, Marion J., Jr. *The Family Revolution in Modern China.* Cambridge, Mass.: Harvard University Press, 1949.

Loewe, Michael. *Everyday Life in Early Imperial China During the Han Period 202 B.C.–A.D. 220.* London: B. T. Batsford, Ltd., 1968.

Mann, Susan. "Widows in the Kinship, Class, and Community Structure of Qing Dynasty China," *Journal of Asian Studies*, 46 (1987), pp. 37–56.

Meskill, Johanna M. *A Chinese Pioneer Family: The Lins of Wufeng, Taiwan, 1729–1895.* Princeton, N.J.: Princeton University Press, 1979.

O'Hara, Albert. *The Position of Woman in Early China.* Taipei, Taiwan, China: Mei Ya Publications, 1971.

Parish, William L., and Martin K. Whyte. *Urban Life in Contemporary China.* Chicago: University of Chicago Press, 1983.

Parish, William L., and Martin King Whyte. *Village and Family in Contemporary China.* Chicago: University of Chicago Press, 1978.

Sidel, Ruth. *Families of Fengsheng: Urban Life in China.* Harmondsworth, England: Penguin, 1974.

Spence, Jonathan D. *The Death of Woman Wang.* Harmondsworth, England: Penguin, 1978.

Stacey, Judith. *Patriarchy and Socialist Revolution in China.* Berkeley: University of California Press, 1983.

Vreeland, Herbert H. *Mongol Community and Kinship Structure.* New Haven, Conn.: Human Relations Area Files Press, 1962.

Wolf, Arthur P., and Chieh-shan Huang. *Marriage and Adoption in China, 1845–1945.* Stanford, Calif.: Stanford University Press, 1980.

Wolf, Margery. *Women and the Family in Rural Taiwan.* Stanford, Calif.: Stanford University Press, 1972.

Wolf, Margery. *Revolution Postponed: Women in Contemporary China.* Stanford, Calif.: Stanford University Press, 1984.

Wolf, Margery, and Roxane Witke, eds. *Women in Chinese Society.* Stanford, Calif.: Stanford University Press, 1975.

Yang, C. K. *Chinese Communist Society: The Family and the Village.* Cambridge: Massachusetts Institute of Technology Press, 1959.

Young, Marilyn B., ed. *Women in China: Studies in Social Change and Feminism.* Ann Arbor: Center for Chinese Studies, University of Michigan, 1973.

JAPAN

Cole, Robert E. *Japanese Blue Collar: The Changing Tradition.* Berkeley: University of California Press, 1971.

Coleman, Samuel. *Family Planning in Japanese Society: Traditional Birth Control in a Modern Urban Culture.* Princeton, N.J.: Princeton University Press, 1983.

Doi, Takeo, trans. by John Bester. *The Anatomy of Dependence.* Tokyo: Kodansha, 1973.

Dore, Ronald P. *City Life in Japan: A Study of a Tokyo Ward.* Berkeley: University of California Press, 1958.

Dore, Ronald P., ed. *Aspects of Social Change in Modern Japan.* Princeton, N.J.: Princeton University Press, 1967.

Eng, Robert Y., and Thomas C. Smith. "Peasant Families and Population Control in Eighteenth-century Japan," *Journal of Interdisciplinary History,* 6 (1975–76), pp. 417–45.

Fruin, W. Mark. "The Family as a Firm and the Firm as a Family in Japan," *Journal of Family History,* 5 (1980), pp. 432–49.

Hanley, Susan B. "Fertility, Mortality, and Life Expectancy in Pre-Modern Japan," *Population Studies,* 28 (1974), pp. 127–42.

Hayami, Akira. "Demographic Analysis of a Village in Tokugawa Japan," *Keio Economic Studies,* 5 (1968), pp. 50–88.

Hendry, Joy. *Marriage in Changing Japan.* New York: St. Martin's Press, 1981.

Imamura, Anne E. *Urban Japanese Housewives at Home and in the Community.* Honolulu: University of Hawaii Press, 1987.

Koyama, Takashi. "Changing Family Composition and the Position of the Aged in the Japanese Family," *International Journal of Comparative Sociology,* 5 (1964), pp. 155–61.

Kurokawa, Minako. "Lineal Orientation in Child Rearing Among Japanese," *Journal of Marriage and Family,* 30 (1968), pp. 129–36.

Lebra, Joyce, Joy Paulson, and Elizabeth Powers, eds. *Women in Changing Japan.* Stanford, Calif.: Stanford University Press, 1976.

Lebra, Takie S. *Japanese Women: Constraint and Fulfillment.* Honolulu: University of Hawaii Press, 1984.

McMullen, I. J. "A Confucian Controversy: Nonagnatic Adoption in Seventeenth and Eighteenth-Century Japan," *Harvard Journal of Asiatic Studies,* 35 (1975), pp. 133–89.

Morris, Ivan. *The World of the Shining Prince: Court Life in Ancient Japan.* Oxford, England: Oxford University Press, 1964.

Nakane, Chie. *Japanese Society.* Berkeley: University of California Press, 1972.

Plath, David W. *Long Engagements: Maturity in Modern Japan.* Stanford, Calif.: Stanford University Press, 1983.

Robins-Mowry, Dorothy. *The Hidden Sun: Women of Modern Japan.* Boulder, Colo.: Westview, 1983.

Silver, Morris. "Births, Marriages, and Income Fluctuations in the United Kingdom and Japan," *Economic Development and Cultural Change,* 14 (1965–66), pp. 302–15.

Smith, Robert J. "The Domestic Cycle in Selected Commoner Families in Urban Japan: 1757–1858," *Journal of Family History,* 3 (1978), pp. 219–35.

Smith, Robert J., and Ella L. Wiswell. *The Women of Suye Mura*. Chicago: University of Chicago Press, 1983.

Vogel, Ezra F. *Japan's New Middle Class: The Salary Man and His Family in a Tokyo Suburb*, 2d ed. Berkeley: University of California Press, 1971.

Wagatsuma, Miroshi, and George A. De Vos. *Heritage of Endurance: Family Patterns and Delinquency Formation in Urban Japan*. Berkeley: University of California Press, 1984.

KOREA

Kendall, Laurel. *Shamans, Housewives, and Other Restless Spirits*. Honolulu: University of Hawaii Press, 1985.

Kendall, Laurel, and Mark Peterson, eds. *Korean Women: View From the Inner Room*. Cushing, Maine: East Rock Press, 1983.

Kim, C. I. Eugene, and Ch'angboh Chee, eds. *Aspects of Social Change in Korea*. Kalamazoo, Mich.: Korea Research and Publications, 1969.

Lee, Mun Woong. *Rural North Korea Under Communism: A Study of Sociocultural Change*. Houston, Texas: Rice University, 1976.

Pak, Ki-Hyuk, and Sidney D. Gamble. *The Changing Korean Village*. Seoul, Korea: Shin-Hung Press, 1975.

SOUTHEAST ASIA

vonBenda-Beckmann, Franz. *Property in Social Continuity: Minangkabau*. The Hague: Martinus Nijhoff, 1979.

Brant, Charles S., and Mi Mi Khaing. "Burmese Kinship and the Life Cycle," *Southwestern Journal of Anthropology*, 7 (1951), pp. 437–54.

Caldwell, J. C. "Fertility Decline and Female Chances of Marriage in Malaya," *Population Studies*, 17 (1963), pp. 20–32.

Carroll, John J., and others. *Philippine Institutions*. Manila: Solidaridad Publishing House, 1970.

Concepción, Mercedes B. "Some Socio-Economic Correlates of Family Size, 1960," *Philippine Sociological Review*, 12 (1964), pp. 16–26.

Firth, Raymond. *Malay Fishermen*, 2d rev. ed. Hamden, Conn.: Archon Books, 1966.

Geertz, Clifford. *Peddlers and Princes: Social Change and Economic Modernization in Two Indonesian Towns*. Chicago: University of Chicago Press, 1963.

Geertz, Hildred. *The Javanese Family*. Glencoe, Ill.: Free Press, 1961.

Geertz, Hildred, and Clifford Geertz. *Kinship in Bali*. Chicago: University of Chicago Press, 1975.

Hainsworth, Geoffrey B., ed. *Southeast Asia: Women, Changing Social Structures, and Cultural Continuity*. Ottawa, Canada: University of Ottawa Press, 1980.

Kuo, Eddie C. Y., and Aline K. Wong, eds. *The Contemporary Family in Singapore*. Athens: Ohio University Press, 1979.

Maretin, J. V. "Disappearance of Matriclan Survivals in Minangkabau Family and Marriage Relations," *Bijdragen Tot de Taal-, Land-, en Volkenkunde*, 117 (1961), pp. 168–95.

Nakamura, Hisako. *Divorce in Java*. Athens: Ohio University Press, 1983.

Potter, Sulamith Heins. *Family Life in a Northern Thai Village*. Berkeley: University of California Press, 1985.

Pye, Lucian W. *Politics, Personality, and Nation Building: Burma's Search for Identity*. New Haven, Conn.: Yale University Press, 1962.

Spiro, Melford E. *Kinship and Marriage in Burma*. Berkeley: University of California Press, 1977.

Van Esterik, Penny, ed. *Women of Southeast Asia*. Detroit, Mich.: Cellar Book Shop, 1982.

Wertheim, W. E. *Indonesian Society in Transition*. The Hague: W. Van Hoeve, 1956.

Youngblood, Robert L. "Female Dominance and Adolescent Filipino Attitude Orientations and School Achievement," *Journal of Asian and African Studies*, 13 (1978, January-April), pp. 65–79.

SOUTH ASIA

Bennett, Lynn. *Dangerous Wives and Sacred Sisters*. New York: Columbia University Press, 1983.

Committee on Women in Asian Studies. *South Asian Women at Home and Abroad: A Guide to Resources*. Minneapolis: Committee on Women in Asian Studies, University of Minnesota, 1984.

von Fürer-Haimendorf, Christoph, ed. *Caste and Kin in Nepal, India, and Ceylon*. London: Asia Publishing House, 1966.

Good, Anthony. "Elder Sister's Daughter Marriage in South Asia," *Journal of Anthropological Research*, 36 (1980), pp. 474–90.

Khan, M. A., and Sirageldin, I. "Son Preference in Pakistan," *Demography*, 14 (1977), pp. 481–95.

Korson, J. Henry. "Dower and Class in an Urban Muslim Community," *Journal of Marriage and Family*, 29 (1967), pp. 527–33.

Levine, Nancy E. "Caste, State, and Ethnic Boundaries in Nepal," *Journal of Asian Studies*, 46 (1987), pp. 71–88.

Mumtaz, Khawar, and Farida Shaheed. *Women of Pakistan*. London: Zed Press, 1987.

INDIA

Ahmad, Imtiaz, ed. *Family, Kinship, and Marriage Among Muslims in India*. Columbia, Mo.: South Asia Books, 1976.

Basham, A. L. *The Wonder That Was India*. London: Macmillan, 1954.

Bebarta, Prafulla C. *Family Type and Fertility in India*. North Quincy, Mass.: Christopher Publishing House, 1977.

Berreman, G. D. "Pahari Polyandry: A Comparison," *American Anthropologist*, 64 (1962), pp. 60–75.

Béteille, André. *Caste, Class, and Power: Changing Patterns of Stratification in a Tanjore Village*. Berkeley: University of California Press, 1965.

Collver, A. "The Family Cycle in India and the United States, *American Sociological Review*, 28 (1963), pp. 86–96.

Dandekar, Hemalata C. *Men to Bombay, Women at Home*. Ann Arbor: Center for South and Southeast Asian Studies, University of Michigan, 1987.

Derrett, J.D.M. *The Death of a Marriage Law*. New Delhi: Vikas Publishing House, 1978.

Dumont, Louis. *Affinity as Value: Marriage Alliance in South India*. Chicago: University of Chicago Press, 1983.

Fox, Richard. *Kin, Clan, Raja, and Rule*. Berkeley: University of California Press, 1971.

Freeman, James M. *Scarcity and Opportunity in an Indian Village*. Menlo Park, Calif.: Cummings Publishing Co., 1977.

Fruzzetti, Lina, and Akos Ostör. *Kinship and Ritual in Bengal*. Columbia, Mo.: South Asia Books, 1984.

Fuller, C. J. *The Nayars Today*. Cambridge, England: Cambridge University Press, 1976.

Inden, Robert B. *Marriage and Rank in Bengali Culture*. Berkeley: University of California Press, 1976.

Inden, Ronald B., and Ralph W. Nicholas. *Kinship in Bengali Culture*. Chicago: University of Chicago Press, 1977.

Ishwaran, K. "Kinship and Distance in Rural India," *International Journal of Comparative Sociology*, 6 (1965), pp. 81–94.

Jha, J. C., and B. B. Chatterjee. "The Changing Family in a Polyandrous Community," *Eastern Anthropologist*, 18 (1965), pp. 64–72.

Kakar, Sudhir. *Indian Childhood: Cultural Ideals and Social Reality*. Delhi, India: Oxford University Press, 1979.

Kakar, Sudhir. *The Inner World: A Psycho-Analytic Study of Childhood and Society in India*. Delhi, India: Oxford University Press, 1978.

Kakar, Sudhir, ed. *Identity and Adulthood*. Delhi, India: Oxford University Press, 1979.

Kapadia, K. M. *Explorations in the Family*. Bombay: Thacker, 1975.

Kapadia, K. M. *Marriage and Family in India*, 3d ed. Oxford, England: Oxford University Press, 1966.

Karve, Irawati. *Kinship Organization in India*, 3d ed. Bombay: Asia Publishing House, 1968.

Kolenda, Pauline M. *Caste in Contemporary India: Beyond Organic Solidarity*. Menlo Park, Calif.: Benjamin/Cummings Publishing Co., 1978.

Kolenda, Pauline M. "Family Structure in the Village of Lonikand, India: 1819, 1958, and 1967," *Contributions to Indian Sociology*, new series 4 (1970), pp. 50–72.

Kurian, George, ed. *The Family in India: A Regional View*. The Hague: Mouton, 1974.

Mukherjee, Ramkrishna. *West Bengal Family Structures, 1946–1966*. Delhi: Macmillan of India, 1976.

Nath, Viswa. "Female Infanticide and the Lewa Kanbis of Gujarat in the Nineteenth Century," *Indian Economic and Social History Review*, 10 (1973), pp. 386–404.

Orenstein, Henry, and Michael Micklin. "The Hindu Joint Family, the Norms and the Numbers," *Pacific Affairs*, 39 (1966), pp. 314–25. Significant for its effort to demonstrate that with then-current Indian life expectancies, if 1 in 4 existing families included 3 generations, then virtually all Indians did in fact experience living in joint families during some portion of their lives.

Ostör, Akos, and others, eds. *Concepts of Person: Kinship, Caste, and Marriage in India.* Cambridge, Mass.: Harvard University Press, 1982.

Qureshi, M. A. *Marriage and Matrimonial Remedies: A Uniform Civil Code for India.* Delhi, India: Concept Publishing Co., 1978.

Sathyavathi, K. "Intrafamilial Interpersonal Environment of Schizophrenic Patients of Hindu Families," *International Journal of Social Psychology,* 21 (1975), pp. 297–302.

Teja, J. S. "Mental Illness and the Family in America and India," *International Journal of Social Psychology,* 24 (1978), pp. 225–31.

Wiser, Charlotte V. *Four Families of Karimpur.* Syracuse, N.Y.: Maxwell School of Citizenship and Public Affairs, Syracuse University, 1978.

Wiser, Charlotte V., and William H. Wiser. *Behind Mud Walls, 1930–1960, With a Sequel—The Village in 1970.* Berkeley: University of California Press, 1971.

ANCIENT NEAR EAST

Adams, R. M. *The Evolution of Urban Society: Early Mesopotamia and Prehispanic Mexico.* London: Aldine Publishing Co., 1966.

Duchesne-Guillemin, Jacques. *Symbols and Values in Zoroastrianism.* New York: Harper and Row, 1966.

Patai, Raphael. *Sex and Family in the Bible and the Middle East.* Garden City, N.Y.: Doubleday, 1959.

Peradotto, John, and J. P. Sullivan, eds. *Women in the Ancient World.* Albany: State University of New York Press, 1983.

Seibert, Ilse. *Women in the Ancient Near East.* New York: A. Schram, 1974.

MIDDLE EAST

Abadan-Unat, Nermin, ed. *Women in Turkish Society.* Leiden, Netherlands: E. J. Brill, 1981.

Alamuddin, N. S., and P. D. Starr. *Crucial Bonds: Marriage Among the Lebanese Druze.* Delmo, N.Y.: Caravan Books, 1980.

Altorki, Soraya. *Women in Saudi Arabia: Ideology and Behavior Among the Elite.* New York: Columbia University Press, 1986.

Azari, Farah, ed. *Women of Iran: The Conflict with Fundamentalist Islam.* London, England: Ithaca Press, 1983.

Beck, Lois, and Nikki R. Keddie, ed. *Women in the Muslim World.* Cambridge, Mass.: Harvard University Press, 1978.

Behnke, Roy S. *The Herders of Cyrenaica: Ecology, Economy, and Kinship.* Urbana: University of Illinois Press, 1980.

Busch, Ruth C. "In-Laws and Out-Laws: A Discussion of Affinal Components of Kinship," *Ethnology,* 11 (1972), pp. 127–31.

Davis, Fanny. *The Ottoman Lady: A Social History from 1718 to 1918.* Westport, Conn.: Greenwood Press, 1986.

Davis, Susan S. *Patience and Power: Women's Lives in a Moroccan Village.* Cambridge, Mass.: Schenkman, 1983.

Dorsky, Susan. *Women of 'Amran: A Middle Eastern Ethnographic Study.* Salt Lake City: University of Utah Press, 1986.

Dwyer, Daisy Hilse. *Images and Self-images: Male and Female in Morocco.* New York: Columbia University Press, 1978.

Eickelman, Christine. *Women and Community in Oman.* New York: Columbia University Press, 1984.

Esposito, John. *Women in Muslim Family Law.* Syracuse, N.Y.: Syracuse University Press, 1982.

Fernea, Elizabeth W., ed. *Women and the Family in the Middle East: New Voices of Change.* Austin: University of Texas Press, 1985.

Fuller, Anne H. *Buarij: Portrait of a Lebanese Muslim Village.* Cambridge, Mass.: Harvard University Press, 1970.

Ghalem, Ali, trans. by G. Kazolias. *A Wife for My Son.* Chicago: Banner Press, 1984.

Al-Haj, Majid. *Social Change and Family Processes: Arab Communities in Shefar-A'm.* Boulder, Colo.: Westview, 1987.

Al-Hibri, Azizah, ed. *Women and Islam.* Oxford, England: Pergamon Press, 1982.

Hilal, Jamal M. "Father's Brother's Daughter Marriage in Arab Communities: A Problem for Sociological Explanation," *Middle East Forum,* 46:4 (1972), pp. 73–84.

Hussain, Frieda, ed. *Muslim Women: The Ideal and Contextual Realities.* New York: St. Martin's Press, 1984.

Ingrams, Doreen. *The Awakened: Women in Iraq.* London: Third World Centre, 1983.

Khuri, Fuad. "Parallel Cousin Marriage as a Nullifier of Intensity of Relationships," *Man,* 5 (1970), pp. 597–618.

Lane, Edward William. *The Manners and Customs of the Modern Egyptians.* London: J. M. Dent, 1836. Reprint. New York: E. P. Dutton, 1923.

Levy, Reuben. *The Social Structure of Islam.* Cambridge, England: Cambridge University Press, 1957.

Mernissi, Fatima. *Beyond the Veil: Male-Female Dynamics in a Modern Muslim Society.* Rev. ed. Bloomington: Indiana University Press, 1987.

Minces, Juliette. *The House of Obedience: Women in Arab Society.* London: Zed Press, 1982.

Musallam, B. F. *Sex and Society in Islam: Birth Control Before the Nineteenth Century.* Cambridge, England: Cambridge University Press, 1983.

Nashat, Guity, ed. *Women and Revolution in Modern Iran.* Boulder, Colo.: Westview, 1984.

Patai, Raphael. *Society, Culture, and Change in the Middle East,* 3d ed. Philadelphia: University of Pennsylvania Press, 1969.

Prothro, Edwin T., and Lutfy Najib Diab. *Changing Family Patterns in the Arab East.* Beirut, Lebanon: American University of Beirut Press, 1974.

Rugh, Andrea. *Family in Contemporary Egypt.* Syracuse, N.Y.: Syracuse University Press, 1983.

El Saadawi, Nawai, trans. by Sherif Hetata. *The Hidden Face of Eve: Women in the Arab World.* New York: Harper and Row, 1982.

Serkel, Ayse Kudat. "Ritual Kinship in Eastern Turkey," *Anthropological Quarterly,* 44 (1971), pp. 37–50.

Shariati, Ali, trans. by Hamid Algar. *On the Sociology of Islam*. Berkeley, Calif.: Mizan Press, 1979.

Spiro, Melford E. *Kibbutz: Venture in Utopia*, new ed. New York: Schocken Books, 1970.

Sweet, Louise E., ed. *Peoples and Cultures of the Middle East*, 2 vols. Garden City, N.Y.: Doubleday, 1970.

Tucker, Judith E. *Women in Nineteenth Century Egypt*. Cambridge, England: Cambridge University Press, 1985.

Utas, Bo, ed. *Women in Islamic Societies: Social Attitudes and Historical Perspectives*. Atlantic Highlands, N.J.: Humanities Press, 1983.

Youssef, Nadia H. "Differential Labor Force Participation of Women in Latin American and Middle Eastern Countries: The Influence of Family Characteristics," *Social Forces*, 51 (1972), pp. 135–53.

MEDITERRANEAN WORLD

Douglass, William A. "The South Italian Family: A Critique," *Journal of Family History*, 5 (1980), pp. 338–59.

Hammel, E. A. "Household Structure in Fourteenth-century Macedonia," *Journal of Family History*, 5 (1980), pp. 242–73.

Laiou, Angeliki E. *Peasant Society in the Late Byzantine Empire*. Princeton, N.J.: Princeton University Press, 1977.

Mogey, John. "Residence, Family, Kinship: Some Recent Research," *Journal of Family History*, 1 (1976), pp. 95–105.

Peristiany, J. G., ed. *Kinship and Modernization in Mediterranean Society*. Rome, Italy: American Universities Field Staff Center for Mediterranean Studies, 1976.

Peristiany, J. G., ed. *Mediterranean Family Structure*. Cambridge, England: Cambridge University Press, 1976.

Pitt-Rivers, Julian, ed. *Mediterranean Countrymen*. The Hague: Mouton, 1963.

WESTERN EUROPE (GENERAL)

Aries, Philippe. *Centuries of Childhood*. London: Jonathan Cape Ltd., 1962.

Aries, Philippe. *The Hour of Our Death*. New York: Knopf, 1981.

Aries, Philippe. *Western Attitudes Toward Death from the Middle Ages to the Present*. Baltimore, Md.: Johns Hopkins University Press, 1974.

Aries, Philippe, and André Bejin, eds. *Western Sexuality: Practice and Precept in Past and Present Times*. Oxford, England: Blackwell, 1985.

Bell, Susan G., and K. M. Offen, eds. *Women, the Family, and Freedom: The Debate in Documents*, 2 vols. Stanford, Calif.: Stanford University Press, 1983.

Bonfield, Lloyd, and others, eds. *The World We Have Gained: Histories of Population and Social Structure*. Oxford, England: Blackwell, 1986.

Boswell, John E. "*Expositio* and *Oblatio*: The Abandonment of Children and the Ancient and Medieval Family," *American Historical Review*, 89 (February, 1984), pp. 10–33.

Elshtain, Jean Bethke, ed. *The Family in Political Thought*. Amherst: University of Massachusetts Press, 1982.

François, M. E. "Adults and Children: Against Evil or Against Each Other," *History of Childhood Quarterly*, 1 (1973–74), pp. 164–77.

Frey, Linda, and others, compilers. *Women in Western European History: A Select Bibliography*, 2 vols. (1982–84); 1st suppl. Westport, Conn.: Greenwood Press, 1986.

Goody, Jack, ed. *The Development of the Family and Marriage in Europe*. Cambridge, England: Cambridge University Press, 1983.

Goody, Jack, Joan Thirsk, and E. P. Thompson, eds. *Family and Inheritance: Rural Society in Western Europe, 1200–1800*. Cambridge, England: Cambridge University Press, 1976.

Guttentag, Marcia, and Paul F. Secord. *Too Many Women? The Sex Ratio Question*. Beverly Hills, Calif.: Sage Publications, 1983.

Hanawalt, Barbara A., ed. *Women and Work in Preindustrial Europe*. Bloomington: Indiana University Press, 1986.

Kaplan, Marion A., ed. *The Marriage Bargain: Women and Dowries in European History*. New York: Haworth Press, 1985.

Langer, William L. "Infanticide: A Historical Survey," *History of Childhood Quarterly*, 1 (1973–74), pp. 353–65; 2 (1974–75), pp. 129–34.

Laslett, Barbara. "A Historical View of the Family as a Private and a Public Institution," *Journal of Marriage and Family*, 35 (1973), pp. 480–92.

Laslett, Peter. *Family Life and Illicit Love in Earlier Generations*. Cambridge, England: Cambridge University Press, 1977.

Laslett, Peter, and Richard Wall, eds. *Household and Family in Past Time*. Cambridge, England: Cambridge University Press, 1972.

Mitterauer, Michael, and Reinhard Sieder, trans. by Karla Oosterveen and Manfred Horzinger. *The European Family: Patriarchy to Partnership from the Middle Ages to the Present*. Oxford, England: Blackwell, 1984.

Rosenberg, Charles E., ed. *The Family in History*. Philadelphia: University of Pennsylvania Press, 1975.

Sommerville, John. *The Rise and Fall of Childhood*. Beverly Hills, Calif.: Sage Publications, 1982.

Stearns, Peter N. *Be a Man! Males in Modern Society*. New York: Holmes and Meier, 1979.

Wall, Richard, and others, eds. *Family Forms in Historic Europe*. Cambridge, England: Cambridge University Press, 1983.

Wheaton, Robert. "The Joint Family in Europe," *Journal of Interdisciplinary History*, 5 (1974–75), pp. 601–28. Significant for pointing out that if 1 in 20 households is three-generational, in a population in which life expectancy at birth is not over 30, then probably a majority of people experience life in a three-generational household at some time.

CLASSICAL GREECE AND ROME

Cameron, A. "The Experience of Greek Children and Ethics," *Classical Review*, 46 (1930), pp. 105–14.

Davies, John K. "Athenian Citizenship: The Descent Group and the Alternatives," *Classical Journal*, 73 (1977–78), pp. 105–21.

Gardner, Jane F. *Women in Roman Law and Society*. Bloomington: Indiana University Press, 1986.

Harrison, Alick R. W. *The Law of Athens: Family and Property*. London: Clarendon Press, 1968.

Hughes, Diane. "From Brideprice to Dowry in Mediterranean Europe," *Journal of Family History*, 3 (1978), pp. 262–96.

Lacey, Walter K. *The Family in Classical Greece*. London: Thames and Hudson, 1968.

Peradotto, John, and J. P. Sullivan, eds. *Women in the Ancient World*. Albany: State University of New York Press, 1983.

Preus, Anthony. "Biomedical Techniques for Influencing Human Reproduction in the Fourth Century B.C.," *Arethusa*, 8 (1975), pp. 237–63.

Rawson, Beryl, ed. *The Family in Ancient Rome: New Perspectives*. Ithaca, N.Y.: Cornell University Press, 1986.

MEDIEVAL WESTERN EUROPE

Bennett, Judith M. *Women in the Medieval English Countryside*. Oxford, England: Oxford University Press, 1987.

Dillard, Heath. *Daughters of the Reconquest: Women in Castilian Town Society, 1100–1300*. Cambridge, England: Cambridge University Press, 1984.

Duby, Georges. *The Knight, the Lady, and the Priest: The Making of Modern Marriage in Medieval France*. London: Allen Lane, 1984.

Fell, Christine, and others. *Women in Anglo-Saxon England and the Impact of 1066*. Bloomington: Indiana University Press, 1984.

Hajdu, Robert. "The Position of Noblewomen in the Pays des Coutumes, 1100–1300," *Journal of Family History*, 5 (1980), pp. 122–44.

Hanawalt, Barbara A. *The Ties That Bound: Peasant Families in Medieval England*. Oxford, England: Oxford University Press, 1986.

Herlihy, David. *Medieval Households*. Cambridge, Mass.: Harvard University Press, 1985.

Herlihy, David. *The Social History of Italy and Western Europe, 700–1500*. London: Variorum Reprints, 1978.

Homans, George C. *English Villagers of the Thirteenth Century*. New York: Russell and Russell, 1941.

Jochens, Jenny M. "The Politics of Reproduction: Medieval Norwegian Kingship," *American Historical Review*, 92 (1987), pp. 327–49.

Kellum, B. A. "Infanticide in the Later Middle Ages," *History of Childhood Quarterly*, 1 (1973–74), pp. 367–88.

Kirshner, Julius, and Suzanne F. Wemple, eds. *Women of the Medieval World*. Oxford, England: Blackwell, 1985.

Leclercq, Jean. *Monks on Marriage: A Twelfth-century View*. Oxford, England: Oxford University Press, 1982.

Leyser, K. "Maternal Kinship in Medieval Germany," *Past and Present*, 49 (1970), pp. 126–34.

Lucas, Angela. *Women in the Middle Ages: Religion, Marriage and Letters*. New York: St. Martin's Press, 1984.

Lynch, Joseph H. *Godparents and Kinship in Early Medieval Europe*. Princeton, N.J.: Princeton University Press, 1986.

Martines, Lauro, ed. *Violence and Civil Disorder in Italian Cities, 1200–1500*. Berkeley: University of California Press, 1973.

Razi, Zvi. *Marriage and Death in a Medieval Parish: Halesowen, 1270–1400*. Cambridge, England: Cambridge University Press, 1980.

Ring, Richard R. "Early Medieval Peasant Households in Central Italy," *Journal of Family History*, 4 (1979), pp. 2–25.

Sheehan, Michael M. "The Formation and Stability of Marriage in Fourteenth-century England: Evidence of an Ely Register," *Medieval Studies*, 33 (1971), pp. 228–63.

Smith, R. M. "The People of Tuscany and Their Families in the Fifteenth Century: Medieval or Mediterranean?" *Journal of Family History*, 6 (1981), pp. 107–28.

Stafford, Pauline. *Queens, Concubines, and Dowagers: The King's Wife in the Early Middle Ages*. Athens: University of Georgia Press, 1983.

Titow, J. Z. *English Rural Society, 1200–1350*. New York: Barnes and Noble, 1960.

Trexler, Richard C. "Florentine Foundlings, 1395–1455," *History of Childhood Quarterly*, 1 (1973–74), pp. 259–284.

Trexler, Richard C. "Infanticide in Renaissance Florence," *History of Childhood Quarterly*. 1 (1973–74), pp. 98–116.

Wemple, Suzanne Fay. *Women in Frankish Society: Marriage and the Cloister, 500 to 900*. Philadelphia: University of Pennsylvania Press, 1981.

MODERN WESTERN EUROPE

Cox, P. R. "International Variations in the Relative Ages of Brides and Grooms," *Journal of Biosocial Science*, 2 (1970), pp. 111–21.

Habakkuk, H. J. *Population Growth and Economic Development Since 1750*. Leicester, England: Leicester University Press, 1971.

Kertzer, David I. "European Peasant Household Structure," *Journal of Family History*, 2 (1977), pp. 333–49.

Klapisch–Zuber, Christine. *Women, Family, and Ritual in Renaissance Italy*. Chicago: University of Chicago Press, 1985.

Levine, David, ed. *Proletarianization and Family History*. New York: Academic Press, 1984.

MacLean, Ian. *The Renaissance Notion of Woman*. Cambridge, England: Cambridge University Press, 1980.

Mosse, George L. *Nationalism and Sexuality: Respectability and Abnormal Sexuality in Modern Europe*. New York: Howard Fertig, 1985.

Ozment, Steven. *When Fathers Ruled: Family Life in Reformation Europe*. Cambridge, Mass.: Harvard University Press, 1983.

Safilios–Rothschild, C. "A Comparison of Power Structure and Marital Satisfaction in Urban Greek and French Families," *Journal of Marriage and the Family*, 29 (1967), pp. 345–52.

Safilios–Rothschild, C., ed. "Macrosociology of the Family: A Symposium," *Journal of Marriage and the Family*, 37 (1975), pp. 854–965.

Shorter, Edward. *The Making of the Modern Family*. New York: Basic Books, 1975.

Smith, J. E., and B. Laslett, eds. "Historical Change in Marriage and the Family," *Sociology and Social Research*, 63 (1979), pp. 425–610.

Tilly, Louise A., and Joan W. Scott. *Women, Work, and Family*. New York: Holt, Rinehart and Winston, 1978.

BRITAIN

Anderson, Michael. "Marriage Patterns in Victorian Britain," *Journal of Family History*, 1 (1976), pp. 55–78.

Bott, Elizabeth. *Family and Social Network*, London: Tavistock Institute of Human Relations, 1978, 2d ed. New York: Free Press, 1971.

Bradley, Leslie. "Seasonality of Marriages in Early Modern England," *Local Population Studies*, 4 (1970), pp. 21–40. This is the first of a series of three; the second, on seasonality of baptisms, appeared in 5 (1970), pp. 18–35, and the third, on seasonality of burials, appeared in 6 (1971), pp. 15–31.

Edwards, W. J. "Marriage Seasonality, 1761–1810," *Local Population Studies*, 19 (1977), pp. 23–27.

Fox, Vivian, and Martin Quitt. *Loving, Parenting, and Dying: The Family Cycle in England and America, Past and Present*. New York: Psychohistory Press, 1981.

Gillis, John R. *For Better, For Worse: British Marriages 1600 to the Present*. Oxford, England: Oxford University Press, 1985.

Hair, P.E.H. "Child Killing and Assault in the Late Tudor Period," *Local Population Studies*, 9 (1972), pp. 43–46.

Hamilton, Roberta. *The Liberation of Women*. London: Allen and Unwin, 1978.

Helmholz, R. H. "Fifteenth-Century Infanticide," *History of Childhood Quarterly*, 2 (1974–75), pp. 379–90.

Horstman, Allen. *Victorian Divorce*. New York: St. Martin's Press, 1985.

Houlbrooke, Ralph A. *The English Family, 1450–1700*. Harlow, England: Longman, 1984.

Kern, Stephen. "Explosive Intimacy in the Victorian Family," *History of Childhood Quarterly*, 1 (1973–74), pp. 437–61.

Levine, David. *Family Formation in an Age of Nascent Capitalism*. New York: Academic Press, 1977.

Loschky, David J., and Donald F. Krier. "Income and Family Size in the Eighteenth Century," *Journal of Economic History*, 29 (1969), pp. 429–48.

Macfarlane, Alan. *Marriage and Love in England: Modes of Reproduction 1300–1840*. Oxford, England: Blackwell, 1985.

Massey, Margaret. "Seasonality in Marriages in the Early Modern Period," *Local Population Studies*, 8 (1972), pp. 48–54.

McLaren, Angus. *Reproductive Rituals: The Perception of Fertility in England*. London: Methuen, 1984.

Outhwaite, R. B. "Age at Marriage in England from the Late Seventeenth to the Nineteenth Century," *Transactions of the Royal Historical Society*, 23 (1973), pp. 55–70.

Prior, Mary, ed. *Women in English Society, 1500–1800*. London: Methuen, 1985.

Rapoport, Rhona, and Robert Rapoport. *Dual-Career Families*. Harmondsworth, England: Pelican, 1971.

Rapoport, Rhona, and Robert Rapoport. *Dual-Career Families Revisited.* Harmondsworth: Pelican, 1977.

Renvoize, Jean. *Web of Violence.* London: Routledge and Kegan Paul, 1978.

Ryerson, Alice. "Model Advice on Child-Rearing in the English Language, 1550–1900," *Harvard Educational Review,* 31 (1961), pp. 302–23.

Schofield, Roger S. "Perinatal Mortality in Hawkshead, Lancashire, 1581–1718," *Local Population Studies,* 4 (1970), pp. 11–16.

Stone, Lawrence. *The Family, Sex, and Marriage in England 1500–1800.* New York: Harper and Row, 1977.

Trumbach, Randolph. *The Rise of the Egalitarian Family.* New York: Academic Press, 1978.

Trustram, Myna. *Women of the Regiment: Marriage and the Victorian Army.* Cambridge, England: Cambridge University Press, 1984.

Vann, Richard. "Wills and the Family in an English Town: Banbury, 1550–1800," *Journal of Family History,* 4 (1979), pp. 346–67.

Wrightson, E. "Infanticide in the Early Seventeenth Century," *Local Population Studies,* 15 (1975), pp. 10–22.

Wrigley, A. E. "A Note on the Lifetime Mobility of Married Women in a Parish Population in the Later Eighteenth Century," *Local Population Studies,* 18 (1977), pp. 22–29.

IRELAND AND SCOTLAND

Arensberg, Conrad M., and Solon T. Kimball. *Family and Community in Ireland,* 2d ed. Cambridge, Mass.: Harvard University Press, 1968.

Carter, Ian. "Marriage Patterns and Social Sectors in Scotland Before the Eighteenth Century," *Scottish Studies,* 17 (1973), pp. 51–60.

Clarkston, L. A. "Household and Family Structure in Armagh City, 1770," *Local Population Studies,* 20 (1978), pp. 14–31.

Cullen, L. M., and T. C. Smout, eds. *Comparative Aspects of Scottish and Irish Economic and Social History, 1600–1900.* Edinburgh, Scotland: John Donald, 1977.

Holley, John C. "The Two Family Economies of Industrialism: Factory Workers in Victorian Scotland," *Journal of Family History,* 6 (1981), pp. 57–69.

Kennedy, R. E. *The Irish: Emigration, Marriage, and Fertility.* Berkeley: University of California Press, 1973.

Soulsby, E. M. "Changing Sex Ratios in the Scottish Border," *Scottish Geographical Magazine,* 88 (1972, April), pp. 5–18.

FRANCE

Berkner, Lutz, and John Shaffer. "The Joint Family in the Nivernais," *Journal of Family History,* 3 (1978), pp. 150–62.

Bideau, Alain. "A Demographic and Social Analysis of Widowhood and Remarriage: Thoissey-en-Dombes, 1670–1840," *Journal of Family History,* 5 (1980), pp. 28–43.

Camp, Wesley D. *Marriage and the Family in France Since the Revolution.* New York: Bookman Associates, 1961.

Flandrin, Jean-Louis, trans. by Richard Southern. *Families in Former Times*. Cambridge, England: Cambridge University Press, 1979.

Hunt, David. *Parents and Children in History*. New York: Basic Books, 1970.

Jeay, Madeleine. "Sexuality and Family in Fifteenth-century France," *Journal of Family History*, 4 (1979), pp. 328–45.

Maranda, Pierre. *French Kinship: Structure and History*. The Hague: Mouton, 1974.

Michel, Andrée. *The Modernization of North African Families in the Paris Area*. The Hague: Mouton, 1974.

Moch, Leslie Page. "Marriage, Migration, and Urban Demographic Structure: A Case from France in the Belle Epoque," *Journal of Family History*, 6 (1981), pp. 70–88.

Ogden, Philip. "Patterns of Marriage Seasonality in Rural France," *Local Population Studies*, 10 (1973), pp. 53–69.

Phillips, Roderick. *Family Breakdown in Late Nineteenth Century France*. Oxford, England: Oxford University Press, 1980.

Segalen, Martine. *Love and Power in the Peasant Family: Rural France in the 19th Century*. Oxford, England: Blackwell, 1983.

Tilly, Louise. "Individual Lives and Family Strategies in the French Proletariat, 1870–1914," *Journal of Family History*, 4 (1979), pp. 137–52.

Tilly, Louise. "The Family Wage Economy of a French Textile City: Roubaix, 1892–1906," *Journal of Family History*, 4 (1979), pp. 381–94.

Traer, James F. *Marriage and Family in Eighteenth-century France*. Ithaca, N.Y.: Cornell University Press, 1980.

Wheaton, Robert, and Tamara K. Hareven, eds. *Family and Sexuality in French History* (1980). A special issue of the *Journal of Family History*.

BELGIUM, NETHERLANDS, SWITZERLAND

Friedl, John. *Kippel: A Changing Village in the Alps*. New York: Holt, Rinehart and Winston, 1974.

Moors, H. G., and others, eds. *Population and Family in the Low Countries*. Leiden, The Netherlands: Nijhoff, 1976.

Netting, Robert M. "Household Dynamics in a Nineteenth-century Swiss Village," *Journal of Family History*, 4 (1979), pp. 39–58.

GERMANY AND AUSTRIA

Franzoi, Barbara. *At the Very Least She Pays the Rent: Women and German Industrialization, 1871–1914*. Westport, Conn.: Greenwood Press, 1985.

Joeres, Ruth-Ellen B., and Mary Jo Maynes, eds. *German Women in the 18th and 19th Centuries*. Bloomington: Indiana University Press, 1985.

Imhof, Arthur E. "Historical Demography as Social History," *Journal of Family History*, 2 (1977), pp. 305–22.

Knodel, John. "The Demography of a Bavarian Village," *Population Studies*, 24 (1970), pp. 353–76.

Knodel, John, and Mary Jo Maynes. "Urban and Rural Marriage Patterns in Imperial Germany," *Journal of Family History*, 1 (1976), pp. 129–68.

Knodel, John, and Etienne Van de Walle. "Breast Feeding, Fertility, and Infant Mortality: An Analysis of Some Early German Data," *Population Studies*, 21 (1967), pp. 109–31.

Mitterauer, Michael. "Marriage Without Co-residence in Rural Carinthia," *Journal of Family History*, 6 (1981), pp. 177–81.

Mitterauer, Michael, and Reinhard Sieder. "The Developmental Process of Domestic Groups," *Journal of Family History*, 4 (1979), pp. 257–84.

Rabbie, Jacob M. "A Cross-Cultural Comparison of Parent-Child Relationships in the United States and West Germany," *British Journal of Social and Clinical Psychology*, 4 (1965), pp. 298–310.

Rebel, Hermann. *Peasant Classes: The Bureaucratization of Property and Family Relations Under Early Habsburg Absolutism, 1511–1636*. Princeton, N.J.: Princeton University Press, 1983.

Rodgers, R. R. "Changes in Parental Behavior Reported by Children in West Germany and the United States," *Human Development*, 14 (1971), pp. 208–24.

Spindler, George D. *Burgbach: Urbanization and Identity*. New York: Holt, Rinehart and Winston, 1973.

SCANDINAVIA AND THE BALTIC

Drake, Michael. *Population and Society in Norway, 1735–1865*. Cambridge, England: Cambridge University Press, 1969.

Dyrvik, Ståle. "Historical Demography in Norway, 1660–1800: A Short Survey," *Scandinavian Economic History Review*, 20 (1972), pp. 27–44.

Lithell, Ulla-Britt. "Breast-Feeding Habits and Their Relation to Infant Mortality and Marital Fertility," *Journal of Family History*, 6 (1981), pp. 182–94.

Plakans, Andrejs. "Identifying Kinfolk Beyond the Household," *Journal of Family History*, 2 (1977), pp. 3–27.

EASTERN EUROPE

Byrnes, Robert F., ed. *Communal Families in the Balkans: The Zadruga*. South Bend, Ind.: Notre Dame University Press, 1976.

Jancar, Barbara Wolfe. *Women Under Communism*. Baltimore, Md.: Johns Hopkins University Press, 1978.

McIntyre, Robert. "The Fertility Response to Abortion Reform in Eastern Europe: Demographic and Economic Implications," *American Economist*, 16 (1972), pp. 45–63. Followed on pp. 64–65 by a comment by Thomas Lindley.

St. Erlich, Vera. *The Family in Transition: A Study of 300 Yugoslav Villages*. Princeton, N.J.: Princeton University Press, 1966.

RUSSIA AND THE SOVIET UNION

Benet, Sula. "Some Changes in Family Structure and Personality Among the Peasants of Great Russia," *Transactions of the New York Academy of Sciences*, 32 (1970), pp. 51–65.

Coale, Ansley J., and others. *Human Fertility in Russia Since the Nineteenth Century.* Princeton, N.J.: Princeton University Press, 1979.

Geiger, Kurt. *The Family in Soviet Russia.* Cambridge, Mass.: Harvard University Press, 1968.

Ransel, David L., ed. *The Family in Imperial Russia.* Urbana: University of Illinois Press, 1978.

SPAIN AND PORTUGAL

Brandes, Stanley H. "*La Soltería,* or Why People Remain Single in Rural Spain," *Journal of Anthropological Research*, 32 (1976), pp. 205–33.

Brettell, Caroline B. *Men Who Migrate, Women Who Wait: Population and History in a Portuguese Parish.* Princeton, N.J.: Princeton University Press, 1987.

Foster, George M. "Cofradía and Compadrazgo in Spain and Spanish America," *Southwestern Journal of Anthropology*, 9 (1953), pp. 1–28.

Livi Bacci, Massimo. "Fertility and Nuptiality in Spain," *Population Studies*, 22 (1968), pp. 83–102, 211–34.

Nader, Helen. *The Mendoza Family in the Spanish Renaissance, 1350 to 1450.* New Brunswick, N.J.: Rutgers University Press, 1979.

Pescatello, Ann M. *Power and Pawn: The Female in Iberian Families, Societies, and Cultures.* Westport, Conn.: Greenwood Press, 1976.

LATIN AMERICA

Adams, R. M. *The Evolution of Urban Society: Early Mesopotamia and Prehispanic Mexico.* London: Aldine Publishers, 1966.

Arrom, S. M. "Marriage Patterns in Mexico City, 1811," *Journal of Family History*, 3 (1978), pp. 376–91.

Belmori, Diana, and others. *Notable Family Networks in Latin America.* Chicago: University of Chicago Press, 1984.

Cancian, Francesca M., Louis Wolf Goodman, and Peter H. Smith, eds. *The Family in Latin America.* (1978). A special issue of the *Journal of Family History.*

Cutright, P., M. Hout, and D. R. Johnson. "Fertility Determinants, 1800–1970," *American Sociological Review*, 41 (1976), pp. 511–26.

Foster, George M. "Cofradía and Compadrazgo in Spain and Spanish America," *Southwestern Journal of Anthropology*, 9 (1953), pp. 1–28.

Hahner, June E., ed. *Women in Latin American History: Their Lives and Views.* Los Angeles: University of California at Los Angeles Press, 1976.

Lavrin, Asuncion, ed. *Latin American Women: Historical Perspectives.* Westport, Conn.: Greenwood Press, 1978.

Pescatello, Ann M., ed. *Female and Male in Latin America: Essays.* Pittsburgh, Pa.: University of Pittsburgh Press, 1973.

Steward, Julian H., and Louis C. Faron. *Native Peoples of South America.* Hightstown, N.J.: McGraw-Hill, 1959.

Tienda, M. "Age and Economic Dependency in Peru: A Family Life-Cycle Analysis," *Journal of Marriage and Family*, 42 (1980), pp. 639–52.

Youssef, Nadia H. "Differential Labor Force Participation of Women in Latin American and Middle Eastern Countries: The Influence of Family Characteristics," *Social Forces*, 51 (1972), pp. 135–53.

CARIBBEAN

Heckscher, Bridget T. "Household Structure and Achievement Orientation in Lower-Class Barbadian Families," *Journal of Marriage and Family*, 29 (1967), pp. 521–26.

Higman, B. W. "African and Creole Slave Family Patterns in Trinidad," *Journal of Family History*, 3 (1978), pp. 163–80.

Martínez-Alier, Verena. *Marriage, Class, and Color in Nineteenth-Century Cuba.* Cambridge, England: Cambridge University Press, 1974.

Rodman, Hyman. "Lower-Class Attitudes Toward 'Deviant' Family Patterns: A Cross-Cultural Study," *Journal of Marriage and Family*, 31 (1969), pp. 315–21.

CANADA, UNITED STATES, AUSTRALIA, AND NEW ZEALAND

Festy, Patrick. "Canada, United States, Australia, and New Zealand: Nuptiality Trends," *Population Studies*, 27 (1973), pp. 479–92.

AUSTRALIA

Grimshaw, Patricia, and others, eds. *Families in Colonial Australia.* London: Allen and Unwin, 1985.

Krupinski, Jerzy, and Alan Stoller, eds. *The Family in Australia: Social, Psychological, and Demographic Aspects*, 2d ed. Rushcutters Bay, New South Wales, Australia: Pergamon Press Australia, 1978.

McDonald, Peter F. *Marriage in Australia, 1880–1971.* Canberra: Australian National University, 1974.

Ruzicka, L. T. "Age at Marriage and Timing of the First Birth," *Population Studies*, 30 (1976), pp. 527–38.

Spencer, Geraldine. "Pre-Marital Pregnancies and Ex-Nuptial Births in Australia, 1911–1966," *Australian and New Zealand Journal of Sociology*, 5 (1969), pp. 121–27.

CANADA

Bouchard, Gerald. "Family Structures and Geographic Mobility at Lateriére, 1851–1935," *Journal of Family History*, 2 (1977), pp. 350–69.

Bouvier, Léon. "The Spacing of Births Among French-Canadian Families: An Historical Approach," *Canadian Review of Sociology and Anthropology*, 5 (1968), pp. 17–26.

Ishwaran, K., ed. *Canadian Families: Ethnic Variations.* Toronto: McGraw-Hill Ryerson, 1980.

Ramu, G. N. *Introduction to Canadian Society: Sociological Analysis.* Toronto: Macmillan of Canada, 1976.

Romaniuk, Anatole, and Victor Piché. "Natality Estimates for the Canadian Indians by Stable Population Models, 1900–1969," *Canadian Review of Sociology and Anthropology*, 9 (1972), pp. 1–20.

Stephenson, Marylee, ed. *Women in Canada*. Toronto: New Press, 1973.

Strong-Boag, Veronica, and Anita Clair Williams, eds. *Rethinking Canada: The Promise of Women's History*. Toronto: Capp Clark Pitman, 1986.

Tepperman, L. "Ethnic Variations in Marriage and Fertility: Canada, 1871," *Canadian Review of Sociology and Anthropology*, 11 (1974), pp. 324–43.

UNITED STATES—GENERAL AND ANGLO-AMERICAN

Bernard, Jessie. *The Future of Marriage*. Cleveland, Ohio: World Publishing, 1972.

Bettelheim, Bruno. "Untying the Family," *Center Magazine*, 9 (1976, September), pp. 5–9, and subsequent discussions by Marilyn Kramer on p. 79 of January 1977 issue and by Wilma Lange Henke on p. 80 of May 1977 issue.

Brooks-Gunn, Jeanne, and Wendy Schempp Matthews. *He and She: How Children Develop Their Sex-Role Identity*. Englewood Cliffs, N.J.: Prentice-Hall, 1979.

Caplow, Theodore, and others. *Middletown Families*. Minneapolis: University of Minnesota Press, 1982.

Carter, Hugh, and Paul G. Glick. *Marriage and Divorce: A Social and Economic Study*. (1970); rev. ed. Cambridge, Mass.: Harvard University Press, 1976.

Census of Population (1980), vol. 1, *Characteristics of the Population*. Washington, D.C.: Government Printing Office.

Chudacoff, Howard P. "The Life Course of Women: Age and Age-Consciousness, 1865–1915," *Journal of Family History*, 5 (1980), pp. 274–92.

Conway, Jill Ker. *The Female Experience in America: A Guide to the History of American Women*, 2 vols. New York: Garland, 1985.

Cornish, E. "Intimacy in an Age of Loneliness: The Future of the Family," *Futurist*, 13 (1979, February), pp. 45–58.

Degler, Carl N. *At Odds: Women and the Family in America*. Oxford, England: Oxford University Press, 1980.

Demos, John. *Past, Present and Personal: The Family and the Life Course in American History*. Oxford, England: Oxford University Press, 1986.

Demos, John, and Sarane Spence Babcock, eds. *Turning Points: Historical and Sociological Essays on the Family*. Chicago: University of Chicago Press, 1978.

Ditz, Toby L. *Property and Kinship: Inheritance in Early Connecticut, 1750–1820*. Princeton, N.J.: Princeton University Press, 1986.

Elder, Glen H., and Richard C. Rockwell. "Marital Timing in Women's Life Patterns," *Journal of Family History*, 1 (1976), pp. 34–53.

Filene, Peter G. *Him/Her/Self: Sex Roles in Modern America*, 2d ed. Baltimore, Md.: Johns Hopkins Press, 1986.

Fox, Vivian, and Martin Quitt. *Loving, Parenting, and Dying: The Family Cycle in England and America, Past and Present*. New York: Psychohistory Press, 1981.

Francoeur, Robert, and Anne Francoeur. "The Pleasure Bond: Reversing the Antisocial Ethic," *Futurist*, 10 (1976, August), pp. 176–80.

Gelles, R. J., and M. A. Straus. "Family Experience and Public Support of the Death Penalty," *American Journal of Orthopsychology*, 45 (1975), pp. 596–613.

Gerstel, Naomi, and Harriet Gross. *Commuter Marriage*. New York: Guilford Press, 1984.

Gordon, Michael, ed. *The American Family in Social-Historical Perspective*, 1st ed. (1973); 2d ed. (1978); 3rd ed. New York: St. Martin's Press, 1983.

Grossberg, Michael. *Governing the Hearth: Law and Family in 19th-Century America*. Chapel Hill: University of North Carolina Press, 1985.

Hareven, Tamara K. *Family Time and Industrial Time*. Cambridge, England: Cambridge University Press, 1981.

Hareven, Tamara K., ed. *History of the Family in American Urban Society* (1975). A special issue of the *Journal of Urban History*.

Hareven, Tamara K., ed. *Transitions*. New York: Academic Press, 1978.

Hertz, Rosanna. *More Equal Than Others: Women and Men in Dual-Career Marriages*. Berkeley: University of California Press, 1986.

Kobrin, Frances E., and Linda J. Waite. *Effects of Childhood Family Structure on Marriage*. Santa Monica, Calif.: Rand, 1984.

Komarovsky, Mirra. *Blue-Collar Marriage*. New York: Random House, 1962.

Lichtman, Allan J., and Joan R. Challinor. *Kin and Communities: Families in America*. Washington, D.C.: Smithsonian Institute Press, 1979.

Litwak, Eugene. "The Extended Family and Geographical Mobility," *American Sociological Review*, 25 (1960), pp. 385–94.

Litwak, Eugene. "The Extended Family and Occupational Mobility," *American Sociological Review*, 25 (1960), pp. 9–21.

Matthaei, Julie A. *An Economic History of Women in America*. New York: Schocken Books, 1982.

Modell, John. "Normative Aspects of American Marriage Timing Since World War II," *Journal of Family History*, 5 (1980), pp. 210–34.

Muncy, Raymond Lee. *Sex and Marriage in Utopian Communities: Nineteenth-century America*. Bloomington: Indiana University Press, 1973.

Nye, F. Ivan. *Role Structure and Analysis of the Family*. Beverly Hills: Sage Publications, 1976.

Nye, F. Ivan, and Felix M. Berardo. *The Family: Its Structure and Interaction*. New York: Macmillan, 1973.

Nye, F. Ivan, and G. McDonald, eds. *Family Policy: A Symposium* (1979). A special issue of *Journal of Marriage and Family*.

Ramey, J. "Multiadult Household: Living Group of the Future?" *Futurist*, 10 (1976, April), pp. 78–83.

Reiss, Ira L. *Family Systems in America*, 3d ed. New York: Holt, Rinehart and Winston, 1980.

Richardson, Herbert W. *Nun, Witch, Playmate: The Americanization of Sex*. New York: Edwin Mellen Press, 1971.

Roemer, Kenneth M. "Sex Roles, Utopia, and Change: The Family in Late Nineteenth Century Utopian Literature," *American Studies*, 13:2 (1972), pp. 33–48.

Rosen, Bernard C. "Family Structure and Achievement Motivation," *American Sociological Review*, 26 (1961), pp. 574–85.

Rossi, Alice, Jerome Kagan, and Tamara K. Hareven, eds. *The Family*. New York: W. W. Norton, 1978.

Rothman, Ellen K. *Hands and Hearts: A History of Courtship in America*. New York: Basic Books, 1986.

Rubin, Lillian. *Worlds of Pain: Life in the Working-Class Family*. New York: Basic Books, 1976.

Ryan, Mary P. *Cradle of the Middle Class: Oneida County 1780–1865*. Cambridge, England: Cambridge University Press, 1981.

Ryan, Mary P. *The Empire of the Mother: American Writing About Domesticity, 1830–1860*. New York: Haworth, 1982.

Ryan, Mary P. *Womanhood in America*, 3d ed. 1984.

Sauer, R. "Attitudes to Abortion in America, 1800–1973," *Population Studies*, 28 (1974), pp. 53–67.

Scanzoni, John H. *Opportunity and the Family*. New York: Free Press, 1970.

Scanzoni, John H. *Sex Roles, Life Styles, and Childbearing*. New York: Free Press, 1975.

Schneider, David M. *American Kinship: A Cultural Account*. Englewood Cliffs, N.J.: Prentice-Hall, 1968.

Schneider, David M., and Calvert B. Cottrell. *The American Kin Universe: A Genealogical Study*. Chicago: University of Chicago Department of Anthropology, 1975.

Schneider, David M., and Raymond Smith. *Class Differences and Sex Roles in American Kinship and Family Structures*. Englewood Cliffs, N.J.: Prentice-Hall, 1973.

Scott, Donald M., and Bernard Wishy, eds. *America's Families: A Documentary History*. New York: Harper and Row, 1982.

Sennett, Richard. *Families Against the City*. Cambridge, Mass.: Harvard, 1970.

Seward, Rudy Ray. *The American Family: A Demographic History*. Beverly Hills, Calif.: Sage, 1978.

Skolnick, Arlene, and Jerome H. Skolnick. *Family in Transition*, 3d ed. (1980); 4th ed. Boston, Mass.: Little, Brown and Co., 1983.

Smith, Daniel Blake. *Inside the Great House*. Ithaca, N.Y.: Cornell University Press, 1980.

Smith, Daniel Scott. "Life Course, Norms, and the Family System of Older Americans in 1900," *Journal of Family History*, 4 (1979), pp. 285–98.

Smith, J. E., and P. R. Kunz. "Polygyny and Fertility in Nineteenth-century America," *Population Studies*, 30 (1976), pp. 465–80.

Smith, J. E., and Barbara Laslett, eds. *Marriage and Family* (1979). A special issue of *Sociology and Social Research*.

Spanier, Graham B., and Paul Glick. "The Life Cycle of American Families: An Expanded Analysis," *Journal of Family History*, 5 (1980), pp. 97–111.

Statistical Abstract of the United States. Washington, D.C.: Government Printing Office, 1986.

Stearns, Carol Z., and Peter W. Stearns. *Anger: The Struggle for Emotional Control in America's History*. Chicago: University of Chicago Press, 1986.

Thornton, Arland, and Deborah Freedman. *The Changing American Family*. Washington, D.C.: Population Reference Bureau, 1983.

Treas, J., and R. J. Walther. "Family Structure and Income Distribution," *Social Forces*, 56 (1978), pp. 866–80.

Troll, Lillian E., and others. *Families in Later Life*. Belmont, Calif.: Wadsworth, 1979.

Uhlenberg, Peter. "Death and the Family," *Journal of Family History*, 5 (1980), pp. 313–20.

Van Wagoner, Richard S. *Mormon Polygamy: A History*. Salt Lake City, Utah: Signature Books, 1986.

Vinovskis, Maris. "An 'Epidemic' of Adolescent Pregnancy? Some Historical Considerations," *Journal of Family History*, 6 (1981), pp. 205–30.

Wells, Robert V. *Revolutions in Americans' Lives*. Westport, Conn.: Greenwood Press, 1982.

Wells, Robert V. *Uncle Sam's Family: Issues and Perspectives on American Demographic History*. Albany: State of New York Press, 1985.

Westoff, Leslie A. *The Second Time Around: Remarriage in America*. New York: Viking Press, 1977.

Young, Leontine. *The Fractured Family*. Hightstown, N.J.: McGraw-Hill, 1973.

UNITED STATES—ETHNIC, INCLUDING HISPANIC

Griswold del Castillo, Richard. *La Familia: Chicano Families in the Urban Southwest, 1848 to the Present*. South Bend, Ind.: Notre Dame University Press, 1984.

Lee, S. C., and Audrey Brattrud. "Marriage Under a Monastic Mode of Life: A Preliminary Report on the Hutterite Family in South Dakota," *Journal of Marriage and Family*, 29 (1967), pp. 512–20.

Mindel, Charles H., and Robert W. Habenstein, eds. *Ethnic Families in America: Patterns and Variations*. New York: Elsevier, 1976.

UNITED STATES—AFRO-AMERICAN AND AMERICAN INDIAN

Axtell, James, ed. *The Indian Peoples of Eastern America: A Documentary History of the Sexes*. Oxford, England: Oxford University Press, 1981.

Dearborn, Mary V. *Pocahontas's Daughters: Gender and Ethnicity in American Culture*. Oxford, England: Oxford University Press, 1986.

Engerman, Stanley L. "Black Fertility and Family Structure in the United States, 1880–1940," *Journal of Family History*, 2 (1977), pp. 117–38.

Gutman, Herbert G. *The Black Family in Slavery and Freedom, 1750–1925*. New York: Pantheon, 1976.

Jones, Jacqueline. *Labor of Love, Labor of Sorrow*. New York: Basic Books, 1985.

McFalls, Joseph, and George Masnick. "Birth Control and the Fertility of the United States Black Population, 1880 to 1980," *Journal of Family History*, 6 (1981), pp. 89–106.

Steckel, Richard H. "Slave Marriage and the Family," *Journal of Family History*, 5 (1980), pp. 406–21.

Wetherell, Charles. "Slave Kinship: A Case Study of the South Carolina Good Hope Plantation, 1835–1856," *Journal of Family History*, 6 (1981), pp. 294–308.

Zollar, Ann Creighton. *A Member of the Family: Strategies for Black Family Continuity*. Chicago: Nelson-Hall, 1985.

Index

abduction, 152, 171, 172, 176, 177
Aborigines of Australia, 37, 44, 54, 100, 280, 281. *See also* Murngin
abortion, 24, 25, 252
absolutism, 191, 192
adoption, 4, 24, 54, 72, 73, 95, 99, 104, 146, 147, 149, 167, 248, 306
adoptive marriage. *See* marriage, adoptive
adultery, 75, 118, 124, 142, 167, 171, 188, 204, 211, 214, 246, 274, 283, 287, 291. *See also* childbearing, extramarital
affinal kin, 258
affinal network, 4, 24, 56, 166
affinal set, 166, 244
affines, 5, 8, 64, 65, 71, 85, 91, 99, 100, 112, 120, 124, 272
Afghanistan, 151, 165
Afikpo, 94, 95, 97, 102
Africa, 8, 10, 11, 19, 21, 27, 33, 45, 50, 65, 127, 129, 132, 140, 189, 193, 197–201, 208–210, 243; central, 92, 96; eastern, 87, 92, 116; northern, 6, 121; southern, 92; sub-Saharan, 57, 65, 77, 79–81, 84–100, 105, 106, 108–110, 119, 120, 131, 263–269, 271, 300; western, 74, 92, 93, 112, 213
African-Americans, 285, 296–302
Africans, 15, 68, 81–99, 137, 263–

269, 271, 272, 275. *See also* Afikpo; Akamba, Akan; Amhara; Ashanti; Barma; Bemba; Bena; Dahomey; Diola; Fang; Fulani; Gonja; Gusii; Herero; Igbo; Jie; Kikuyu; Kpelle; !Kung; Lele; LoDagaa; LoDagaba; Lovedu; LoWiili; Lozi; Malagasy; Mandinka; Masai; Mbuti; Mongo; Ndembu; Nuer; Nyamwezi; Nyaro; Rukuba; Samburu; Suku; Tale (Tallensi); Tiv; Tonga (Zambia); Tswana; Tullushi; Turkana; Yako; Yoruba; Zande; Zulu
age-grade, 116, 122, 123, 125, 137
agnate amnesia, 72, 99, 104, 124
agnates, 5, 6, 11, 72, 99–101, 104–106, 114, 120, 124, 164, 175, 180
agriculturalists, 8–11, 43, 45, 46, 49, 52, 57, 59, 62, 67, 69, 70, 79, 84, 86, 87, 93, 108–112, 118, 124, 126, 127, 180, 305, 306. *See also* agriculture
agriculture, 6, 38, 45–47, 49, 55–59, 66, 71, 77, 83–86, 89, 107, 109–112, 160. *See also* hoe agriculture; irrigated agriculture; plow agriculture; settled agriculture; shifting cultivation
Akamba, 97
Akan, 111
Albania, Albanians, 34, 165, 228, 230, 231

About the Author

G. ROBINA QUALE is Professor of History at Albion College, Michigan. Her earlier works include *Eastern Civilizations* and an article in the *Indiana Social Science Quarterly* on myths of nation-building. Professor Quale is a member of the American Historical Association, the International Society for the Comparative Study of Civilizations, and the World History Association.